LEARNING BIBLICAL HEBREW

Reading for Comprehension

An Introductory Grammar

LEARNING BIBLICAL HEBREW

Reading for Comprehension

An Introductory Grammar

Karl V. Kutz and Rebekah L. Josberger

LEXHAM PRESS

Learning Biblical Hebrew: Reading for Comprehension—An Introductory Grammar

Lexham Press, 1313 Commercial St., Bellingham, WA 98225
LexhamPress.com

Unless otherwise noted, Scripture quotations are the author's own translation.

Print ISBN 9781683590842
Digital ISBN 9781683590859

Lexham Editorial Team: Douglas Mangum, Abby Salinger, Justin Marr, James Spinti, Russell Meeks, Elliot Ritzema

Typesetting: Andy Kerr, Abigail Stocker, Anna Fejes
Cover Design: Peter Park
Cover Photo: The Great Isaiah Scroll, cols. 5–6.
Photo © The Israel Museum, Jerusalem, by Ardon Bar-Hama

Contents

CHAPTER 10

CHAPTER 11

CHAPTER 12

CHAPTER 13

CHAPTER 28

II-*Waw/Yod* Verbs: *Niphal—Hophal* Stems 353

CHAPTER 29

Geminate Verbs 367

CHAPTER 30

I-*Nun* Verbs 381

List of Tables

List of Verb Paradigms

Preface

If you are reading this preface, you are probably curious about one of two things—can this grammar help you learn Hebrew, or can this grammar help you teach Hebrew? Whichever question you identify with, you already have won our hearts, as we have spent our lives devoted to these same questions.

TO THE POTENTIAL STUDENT

Welcome to one of the most grueling and rewarding tasks you ever will undertake. Learning Hebrew is often perceived to be a highly academic endeavor, reserved for the elite. But it does not need to be that way. In this grammar we will introduce you to a quirky, vibrant, expressive, and sometimes frustrating language. It takes hard work, and it takes time. But if you are reading this preface, you are sufficiently equipped. You have already learned one language (English), and you can learn another. Here are a few things we want you to know about Hebrew—whether or not you end up using this grammar.

1. Hebrew is alive. Whatever method you choose for learning Hebrew, do not let anyone (even us) strip it down to nothing more than facts and paradigms. It is fluid, artistic, and vivid. Like all languages, it is dynamic, and, as our students like to joke, it seems to have a mind of its own. Sometimes you will love it; sometimes you will hate it. You can learn to understand and predict the broad patterns and concepts that give it coherence despite its anomalies, but it will always sneak up on you and surprise you.

2. You do not need to know Hebrew to have access to the Scriptures. Further, do not expect knowledge of Hebrew

to resolve all the problems or tensions you find in the biblical text. God's communication with his people took place within the imperfections and complications of human language. Reading the text in Hebrew helps you to slow down and notice things you never saw before; the vivid and sometimes unexpected wording prompts you to see the text afresh; and the natural limits of word meaning and flow of thought often clarify what the text means. But when you learn Hebrew you will discover that the text is complex. If anything, your study of Hebrew will promote personal humility and a desire to return to the text over and over again to search out its meaning.

3. You can learn Hebrew! Your greatest obstacle will be your own fear of failure and preconceived notions of what success looks like. Learning a language involves mistakes and failure (sometimes lots of failure) before you achieve success. It also requires consistency and discipline rather than short-term achievement. But if you are willing to work at the process, you will succeed. It is not just the brilliant, linguistically-minded students who thrive. Students who would never identify themselves as scholars or linguists surprise themselves by falling in love with the language and more deeply in love with Scripture and its Author. The purpose of this grammar is to teach you Hebrew regardless of your vocation or profession. If you work hard you will not only learn to read Hebrew, but you will have an understanding of the language that allows you to read the text for the rest of your life—and every time you read, you will learn more.

TO HEBREW TEACHERS

In a field where there are nearly as many Hebrew textbooks as there are Hebrew programs, you may wonder, "Why this grammar?" For us, the answer is simple—our students. For over twenty years this method has been used to teach students to read Hebrew. Our students come from every type of background, represent a varied propensity for languages and academics, and have different long-term goals. But, they all share the same result: they now read Hebrew. They read well; they love the language; and they retain their skills long after they leave the classroom. So what philosophies drive this particular approach to learning Hebrew?

1. Teach for long-term retention. Too often Hebrew is viewed by students as their most difficult class and the least used after graduation. As teachers, neither of us want to contribute to that view. We know students will have to work hard, but we want them to walk away with a skill they can use the rest of their lives. Long-term retention is directly linked to how easily students can read and how quickly they can access the text without extensive recourse to aids. The key factors in promoting long-term skill are a strong vocabulary base and broad exposure to the text. Further, students retain more when their learning is based on understanding rather than rote memory. Of course, memorization is a necessary component of language learning, but the need for rote memorization is reduced by introducing advanced concepts in a manner that beginning students can understand and by reiterating and building on those concepts throughout their language learning. In short, rather than trying to simplify the process for students, we push them to learn as much as they can about the language so that they *know* it like one knows a person rather than *learn about* it like one studies facts.

2. Read biblical text as soon and as much as possible. This grammar is accompanied by a graded reader that helps students read large portions of biblical text (Joseph narrative, Ruth, Jonah). By the fourth lesson each grammar lesson is accompanied by a full chapter of biblical text. Early chapters are adapted and glossed to accommodate the students' skill set but are not limited in length. The graded reader is adapted from the biblical text so that the student is exposed not just to vocabulary and grammar

but to syntax, word order, and Hebrew thought. Further, the continuity of narrative creates a flow of thought that allows the student to anticipate what should come next, promoting an instinctual understanding of the language to accompany their growing grammatical knowledge. More importantly, the student gets to do what they want to do most—read the biblical text.

3. Allow room for failure. The grammar is designed to provide students safety to fail as they learn. The explanations of grammatical concepts are rather comprehensive even when the student is only expected to retain a few key principles. Success is not determined by mastering all the details. Likewise, the exercises are created so that students can practice what they have learned in an environment where their mistakes promote learning. Students are given credit for self-corrected assignments rather than based on their accuracy in a first attempt. Since people learn to read at different rates, students are given credit for completing assignments based on time spent rather than volume completed. Students are encouraged to work on assignments in community, where they can benefit from one another's strengths—and where they can both celebrate and commiserate, depending on the day's task. In short, student success is enhanced by students learning in groups, doing homework together, meeting with advanced students for tutoring, and experiencing faculty mentoring (which often involves letting them see the teacher learn, too).

This grammar may not be for everyone. It is aggressive. It assumes that the ability to use Hebrew resources requires an understanding of Hebrew language to guide their use. But it is also forgiving, viewing the study of Hebrew as a life-long process and providing a learning environment—for teachers and students alike—that can be returned to again and again.

Acknowledgements

To our students—this grammar is both for you and from you. Though we cannot mention you all by name, your passion for Hebrew and desire to learn have constantly refined and shaped how we teach. Your encouragement to bring this text to print has been both relentless and empowering. Thank you for countless hours of dialogue about Hebrew pedagogy and the meaning of the text, your outrageous humor, and the joy of being in relationship with you while reading and applying the Hebrew Scriptures.

Special thanks to Haley Kirkpatrick for countless hours entering and editing the workbook and to the many students who showed up last minute to edit, encourage, and bring coffee. We are humbled by your support and amazed by the questions you asked and errors you caught. And to Doug Mangum, our editor at Lexham, thank you for your excitement about this project and your advice, hard work, and attention to detail. We are so proud of the result. And finally, to Jim, Mia, Amanda, Emily, and Haven—thanks for supporting this process while reminding us that there is more to life than Hebrew.

To our mentors and teachers, Michael Fox and Daniel Block—this grammar is dedicated to you, your impact on us, and the legacy you are imparting to a new generation of scholars.

Abbreviations

*	historic form or non-existent form (not in Biblical Hebrew)
abs.	absolute
acc.	accusative
act.	active
adj.	adjective
adv.	adverb
BDB	Brown, Francis, S. R. Driver, and Charles A. Briggs. *A Hebrew and English Lexicon of the Old Testament*. Oxford: Clarendon, 1906
BHS	*Biblia Hebraica Stuttgartensia*. Edited by Karl Elliger and Wilhelm Rudolph. Stuttgart: Deutsche Bibelgesellschaft, 1983
C	consonant
c(.)	common
ch(s).	chapter(s)
coh.	cohortative
conj.	conjunction
consec.	consecutive
cst.	construct
def. art.	definite article
dir. obj.	direct object
du.	dual
E.T.	English Text
f(.)	feminine
H	Hebrew
GKC	*Gesenius' Hebrew Grammar*. Edited by Emil Kautzsch. Translated by A. E. Cowley. 2nd ed. Oxford: Clarendon, 1910
GNT	Greek New Testament
hiph.	*hiphil*
hithp.	*hithpael*
hoph.	*hophal*
HS	*Hebrew Studies*

impf.	imperfect
impv.	imperative
ind. obj.	indirect object
inf. abs.	infinitive absolute
inf. cst.	infinitive construct
irreg.	irregular
JHS	*Journal of Hebrew Scriptures*
Joüon	Joüon, Paul, and T. Muraoka. *A Grammar of Biblical Hebrew*. Revised English ed. Roma: Pontificio istituto biblico, 2006
juss.	jussive
lit.	literally
LXX	Septuagint
m(.)	masculine
MS(S)	manuscript(s)
MT	Masoretic Text
N/A	not applicable
n.	noun
neg.	negative
niph.	*niphal*
NT	New Testament
num.	number
obj.	object
OT	Old Testament
p/pl.	plural
pass.	passive
pers.	person
pf.	perfect
pi.	*piel*
p.n.	proper name
prep.	preposition
pron.	pronoun
ptc.	participle
pu.	*pual*
refl.	reflexive
rel.	relative
s/sg.	singular

subj.	subject
suff.	suffix
syll.	syllable
trans.	translated by
v(v).	verse(s)
V	vowel
vb.	verb
Waltke-O'Connor	*An Introduction to Biblical Hebrew Syntax*. Bruce K. Waltke and Michael O'Connor. Winona Lake, IN: Eisenbrauns, 1990

CHAPTER 1

The Hebrew Alphabet

The Hebrew characters that are used today are referred to as square script and are borrowed from Aramaic. The earliest Hebrew texts used the Phoenician alphabet prevalent throughout Canaan. This ancient Hebrew script is called Paleo-Hebrew. Paleo-Hebrew continued in use until the time of the Babylonian exile (mid-sixth century BCE) when the Jewish people began using Aramaic, the diplomatic and trade language of both the Babylonian and Persian Empires. The use of Aramaic continued after their return to Judea, and the Aramaic square script was adopted for their own native Hebrew language. The Paleo-Hebrew script can still be seen in ancient inscriptions, coins, and a number of biblical fragments among the Dead Sea Scrolls. However, most of the manuscripts of the Hebrew Bible utilize some form of the square script borrowed from Aramaic. This Hebrew square script is also used in modern printed editions of the Hebrew Bible.

WHAT DOES THE ALPHABET LOOK LIKE?

The Paleo-Hebrew letters are shown below with the corresponding Hebrew square script letters printed above them. (Hebrew is read from right to left as illustrated by the arrow below.)

right to left

The Paleo-Hebrew characters originally reflected the shape of an object and were used to represent the first sound in the object's name. For example, the Paleo-Hebrew 𐤊 is the drawing of a "hand," the Hebrew name for which is *kaph*. Thus, the symbol 𐤊 is called *kaph* and represents the "k" sound. The names of the letters continued in use even after the adoption of the square script.

Table 1.1 below presents the Hebrew alphabet together with the name of each character. For Hebrew letters that extend below the line, a dotted line has been added to the table to give you a perspective on length. These longer characters include the ק (*qoph*) and the final forms (except *mem*) that are highlighted by boxes.

Table 1.1: The Hebrew Alphabet†

ו	ה	ד	ג	ב	א
vav	*heh*	*dalet*	*gimel*	*bet*	*aleph*
ך	כ	י	ט	ח	ז
final *kaph*	*kaph*	*yod*	*tet*	*ḥet*	*zayin*
ס	ן	נ	ם	מ	ל
samek	final *nun*	*nun*	final *mem*	*mem*	*lamed*
ק	ץ	צ	ף	פ	ע
qoph	final *tsade*	*tsade*	final *pe*	*pe*	*ayin*
		ת	שׁ	שׂ	ר
		tav	*shin*	*sin*	*resh*

† Boxes highlight final forms

Final Forms

Five Hebrew characters have two distinct forms—a standard form and a final form. The final form is used only when the letter appears at the end of a word, for example, מלך (NOT מלכ). With the exception of the final *mem* (ם), these final forms simply pivot the lower leg of the letter so that it extends below the line.[1]

Easily Confused Letters

When learning to write and recognize Hebrew consonants, watch out for letters that are frequently confused due to similar shape. Subtle differences between a curve and a projection (ר vs. ד), the length of a line (ו vs. ן), or the angles of a stroke (ע vs. צ) are essential for distinguishing these characters. Do not feel discouraged if it takes a bit to get accustomed to identifying each character. They will soon become familiar.

Table 1.2: Easily Confused Letters

פ *pe*	כ *kaph*	ב *bet*		ן final *nun*	י *yod*	ז *zayin*	ו *vav*
ך final *kaph*	ר *resh*	ד *dalet*	צ *tsade*	ע *ayin*		מ *mem*	ט *tet*
ת *tav*	ח *ḥet*	ה *heh*	ם final *mem*	ס *samek*		נ *nun*	ג *gimel*

1. In early manuscripts like the Dead Sea Scrolls the final *mem* drops below the line as well. However, in later manuscripts and printed editions it has the same baseline as regular forms. The Dead Sea Scrolls sometimes display distinctions between other medial and final letters that are no longer preserved. For example, the final *bet* sometimes appears with a longer baseline than that found in medial *bet* (e.g., line 5 of 4Q71).

WHAT DOES THE ALPHABET SOUND LIKE?

Table 1.3 below provides a description of the Hebrew alphabet. Included in this chart are the Hebrew letter, its name, and its pronunciation. The name of each Hebrew letter begins with the sound that is used in pronunciation. For example, the *samek* (ס) sounds like /s/. Learning the names of the letters helps you remember their sound.

Throughout the grammar the names of the letters are represented with simple English spelling. However, the chart below includes some phonetic detail so that you can learn to pronounce the names correctly. The symbol ḥ indicates a rough /h/ sound, like when you try to clear your throat. The symbol ē sounds like the long vowel in "th<u>ey</u>," and the symbol ī sounds like the vowel in "sk<u>i</u>." For example, *bēt* is pronounced like the English word "bait," and *sīn* is pronounced like the word "seen." When pronouncing the names of these letters you should be aware that the accent is always on the first syllable (e.g., *áleph, bét, gímel, dálet*, etc.).[2] Do not be confused when some Hebrew consonants have no English equivalent.

Table 1.3: Pronunciation Equivalents for the Hebrew Alphabet

Letter	Name	Pronunciation	
א	*aleph*	/ /	*not heard in English*
בּ/ב	*bēt*	/b/	as in *boy* (בּ) and /v/ as in *verse* (ב)
גּ/ג	*gimel*	/g/	as in *girl*
דּ/ד	*dalet*	/d/	as in *door*
ה	*hēh*	/h/	as in *help*
ו	*vav* (*waw*)	/v/	as in *verse* (originally this letter was pronounced as /w/ and will be spelled as *waw* in future chapters.)

2. A system of transliteration is commonly used in commentaries and technical works when English characters are used in place of the actual Hebrew font (with diacritic marks to distinguish similar sounds). This transliteration system is discussed in appendix 5.

ז		*zayin*	/z/	as in *zoo*
ח		*ḥēt*	/ḥ/	this is a rough /h/ sound (like when you try to clear your throat)
ט		*tēt*	/t/	as in *top*
י		*yōd*	/y/	as in *yard*
כ/כּ	ך	*kaph*	/c/	as in *cup* (כּ) and /ch/ as in the Scottish word for lake—e.g., *"Loch Ness"* (כ).
ל		*lamed*	/l/	as in *lake*
מ	ם	*mēm*	/m/	as in *man*
נ	ן	*nūn*	/n/	as in *next*
ס		*samek*	/s/	as in *sand*
ע		*ayin*	/ /	*not heard in English*
פ/פּ	ף	*pē*	/p/	as in *park* (פּ) and /ph/ as in *phrase* (פ)
צ	ץ	*tsadē*	/ts/	as in *nets*
ק		*qōph*	/k/	as in *conquer* (sounds similar to כ, *kaph*, but is pronounced further back in the throat)
ר		*rēsh*	/r/	as in *role* (roll the /r/ with the tongue in the front of the mouth)†
שׂ		*sīn*	/s/	as in *sand* (sounds the same as ס, *samek*)‡
שׁ		*shīn*	/sh/	as in *ship*
ת/תּ		*tav*	/t/	as in *top* (sounds the same as ט, *tēt*)

† Some scholars suggest that the ר /r/ is pronounced in the back of the throat like a guttural (analogous to French or German /r/).

‡ Notice that the dot is on the left side of the consonant for שׂ *(sin)* and on the right side of the consonant for שׁ *(shin)*. To help you remember this, keep in mind that "sin is never right."

The Hebrew alphabet is different from the English alphabet in that it is made up only of consonants and has no vowel letters. Vowel sounds are naturally used when pronouncing words, but they are not represented by the alphabet itself. Originally, when reading a Hebrew text aloud, a person simply supplied the vowels for each word based on his or her familiarity with the language. Eventually vowel notations were added to help the reader know how the text was supposed to be read. We will discuss the vowels in the next chapter.

SPECIAL GROUPS OF LETTERS

There are a few groups of letters that share similar characteristics and will figure prominently in the chapters that follow.

BeGaD KePhaT Letters

One important group of related letters is the *BeGaD KePhaT* letters—בגד כפת. These six letters are listed in the pronunciation table above both with and without a dot. This dot is called a *dagesh*. These dots were added to the text, together with the vowel notations, in order to accurately reflect an important aspect of pronunciation. The dot in these six letters indicates a hard pronunciation (a full stop of air) in contrast with the soft pronunciation of that consonant without the dot (e.g., פּ /p/ vs. פ /ph/). These six letters can be remembered with the mnemonic *BeGaD KePhaT* (בגד כפת).

The *BeGaD KePhaT* letters can all appear with or without the dot, but modern pronunciation maintains the distinction between hard and soft sounds in only three of these letters, namely the *bet*, *kaph*, and *pe* (see table 1.4 for pronunciation).[3]

Gutturals

A second important group of consonants are the gutturals: א, ה, ח, and ע. The term *guttural* indicates a sound produced in the back of the throat. The letter ר is also associated with the gutturals because it behaves similarly. We will discuss these letters more fully in future lessons. For now, simply learn to identify the four gutturals א, ה, ח, ע, and associated letter ר.

3. This grammar follows Modern Hebrew pronunciation, which no longer makes a distinction between the hard and soft pronunciation of ג, ד, and ת. However, some Hebrew programs encourage their students to maintain a distinction for all these characters, distinguishing גּ (as in **g**irl) from ג (as in massa**g**e), דּ (as in **d**oor) from ד (as in **th**is), and תּ (as in **t**op) from ת (as in **th**eme).

Table 1.4: Modern Pronunciation of *BeGaD KePhaT* Letters

Hard and soft			*No distinction*		
בּ	hard b	as in **b**oy	ג/גּ	g	as in **g**irl
ב	soft b	as in **v**erse			
כּ	hard k	as in **c**up	ד/דּ	d	as in **d**oor
כ	soft k	as in lo**ch**			
פּ	hard p	as in **p**ark	ת/תּ	t	as in **t**op
פ	soft p	as in **ph**rase			

WRITING THE HEBREW ALPHABET

Hebrew Square Script

Learning to write the characters of the Hebrew square script by hand will help you notice the distinctions between similar characters and reinforce your familiarity with the printed text. You do not need to reproduce the fancy calligraphy of printed Hebrew fonts. Handwritten characters can be produced in a much simpler form. Table 1.5 shows you how to write out the Hebrew square script by hand.

Hebrew Cursive (Optional)

Some students take advantage of the Hebrew cursive script (table 1.6). The advantage of cursive script is that it follows the flow of the hand and allows the writer to make each consonant with fewer strokes. As a result, it allows you to write more quickly and efficiently. You are welcome to learn the cursive script, but you must first master the square script, which more closely matches the shape of the letters in the biblical text.

Table 1.5: Writing the Hebrew Square Script†

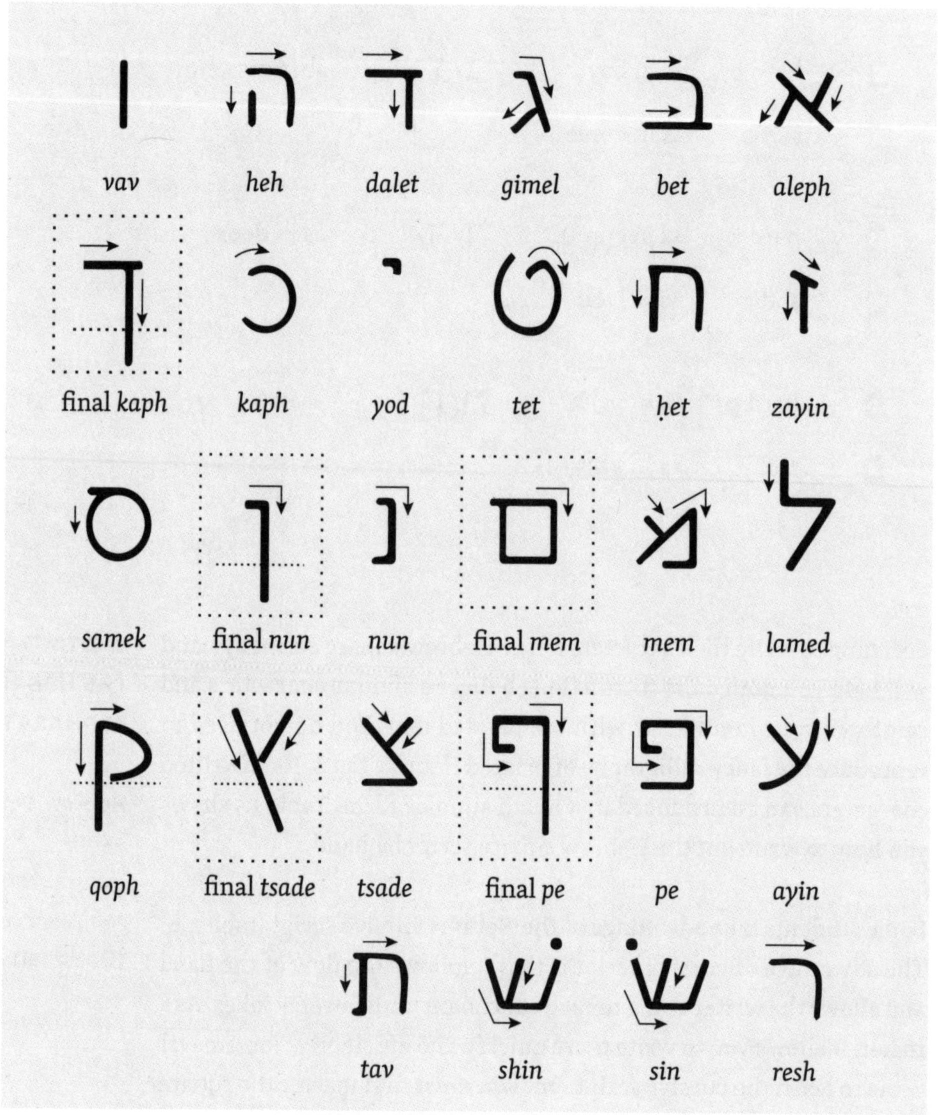

† Boxes highlight final forms

Table 1.6: Writing in Hebrew Cursive†

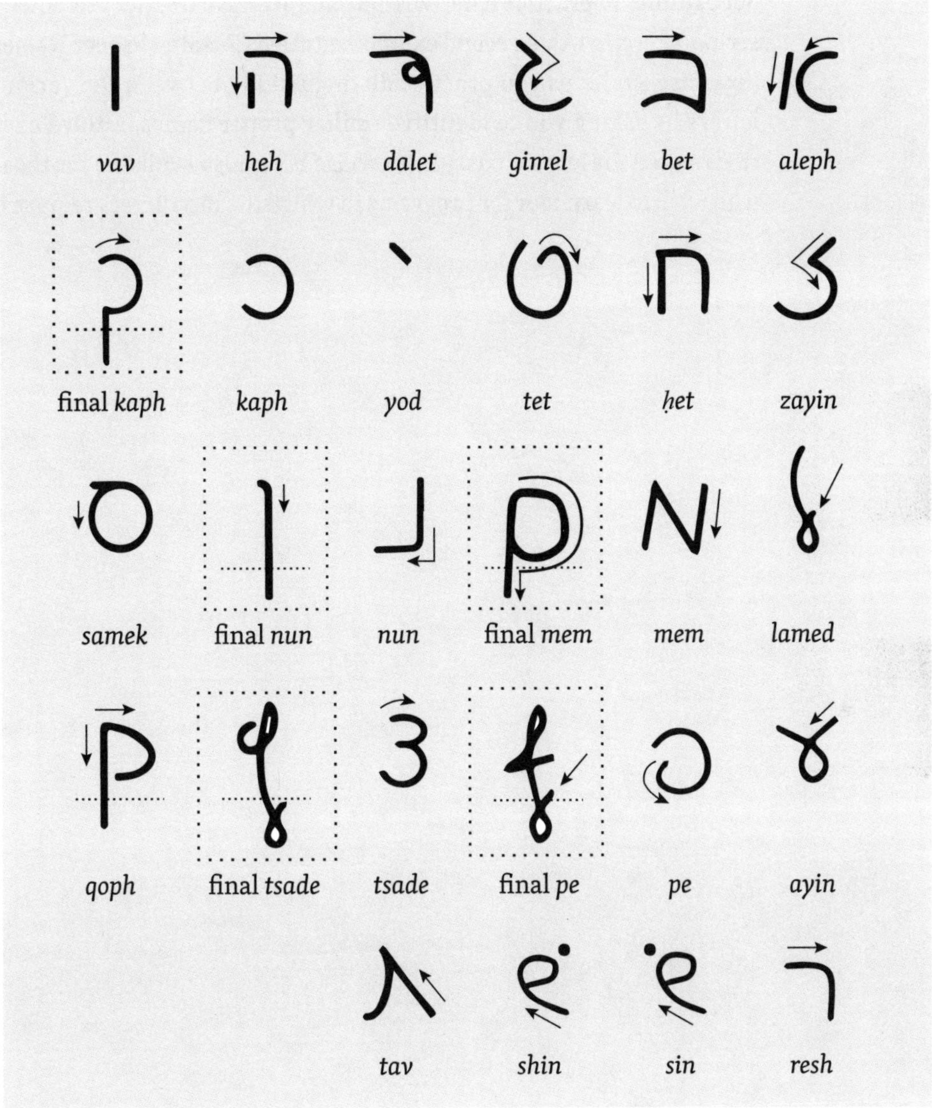

† Boxes highlight final forms

EXERCISES FOR CHAPTER 1

The workbook includes several exercises to help you become acquainted with the Hebrew alphabet. The first exercise provides you with an opportunity to practice hand-written characters in the Hebrew square script (exercise 1A). A second exercise entitled "Reading Proper Names" (exercise 1B) helps you practice distinguishing between the various letters by asking you to identify familiar proper names. A third exercise related to Hebrew cursive (exercise 1C) is also available for those who wish to learn it or for programs in which the instructors require it.

CHAPTER 2

Hebrew Vowels

As noted earlier, the Hebrew alphabet does not include vowels. The vowel sounds are supplied by the reader based on familiarity with the Hebrew language and with the text. The desire for clarity and for the preservation of longstanding reading traditions of the biblical text eventually led to innovations that would mark the presence of vowels.

HOW ARE VOWELS REPRESENTED?

Vowel Markers

The first innovation for marking the presence of vowels involved the use of three existing consonants— ו (*waw*), י (*yod*), and ה (*heh*)—to serve as *vowel markers*.[1] If you slowly pronounce the vowels as they sound in the words "they" and "ski," you can hear the subtle hint of a /y/ sound after each vowel. In the words "so" and "true," you can hear a subtle /w/ sound. In a similar manner you can hear the hint of an /h/ sound at the end of the vowel in the word "mocha." Based on this affinity in sound, Hebrew scribes eventually began to insert the characters ו (w), י (y), and ה (h) to alert the reader to the presence of vowel sounds. Thus the scribes began to represent vowel sounds in a purely consonantal text. When used to indicate the presence of a vowel, these three letters do not function as true consonants. Instead they function as vowel markers (called *matres lectionis* in some grammars).

The insertion of vowel markers helped to alleviate confusion in reading. Without vowel markers, words that should be pronounced

1. Remember that in chapter 1 the name of the Hebrew character *waw* was spelled as ***vav*** due to our focus on how the letter is pronounced. In all other discussions it will be written as ***waw*** (though still pronounced *vav*) to serve as a constant reminder that this character was originally pronounced as /w/. This older pronunciation /w/ will help you understand its use as a vowel marker.

differently are spelled the same. Vowel markers alert the reader to the presence of a vowel sound and ensure that the correct word is read.

Hebrew word	Without vowel markers		Vowel markers added
"king" (*melek*)	מלך	→	מלך
"queen" (*malka*)	מלך	→	מלכה
"they ruled" (*mal^eku*)	מלך	→	מלכו

The text of Genesis 1:1–2 illustrates the use of vowel markers. The letters in red are not functioning as consonants, but instead serve to mark the presence of vowel sounds (i.e., they are vowel markers).

u a i i
בראשית ברא אלהים את השמים ואת הארץ והארץ היתה תהו
ובהו וחשך על פני תהום ורוח אלהים מרחפת על פני המים
e i u o e u

For now, know that the letters ו (*waw*), י (*yod*), and ה (*heh*) can be used as vowel markers. Later we will show you how to tell when these letters are used as vowel markers and when they are true consonants.

Vowel Pointing

Eventually the consonantal text was standardized and considered unchangeable. Any further attempt to preserve the ancient oral reading traditions required an entirely different set of notations—one that would not interfere with the consonants. The solution was to develop a system of vowel notations that were added above or below the letters without altering the consonantal text.

At one time there were three different vowel notation systems in use, each one with its own special set of symbols. Table 2.1 displays these various vowel systems using boxes to show how the vowels are positioned in relationship to the Hebrew consonants.

Table 2.1: Early Systems of Hebrew Vowel Notation

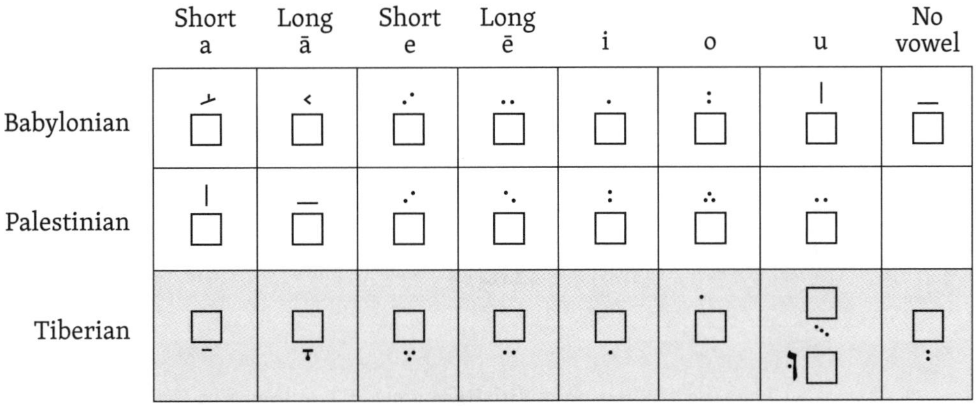

The Tiberian system eventually became the standard system of vowel pointing and is represented in printed editions of the Hebrew Bible today.

Vowel Placement

In the Tiberian system vowels are placed below or to the left of the consonants. The majority of vowels appear directly beneath the letter (i.e., בָ). The long /ō/ is placed in the upper left hand corner of the Hebrew character (בֹ) and the long /ū/ is represented by a dot inside the following vowel marker (בוּ). When these vowels are put into a Hebrew sentence, they look like this.[2]

Gen 1:1

בראשית ברא אלהים את השמים ואת הארץ *Before*

בְּרֵאשִׁית בָּרָא אֱלֹהִים אֵת הַשָּׁמַיִם וְאֵת הָאָרֶץ *After*

2. The pointing system identifies more than just vowel sounds. For example, it distinguishes between *sin* and *shin* (see בראשית above). For now, focus on the vowels.

Hebrew is read from right to left, and vowels follow consonants. In other words, begin with a consonant, look for a vowel notation, and proceed to the next consonant. For example, when you encounter the word הֶעָפָר, the *heh* is pronounced first together with the vowel below it.

he-ā-phār

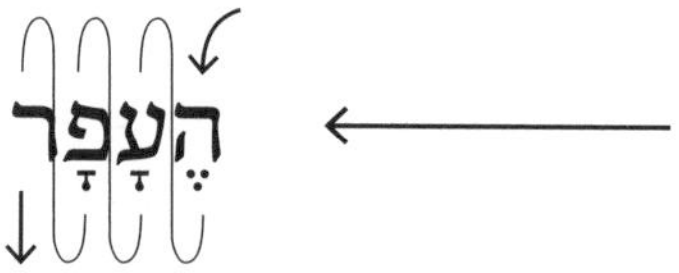

The silent *ayin* is next with its vowel (-*ā*-), followed by the *pe* plus vowel and the last letter that has no vowel of its own (-*phār*). In the beginning it is entirely natural to read Hebrew one syllable at a time. Together the syllables produce *he-ā-phār* ("the dust").

Remember, not all vowels appear underneath the consonant. If a consonant does not have a vowel beneath it, look to the upper left and then proceed to the next consonant.

ḥō-shek *qō-desh*

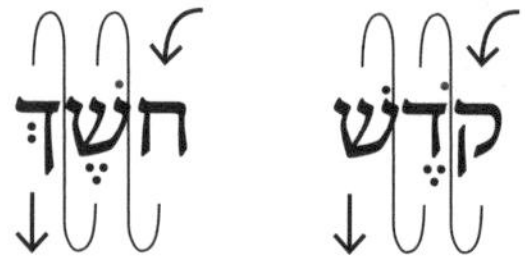

Thus, קֹדֶשׁ is pronounced *qōdesh* ("holiness"). Sometimes the vowel at the upper left overlaps the dot of a *shin* (שׁ), in which case it often does double duty for both the consonant and the vowel. Thus the word חֹשֶׁךְ is pronounced *ḥōshek* ("darkness").

HOW ARE THE VOWELS PRONOUNCED?

There are ten vowels used in Hebrew. The diagram below presents the full range of Hebrew vowels.

Table 2.2: The Hebrew Vowels

		Short Vowels	*Name (Sound)*	**Long Vowels**	*Name (Sound)*
a-class	a	□ַ	*pataḥ* (ball)	□ָ □ָה	*qamets* (ball)
i-class	e	□ֶ	*segol* (pet)	□ֵ □ֵי	*tsere* (they)
	i	□ִ	*ḥireq* (pit)	□ִי	*ḥireq yod* (ski)
u-class	o	□ָ	*qamets qaton* (hope) "short *qamets*"	□ֹ □וֹ	*ḥolem* (hope)
	u	□ֻ	*qibbuts* (rule)	□וּ	*shureq* (rule)

Learn to identify the vowels by name, length, sound, and vowel class. For example, the vowel ◌ֶ (*segol*) is a short /e/ that sounds like the vowel in "pet" and is an i-class vowel. Many vowels have the same basic sound whether short or long, although they retain a visual distinction (e.g., ◌ֻ and וּ both sound like /u/ in "rule"). Further, recognize that long vowels can occur with or without a vowel marker (discussed in more depth in ch. 5). One difficulty that students face is that the same vowel notation is used to represent both long /a/ and short /o/.[3] We will teach you how to distinguish these two vowels later. For now, assume the symbol ◌ָ represents a long /a/ unless explicitly indicated.

Another difficulty that students face is the expectation that /a/, /e/, and /i/ will sound like they do in English. Note carefully that /a/ is pronounced like the /ah/ in ball for both long and short vowels (NOT like

3. Historically long /a/ and short /o/ were distinct in sound (as represented in the pronunciation chart above). This distinction is preserved in the Ashkenazi reading tradition. However, the Hebrew scribes who put in the Tiberian vowel pointing did not hear any distinction in sound between long /a/ and short /o/. (Just as we hear little difference between the vowels in the words "ball" and "hop.") As a result, they naturally used the same vowel symbol to represent both vowels. This historic distinction was adopted as the official pronunciation for Modern Hebrew and is followed in this grammar.

b<u>a</u>t or b<u>ai</u>t). Likewise, long ē (*tsere*) is pronounced like the /ey/ in th<u>ey</u> (NOT like s<u>ee</u>), and long ī (*ḥireq yod*) is pronounced as in sk<u>i</u> like an English ē (NOT like the English ī in k<u>i</u>te).

MARKING THE ABSENCE OF A VOWEL (SHEWA)

The Hebrew vowel system requires all but final consonants to have some kind of vowel notation. Thus the system requires a symbol to designate the *absence of a vowel*. The symbol chosen to represent a vowelless consonant is called a *shewa* (ְ). Hebrew has two types of *shewa*, simple *shewa* (ְ) and composite *shewa* (ֲ, ֱ, ֳ), that both indicate the absence of a vowel. A simple *shewa* (ְ) is sometimes silent. However, when a slight sound is needed for the transition between consonants, the simple *shewa* has a very short sound as when "because" is pronounced *b'cause*.[4] The composite *shewa* is also used to indicate a specific quality—a-class composite-*shewa* (ֲ), the i-class composite-*shewa* (ֱ), and the u-class composite-*shewa* (ֳ)—each are pronounced like an abrupt short vowel.[5]

Table 2.3: Types of *Shewas*

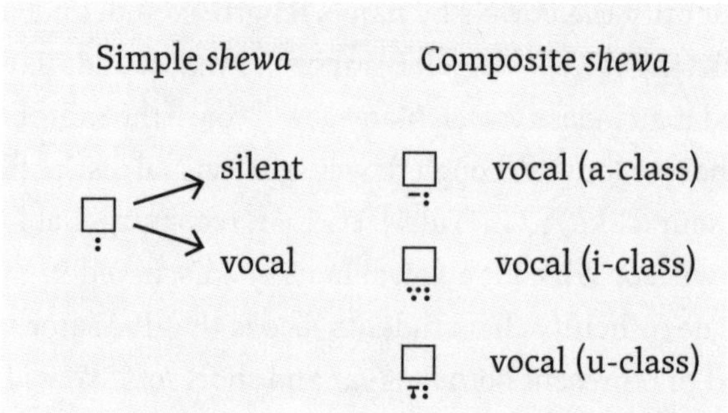

Regardless of its appearance, **a *shewa* is a *shewa* is a *shewa*.** A *shewa* always represents the absence of a vowel, even when you occasionally hear a sound.[6]

4. In many cases the composite *shewa* is used with gutturals (א, ה, ח, ע) to ensure that the guttural is not lost in pronunciation; e.g., the word אֲדָמָה is read as *adāmā* ("ground").

5. The Hebrew names for the composite *shewa* are *ḥateph-pataḥ* (ֲ), *ḥateph-segol* (ֱ), and *ḥateph-qamets* (ֳ)—i.e., "hurried *pataḥ*," etc. Notice that there is one composite *shewa* for each vowel class.

6. Cf. Joüon §8a. Some choose to describe the *shewa* as a half vowel or reduced vowel because they are trying to capture the fact that it is sometimes voiced (e.g., GKC §10a). While this may be helpful for students in terms of clarifying sound, it presents problems later on when we begin discussing syllable structure and historic vowel changes.

Distinguishing Silent Shewa and Vocal Shewa

As reflected in the table above, composite *shewas* (◌ֲ, ◌ֱ, and ◌ֳ) are always vocal. However, the simple *shewa* (◌ְ) can be either silent or vocal. The use of silent *shewa* versus vocal *shewa* is driven entirely by the demands of pronunciation. The following table will help you learn to distinguish when conditions demand a sound (vocal) and when they do not (silent). These principles are largely intuitive, and future chapters will revisit and clarify the use of *shewa* once you have more understanding of Hebrew word structure. For now allow these principles to guide your pronunciation of Hebrew words.

Table 2.4: Distinguishing Silent *Shewa* and Vocal *Shewa*

1. *Shewa* under the first consonant of a word is vocal.

   מְלָכִים — *m*^{e}*lākīm*

2. *Shewa* under the final consonant of a word is silent.

   מֶלֶךְ — *melek*

3. *Shewa* in the middle of a word—after a long vowel, *shewa* is vocal; after a short vowel, *shewa* is silent.

   יֵלְכוּ — *yē-l*^{e}*kū*

   מַמְלָכָה — *mam-lākā*

4. Double-*shewa* at the front of a word is impossible.

5. Double-*shewa* at the end of a word is silent.

   קָטַלְתְּ — *qātalt*

6. Double-*shewa* in the middle of a word—the first is silent, the second is vocal.

   מַמְלְכוֹת — *mam-l*^{e}*kōt*

1) Shewa under the first consonant of a word is vocal.

A *shewa* under the first consonant of a word is always a vocal *shewa*. A vowelless letter at the front of a word requires a quick shift in sound in order to distinctly pronounce each of the first two consonants. For example, מְלָכִים is pronounced as *mᵉlākīm*. The vocal *shewa* is simply a product of the demands of pronunciation.

2) Shewa under the final consonant of a word is silent.

A *shewa* under the final consonant of a word is always silent. No additional sound is required because there is no transition into another consonant. For example, the word מֶ֫לֶךְ ("king") is pronounced *melek*, with no sound voiced with the *shewa*. Notice once again that the distinction between silent and vocal *shewa* is driven by the demands of pronunciation.

3) Shewa in the middle of a word—after a long vowel, shewa is vocal; after a short vowel, shewa is silent.

If you find a *shewa* under a consonant in the middle of the word, you will need some other guidelines for determining whether it is vocal or silent. Until you acquire a better understanding of Hebrew syllables and word structure, consider a *shewa* after a long vowel to be vocal and a *shewa* after a short vowel to be silent.

After <u>L</u>ONG vowels: *shewa* is <u>L</u>OUD (vocal)
After <u>SH</u>ORT vowels: *shewa* is <u>Shhh</u>! (silent)

For example, the word יֵלְכוּ is pronounced as *yē-lᵉkū*. The vowel before the *shewa* is long /ē/, so the *shewa* should be vocal. You must make a short sound as you transition from the ל to the כ. On the other hand, the word מַמְלָכָה is pronounced as *mam-lākā*. The vowel before the *shewa* is short /a/, so the *shewa* is silent. No vowel sound is heard after the second מ.

4) Double-shewa at the front of a word is impossible.

Two *shewas* cannot stand together at the front of a word. If you think about this for a moment, the reason will become clear. Try to pronounce מְלְכֵי*[7] without a sound between the first three consonants (*mlkē*). Hebrew does not allow for this type of consonant cluster. As a result, you will never find two *shewas* at the front of a word.

5) Double-shewa at the end of a word is silent.

You will, however, find two *shewas* together at the end of a word. When you do, they will both be silent. Once again, this makes sense. We often finish words with two vowelless consonants in English (e.g., *bolt* or *card*). When you encounter the word קָטַלְתְּ, treat the final *shewas* as silent and pronounce the word as *qatalt*.

6) Double-shewa in the middle of a word—the first is silent, the second is vocal.

When two *shewas* occur side-by-side in the middle of a word, the first *shewa* is silent and the second *shewa* is vocal. Or, as our students like to say, "the first one does the walking and the second does the talking." Hebrew does not allow three consonants in a row without an intervening vowel sound. Thus a word like מַמְלְכוֹת, is pronounced *mam-l*^{e}*kōt*. When you encounter double *shewas* in the middle of a word, the first is silent, the second is vocal. Notice that all three rules about double-*shewa* are a by-product of the natural limitations of pronunciation.

ADDITIONAL NOTATIONS IN THE POINTING

The Hebrew vocalization system contains another key element besides the vowels and *shewas*. As you may remember, Hebrew letters sometimes appear with a dot inside them. So far you have only learned one kind of dot, the *dagesh lene* that marks the hard pronunciation of certain letters.[8] However, there are actually three types of dots. These are referred to as *dagesh lene* (*BeGaD KePhaT* dot), *dagesh forte* (doubling dot), and *mappiq* (h-dot).

7. Note that the asterisk * is used to indicate reconstructed historic forms or forms not actually found in Biblical Hebrew.

8. Remember that the hard and soft distinction with the letters ג, ד, and ת is no longer heard in our modern pronunciation. As a result, these three letters are now pronounced hard even when they have no *dagesh*.

Dagesh Lene ("BeGaD KePhaT Dot")

The *dagesh lene* is used to mark the hard pronunciation of בגד כפת (the "*BeGaD KePhaT* letters"). The hard pronunciation is used at the beginning of a word or syllable where a "plosive" or hard pronunciation would be expected (e.g., פּ = p). The soft pronunciation follows a vowel sound and is linked to the flow of air that is initiated by the preceding vowel (e.g., פ = ph). To identify a *dagesh lene* confirm these two conditions: 1) It only occurs in a *BeGaD KePhaT* letter, and 2) it never follows a vowel. Because the function of the *dagesh lene* is purely related to sound, it is the simplest of the dots to master.

1. It only occurs in the *BeGaD KePhaT* letters (בגד כפת).
2. It never follows a vowel.

Once you learn these principles it will not surprise you to see the *dagesh lene* in *BeGaD KePhaT* letters either at the beginning of words or following silent *shewa*.[9]

Dagesh Forte ("Doubling Dot")

The second type of dot is called a *dagesh forte*[10] and is used to mark the presence of a doubled consonant. Hebrew expresses a doubled consonant with a *dagesh* rather than writing the consonant twice (e.g., חִטְטֵא* is written as חִטֵּא). Since it reflects a doubled consonant, you can also refer to the *dagesh forte* as a doubling dot.

The *dagesh forte* implies the presence of two identical consonants with only one vowel pointing (either a vowel or *shewa*). Every *dagesh forte* has an implicit silent *shewa* with the first of the doubled consonants. For pronunciation you will need to voice the consonant once with silent *shewa* and a second time with the vowel pointing provided. Thus in the example חִטֵּא you should pronounce the ט twice (חִטְטֵא* pronounced *ḥit-tē*). The same is true when a doubled consonant appears with a *shewa*. The word יִסְּדוּ has two *sameks* (= יִסְסְדוּ*). Since the doubled consonant with *shewa* is the equivalent of two *shewas* side-by-side, the first is silent (the implicit *shewa*) and the second is vocal (the visible *shewa*). The word יִסְּדוּ (= יִסְסְדוּ*) is thus pronounced *yis-sᵉdū*.

9. When a *BeGaD KePhaT* letter at the beginning of a word does not have a *dagesh lene*, it is because the preceding word ends in a vowel and the two words are syntactically linked (i.e., closely associated in a phrase).

10. The term *dagesh lene* is the "weaker *dagesh*" (Latin *lene*) that designates only hard pronunciation. The term *dagesh forte* is the "stronger *dagesh*" (Latin *forte*) where you find doubling (plus hard pronunciation where applicable).

Dagesh Forte with Gutturals

As a rule gutturals and *resh* (א, ה, ח, ע, and ר) do not take *dagesh forte*. It is difficult to double a consonant that is pronounced in the back of the throat.

Dagesh Forte with "Skin 'em Levi" Letters

One group of consonants that take *dagesh forte* can lose that *dagesh* under special conditions. The mnemonic *Skin 'em Levi* or קנמ לוי-"s" (where the "s" = the sounds ס, צ, שׂ, שׁ) will help you remember the consonants included in this group. These *Skin 'em Levi* letters frequently (though inconsistently) lose *dagesh forte* when they are followed by a *shewa*.

Dagesh Forte in BeGaD KePhaT Letters

Although *dagesh lene* and *dagesh forte* both appear as a dot, it is possible to tell them apart. If a dot appears in a letter that is not a *BeGaD KePhaT* letter, it must be a *dagesh forte*.[11] However, a *dagesh* in a *BeGaD KePhaT* letter can create potential confusion because these letters can take either type of *dagesh*. Since a *dagesh lene* never follows a vowel, a *dagesh* following a vowel is *forte*. If it does not follow a vowel, it is *lene*.

After a vowel sound	→	***Dagesh forte***
After a *shewa*	→	***Dagesh lene***

Both types of *dagesh* will cause a *BeGaD KePhaT* letter to be pronounced with a hard sound.

Mappiq ("H-Dot")

The third type of dot is called a *mappiq*. The *mappiq* is used to indicate that a *heh* (ה) at the end of a word is a true consonant rather than a vowel marker.[12] When the *mappiq* is present, it affects both pronunciation and meaning. A *heh* (ה) with a *mappiq* is pronounced with a slight aspiration so that the consonant is noticeable. You should hear a subtle difference between מַלְכָּה ("queen") and מַלְכָּהּ ("her king"). These two words, which have identical letters, are distinguished with regard to sound and meaning.

11. Unless it is the *mappiq* or h-dot discussed below, but *mappiq* is seen in final ה.

12. Hebrew manuscripts also use *mappiq* to indicate that א, ו, and י are functioning as consonants. In printed editions of the Hebrew Bible you will see this only with ה and א (e.g., וַיָּבִיאּוּ). Cf. GKC §14d.

◌ָהּ	Consonant	pronounced *āh*
◌ָה	Vowel marker	pronounced *ā*

As you learn more Hebrew you will see how the *mappiq* marks a difference in meaning. At this point you simply need to think about pronunciation.

RECOGNIZING VOWEL MARKERS

The letters used to indicate the presence of vowels are *heh* (ה), *waw* (ו), and *yod* (י). The *heh* (ה) is always a consonant unless it appears at the end of the word without a *mappiq*. Determining when ו and י act as vowel markers or as true consonants requires closer attention to the surrounding vowel pointing. Two principles for identifying a vowel marker are:

1. Vowel markers always have affinity with the vowels they represent.
2. Every Hebrew consonant has one, and only one, vowel notation.

1) Vowel markers always have affinity with the vowels they represent.

Vowel markers always have affinity with the vowels they represent. Although final ה can be used to represent a number of different vowels (◌ָה, ◌ֶה, ◌ֵה, and ◌ֹה), by contrast the י serves only i-class vowels (e.g., ◌ִי, ◌ֵי, ◌ֶי), and ו serves only u-class vowels (e.g., וּ, וֹ). If you pronounce each of these vowel sounds, you can hear the subtle /h/, /y/, or /w/ sound at the end of the vowel. For example, if you say the words "they" or "ski," you can hear the hint of a /y/ sound with the vowel. The letter י is thus the natural choice to serve as a vowel marker for i-class vowels (◌ִי, ◌ֵי, ◌ֶי). Likewise you can hear the hint of a /w/ sound with the vowels in the words "hope" and "rule." As a result, the letter *waw* is used as a vowel marker for u-class vowels (וֹ, וּ). If ו or י follows an incompatible vowel, it cannot be a vowel marker.

◌ֵי	Compatible *yod*	=	*vowel + vowel marker*
◌ָי	Incompatible *yod*	=	vowel + consonant

When a *waw* or *yod* is a consonant, it is pronounced /v/ or /y/. When it is a vowel marker, simply pronounce the vowel.

2) Every Hebrew consonant has one, and only one, vowel notation.

Every consonant requires a vowel notation (a vowel or *shewa*) except the last letter of a word.[13] Moreover, every consonant has *only one* vowel notation.[14] To distinguish a vowel marker from a consonant, consider each element of the word in order. For example, in the word מְצַוְּךָ the ו could be either a *shureq* (long u-class vowel) or a *waw* (consonant) with a doubling dot. This word begins with consonant + vowel notation (מְ) + consonant + vowel notation (צַ). The next letter (וּ) *must* be a consonant because Hebrew cannot have two vowels in a row. Equally true, the *shewa* under the *waw* (וְ) must belong to a consonant. This וּ must be a doubled *waw* (*dagesh forte*), not a vowel. The word מְצַוְּךָ ("commanding you") is pronounced *m^e-tsav-v^e-kā* (NOT *m^e-tsaū-kā*).

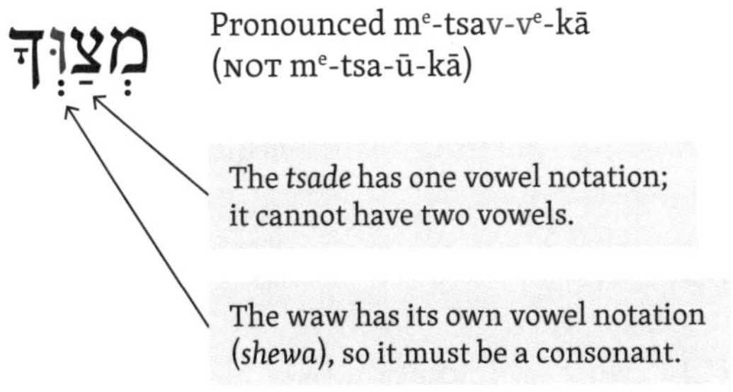

In a second example, the *yod* in שִׂים could be either a *ḥireq yod* (long i-class vowel) or a *yod* (consonant). The word begins with consonant + vowel notation (שִׂ). Based on the example above, you would expect a consonant to follow and might identify the *yod* as that consonant.

13. A final letter can have a vowel notation, but does not require one (e.g., קָטַלְתָּ).

14. Words like רוּחַ (pronounced *rū-aḥ*) are not really an exception. As we will see in ch. 3, this short /a/ sound is a helping vowel added only to transition from the long vowel in the front of the mouth to the guttural in the back of the throat. It is merely there to smooth pronunciation.

However, every consonant except the last letter in a word must have a vowel notation following it. Since *yod* has no vowel notation following it, it cannot be a consonant. It is a vowel marker. The word שִׂים ("to put") is pronounced *sim,* as in "seem" (NOT *si-ym*).

שִׂים Pronounced sīm (NOT si-ym)

The vowel with *sin* shares affinity with *yod* (as in 'ski' where you hear a subtle /y/).

The *yod* has no vowel notation, so it cannot be a consonant.

QUIESCENT ALEPH

Another letter that does not always function as a consonant is *aleph* (א). You have already learned that *aleph* is a silent letter. Though silent, when *aleph* carries a vowel, it is functioning as a consonant (e.g., מָאַס = *ma-as*). However, sometimes *aleph* appears without any vowel notation (neither vowel nor *shewa*). The lack of vowel notation indicates that *aleph* is not only silent but has lost its consonantal value. This *aleph* is not represented at all in pronunciation and appears in the text only to preserve the original spelling of the word. This use of the letter is called "quiescent" *aleph*. When you see *aleph* in the text without any vowel notation, it is not functioning as a consonant. An *aleph* in the middle of a word can be quiescent (e.g., רֵאשִׁית = *rē-shīt* "beginning"), and an *aleph* in final position is always quiescent (e.g., בָּרָא = *bara*).

מָאַס	With vowel notation (אַ)	=	Consonantal *aleph*
רֵאשִׁית	No vowel notation (א)	=	Quiescent *aleph*

EXERCISE FOR CHAPTER 2

Exercise 2 in the workbook will help you practice recognizing the various vowels and distinguishing between vocal and silent *shewa*.

CHAPTER 3

Syllables and Reading Hebrew

Now that you have an introduction to Hebrew consonants and vowels, it is time to start putting them together so that you can read the Hebrew text aloud. In order to do this correctly you must learn to identify the individual consonant-vowel units (called *syllables*) that make up each word and learn to stress the appropriate syllable. For example, in English we pronounce the word "history" as a combination of the syllables *his-to-ry*, and we stress the first syllable (*his'-to-ry*). To read Hebrew properly you must correctly identify the syllables and pronounce them in sequence with the appropriate stress.

While the immediate outcome of this chapter is that you will be able to read Hebrew words aloud, the ultimate goal is broader than pronunciation. In studying syllabification (the breaking down of words into smaller units of sound, called syllables) we are laying the groundwork for a more developed understanding of the formation and behavior of Hebrew words. This fundamental understanding of word structure will enable you to recognize and even anticipate the changes that will occur within Hebrew words as they are altered to communicate additional components of meaning. The practical outcome of this understanding of word structure is the enhancement of reading speed and comprehension, and a substantial reduction in the amount of required memory work.

As we walk through this chapter we will help you learn pronunciation by including an English representation of the sounds we are discussing. As we do so we will show you where the syllable breaks occur (e.g., מֶ֫|לֶךְ = *me´-lek*).[1]

WHAT IS A SYLLABLE?

In English we think of syllables as isolated units of sound within a word. The concept is much the same in Hebrew. These units of sound in Hebrew words are driven primarily by the relationship between consonants and vowels and follow predictable patterns.

Consonant + Vowel (+ Consonant)

As a general rule,[2] ***Hebrew syllables begin with a consonant and have only one vowel.*** A Hebrew syllable can end with that vowel or include an additional consonant. To simplify matters we talk about two types of syllables, those comprised of a *consonant + vowel* (CV) and those comprised of a *consonant + vowel + consonant* (CVC). If the syllable ends with a vowel, then that syllable is called an *open* syllable. If a syllable ends with a consonant, it is said to be *closed*. In other words, the vowel is closed in.

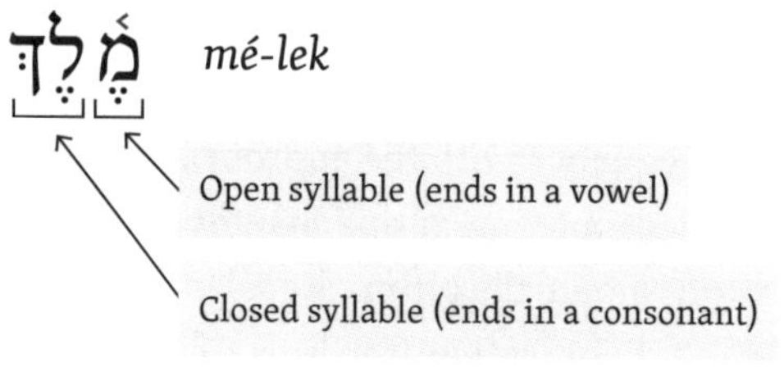

Once these syllables are put together to make up a Hebrew word, one syllable in each word will be *accented*. By this we mean that you will put more stress on one syllable than you do on the other syllables. Notice again the English word "history" that we mentioned in the opening paragraph. As you say this word you will hear a slight rise in the tone of your voice when you pronounce the first syllable (*his´-to-ry*). This is the kind of stress you will need to make with accented syllables in Hebrew.

1. The representation of pronunciation is different than formal transliteration. Transliteration, while more precise, is less helpful for identifying pronunciation for beginning students. For example, the transliteration of דָּבָר is *dāḇār*, but its pronunciation is represented more simply as *dā-vār´*. In this grammar consonants are represented for sound and vowels marked only as long or short.

2. One thing that you may as well come to accept is that ***there is an exception to every Hebrew rule***. Language is alive; it grows and changes and can be as unpredictable as the people who speak it. When describing language, grammarians can trace patterns and help students to understand general behavioral principles by setting forth what we call "rules," but these "rules" are really more like descriptive guidelines.

In Hebrew words, the accent falls either on the last syllable or on the second-to-last syllable. Of these, the most common position for the accent is on the last syllable. When you see a Hebrew word in this grammar, assume that the accent is on the final syllable unless otherwise marked. When the accent falls on the second-to-last syllable, it will be marked with the symbol ˂ above the first consonant of that syllable.[3]

דָבָר **Unmarked—Accent the last syllable** (*dā-vār′*)

מֶ֫לֶךְ **Marked—Accent the second-to-last syllable** (*me′-lek*)

In Hebrew it is customary to identify a syllable based on whether it is open or closed and on its relationship to the accent. As a result, we end up with four types of syllables: (1) *closed unaccented*, (2) *open unaccented*, (3) *closed accented*, and (4) *open accented*.

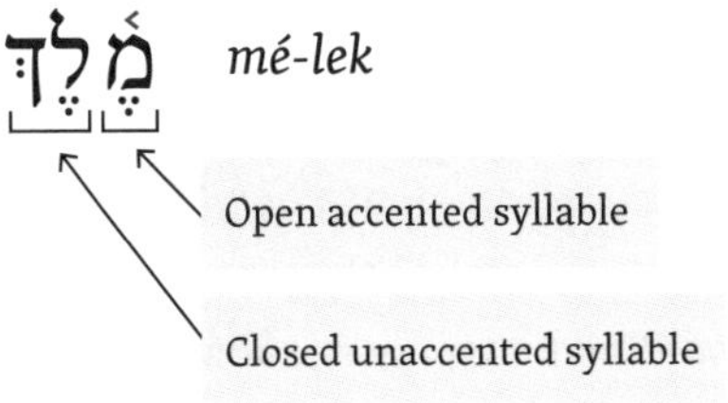

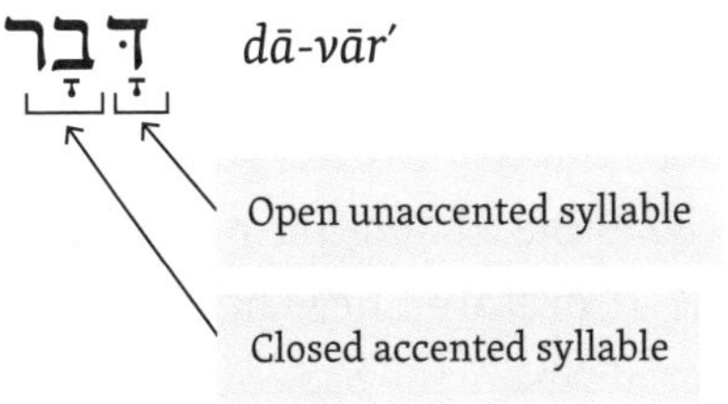

Exceptions

Two exceptions seem to violate the principle that *a Hebrew syllable begins with a consonant and has only one vowel.* These exceptions are not something you need to memorize. You will become familiar with them through exposure.

3. When you begin translating from the Hebrew Bible, you will find that the accents in the Hebrew Bible take a different form than the accent mark used in this grammar, but they will be easy to spot once you know your vowels. If the marks you see do not look like vowels, then the notations are accents.

Exception #1: Shureq (וּ) at the beginning of a word is treated as its own syllable.

The only exception to the rule that *every syllable starts with a consonant* is when וּ (*shureq*) appears at the beginning of a Hebrew word. Initial *shureq* occurs with some frequency because וּ at the beginning of a word marks the presence of the conjunction "and." (Normally the conjunction "and" is marked by וְ but is replaced by וּ on occasion.) This initial וּ is always treated as its own syllable. The following consonant begins a new syllable. For example, the word וּמֶ֫לֶךְ ("and king") must be pronounced as *ū-mé-lek* (NOT *ūm-e-lek*). Even if the first consonant has a *shewa*, that consonant must begin a new syllable. The word וּשְׁמוּאֵל ("and Samuel") is pronounced *ū-sh*^{e}*-mū-ēl* (NOT *ūsh-mū-ēl*). Remember that initial וּ always starts its own syllable and always stands alone.

וּמֶ֫לֶךְ *ū-mé-lek*

וּשְׁמוּאֵל *ū-sh*^{e}*-mū-ēl*

Exception #2: Furtive pataḥ is merely a helping vowel.

One other scenario seems to violate the principle that *a Hebrew syllable begins with a consonant and has only one vowel.* When a Hebrew word ends with the gutturals ה, ח, or ע, a *pataḥ* is sometimes added *before* the guttural to ease pronunciation.[4] This *pataḥ* is called furtive *pataḥ* ("subtle *pataḥ*"). It is a helping vowel and is not considered in determining syllables. It is difficult to pronounce a guttural immediately after a vowel that is produced in the front of the mouth (like long /ō/ or /ū/). Since gutturals like ה, ח, or ע are voiced in the back of the throat, the *pataḥ*, which is also produced in the back of the throat, eases this transition. The word רוּחַ must be treated as a single syllable word with no syllable break and is pronounced *rūaḥ* (NOT *rū-ḥa*).[5]

4. Because an א at the end of a word is quiescent, there is no guttural sound to transition into, and furtive *pataḥ* is not needed.

5. Thanks to advances in typesetting, modern texts place the furtive *pataḥ* a little to the right of the final consonant to help you see that it is only a helping vowel (e.g., רוּחַ). In older texts it sometimes appears directly under the consonant (רוּחַ).

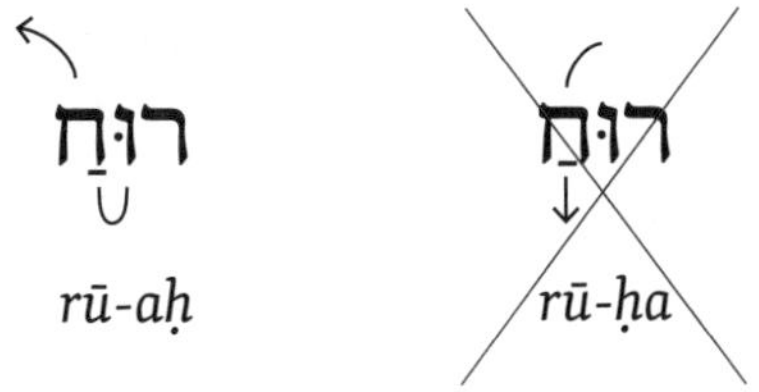

If a *pataḥ* appears to be the final element of a word, it must be a furtive *pataḥ*.

DETERMINING HEBREW SYLLABLES

In principle, identifying syllables is fairly simple. In fact, much of it is intuitive. For example, when you see מַלְכָּה, you are most likely going to pronounce it *mal-kā* because that is the easiest way to put these letters together. When you see מְלָכָה, you would likely pronounce it *m*[e]*-lā-kā* even if you do not remember that *shewas* at the beginning of the word are vocal. You will pronounce this *shewa* because you need a sound to connect the מ to the ל. However, sometimes relying on intuition is not enough. For example, חָכְמָה can be pronounced *hok-mā* with the first vowel functioning as short /o/, or *ḥā-k*[e]*-mā* with the first vowel functioning as long /ā/.[6] Fortunately, predictable patterns enable you to pronounce Hebrew words accurately and with confidence. In most cases, understanding syllable structure will suffice.

Basic Syllable Structure

The principle that *every syllable begins with a consonant and has one and only one vowel* is usually sufficient for identifying syllables. The beginning of a word obviously marks the start of a syllable. The first consonant will have either a vowel or a *shewa* associated with it. Every subsequent consonant that has a vowel begins a new syllable. For example, in the word מֶ֫לֶךְ the מ must begin a syllable because it starts the word. The ל must also begin a syllable because it has its own vowel. As a result, the word מֶ֫לֶךְ must be pronounced as *mé-lek* (NOT *mel-ek*) because a syllable does not begin with a vowel. Based on this analysis

6. In this example, both pronunciations are possible, but they have different meanings. Context will help you determine which you should use.

of the syllables we can identify the first syllable as an open accented syllable (i.e., מֶ֫|לֶךְ) and the second syllable as a closed unaccented syllable (i.e., מֶ֫|לֶךְ).

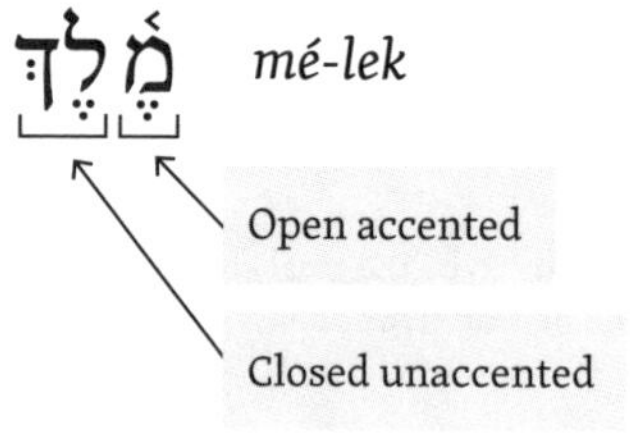

With the word מֶ֫לֶךְ, the presence of a second vowel demands a second syllable. The basic patterns of syllable structure guide you in your pronunciation. However, sometimes a consonant does not have a vowel and is marked instead with a *shewa* (ְ). To pronounce these syllables properly, you will need to determine whether the *shewa* is silent or vocal.

In chapter 2, you learned that *shewa* after a short vowel is silent, and *shewa* after a long vowel is vocal (long = loud; short = shhh!). In this chapter you will see that these distinctions are actually related to syllabification. Just as *shewa* at the beginning of a word is vocal, *shewa* at the beginning of a syllable must be vocal. A *shewa* at the end of a syllable is silent. Pronunciation is driven by whether the consonant with the *shewa* closes the current syllable or opens a new one. To answer this question you need more information about syllable patterns.

Unaccented Syllables Follow Predictable Patterns

In the presentation above we discussed two types of syllables, accented and unaccented. Accented syllables are unpredictable because they take either long or short vowels and can be open or closed.[7] On the other hand, unaccented syllables are predictable. ***Closed unaccented syllables take short vowels.*** This one principle can be applied in four settings: 1) Closed unaccented syllables take short vowels. 2) Conversely, open unaccented syllables take long vowels. 3) A short vowel in an unaccented syllable means the syllable is closed. And conversely, 4) a long vowel in an unaccented syllable means the syllable is open.

7. Determining whether accented syllables are open or closed is not a problem. Most accented syllables are part of endings you will memorize and/or appear at the end of the word.

In Unaccented Syllables

Closed syllable	→	Short vowel
Open syllable	→	Long vowel

Likewise

Short vowel	→	Closed syllable
Long vowel	→	Open syllable

If you can remember the simple phrase, *closed unaccented syllables take short vowels*, you will know what to expect in any unaccented syllable.[8]

Take the word מַלְכָּה for example. The מ obviously begins the syllable. The accompanying vowel is *pataḥ* (short /a/). When unaccented, *short* vowels occur in *closed* syllables. Thus, you immediately know that you need the ל to close the syllable. Since the ל closes the syllable, the *shewa* must be silent because there is no vowel sound at the end of a closed syllable.

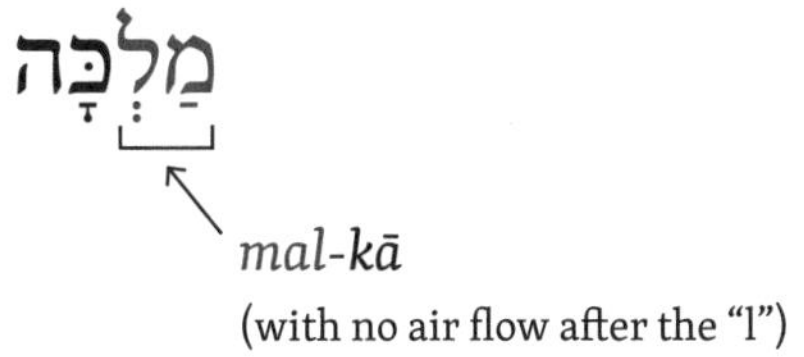

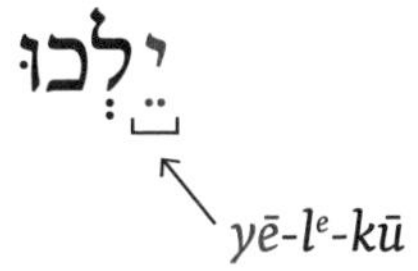

Similarly, consider the word יֵלְכוּ. The vowel with the *yod* is a *tsere*, a long /ē/ vowel. When unaccented, long vowels demand open syllables. Thus, the syllable must end with the *tsere* and the ל must start a new syllable—meaning that the *shewa* with this ל must be vocal.

In this grammar, we will treat vocal *shewas* as standing alone in their own syllable. Technically **a *shewa* is a *shewa* is a *shewa*,** meaning that a *shewa* is never a vowel, making it awkward to treat vocal *shewa* as its own syllable. However, because the abbreviated sound of a vocal

8. It may be helpful to think of a short vowel as being smaller—happiest when nestled snuggly between two consonants. A long vowel, on the other hand, is strong and throws off the constraints of the following consonant. This does not necessarily reflect the nature of the vowels but can be a helpful way to remember how they behave.

shewa sounds like a syllable, it will be easier to treat vocal *shewa* as occurring in its own syllable. Moreover, a vocal *shewa* often reflects a historic syllable in which a historic vowel has been lost. Treating the vocal *shewa* as standing in its own syllable will thus prepare you for anticipating the vowel changes we will discuss in the next chapter. The final syllabification of יֵלְכוּ is יֵ | לְ | כוּ.

HOW SYLLABLES AND POINTING WORK TOGETHER

Right now you have a basic understanding of nearly all Hebrew syllables. In fact, you know more than you think you know. One of our goals in this grammar is not just to teach you facts but also to help you integrate them so that you come away with an understanding of how the language works. In the discussion that follows you will see that vowel length, *shewa*, and *dagesh* are interrelated and are directly affected by syllabification.

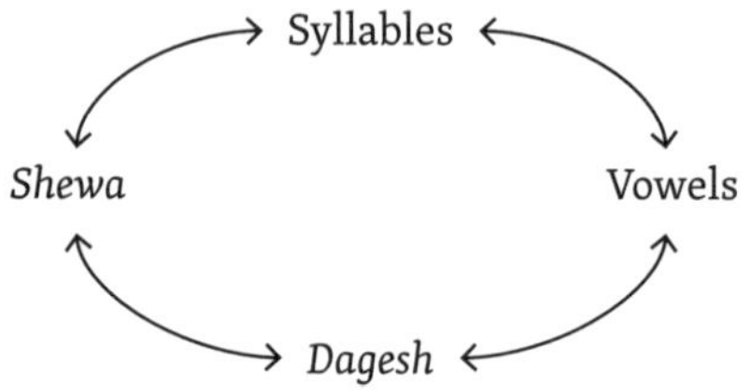

Syllables and Shewa

In chapter 2 we discussed two types of simple *shewa* (ְ): vocal *shewa* and silent *shewa*. To distinguish them you learned the general principle that *after a long vowel,* shewa *is vocal* and *after a short vowel,* shewa *is silent*. Now that you are beginning to understand syllables and basic Hebrew word structure, you should be able to see *why* the *shewa* behaves the way it does. The difference between the vocal and silent *shewa* is its placement within the syllable. *A vocal* shewa *begins a syllable and a silent* shewa *closes a syllable*. It makes sense that a *shewa* that begins a syllable will have a sound because a small sound helps to move you from one consonant to the next (e.g., מְלָכָה *m^{e}-lā-kā*). Similarly, a *shewa* that ends a syllable will be silent where the sound stops, so no airflow is needed to move you to the next sound (e.g., מַלְכָּה *mal-kā*). This is why *shewa* (ְ) is vocal after an unaccented long vowel (which must occur in an open syllable) and silent after an unaccented short vowel (which you now know must occur in a closed syllable).[9]

9. A composite *shewa* is naturally heard regardless of whether it opens or closes a syllable.

Syllables and Dagesh

The principle that *closed unaccented syllables take short vowels* has implications for the relationship between syllables and *dagesh*. This relationship applies to *dagesh lene, dagesh forte,* and the loss of *dagesh forte* in the *Skin 'em Levi* letters.

mal-kā

yē-l^{e}-khū

Dagesh Lene

In chapter 2 you saw that *dagesh lene* follows a silent *shewa*. A silent *shewa* appears at the end of a closed syllable. A closed syllable creates a full stop in sound. Without a vowel sound there is no airflow to soften the following *BeGaD KePhaT* letter, so it takes a hard, plosive sound (e.g., כּ = *k*). As a result, when you see a *dagesh lene* in the middle of a word you can count on the fact that the preceding syllable is closed. Perhaps it would help to think of the *dagesh lene* as a plug that stops the flow of air. Conversely, after an open syllable the airflow of the vowel continues through the following consonant. If this consonant is a *BeGaD KePhaT* letter, then it will produce a softer sound, the one that results from airflow (e.g., כ = *ch* as in Lo<u>ch</u> Ness).[10]

Dagesh Forte

Unlike *dagesh lene*, the *dagesh forte* always follows a vowel. Because *dagesh forte* represents a doubled consonant, the first consonant closes the preceding syllable and the second consonant opens the following syllable. The first closed syllable must have a vowel, which explains why a *dagesh forte* always follows a vowel. As a result, the syllable division in a word with *dagesh forte* should be pronounced as in the example below.

10. Remember that only three *BeGaD KePhaT* letters maintain the hard and soft distinction—*bet, kaph,* and *pe* (בּ = *b*, ב = *v*, כּ =*k*, כ = *kh* as in Loch Ness, פּ = *p*, and פ = *ph*).

חִטֵּא (=חִט|טֵּא*)

ḥit-tē

Skin 'em Levi—Loss of Dagesh Forte

Sometimes you will not see a *dagesh forte* in the text where there should be one. By the time the Masoretes inserted pointing to preserve pronunciation, some doubled consonants were no longer heard. The loss of doubling happened only with certain letters and only when they are followed by *shewa*. As introduced in chapter 2 (see page 21), the mnemonic *Skin 'em Levi* will help you remember which consonants can lose *dagesh forte* when followed by *shewa*. In such cases, the syllable structure and vowel length still behave as if the consonant is doubled. The preceding vowel will be short because the syllable is still theoretically closed. The *shewa* is vocal because the consonant is still theoretically doubled. You do not yet know when to expect this phenomenon, but we will review it again each time it becomes relevant.

One of the most common verbs (וַיְהִי) is affected by the *Skin 'em Levi* principle.[11] This verb is formed by adding *waw*, *pataḥ*, and doubling dot to the beginning of the word (וַ□). However, when attached to a verb that begins with a vowelless *yod* (one of the *Skin 'em Levi* letters), the expected form וַיְּהִי* (with *dagesh*) will instead appear as וַיְהִי (without *dagesh*). When you pronounce this word you will not double the *yod*, but you will pronounce the *shewa* as vocal. The *pataḥ* (short /a/) is still in a theoretically closed syllable. The *shewa* is vocal because the *yod* is still theoretically doubled. Thus וַיְהִי is pronounced *wa-y*^{e}*-hī* (NOT *way-hī*).

Loss of *Dagesh Forte* with *Skin 'em Levi* Letters

Historic pattern	וַיְּהִי*	*way-y*^{e}*-hī*
Hebrew text	וַיְהִי	*wa-y*^{e}*-hī*

11. This verb will be introduced in ch. 4.

Syllables and Vowels

As we saw at the beginning of the chapter, syllables and vowel length are directly related. We have learned that *closed unaccented syllables take short vowels* and that open unaccented syllables take long vowels. As a result, we can infer that a short unaccented vowel must stand in a closed syllable and that a long unaccented vowel must stand in an open syllable. In most cases the length of the vowel is clear from the vowel pointing (e.g., *segol* ֶ is short and *tsere* ֵ is long), enabling you to determine the syllabification.

Distinguishing Qamets and Qamets Qaton (Long /ā/ and Short /o/)

In chapter 2 we encountered two vowels that are identical in appearance (ָ)—long /ā/ and short /o/. At the time we did not teach you how to tell the difference between them because you first needed to understand the principles of syllabification. The key to distinguishing them is that *short /o/ always occurs in closed unaccented syllables.* (Both closed *and* unaccented criteria must be met in order to have short /o/.) Since the vowel itself does not clearly delineate length, you must identify the syllable as closed unaccented by other means in order to determine when the vowel is short.

Distinguished by Accent

In many cases the location of the accent will help you spot short /o/. For example, the word וַיָּ֫מָת is pronounced *way-yā′-mot* (NOT as *way-yā′-māt* or *way-yo′-māt*). Since the ָ vowel under the *yod* is accented (וַיָּ֫מָת), it must be a long /ā/. Short /o/ only occurs in *closed unaccented* syllables. The final syllable is closed and unaccented (וַיָּ֫מָת) and must be pronounced with the short /o/ sound (*way-yā′-mot*).

In the example above, the short /o/ is recognizable because it clearly stands in a closed unaccented syllable. However, sometimes you will need other indicators to help confirm that a syllable is closed. Fortunately, several features help you identify closed unaccented syllables. These indicators include the *dagesh lene*, the *maqqeph*, the *metheg*, and the composite *shewa*.

Distinguished by Dagesh Lene

A *dagesh lene* (*BeGaD KePhaT* dot) can help distinguish a short /o/ from a long /ā/. You have learned that a *dagesh lene* results from a lack of airflow and follows a silent *shewa*. Thus a *dagesh lene* in the middle of word follows a closed syllable. If that closed syllable has the vowel ָ and is unaccented, then that vowel is a short /o/ and should be pronounced accordingly. For example, the word הָפְדֵּה is pronounced *hoph-dē* (NOT *hā-phᵉ-dē*).

Using *Dagesh Lene* to Identify Short /o/

הָפְדֵּה	הָפְדֵּה	הָפְדֵּה	הָפְדֵּה	Pronounced *hoph-dē*
1) *Dagesh lene* follows silent *shewa* →	2) Silent *shewa* indicates closed syll. →	3) Accent on final syllable →	4) Closed unacc. syllable	

Distinguished by Maqqeph

Another way to spot short /o/ is by understanding the use of the Hebrew *maqqeph*. The *maqqeph* looks like a dash (־) and indicates a close relationship between two words. When words are joined with *maqqeph*, these words are pronounced as a single unit, as if they were one word. The first word gives up its accent and, as a result, all the syllables in that word are unaccented. For example, in כָּל־הָעָם (*kol-hā-ām*) the *maqqeph* removes the accent from the first word. Thus the vowel in this word stands in a closed unaccented syllable and must be a short /o/ (*kol-hā-ām*).

Using *Maqqeph* to Identify Short /o/

כָּל־הָעָם	כָּל־הָעָם	כָּל־הָעָם	Pronounced *kol-hā-ām*
1) *Maqqeph* removes accent from first word →	2) Closed unacc. syllable requires a short vowel →	3) Open unacc. & closed accented syll indicate long /ā/	

The *maqqeph* does not affect meaning. The same book, and even the same verse, may present a phrase both with and without the *maqqeph*. So כֹּל הָעָם (*kōl´ hā-ām´*) and כָּל־הָעָם (*kol-hā-ām´*) are similar in pronunciation and mean the same thing—"all the people."

Distinguished by Metheg

In some cases the Masoretes inserted a short vertical line (ֽ), called a *metheg* ("bridle"), to aid in pronunciation.[12] Like its name, think of the *metheg* as a bridle on a horse. When it appears with a *qamets* (ָ), imagine that the *metheg* holds you back and keeps you from rushing forward to the next consonant. Thus you will read the long /ā/ with a *metheg*, not the short /o/. Whenever you see a *metheg* with *qamets*, default to reading the vowel as long /ā/. The difficulty with the *metheg* is that long /ā/ often appears without it.

Using *Metheg* to Rule Out Short /o/

אָֽכְלָה

Pronounced
ā-kᵉ-lā

Metheg indicates long /ā/

Distinguished by Composite Shewa

Another helpful indicator for spotting short /o/ is its placement immediately before the u-class composite *shewa* (ָ ֳ). The vowel class of the composite *shewa* is usually determined by the vowel that precedes it. For example, the a-class composite *shewa* (ֲ) follows a *pataḥ* (ַ ֲ), the i-class composite *shewa* (ֱ) follows a *segol* (ֶ ֱ), and the u-class composite *shewa* (ֳ) follows a *qamets qaton* (ָ ֳ). Thus, when you see the sequence ָ ֳ recognize that the vowel classes match. Since ֳ always reflects a u-class composite *shewa*, the preceding vowel must likewise be a u-class vowel. For example, the word מָעֳמָד is pronounced *moᵒ-mād* (NOT *māᵒ-mād*).

As it relates to syllabification, remember that short /o/ only occurs in a closed unaccented syllable. Therefore, having determined that the first vowel in מָעֳמָד is a short /o/, it follows that the composite *shewa* must be closing the syllable (מָעֳ|מָד). This is true despite the fact that composite *shewa* is always pronounced (vocal). It is used in place of a silent *shewa* because the guttural requires some additional sound.

12. A *metheg* can be used for other things besides marking syllables and vowel length and is used in syllables with any type of vowel. In the vast majority of its occurrences, the *metheg* serves as a musical notation with little relevance to pronunciation. However, when it is used with the *qamets* it is a helpful indicator of vowel length.

Using Composite *Shewa* to Identify Short /o/

מָעֳמָד	מָעֳמָד	מָעֳמָד	מָעֳמָד	Pronounced *mo^{o}-mād*
1) U-class composite *shewa* →	2) Preceding vowel is u-class (short /o/) →	3) Short vowel in unacc. syll. = closed syll. →	4) Accented syll. = long /ā/	

Having a composite *shewa* at the end of a syllable may seem odd. But this is why we learn to identify syllables on the basis of syllable type (open vs. closed), not on the basis of sound (vocal *shewa* vs. silent *shewa*). Remember a *shewa* is a *shewa* is a *shewa*. Pronunciation is a by-product of the *shewa*'s environment or character. When a regular *shewa* opens a syllable it is vocal because of its environment—the mouth must make a transition between consonants. When a regular *shewa* closes a syllable it is silent because of its environment—the syllable is finished. A composite *shewa* can likewise be used to either open or close a syllable. It just happens to always be vocal because the environment—the gutturals require some kind of sound.

Distinguished Based on Familiarity with Hebrew

Although the principles stated above help in reading Hebrew aloud and understanding the syllabification of words, even these are not always sufficient. Your growing familiarity with Hebrew will help you recognize patterns that aid in pronunciation. In other words, distinguishing between long /ā/ and short /o/ is not something you master quickly. Your ability will grow in proportion to your Hebrew knowledge.

1) Relying on Vocabulary

Sometimes it is only your familiarity with vocabulary that helps you to distinguish between long /ā/ and short /o/. For example, based on what we just learned above, you would expect the pattern ◌ָ◌ֳ to reflect two /o/ sounds. Yet the name נָאֳמִי is pronounced *Nā^{o}-mī* (NOT *No^{o}-mī*). You know that this word is pronounced with an initial long /ā/ only because that is how you learned Naomi's name.

Distinguishing Based on Familiar Vocabulary

נָאֳמִי

Pronounced
Nāº-mī

Familiar proper name (Naomi)

Likewise, Hebrew vocabulary words that you learn will allow you to anticipate that certain words must have a short /o/, even when it would otherwise be unclear or unexpected based on syllable patterns. For example, אֹ֫זֶן ("ear") and אָזְנֵי ("ears of") are variations of the same noun and should have the same class of vowel. Since אֹ֫זֶן is pronounced *ō′-zen*, we know that אָזְנֵי ("ears of") should be pronounced *oz-nē* (with short /o/ and silent *shewa*).

Some words seem to "break the rules" entirely, containing short /o/ in an open syllable. For example, the word קָדָשִׁים ("holy things") is pronounced *qo-dā-shīm* because it is based on the Hebrew word קֹ֫דֶשׁ ("holiness" pronounced *qō′-desh*), despite the fact that the first vowel is in an open syllable.

Distinguishing Based on Familiar Vocabulary

אָזְנֵי

Pronounced
oz-nē

Derived from the noun אֹ֫זֶן (*ō′-zen*)

קָדָשִׁים

Pronounced
qo-dā-shīm

Derived from the noun קֹ֫דֶשׁ (*qō′-desh*)

2) Relying on Grammatical Forms

You will find that a knowledge of various structural patterns (e.g., noun patterns, verb paradigms) will be a tremendous asset to you in pronunciation. At this point you have not learned any word formation patterns to guide you, but you will soon. Knowing from context if a word is a noun or a verb can help you to distinguish between long /ā/ and short /o/. In this discussion we will use the word חָכְמָה because this word can be either a verb ("she was wise") or a noun ("wisdom").

Based on structure alone, the word חָכְמָה could be pronounced either as *ḥā-k^{e}-mā* or as *ḥok-mā*. Unless the word includes a *metheg* (e.g., חָֽכְמָה = *ḥā-k^{e}-mā*), context will be the only guide to pronunciation. If you expect a verb, then you will vocalize חָכְמָה as *ḥā-k^{e}-mā* ("she was wise") based on the fact that the basic verb formation takes an a-class vowel. But if you expect a noun, then you will vocalize חָכְמָה as *ḥok-mā* ("wisdom"), following a common noun pattern.

Distinguishing Based on Grammatical Form

חָ|כְ|מָה — Pronounced *ḥā-k^{e}-mā*	חָכְ|מָה — Pronounced *ḥok-mā*
Verb pattern (determined by context)	Noun pattern (determined by context)

SUMMARY You now have the tools necessary for syllabification. Although we have covered a broad range of ideas in this chapter, they all boil down into two basic principles:

- ***Every syllable begins with a consonant and has only one vowel.*** *(Exceptions: The conjunction* וּ *and furtive* pataḥ.*)*
- ***Closed unaccented syllables take short vowels.***

These principles will enable you to correctly pronounce Hebrew words. Though you may not always succeed at the first attempt, your boldness to voice what you see and learn in the process will contribute to your ultimate success.

EXERCISES FOR CHAPTER 3 The workbook includes several exercises to help you correctly determine the syllable structure and vocalization of Hebrew words. Exercise 3A provides practice in syllable division. Exercise 3B focuses on reading aloud the text of Gen 1:1–5 and Deut 6:4–9. Exercise 3C demonstrates the value and contribution of oral reading by highlighting some poetic wordplays from Isaiah that enhance the effectiveness of the prophet's message.

Now that you can pronounce Hebrew words, it is time to begin learning vocabulary. The first vocabulary list appears in the workbook above the translation exercise for chapter 4. Vocabulary lists sometimes provide more than one possible English definition for each word. Not every possible definition is equally applicable to every English context. As you study your vocabulary, envision the common core idea behind all the translation options in order to understand what lies at the heart of the Hebrew word. Understand that different contexts may require that you choose different English words to accurately express the concept. For example, "*keep* the Torah" and "*guard* the prisoner" would both be represented by the same Hebrew word (שָׁמַר). However, using the same English word in both contexts might be awkward. As you learn vocabulary, recognize both the core concept and the various ways an idea can be expressed in English.

CHAPTER 4

Gender and Number, Definite Article and Conjunction

Now that you have learned to identify the consonants, vowels, and syllables necessary for correctly pronouncing Hebrew words, it is time to learn how these Hebrew words are created. This chapter introduces you to the triconsonantal roots that form the basis of Hebrew words and convey their core meaning and presents some of the basic components that are added to the front and back of words to augment that meaning.

ROOTS AND ADDITIONAL COMPONENTS OF MEANING

In the Hebrew language most words have a three-consonant base called a *root* that provides the core of meaning. This root is essentially an abstract concept represented only by consonants (e.g., שׁמע "to hear"). In order to form actual words, the root must be combined together with vowel patterns that refine this meaning. Consonants can also be attached to the front and/or back of the root to further modify meaning. In this way, the abstract concept of the root is supplemented by vowel patterns and/or added consonants to create verbs, nouns, and adjectives that are related to the core idea of the root. For example, the following verbs (vb.) and nouns (n.) are all formed from the root שׁמע.

שָׁמַע	vb. "he heard"	שֵׁמַע	n. "report"
מִשְׁמָע	n. "thing heard"	הַשְׁמָעוּת	n. "causing to hear"

Because the root is merely an abstraction and can never be vocalized without the vowel patterns necessary to pronounce it, you will never memorize just the root consonants. Hebrew grammars teach vocabulary using a simple form of the verb as a representation of the core meaning. For example, the word שָׁמַע is listed in your vocabulary with the definition "to hear," even though this form technically means "he heard." In your vocabulary you can concentrate on the abstract meaning ("to hear") because we will learn the various verb forms separately. All other vocabulary words derived from these roots (e.g., nouns, adjectives, adverbs) will appear in your vocabulary as fully developed words like those represented above (e.g., מִשְׁמָע "thing heard").

Recognizing the triconsonantal root in the words you encounter allows you to make associations between words that are related in meaning so that you can build your vocabulary. It also helps you more quickly discern the meaning or function of individual Hebrew words based on the vowel patterns and additional consonants that are used in the formation of these words. Eventually you should reach a point where you can intuitively sense the meaning of an unfamiliar word because you recognize either the base meaning of the root or a familiar word structure.

Sometimes a word in the text does not preserve all three letters of the root to which it is related. For example, the vocabulary word רַב ("much, many") comes from a root you will later learn as רָבַב ("to be much, many"). Other forms of this word evidence all three letters (e.g., plural רְבָבִים = רַבִּים). Other roots that frequently lose one or more letters when you encounter them in the text include roots that start with *nun* (e.g., נָתַן), roots that end with a *heh* (e.g., רָאָה), and roots that have *waw* or *yod* in them (e.g., שִׂים). Note the following examples:

נָתַן	"to give"	→	תֵּן	"give!"
רָאָה	"to see"	→	רָאוּ	"they see"
שִׂים	"to put"	→	שָׂם	"he put"

You will eventually learn the principles of how to recognize these irregular roots. Until then the translation exercises include glosses that identify the weak roots.[1] For now you should simply realize that whether you can see all the letters or not, a three-consonant root is at the core of most words. You should always strive to make associations between the words you encounter in the text and the vocabulary you already know.

ADDITIONS TO HEBREW NOUNS AND ADJECTIVES

Nouns and adjectives are two of the most basic parts of speech. A noun is a word that identifies a person (e.g., girl), place (e.g., Jerusalem), object (e.g., book), or idea (e.g., righteousness). Adjectives describe the attributes of nouns (e.g., a holy book). Hebrew adjectives can also be used in place of nouns. For example, the Hebrew expression "the holy of Israel" means "the Holy One of Israel."[2]

The Hebrew nouns and adjectives that you encounter in your vocabulary do not always appear exactly as you memorized them. Additional components of meaning are often attached directly to the front or back of the word. For example, Hebrew attaches endings to mark words as plural. We do a similar thing in English (e.g., hills, patches, oxen). In Hebrew other elements can be added directly to Hebrew nouns to communicate concepts that English reflects by means of separate words. These include the definite article (i.e., the), prepositions (e.g., to, in, from), the conjunction (e.g., and, but), and possessive pronouns (e.g., his, her, their, your).

In this chapter we will look at three of these building-block forms: the markings for gender and number, the definite article ("the"), and the conjunction ("and"). You will be introduced to the rest of the items in the chapters to come.[3]

GENDER AND NUMBER

Hebrew has several endings that mark a word for gender and number. Most students find the discussion about number to be more familiar than the concept of gender. As a result, we will first examine how Hebrew identifies the number of items or persons intended

1. The translation exercises provide definitions (glosses) for words not in your vocabulary. When all three root letters are not visible we provide the full root so that you can make the association with your vocabulary.

2. The function of nouns and adjectives will be discussed more in ch. 6.

3. These "building blocks" have predictable guidelines that define their use. Since multiple components can be added to the same word, each component is added in a particular order and has a fixed position where it is attached to the word. E.g., the conjunction ("and"), preposition (e.g., "in"), and definite article ("the") are added in a particular sequence. Like in English, you would never see "the and in dream," but rather "and in the dream" (וּבַחֲלוֹם = וּ + בְּ + [הַ] + חֲלוֹם).

(grammatical number) and then discuss how Hebrew clarifies the relationship between words in a sentence (grammatical gender).

Significance of Grammatical Number

You are already familiar with the concepts of singular and plural from your understanding of English (e.g., day vs. days). Hebrew can designate items not only as singular and plural but also as dual. A dual ending specifies that exactly two items are being referenced. The dual ending is often used with objects that exist in pairs (e.g., hands, eyes, ears). When the dual is used this way, it need not be explicitly translated because the English plural conveys the concept sufficiently; for example, "the voice is the voice of Jacob, but the *hands* [dual in Hebrew] are the hands of Esau" (Gen 27:22). However, the dual ending can be used to indicate precisely two of a particular item without actually using the number "two." When the dual is used this way, your English translation should represent a sensitivity to the dual ending; for example, "The Lord has given you the Sabbath; therefore on the sixth day he gives you bread for *two days* [dual]" (Exod 16:29).

While we are discussing issues of translation, you should be aware that languages use singular and plural concepts differently. Sometimes Hebrew uses plurals where English does not and vice versa. For example, the Hebrew word זֶ֫רַע ("seed") is a singular noun, but it conveys a collective idea and in many cases should be translated with an English plural; for example, "all the *descendants* [seed] of Ephraim" (Jer 7:15). Conversely, a Hebrew plural like אֱלֹהִים ("God") may need to be translated as a singular concept in English (e.g., "God" NOT "gods").[4] A good translation is sensitive to both languages. A translator must understand what the Hebrew says and then express that thought with a translation that accurately reflects meaning to an English reader.

Significance of Grammatical Gender

Hebrew also marks nouns and adjectives for gender. In English we tend to understand the concept of gender according to physical gender: "he" = male, "she" = female, "it" = no gender (or neutral). Hebrew, on the

4. The Hebrew use of the grammatical plural to represent concepts that are expressed in the singular in English is frequently seen in the expression of: (1) ideas composed of parts (e.g., פָּנִים "face" and חַיִּים "life"), (2) abstract qualities (e.g., בְּתוּלִים "virginity" and כִּפֻּרִים "atonement"), and (3) respect (e.g., אֲדֹנִים "master" and אֱלֹהִים "God").

other hand, uses gender to designate words as masculine or feminine based primarily on grammatical gender. In English we see occasional remnants of the concept of grammatical gender when we refer to countries or ships as feminine (e.g., "America, long may *she* endure!").

When we speak of *grammatical gender*, we are referring to the practice of classifying words as masculine (m.) or feminine (f.), regardless of whether or not they reflect biological gender. Hebrew has only two genders (masculine and feminine) and does not have a separate classification for the grammatical "neuter." In other words, instead of "it," Hebrew uses "he" or "she" even to refer to items without biological gender. Words with no inherent biological gender are likewise classified as either masculine or feminine. Hebrew uses a combination of distinct endings to identify words as masculine and feminine—for example, אִישׁ ("man" = no ending) and אִשָּׁה ("woman" = ָה ending). The nouns סֵבֶל (m.) and סִבְלָה (f.) share a common meaning ("burden") that has no inherent gender but are marked as masculine and feminine by endings similar to words like אִישׁ and אִשָּׁה. The gender of סֵבֶל and סִבְלָה has no effect on meaning. The grammatical gender in these words impacts form only and can function to signal relationship with other words in the sentence.[5]

Because gender endings are primarily about structural patterns, the gender of words is usually apparent from the form of the word. However, this is not always the case, and you will need to be aware of grammatical gender when you learn your vocabulary words. For example, the word אֶרֶץ "land" (f.) is feminine even though it does not take the ָה ending. Further, some irregular nouns exhibit a mixed form. For example, feminine endings are sometimes used on masculine nouns and vice versa (e.g., אָבוֹת "fathers" = אָב + feminine plural ending וֹת). While these exceptions exist, you can usually identify the gender of a word by its ending.

As in many languages, the masculine form is the default gender. In other words, the masculine gender is typically used if a group of people or items is mixed in regards to gender. The masculine form can be used for groups of men or for groups composed of both males

5. E.g., a feminine verb should have a feminine noun as the subject.

and females. When the feminine gender is used to refer to persons, it exclusively refers to females.

Gender and Number Endings

In Hebrew the gender and number endings are linked. The chart below presents the endings for designating gender and number. The symbol □□□ is used to represent any given Hebrew word so that you can focus just on the endings. The word סוּס (*horse*) is also included to illustrate how these endings can affect meaning. Learn these endings well.

Table 4.1: Gender and Number Endings

	Masculine		Feminine	
Singular	□□□	סוּס "horse"	□□□ָה	סוּסָה "mare"
Plural	□□□ִים	סוּסִים "horses"	□□□וֹת	סוּסוֹת "mares"
Dual	□□□ַ֫יִם	סוּסַ֫יִם "two horses"	□□□ָתַ֫יִם	סוּסָתַ֫יִם "two mares"

DEFINITE ARTICLE

Understanding Definiteness in Hebrew and English

Most languages have a way to indicate that a particular person or object is in mind. In Hebrew this specificity is often conveyed by means of a definite article; a small prefix usually translated as "the." English has two types of articles, definite ("the") and indefinite ("a" or "an"). Hebrew only has a definite article. This means that if an object is left without a definite article, the word usually indicates an unspecified object represented in English by an indefinite article (e.g., "*a* man") or a generic label (e.g., "man" = mankind).

As we saw with gender and number, there is never an exact overlap in how languages express concepts. Hebrew sometimes uses a definite article where English will not. In other instances English requires a definite article for a sentence to make sense when the Hebrew text does not have one. So the presence of a definite article in Hebrew does not necessarily mean that you should reproduce one in your English translation. For example, in Hebrew the definite article sometimes requires a totally different word in English. You might encounter something like, "This day [lit. *the* day] you have turned from the Lord" (Josh 22:18). Other times you will leave out the definite article when you translate in order for your English sentence to make sense. For example, "And Asa did what was good [lit. *the* good] . . . in the eyes of the Lord his God" (2 Chr 14:2).

You do not need to memorize rules for translating the definite article. For now, when you see an article in the Hebrew text, simply represent it in your English translation (i.e., "the"), even if it creates a sentence that is a little awkward. This will help you begin to consciously acknowledge the presence of the article and think about its significance. As you progress, carefully consider the implications of the article, both in the text and in your translation. Why is it there? How will it affect the English reader? Think about the context and find a suitable translation for what the author is trying to say.

Recognizing the Definite Article

In Hebrew the definite article is attached directly to the word and is represented by a prefixed ה together with a particular set of vowels. The standard form of the definite article is ◌ַה (a prefixed ה + *pataḥ* + doubling of the next consonant). The doubling dot creates a stable closed unaccented syllable at the front of the word, protecting the short /a/ vowel. This pattern is stable as long as you can double the first consonant of the word to which the article is attached.

Standard form הַ◌ּ הַשָּׁלוֹם

However, we have learned that certain letters do not accept the doubling dot (namely, the gutturals and ר). When the first consonant of the word cannot be doubled, then the article becomes an open syllable. Since *closed* unaccented syllables take short vowels, *open* unaccented syllables must take long vowels. Thus the principles we have learned regarding syllabification and vowels apply directly to the vocalization of the definite article. There are two ways the vowel responds when left in this open syllable. When the article is attached to words that begin with the gutturals א, ע, and ר, the vowel will lengthen (□הָ). In other words, it compensates for the open syllable created by the absence of doubling and lengthens the vowel (what we call *compensatory lengthening*).

Gutturals ר ע א	□הָ	הָאִישׁ	Compensatory lengthening

The H-gutturals (ה, ח) will simply leave the vowel alone (□הַ). You can perhaps think of this as if they act like they are doubled even when they are not (called *implicit doubling* or *virtual doubling*). Remembering this concept as *"h"onorary doubling* may help you make the association with the letters *heh* and *ḥet*. With these consonants the definite article will act as if all the regular conditions are met, and you will see no modification of the vowel at all (□הַ).

H-consonants	□הַ	הַחֲלוֹם	Vowel remains unchanged

Even less frequently you will encounter the definite article vocalized with a *segol* (□הֶ). At this point you need only recognize that □הֶ is a legitimate form of the definite article used only with gutturals with *qamets* (long /ā/).[6]

Some gutturals with *qamets*	□הֶ	הֶעָפָ֫ר	Change to *segol*

It is important that you learn these vowel patterns because Hebrew has many uses of a prefixed ה besides just the definite article. When ה is used for functions other than the definite article, the vowels will usually be different. You must learn to associate the definite article with more than just the consonant ה. If you learn the standard form (□הַ) and understand why changes are made to the vowel when a word begins with a guttural (closed syllable → open syllable), you should

6. When the article is attached to words beginning with הָ, חָ, or עָ (note the *qamets*), the article will shift its vowel to *segol* (e.g., הֶהָרִ֫ים "the mountains"), *except* when the הָ֫ or עָ֫ is in the accented syllable resulting in an article with *qamets* (e.g., הָהָ֫ר "the mountain").

always be able to recognize the definite article. However, if the relationship between syllabification and vowel changes does not yet make perfect sense to you, do not worry. For now, simply memorize the four options for the definite article. The principles of syllabification and vowel change will become familiar to you in time. They are embedded throughout the grammar and reflect a deeper understanding of how Hebrew works that can take time to catch. The following table summarizes the principles outlined above.

Table 4.2: Basic Rules for the Definite Article

		הַ⊡	Standard form
ר א ע	→	הָ□	Compensatory lengthening
ה ח	→	הַ□	"H"onorary doubling
Gָ	→	הֶ□	Usually changes to *segol*

CONJUNCTION ("AND")

Conjunctions are words that "conjoin" or link words and ideas together. In Hebrew, the most common conjunction is represented by the letter *waw* (ו) and is attached directly to the beginning of a word (e.g., וְשָׁלוֹם). This conjunction is vocalized differently depending on the type of word to which it is attached. Regardless of how it is vocalized, whenever you see a word beginning with *waw* (ו) you can initially translate it as "and." After you grapple with what the text is trying to say, you may then find that you have to adjust your translation to fit the context. Based on the context there are a variety of ways that you can translate this conjunction (e.g., and, but, then, now, so). It may seem odd to have so many translation options, but this conjunction simply signals a connection between words or clauses. Hebrew relies on context to clarify the exact nature of that connection. It is the reader's responsibility to figure out the implicit relationship between these words and clauses.

It should come as no surprise that the vowels associated with the conjunction vary depending on the word to which the conjunction is attached. The conjunction has no vowel of its own; it is simply a *waw* (ו). As a result it will usually appear with a simple *shewa* (וְ) unless the word to which it is attached has a preference or need for a particular vowel. The following principles summarize the vocalization of the conjunction in different contexts, but the overall guiding principle is that the conjunction does not have its own vocalization—it adjusts depending on the vocalization of the following word.

Standard Form

The standard Hebrew conjunction consists of the letter ו with a simple vocal *shewa* attached to the beginning of a word (וְ□□□).

Standard form   וְ□□□   וְשָׁלוֹם

"BuMP-Shewa" Rule

When attached to words beginning with בּ, מ, פּ, or to any consonants with a simple *shewa*, the conjunction will be vocalized as וּ (long ū). Remember the mnemonic—"BuMP-*Shewa*." Since the conjunction has no vocalization of its own, it adapts itself to the demands of the word to which it is attached. The consonants בּ, מ, and פּ are pronounced with the lips up at the front of the mouth where the u-class vowel is produced. As a result, the u-class vowel was a natural choice for transitioning from the conjunction into these consonants.

The same u-class vowel is also used before words that start with *shewa* because two vocal *shewas* in a row would leave you with three consonants before you reach the first vowel (וְשְׁמוּאֵל* *vshmū-ēl* → וּשְׁמוּאֵל).

	וּב□□	וּבֵית
	וּמ□□	וּמָקוֹם
BuMP-*Shewa*	וּפ□□	וּפֶן
	וּ□ְ□□	וּשְׁמוּאֵל

Before Shewa

Connecting the conjunction to words that begin with *shewa* requires further explanation. The conjunction attaches differently to simple *shewa* (◌ְ) than to composite *shewa* (◌ֲ, ◌ֱ, ◌ֳ), and a few consonants further influence the connection. For now, memorize the features, but the conjunction is common and quickly becomes second nature.

a) Simple Shewa Follows the "BuMP-Shewa" Rule

For most words beginning with regular *shewa* (□ְ□□) the "BuMP-*Shewa*" rule is used as described above (e.g., וְשְׁמוּאֵל* → וּשְׁמוּאֵל).

b) Composite Shewa Requires Matching Vowels

The conjunction takes a different vocalization before a composite *shewa.* Remember that the conjunction has no vocalization of its own and takes its cue from the word that follows. In cases where the conjunction is joined to a word starting with a composite *shewa*, the vowel with the conjunction matches that of the composite *shewa.*

	וַ□ֲ□□	וַאֲנִי	
Matching	וֶ□ֱ□□	וֶאֱדוֹם	Vowels determined by the composite *shewa*
	וָ□ֳ□□	וָחֳלִי	

c) Yod + Shewa Changes to Ḥireq Yod

Words that begin with *yod* and *shewa* respond differently. Again, remember that the conjunction has no vocalization of its own and adapts itself to the demands of the word to which it is attached. If the *yod* (י) has its own vowel, the conjunction will attach according to its standard pattern (e.g., וְיָד "***and*** a hand"). If the *yod* has no vowel (represented by *shewa*), the conjunction is free to choose one. This vowel choice is driven by the *yod's* preference for i-class vowels because this vowel class has the closest affinity in sound. If you remember what you learned about vowel markers, you can anticipate that the most common vowel to associate with *yod* is a long i-class vowel, in this case *ḥireq yod* (ִי). Therefore, a word like יְהוּדָה ("Judah") becomes וִיהוּדָה ("***and*** Judah"). If that explanation does not come as second nature to you yet, you can visualize this in the following fashion: Yod *plus* shewa *will throw a dot and drop a* shewa.

1. Adding a regular *shewa* to the word יְהוּדָה results in a consonant cluster at the front of the word that is impossible to pronounce (e.g., וְיְהוּדָה* *vyhūdā*). You cannot have three consonants in a row before you get to a vowel. The conjunction needs a vowel to help break up the consonant cluster.

2. The short /i/ is used with the *yod* (י) because it has a close affinity with the *yod*, unlike the long /ū/ that is used with *shewa* in the "B<u>u</u>MP-*Shewa* Rule" (*uy*, pronounced "ooee," is awkward). It may help to envision dropping one of the dots in the *shewa* under the conjunction (וְיְהוּדָה* → וִיְהוּדָה*).

3. Once the conjunction is vocalized with a short /i/, the short /i/ and vowelless *yod* (וִיְהוּדָה*) merge together (or *coalesce*) into a long /ī/. As a result, the *yod* is no longer serving as a consonant. It is a vowel marker, and the *shewa* must be dropped. (Remember that vowel markers never have their own vowel notations.) The final form is written with an initial long vowel (וִיְהוּדָה* → וִיהוּדָה). Even though the *yod* is functioning as a vowel marker, it

is reflecting a historic consonant and marks the start of the word to which the conjunction is attached. The word is still יְהוּדָה (NOT הוּדָה).

Special Cases Using Qamets

Before an accented syllable you will occasionally see the conjunction with *qamets* (e.g., Gen 1:2 תֹּהוּ וָבֹהוּ; Gen 2:9 טוֹב וָרָע). This is especially true when the words are paired closely together in the context.

Names of God

The principles listed above for the vocalization of the conjunction are sufficient for most of the words you will encounter. However, the words אֱלֹהִים ("God, gods") and אֲדֹנָי ("Lord") have a special vocalization worth noting. According to the rules you have learned, the composite *shewa* at the front of each of these words should produce the forms וֶאֱלֹהִים* and וַאֲדֹנָי*. However, these words experience an additional modification. You have learned that a vowelless *aleph* can quiesce (lose its consonantal value). This can happen even if the *shewa* is a composite *shewa*. (Remember, a *shewa* is a *shewa* is a *shewa*.) When the *aleph* quiesces in the word אֲדֹנָי, the vowel under the conjunction is left in an open syllable (e.g., וַאֲדֹנָי* → וַאדֹנָי). In the case of וַאדֹנָי there is no further change (despite the fact that open syllables prefer long vowels). The word וֶאֱלֹהִים responds in the same fashion, except that the vowel under the conjunction lengthens to accommodate the open syllable (e.g., וֶאֱלֹהִים* → וֶאלֹהִים* → וֵאלֹהִים).

	וֶאֱלֹהִים*	→	וֵאלֹהִים
Names of God (*aleph* quiesces)	וַאֲדֹנָי*	→	וַאדֹנָי
			(וַיהוה)

The divine name יהוה must also be included in this discussion because the Hebrew reading tradition typically substitutes אֲדֹנָי in place of pronouncing God's personal name (see exercise for ch. 3). As a result, the vocalization of יהוה matches the vocalization for וַאדֹנָי (i.e., וַיהוָה) so as to remind you to read it properly.[7]

7. Although God's personal name is usually vocalized using אֲדֹנָי (i.e., יְהוָה or יְהֹוָה), it is sometimes vocalized using אֱלֹהִים (i.e., יֱהוִה or יֱהֹוִה). However, there are no instances of the second vocalization with the conjunction.

Table 4.3: Rules for Conjunctions

STANDARD	THE "BuMP-*Shewa*" RULE (Before ב מ פ & *Shewa*)
וְ□□□	וּב□□
	וּמ□□
	וּפ□□
	וּ□ְ□□
BEFORE COMPOSITE *SHEWA* (Matching)	**BEFORE *YOD* + *SHEWA* (*Ḥireq yod*)†**
וַ□ֲ□□	וִי□□
וֶ□ֱ□□	
וָ□ֳ□□	
BEFORE ACCENT	וָ□֫□□
NAMES OF GOD	וֵאלֹהִים, וַאדֹנָי, וַיהוָה

† Remember, וִיהוּדָה → וִיְהוּדָה* → וְיְהוּדָה*.

BASIC GRAMMAR FOR TRANSLATING

Now that you have begun learning Hebrew vocabulary and have learned a few of the basic elements of Hebrew nouns and adjectives, it is time to begin translating. Before you can translate, we must first introduce a few simple verb forms so that you can read basic sentences. This introduction gives you the tools to complete the translation exercises.

Basic Verb Formation

Your current vocabulary already includes some Hebrew verbs (e.g., שָׁמַר "to keep, guard"). Although the definitions give the concept at the core of each root, these forms are actually fully conjugated verbs with an inherent subject (e.g., שָׁמַר = "***he*** kept").

VOCABULARY CARD	IN HEBREW TEXT
שָׁמַר *to keep, guard*	שָׁמַר אֶת־הַצֹּאן "***He kept*** the flock"

For now, the translations include two types of verbs, the *perfect* and *imperfect*. We use the perfect to describe actions that occurred in the past and the imperfect for actions that occur in the present or future.[8]

Perfects and Waw Consecutive Perfects

Perfects are formed by adding elements to the *end* of the word to indicate the subject (i.e., who is doing the action) and are generally translated as a simple past tense. For example, the verb שָׁמַר signifies that "he" is doing the action and can be translated as "he kept." A verb like שָׁמַר can be given endings to indicate different subjects. In this chapter we introduce only three forms: "***he*** kept" (שָׁמַר), "***she*** kept" (שָֽׁמְרָה), and "***they*** kept" (שָֽׁמְרוּ).[9]

Perfects

"***he*** kept"	שָׁמַר
"***she*** kept"	שָֽׁמְרָה
"***they*** kept"	שָֽׁמְרוּ

8. In subsequent chapters you will learn that *perfects* view action as a *completed* event. Most actions viewed from this perspective tend to be in the past. Thus we can generally translate perfects as past tense. Likewise, *imperfects* view action as an *incomplete* event. Most actions viewed from this perspective tend to be in the present or future. Thus we can generally translate imperfects with an English present or future tense.

9. Remember that the *metheg* in the first syllable of the feminine and plural forms (i.e., the short vertical marking) lets you know this syllable should be pronounced open. Therefore, the vowel is a long /ā/ and the *shewa* is vocal (e.g., *shā-mᵉ-rā* and *shā-mᵉ-rū*). In the Hebrew text you may not always see the *metheg*, but these verbs will always follow the same pattern of pronunciation.

Because of the way that Hebrew tells stories, we must also introduce you to a concept that many English speakers consider odd—the "*waw* consecutive." While a conjunction can appear at the front of a verb to simply mean "and" (e.g., וְשָׁמַר "**and** he kept"), a *waw* added to the front of these verbs can also signal that the verb conveys the *opposite* of what you expect. For example, שָׁמַר means "he kept," but וְשָׁמַר can mean "and he will keep." The simple perfect and the *waw* consecutive perfect are the two forms of the perfect you will encounter in the translation exercises until chapter 17.

Table 4.4: Translating Perfects

Perfect	*Waw* Consecutive Perfect
שָׁמַר "he kept"	וְשָׁמַר "**and** he **will keep**"
שָׁמְרָה "she kept"	וְשָׁמְרָה "**and** she **will keep**"
שָׁמְרוּ "they kept"	וְשָׁמְרוּ "**and** they **will keep**"

Imperfects and Waw Consecutive Imperfects

Imperfects are formed by adding a letter to the *front* of the word (although they can have an ending too) and are generally translated as present or future tense. Again, this chapter introduces only three forms: "***he*** will keep" (יִשְׁמֹר), "***she*** will keep" (תִּשְׁמֹר), and "***they*** will keep" (יִשְׁמְרוּ). Notice that the singulars depicted here have no ending, but the plural has the same plural ending as the perfect.

Imperfects

"***he*** will keep"	יִשְׁמֹר
"***she*** will keep"	תִּשְׁמֹר

"***they*** (m.) will keep" יִשְׁמְרוּ

The imperfect, like the perfect, can appear alone or with the conjunction attached. You can tell the difference between the two conjunctions based on form. The simple conjunction ("and") follows the pattern you have already learned for the conjunction וְ (e.g., וְיִשְׁמֹר "***and*** he will keep"). The *waw* consecutive appears with the same vowel pointing you learned for the article (*pataḥ* + doubling) and signals that you will translate it the opposite of how you would translate an imperfect (e.g., וַיִּשְׁמֹר "***and*** he ***kept***").

Table 4.5: Translating Imperfects

Imperfect	Simple Conjunction Imperfect	*Waw* Consecutive Imperfect
יִשְׁמֹר "he will keep"	וְיִשְׁמֹר "***and*** he will keep"	וַיִּשְׁמֹר "***and*** he ***kept***"
תִּשְׁמֹר "she will keep"	וְתִשְׁמֹר "***and*** she will keep"	וַתִּשְׁמֹר "***and*** she ***kept***"
יִשְׁמְרוּ "they will keep"	וְיִשְׁמְרוּ "***and*** they will keep"	וַיִּשְׁמְרוּ "***and*** they ***kept***"

For now, feel free to refer to the above charts every time you translate until it becomes second nature. Do not worry about mastering these forms at this point. They are provided so that we can present the translation exercises as close to the biblical text as possible.

Do not be concerned if you encounter verbs that have slightly different vowels (e.g., שָׂנֵא "he hated") or no longer have all the consonants visible (e.g., בָּא "he came," from בוֹא). When a word does not contain all three root letters, the root will be provided in parentheses below the word. Translate based on the vocabulary meaning of the root and the subject implied by what is attached to the beginning and/or end of the root.

Word Order As you begin to translate, you will find that the verb is usually placed first because it already has an embedded subject (i.e., וַיִּשְׁמֹר = "and *he* kept"). If the author wishes to clarify the specific person doing the action, the standard way to do this is to restate the subject immediately after the verb. For example, the clause וַיִּשְׁמֹר יוֹסֵף expresses the following ideas: "and *he* kept, [namely] Joseph." When translating, you should express this according to English word order as "and Joseph kept." This verb + subject sequence is the standard pattern for Hebrew narrative.

וַיִּשְׁמֹר יוֹסֵף "And Joseph kept"

(lit. "and he kept, [namely] Joseph")

Although the standard word order for Hebrew narrative is verb + subject, the author may choose to place some other part of the sentence in the initial position (*fronting*). Placing the subject first is often used to signal information that provides background for the story. You have already seen an example of this in v. 2 of your assigned reading from Genesis 1:1–5.[10] The italicized nouns in the English translation below are placed first in the Hebrew clause to signal background information that is not part of the narrative sequence.

1	In the beginning God created (pf.)	בְּרֵאשִׁית בָּרָא אֱלֹהִים
	the heavens and the earth.	אֵת הַשָּׁמַיִם וְאֵת הָאָרֶץ׃
2	***And the earth*** was (pf.) formless and void	וְהָאָרֶץ הָיְתָה תֹהוּ וָבֹהוּ
	and darkness was over the face of the deep	וְחֹשֶׁךְ עַל־פְּנֵי תְהוֹם
	and the breath of God was hovering (ptc.)	וְרוּחַ אֱלֹהִים מְרַחֶפֶת
	over the surface of the waters.	עַל־פְּנֵי הַמָּיִם׃

10. See exercise 3B of the workbook.

3 And God said, "Let there be light."	וַיֹּאמֶר אֱלֹהִים יְהִי אוֹר
And there was light.	וַֽיְהִי־אוֹר׃

The author may also place some other item at the front of the sentence to focus the reader's attention. This use of fronting should not be simplistically labeled as "emphasis." It is more nuanced than that. A good example of this is again seen in the reading from Genesis 1.

5 And God called the light day	וַיִּקְרָא אֱלֹהִים לָאוֹר יוֹם
and ***the darkness*** he called (pf.) night.	וְלַחֹשֶׁךְ קָרָא לָיְלָה
And there was evening	וַֽיְהִי־עֶרֶב
and there was morning—day one.	וַֽיְהִי־בֹקֶר יוֹם אֶחָד׃

The point of this verse is not that the author was emphasizing darkness. The fronting of the word "darkness" simply places the words "light" and "darkness" in closer proximity so the reader experiences the link more clearly.

As you read, anticipate the standard narrative sequence of verb + subject. When you have a departure from this word order, learn to hear the inflection of the author's voice as he tells his story.

EXERCISES FOR CHAPTER 4

Based on the principles for vocalizing the definite article and conjunction (see tables 4.2 and 4.4), complete exercises 4A and 4B, which give you opportunity to practice adding definite articles and conjunctions to various Hebrew words. Then complete the translation exercise for chapter 4 that appears in the companion workbook. Use tables 4.5 and 4.6 as needed to guide your translation of the verbs.

CHAPTER 5

Vowel Changes in Hebrew Nouns

In the last chapter you learned that the meaning of a Hebrew word is enhanced by attaching endings that indicate gender and number. This system is complicated by the fact that when you add endings, the vowels within the word will often change. As a result, the plural of חָכָם ("wise man") is חֲכָמִים ("wise men"). Likewise, other forms that you have not yet learned will produce words like חֲכַם־‹ ("wise man of") and חַכְמֵי־‹ ("wise men of").[1] There are different combinations of vowels in each of these forms despite the fact that they are formed from the same Hebrew word. These changes can make words difficult to recognize.

The difficulty created by shifting vowels is greatly simplified if you understand the historical development that explains how and why these vowels change. For example, the words חָכָם, חֲכָמִים, חֲכַם־‹ and חַכְמֵי־‹ all originate from a single historic חַכַם*, and these vowel changes are governed by predictable rules.[2] In this chapter we will expand your understanding of the Hebrew vowel system and its development through time—including historic vowel length and the rules for vowel change. We will then show you how to walk through the steps of identifying the historic form, attaching endings, and applying the vowel rules so that you can recognize vocabulary words even when endings have caused the vowels to shift.

1. The vowel changes cannot be fully illustrated using only the gender and number endings you just learned. The discussion in this chapter also requires endings that you do not yet know. Do not worry about identifying the endings if they do not look familiar to you. Instead focus on what happens with the vowels in each syllable.

2. As noted in ch. 2, the asterisk * is used to indicate reconstructed historic forms not found in Biblical Hebrew.

HISTORIC VOWELS Hebrew vowels were historically either long or short and maintained their place in a word regardless of what endings were added.[3] However, historic short vowels eventually began to lengthen or drop in certain contexts while long vowels remained constant in all forms of the word. Discussing Hebrew words in terms of their "historic" vowels helps explain the forms that appear in Biblical Hebrew.[4] These historic vowels are highlighted by the two bold columns in the table below. The horizontal rows represent the relationship between the historic vowels and the vowels you now see in the Hebrew text. In each example the symbol □ represents any given Hebrew consonant.

Table 5.1: Changes in Historic Vowels

Proto-Semitic		Reduced	**HISTORIC SHORT**	Lengthened	**HISTORIC LONG**
a-class	a	□ְ or □ֲ ←	□ַ	→ □ָ	□ָ (rare)
i-class	e i	□ְ or □ֱ ←	□ֶ □ִ	→ □ֵ	†□ֶי □ֵי □ִי
u-class	o u	□ְ or □ֳ ←	□ָ □ֻ	→ □ֹ	□וֹ □וּ

† When *segol* (a short vowel) appears with a vowel marker, either י or ה, it is a historic long vowel.

(modified from Manuel, "Notes")

3. We are indebted to Paul Manuel ("Notes on Hebrew Grammar," [unpublished instructor's notes for Hebrew 103, University of Wisconsin-Madison, fall, 1988]) for much of how we view and present the vowel changes in Biblical Hebrew.

4. Strictly speaking, some of these vowels are "historic" because they were always long. Others are "historic" only in the sense that they became long in the period before Biblical Hebrew. The *ḥolem waw* (וֹ) appeared as a replacement for the historical long a-class vowel, and both *ḥolem waw* (וֹ) and *tsere/segol yod* (ֵי or ֶי) resulted from the contraction of *pataḥ* and *waw/yod* (ַו → וֹ and ַי → ֵי). Regardless of when they became unchangeable long vowels, it is helpful to think of them as "historic" to reinforce the fact that all words develop from vowel patterns that preexisted Biblical Hebrew.

As indicated by the isolation of the column to the right, historic long vowels never change. (They can also be referred to as unchangeable vowels.) The unchangeable vowels are generally identified by the use of vowel markers (i.e., ◌ֶי, ◌ֵי, ◌ִי, וֹ, וּ), although these vowels can appear without vowel markers.[5] The Hebrew Masoretic Text maintains a fairly consistent distinction between historic long vowels (with vowel markers) and lengthened short vowels (without vowel markers). For now, rely on the vowel markers to signal the presence of unchangeable long vowels. We will refer to the isolated column as "historic long" or "unchangeable long" and refer to the lengthened short vowels simply as "long."

The historic short vowels were able to change. As indicated by the arrows, the columns on either side of the historic short vowels are the result of short vowels lengthening or reducing. Short vowels reduce to *shewa*, remain short, or upgrade to a long vowel depending on the environment of the word. In other words, short vowels can become long, or short vowels can reduce to *shewa*, but vowels NEVER shift from *shewa* to long or long to *shewa*.

When vowels remain short, the i-class vowels *segol* ◌ֶ and *ḥireq* ◌ִ are often interchangeable. The u-class vowels often vary depending on the environment of the syllable. Hebrew usually reserves short u-class *qibbuts* ◌ֻ for use before doubled consonants and *qamets qaton* ◌ָ for all other cases. To remember this tendency, think of *qibbuts* preceding a *dagesh* as the "connect four" rule (e.g., ◌ּ◌ֻ).

The historic long /ā/ that is shaded in the chart above is so rare that it almost never occurs, being replaced instead with long /ō/.[6] Therefore, you should assume that any a-class *qamets* originated from a short /a/ (*pataḥ*). In later chapters you will learn that some of the

5. Historic long vowels sometimes appear in the Masoretic text without a vowel marker. When historic long vowels appear without vowel markers they are described as *defectively written* in contrast to those that have the expected *plene spelling* (or *full spelling*). As you learn Hebrew well enough to know when to expect an unchangeable long vowel, you will recognize defective spellings.

6. A historic long /ā/ is very rare because most of these vowels shifted to long /ō/ in the period before Biblical Hebrew in a process called *Canaanite Shift*. The term derives its name from the fact that this vowel shift is unique to the languages of ancient Canaan. For example, the Hebrew term קֹטֵל appears as קָטֵל in Aramaic (a non-Canaanite Semitic language).

other unchangeable long vowels result from the combination of a short vowel plus *waw* or *yod*.

RULES FOR VOWEL CHANGE

We have already shown you that the vowels can change, now we will show you how and when they change. Hebrew words alter historic short vowels based on the type of syllable (open or closed) and its relationship to the accent. We will refer to the syllable immediately before the accent as the *near syllable* and the syllables further removed from the accent as *distant syllables*.[7] For example, a word like אֱלֹהִ֫ים would be identified as having an accented syllable (אֱ|לֹ|הִ֫ים), a near open syllable (אֱ|לֹ|הִ֫ים), and a distant open syllable (אֱ|לֹ|הִ֫ים).

Eventually you will be able to visualize the structure of these words in your head. For now you will probably need to write these words down and manually divide the syllables. To do this you should mark the accent and identify the syllables as you work your way from the accent to the front of the word. Remember that in this grammar, if a word is unmarked, the accent falls on the final syllable.

N D[1]

אֱ|לֹ|הִ֫ים

<	= Accented
N	= Near syllable (first syllable before the accent)
D^1 D^2 D^3	= Distant syllables (two or more syllables before the accent)

Three simple rules govern vowel changes in Hebrew words. These rules apply only to historic short vowels[8] in unaccented syllables.[9] Keep in mind that the first rule addresses all *closed* unaccented syllables (whether near, distant, or even following the accented syllable). The second and third rules address *open* unaccented syllables depending on their relationship to the accent (near or distant).

7. Many grammars use the terms *tonic* (i.e., the syllable with the accent or "tone"), *pretonic* (one syllable before the accent), and *propretonic* (two or more syllables before the accent).

8. Remember that only historic short vowels can change.

9. The vowel rules do not address accented syllables because accented syllables are unpredictable. As a general rule, accented syllables tend to lengthen historic short vowels. However, in most cases the accented syllables are known by the forms students memorize (e.g., gender and number endings).

Table 5.2: Rules for Vowel Change

1. **Closed** unaccented syllables require short vowels.
2. Near **open** syllables (1 syllable before the accent):
   a. Lengthen for Nouns.
   b. Reduce for Verbs—but lengthen a-class vowels and preformative vowels.†
3. Distant **open** syllables reduce (2+ before the accent)

(modified from Manuel, "Notes")

† The second part of the rule is presented so that you can see the whole picture, but it is not utilized until we begin discussing verbs (ch. 12).

Rule #1 applies to all closed unaccented syllables regardless of their place in the word (near, distant, or even after the accent). Rule #2 deals with vowel changes in the syllable immediately before the accent. In nouns, a historic short vowel will lengthen. This syllable will respond differently in verbs. We will explain the application for verbs more fully once we start learning the verb paradigms. For now focus on how the vowel rules relate to nouns and adjectives. As stated by rule #3, distant open syllables respond the same in all Hebrew words; they reduce to *shewa* whenever possible.

The importance of these rules can be seen when you observe what happens when you attach endings. In its dictionary form the word has a defined accent and syllable structure. When you add endings the accent moves further to the end of the word and the syllable structure is often affected—near syllables can become distant, closed syllables can become open, and vowels shift. However, all vowel changes are governed by the rules above.

HISTORIC FORMS

As mentioned above, you are going to be confronted with words that do not look like what you learned. In our earlier example you saw that the word חָכָם ("wise man") can appear as חֲכָמִים ("wise men"), חֲכַם־ ("wise man of"), or חַכְמֵי־ ("wise men of"). None of these words can be explained by applying the vowel rules to חָכָם. As noted in previous sections, the long vowel in חָכָם could never have reduced to the *shewa* seen in חֲכָמִים. Vowels only shift one step (short to reduced or short to long, *not* long to reduced).

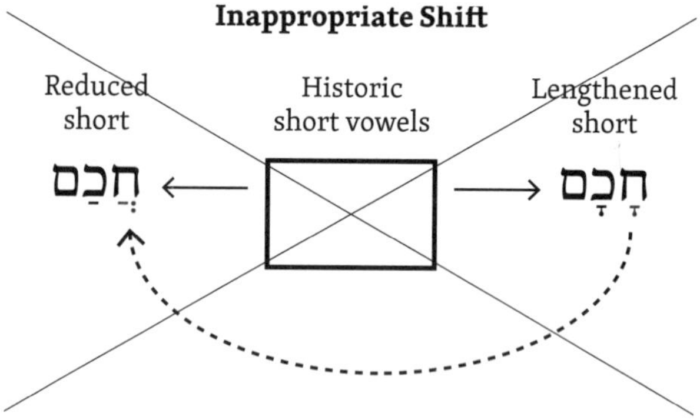

This does not mean that the vowel rules do not work. They simply have to be applied correctly. Since there are no vowel markers in the word חָכָם (that would signify unchangeable long vowels) and since both vowels fluctuate in the various forms you see in the text, these vowels must have been historic short vowels. An historic חַכַם* is the point of origin for all four words. The illustration below depicts the vowel shifts in a layout similar to the vowel chart (table 5.1) so that you can see the single-step transition from short to reduced or short to long.

Accurate Shift

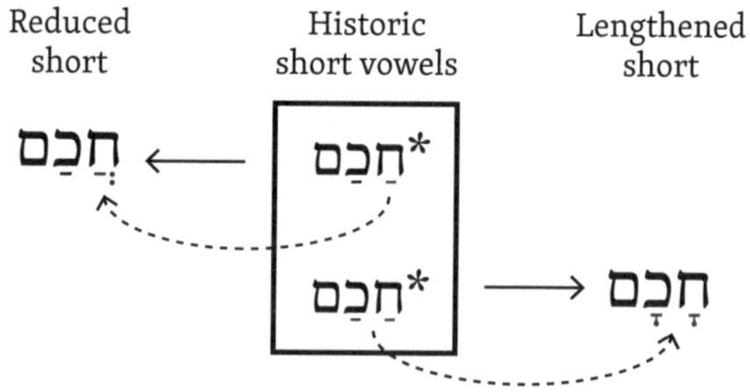

Keep in mind that this historic form חַכַם* is not a form you will ever see in the biblical text. This shift is actually something that occurred in the development of Hebrew prior to the current vocalization of the Hebrew Bible. In other words, it predates the biblical text.

Table 5.3: Moving from Historical to Biblical Form

Historic Form	חֲכַם*			
Hebrew Bible	חָכָם	חֲכַם־◻	חַכְמֵי־◻	חֲכָמִים
	"a wise man"	"wise man of"	"wise men of"	"wise men"
First vowel:	*Short lengthens*	*Short reduces*	*Short stays*	*Short reduces*
Second vowel:	*Short lengthens*	*Short stays*	*Short reduces*	*Short lengthens*

Through the course of time, the word חֲכַם* was affected by the syllables and accent in predictable ways according to the vowel rules outlined above. It might seem crazy to have you reconstruct a form you will never see. However, this historic form will help you predict all the vowel changes you encounter when attaching an ending to a Hebrew word. This eliminates the need for rote memorization of multiple, seemingly random vowel patterns.

These subtle vowel changes in the word חָכָם may not seem like a big deal to you right now. To some degree you may be tempted to rely on your ability to spot familiar roots (חֲכָמִים) and endings (חֲכָמִים). But what you have not yet learned is that there are other Hebrew words that can be easily confused if you are not aware of the principles of vowel changes. For example, you must eventually be able to distinguish between the adjective "wise woman" (חֲכָמָה *ḥ*ᵃ*-kā-mā*), the noun "wisdom" (חָכְמָה *ḥok-mā*), and the verb "she was wise" (חָֽכְמָה *ḥā-k*ᵉ*-mā*). Since your goal is not to simply get the gist of what the author says, but to read the Hebrew text with care and precision, you must pay attention to the subtle details that guide your interpretation.

FINDING THE HISTORIC FORM

You have seen that historic forms are important because they account for all the vowel changes that take place in Hebrew words and that the vowel rules govern how those changes take place. As you learn vocabulary you should begin to consciously identify the historic forms for yourself. You can determine the historic form with the information you already know.

Identifying the Historic Length of Vowels

If a word has vowels with vowel markers, these are historic long vowels that will remain unchanged. In general, all other vowels go back to historic short vowels, and should be visualized as such. It will be easiest if you consistently visualize short /a/ as a *pataḥ* (ַ), short /i, e/ as a *ḥireq* (ִ), and short /o, u/ as a *qibbuts* (ֻ).[10] Although certain vowel classes are represented by more than one vowel (e.g., short i-class is represented by short /i/ ִ and short /e/ ֶ), we are only trying to approximate the historic form, so the vowel class is what really matters.

Biblical Hebrew		Historic form
שָׁ|לוֹם	→	*שַׁלוֹם
זָ|קֵן	→	*זַקִן
כֹּל	→	*כֻּל

Identifying the Historic Form Reflected by a Shewa

Analyzing words with a *shewa* in them may cause you a little more difficulty because a *shewa* could reflect either a historic short vowel or an original *shewa* (i.e., no vowel). Furthermore, any *shewa* that evidences a historic short vowel could be derived from any one of the three vowel classes (a-class, i-class, or u-class).

Shewa in a Near Syllable—Historic Shewa

If a noun or adjective has a *shewa* immediately in front of the accent, that *shewa* was always a *shewa*. A historic vowel would have lengthened according to rule #2 (*near open syllables lengthen in nouns*). This *shewa* is a historic *shewa*, and historic *shewas* are unchanging. This *shewa* will be present in every word derived from the historic form.

10. The use of *qibbuts* is especially important so that your visualization of the word does not confuse short /o/ and long /ā/ (both of which are represented by ָ).

Biblical Hebrew		Historic form
מִשְׁ|פָּט	→	*מִשְׁפַּט

Shewa in a Distant Syllable—Historic Vowel or Historic Shewa

Shewas that are further removed from the accent could reflect either historic *shewas* or historic short vowels that have reduced (rule #3: *Distant open syllables reduce* *חַכַמִים → חֲכָמִים). If a distant *shewa* is under the first consonant of the word (not counting prefixes), then this *shewa* represents a historic short vowel that has reduced.[11] The historic form you reconstruct should include a historic short vowel in that syllable.

Biblical Hebrew		Historic form[12]
N D		
אֲ|דָ|מָה	→	*אַ|דַ|מַה

If a distant *shewa* is not at the front of the word, but instead is preceded by another consonant, then that *shewa* could either reflect a historic *shewa* or a reduced short vowel. In order to determine which option is correct, you must rely on your familiarity with other forms of the same word. For example, the word מַלְאָכִים ("angels") taken in isolation could stem from a historic *מַלְ|אַךְ or *מַ|לַ|אַךְ. Both options are possible. However, the vocabulary form without endings gives you an additional piece of data. The word מַלְאָךְ has a *shewa* immediately before the accent. We learned above that a *shewa* in a near syllable is always a historic *shewa* (rule #2: *In near open syllables short vowels would lengthen*). Historic *shewas* do not change. That means this *shewa* must appear in all forms of this word. The historic form is thus *מַלְ|אַךְ (NOT *מַ|לַ|אַךְ).

11. Prefixes (e.g., definite articles and conjunctions) are always added to the word after it has undergone modification of vowels.

12. We will see later that the historic form is actually *אַ|דַ|מַת, but for now this illustrates the principles for determining historic vowels.

Biblical Hebrew	Possible historic forms	Additional form
N D מַ|לְ|אָ|כִים →	*מַלְ|אַךְ	(מַלְאָךְ ←)
↘	~~*מַ|לַ|אַךְ~~	"angel, messenger"

Conversely, the word אַדְמַת־ ("ground of") could stem from a historic *אַ|דַ|מַת or *אַדְ|מַת. Theoretically, both options are possible. However, the vocabulary form אֲדָמָה ("ground") indicates that the second consonant of this word did indeed have a historic vowel. If a syllable has a vowel in one form of this word, it evidences a historic vowel. The historic form of this word must be *אַ|דַ|מַת (NOT *אַדְ|מַת). Because all forms are generated from a single historic form, alternate forms of the same word can help you identify the historic vowels.

Biblical Hebrew	Possible historic forms	Additional form
N D אַ|דְ|מַת־ →	~~*אַדְ|מַת~~	
↘	*אַ|דַ|מַת	(אֲדָמָה ←) "ground"

Identifying the Vowel Class Reflected in a Shewa

If a *shewa* does indeed reflect the presence of a historic short vowel, it could derive from any of the three vowel classes (a-class, i-class, or u-class). If you are dealing with a composite *shewa*, it will generally guide your decision and tell you what short vowel to use. With a-class ֲ assume historic short /a/. With i-class ֱ assume historic short /i/. With u-class ֳ assume historic short /u/. If you are confronted with a regular *shewa*, be aware that Hebrew has a strong preference for a-class vowels. Unless there is other evidence to the contrary, assume that the historic short vowel from which a shewa reduces was short /a/. This will be correct more often than not and will serve you well in understanding the changes that occur.

HOW TO ADD ENDINGS TO HEBREW NOUNS

Now that you can find the historic form and know the vowel rules, it is time to put all the pieces together. Remember that your vocabulary form is not the base to which endings are attached. Rather, the endings are attached to historic forms. (Endings were attached long before vowels changed to those found in Biblical Hebrew.) The illustration from p. 69 is repeated below to demonstrate the process of applying the Hebrew vowel rules. This process involves three steps:

1. Move from vocabulary form back to the historic form (חָכָם → חַכַם*)
2. Attach the ending to the historic form (חַכַם* → חַכַמִים*)
3. Apply the vowel rules by starting with the syllable closest to the accent (חַכַמִים* → חֲכָמִים)

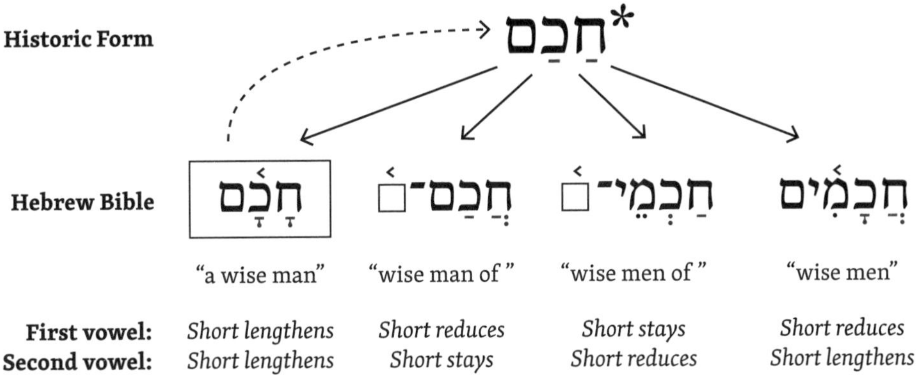

If you could simply move from your vocabulary word to the form with the endings, this whole process would not be necessary. In order to generate words you must first work backward from your vocabulary word to the historic form, then you can use the historic form to generate the forms with endings. Do not panic about mastering this material, simply seek to understand each step as it is explained.

Example 1

To make the word זָקֵן ("old") into a masculine plural ("old men"), you must follow the steps outlined above. The diagrams below illustrate each stage of this process.

Step 1: Move from vocabulary form back to the historic form.

Biblical Hebrew		Historic form
זָ|קֵן	→	*זַ|קִן

No vowel markers
(historic short)

Step 2: Attach the ending to the historic form and adjust syllables.

Historic form		Ending added
*זַ|קִן	→	*זַ|קִ|נִים

Step 3: Apply the vowel rules
(starting with the syllable closest to the accent).

Historic form plus ending		Biblical Hebrew
N D *זַ|קִ|נִים	→	זְקֵנִים

Rule #2: Near open syllables lengthen

Rule #3: Distant open syllables reduce

Rule #1 (*closed unaccented syllables take short vowels*) does not apply to any of the syllables in this word because both syllables are open. Rules #2–3 state that *near open syllables lengthen* and *distant open syllables reduce*. As a result, the historic short /i/ lengthens to *tsere* and the historic short /a/ reduces to *shewa*.

Example 2 You will sometimes run into a situation where applying the vowel rules to multiple distant syllables (D^1, D^2, etc.) would result in two *shewas* at the beginning of the word (e.g., חֲכַמֵי־* → חֲכְמֵי־*). As we saw in chapter 2, this situation is not acceptable in Hebrew. When it occurs, Hebrew will not allow the second distant syllable (D^2) to reduce but will retain the historic short vowel in order to maintain a suitable word structure (a closed unaccented syllable). For example, note how the word חָכָם ("wise") relates to חַכְמֵי־ ("wise men of").

Step 1: Move from vocabulary form back to the historic form.

Biblical Hebrew		Historic form
חָ|כָם	→	*חַ|כַם
No vowel markers (historic short)		

Step 2: Attach the ending to the historic form and adjust syllables.

Historic form		Ending added
*חַ|כַם	→	*חַ|כַ|מֵי־□

Step 3: Apply the vowel rules
(starting with the syllable closest to the accent).

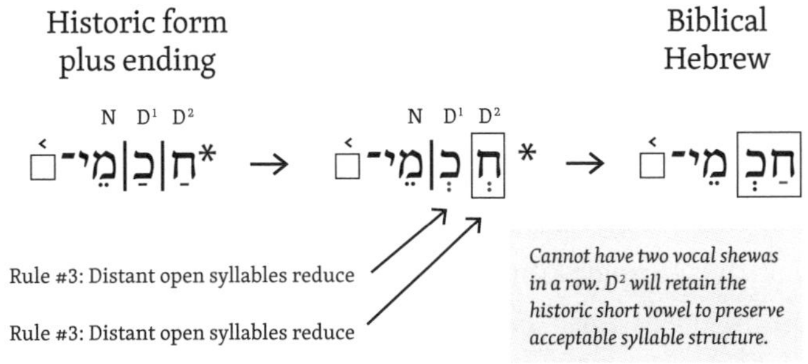

In this word we are presented with two distant open syllables (D¹ and D²). Rule #3 that tells us that *distant open syllables reduce.* The vowel in D¹ will thus reduce to a *shewa* (חַ|כְ|מֵי־). But at this point we have a small problem. If we try to reduce D² based on the same rule (*distant open syllables reduce*), the two vocal *shewas* produce a consonant cluster (*חֲכְמֵי־). Hebrew does not allow two vocal *shewas* in a row. As a result, the initial syllable must retain its historic short vowel in order to create a stable syllable (closed unaccented).

Understanding the historical development of Hebrew words will allow you to recognize vocabulary more quickly and translate with greater precision and confidence—even when vowel changes take place. This skill will take time and practice to develop, but it will save you the labor of rote memorization, will apply to all aspects of Hebrew grammar, and is a skill that you will retain even if your recollection of vocabulary fades.

SPECIAL CONSIDERATIONS FOR SEGOLATE NOUNS

On occasion you may encounter words in the biblical text that seem to contradict the vowel rules. However, the problem is not the vowel rules. The incongruity is caused by additional factors that affect the transition from the historic form to the forms in the biblical text. These extra steps obscure the connection between vocabulary form and historic form.

One of the most common examples of words that do not seem to fit the vowel rules are *segolate nouns*. Segolate nouns are fairly simple for students to identify because of their unique appearance. They are accented on the second to last syllable of the word and have a short vowel in the final syllable (usually *segol*, although a *pataḥ* can be used in close proximity to a guttural since gutturals prefer a-class vowels).

נַ֫עַר בֹּ֫קֶר סֵ֫פֶר מֶ֫לֶךְ

You might expect the historic form of these words to contain two historic short vowels (e.g., assuming that מֶ֫לֶךְ comes from historic מְ֫לִךְ*). However, that form does not explain other forms of this word and determining the historic form requires a few extra steps..

Singular Segolates (One-syllable Historic Form)

Segolate nouns were historically single-syllable words with a final consonant cluster—CvCC (e.g., מַ֫לְךְ*). Because Hebrew does not like consonant clusters, a helping vowel was inserted between the final two consonants to ease pronunciation (e.g., מַ֫לֶךְ*). The vowel in the accented syllable (the original vowel) was then either harmonized with the helping vowel (for historic a-class patterns, e.g., מַ֫לֶךְ* → מֶ֫לֶךְ) or that vowel was lengthened (for i-class and u-class patterns, e.g., סִ֫פֶר* → סֵ֫פֶר and בֻּ֫קֶר* → בֹּ֫קֶר).

Table 5.4: Development of the Segolate Lexical Form

Historic singular (one syllable)		Helping vowel added		LEXICAL FORM (with harmonization or lengthening)
*מַלְךְ	→	*מַ֫לֶךְ	→	מֶ֫לֶךְ
*סִפְר	→	*סִ֫פֶר	→	סֵ֫פֶר
*בֻּקְר	→	*בֻּ֫קֶר	→	בֹּ֫קֶר

Plural Segolates (Two-Syllable Historic Form)

Segolate nouns use a different historic form for the plural. When you are talking about plural objects (e.g., "kings"), the segolates shift to a historic form with *two* vowels, forming a bisyllabic base (two syllables). The second vowel is always an a-class vowel, regardless of the vowel in the first syllable. For example, the plurals of מֶ֫לֶךְ, סֵ֫פֶר, and בֹּ֫קֶר are formed off the historic forms *סִפַר, *מַלַךְ, and *בֻּקַר respectively.

Table 5.5: Historic Forms of Segolate Singulars and Plurals

Historic singular (One syllable)	Historic plural (Two syllables)
*מַלְךְ	*מַלַךְ
*סִפְר	*סִפַר
*בֻּקְר	*בֻּקַר

The historic forms are then adjusted in keeping with the vowel rules to produce the forms you commonly see in the Hebrew Bible: מְלָכִים ("kings"), סְפָרִים ("books"), and בְּקָרִים ("mornings"). These distinctive monosyllabic singulars and bisyllabic plurals depicted in the table above serve as the base for all the segholate forms you encounter.[13]

Historic form		Historic form plus ending		Biblical Hebrew
		N D		
*מַלְךְ	→	*מַ|לַ|כִים	→	מְלָכִים

Rule #2: Near open syllables lengthen

Rule #3: Distant open syllables reduce

This distinction also explains why two nearly identical forms, the singular מַלְכִּי ("my king") and plural מַלְכֵי ("kings of"), differ in regard to *dagesh lene*. The *dagesh lene* is present in the singular because it follows the silent *shewa* of a historically closed syllable. Conversely, the plural lacks *dagesh lene* because the *kaph* was preceded by a historic vowel.

Summary of Segolate Nouns

We are aware that the principles for segolate nouns are rather complex and require you to think in completely new ways. As a first-year student you should take away at least these core ideas: (1) Segolate vocabulary will not directly give you the historic forms. (2) Singular segolate nouns derive from a one-syllable historic form represented by *מַלְךְ (*singular = one*). (3) Plural segolate nouns derive from a two-syllable historic form represented by *מַלַךְ (*plural = two*). Remember that the second vowel of the plural will always be an a-class vowel. Remember also that words generated from the plural form will never take a *dagesh lene* in the third consonant because of the historic vowel pattern. Once you know these simple elements, segolates follow the vowel rules just like every other noun.

13. It may be helpful to think of segolate patterns as 1 syllable = 1 (singular) and 2 syllables = 2 (plural).

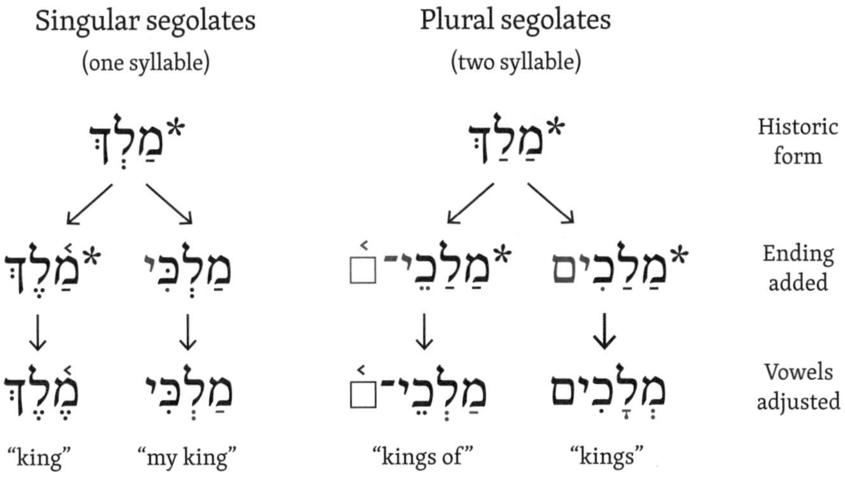

This chapter can be overwhelming. While you should strive to understand each explanation, only a few elements must be mastered:

- Vowel chart (table 5.1) — The interrelationship between Hebrew vowels
- Vowel rules (table 5.2) — (1) Closed unaccented syllables take short vowels, (2) near open syllables lengthen in nouns, and (3) distant open syllables reduce.
- The steps for adding endings to nouns and adjectives — (1) Find the historic form, (2) add the endings, and (3) apply the vowel rules (as reviewed in the examples on pp. 70–79).
- The historic forms of the segolate nouns are represented by *מַלְךְ (*singular = one syllable*) and *מַלַךְ (*plural = two syllables*).

EXERCISE FOR CHAPTER 5

The best way to understand the principles of vowel change is to practice applying them. The workbook includes an exercise that will help you do this. Skim back through the material you learned in chapter 4 and the principles of vowel change in this chapter (particularly as demonstrated in the examples on pp. 70–79). Then complete the exercise in the workbook entitled "Vowel Changes with Gender and Number Endings" (exercise 5). As you complete this exercise you will also be asked to attach prefixes such as the definite article and the conjunction. Be sure to add these prefixes *after* you have produced the final form of the word. It is expected that you will make errors as you complete these exercises. Those errors are part of the learning process. Correct them and seek to understand why you made your mistakes.

CHAPTER 6

Noun and Adjective Function

Although you received a basic introduction to nouns and adjectives in chapter 4 when we discussed gender and number endings, there are a few other details for you to learn. A noun is a word that identifies a person (e.g., girl), place (e.g., Jerusalem), object (e.g., book), or idea (e.g., righteousness). Adjectives describe the attributes of nouns (e.g., a *holy* book). In Hebrew, adjectives can also be used in place of nouns. For example, the Hebrew expression "the *holy* of Israel" means "the *Holy One* of Israel." This chapter explains how to recognize the relationship between nouns and adjectives and presents an overview of how nouns and adjectives function in Hebrew sentences.

HEBREW ADJECTIVES

Adjectives Must Agree with the Noun They Modify

Adjectives are words that describe some quality or attribute of a noun (e.g., good, bad, tall, short). The close link between an adjective and the noun it modifies requires that the adjective agree with that noun in both gender and number. That is why the gender and number endings are attached to both nouns and adjectives. For example, the phrase "good kings" would be expressed in Hebrew as מְלָכִים טוֹבִים while a "good queen" would be expressed as מַלְכָּה טוֹבָה. In each phrase the adjective agrees with the noun in gender and number.

You will sometimes run across irregular nouns whose appearance does not match their grammatical gender. Please note that the adjective must agree with the actual gender and number of the noun, not its form. For example, the word אָבוֹת ("fathers") uses a plural ending that normally appears on feminine nouns. However, אָבוֹת it is a masculine plural noun and must be modified by a masculine plural adjective like טוֹבִים (NOT טוֹבוֹת). Similarly, the phrase אֶ֫רֶץ טוֹבָה uses a feminine adjective because the word אֶ֫רֶץ is a feminine noun even though it does not end with the typical feminine ending. One must match the grammatical gender, not the form or appearance of the word.

Attributive and Predicate Use of Adjectives

One of the goals of this grammar is to teach students how to read and understand Hebrew as a living language, without having to translate. However, we recognize that students need to rely upon English as a starting point to understand what they read. The following paragraphs discuss adjectives in a more abstract sense and then provide guidelines to explain how placement and definiteness help determine the relationship between the noun and adjective. But first focus on instinctively recognizing this relationship as you read.

Intuitive Reading

By definition all adjectives must describe a noun. Sometimes the noun will be included explicitly in the sentence. Sometimes the noun is not included in the sentence, and the reader must understand the implied person or object that the author has in mind.[1] Either way, an adjective is always linked to a nominal idea, and your job as a reader is to determine the relationship between the adjective and the noun.

When you read, you should provisionally identify each adjective as describing something generic. If you have a sentence that states—

אָמַר הַמֶּ֫לֶךְ הַטּוֹב אֶל־הָאִישׁ

הַטּוֹב	הַמֶּ֫לֶךְ
"the good [one]"	"the king"

—you read "the king, the good [one], spoke to the man." You know that the word "good" must describe someone or something, and since Hebrew has already provided a noun that agrees with the adjective, you assume that the king is what is being described. Hopefully you will understand the best way to translate this in English because you understand what the Hebrew is trying to say. While you will think in

1. When a noun is present grammarians refer to the adjective as having *adjectival* function. When the noun is not present in the sentence, grammarians refer to the adjective as having *substantival* function because it is used in place of the noun. We use substantive adjectives in English too. Consider the common expression "My favorite is. . . ." The word "favorite" is an adjective, but is being used in place of a word that has "substance" (i.e., a noun).

Hebrew, "the king, the good [one]," you will translate this for English readers as "the good king."

Likewise, if you have a sentence that states —

שָׁמַע כִּי הַמֶּ֫לֶךְ טוֹב

"a good [one]" "the king"

—you once again know that the word "good" describes something, and since Hebrew has already provided a noun that agrees with the adjective, you know that it is probably describing the king. So you read, "He heard that the king, a good [one]." As you conceptualize this in Hebrew, you understand that there is a link between "king" and "good" but you pick up on the disparity in the grammar. One has a definite article and the other does not. If you pause and think about this phrase, you will realize that you already have a meaning in mind. In English the only way to make sense of this phrase is to provide some form of the verb "to be." Thus you would translate this as "He heard that the king was a good [one]" or more simply, "that the king was good."

As a third example, consider the adjective in the following sentence.

קָרָא אֶל־הַטּוֹב

"the good [one]"

Again begin with the knowledge that the word "good" must describe someone or something. This sentence does not provide a noun to identify who or what is being described, so you leave it abstract, "he called to the good [one]." Context will usually give more clues as to how this should be translated. In this case we would probably choose to translate this as "he called to the good man."[2] Learn to treat every adjective as an attribute inseparably bound to a nominal idea and let context determine what that relationship is.

2. Notice that English translations will sometimes translate by adding nouns that are not formally in the Hebrew text. This is not only appropriate but necessary since Hebrew and English have different expectations of what elements must be included for a sentence to make sense.

In our final example you will see how important context is in determining the relationship between the noun and adjective. Exodus 9:27 states—

יהוה הַצַּדִּיק וַאֲנִי וְעַמִּי הָרְשָׁעִים

הַצַּדִּיק	יהוה
the righteous [one]	the LORD

When you read the first phrase, you should see in your mind "the LORD, the righteous [one]." Like the first example above, the sentence provides the noun that the adjective is describing. Thus when translating you could express these first two words as "The righteous LORD." However, the verse continues "and I and my people, the wicked [ones]."

הָרְשָׁעִים	וְעַמִּי	וַאֲנִי	הַצַּדִּיק	יהוה
the wicked [ones]	and my people	and I	the righteous [one]	the LORD

In the context of the whole verse, the phrase "the righteous [one]" parallels "the wicked [ones]." Your initial translation "the righteous LORD" makes no sense in the context and is in fact blasphemous: "the righteous LORD and I and my people are the wicked ones." The context demands that you interpret the sentence so that the first two words represent the same grammatical structure as the last three words. You must translate the verse as, "The LORD is the righteous one, and I and my people are the wicked ones." However, if you can learn to read Hebrew for its own sake and not get stuck "decoding" you will see the parallelism yourself: "the LORD, the righteous [one] and I and my people, the wicked [ones]." Obviously when translating you will have to smooth this out for an English audience.

Formal Distinctions

Grammarians use specific terminology and a set of rules to describe the function of adjectives. They divide adjectives into two categories: attributive adjectives and predicate adjectives. This concept can be confusing to students since every adjective describes an attribute of a noun. The following nuanced definition will help you to understand the distinction between these two types of adjectives.

An *attributive adjective* is closely bound to the noun it modifies and appears in the same syntactical slot in the sentence as the noun itself. If the noun is the subject of the sentence, then the noun and adjective together will create the complete subject (e.g., "A *good king* took the throne"). Similarly, if the noun serves as the direct object, the pair will create a more complete picture of the object ("God gave them *a good king*"). This applies to any noun function in a sentence. Since the function of this type of adjective is limited to conveying an attribute of the noun, grammars refer to this type of adjective as an *attributive adjective.*

Predicate adjectives also reflect an attribute of the noun but do so from a different grammatical slot in the sentence. As the name "predicate" suggests, a predicate adjective serves as the verbal side (or *predicate* side) of the sentence (e.g., "The king *is good*"). These types of sentences correspond to English sentences with the verb "to be" (e.g., is, are, was, were), whether this Hebrew verb is stated הַמֶּ֫לֶךְ הָיָה טוֹב ("The king is a good [one]") or merely implied הַמֶּ֫לֶךְ טוֹב ("The king, a good [one]"). Both mean, "The king is good," and should be translated as such. Though the Hebrew predicate adjective is not a verb, it is part of the verbal side of the sentence (predicate) and English demands that a verb be supplied.

The word order of the adjective and noun can provide some help in distinguishing between attributive and predicative adjectives. Predicate adjectives can appear either before or after the noun[3] and are not limited by agreement in definiteness.[4] On the other hand, attributive adjectives are more common but are limited in the form they can appear in the text. An attributive adjective *always follows* the noun it

3. The fact that a predicate adjective can be placed either before or after the noun is not a question of meaning but rather of focus. It is possible that the placement of a predicate adjective is merely stylistic, but you should consider the fact that the author is stressing something specific through his word order. An expression like יהוה טוֹב ("the Lord is good") may perhaps identify the Lord as the one who is good in contrast to other gods or individuals, while the expression טוֹב יהוה ("Good is the Lord") could suggest that he is in fact good when circumstances could lead one to assume that he is harsh or evil. Consider Ps 73:1 where the rest of the psalm suggests that the author wishes to assert the goodness of God when circumstances seem to suggest otherwise: אַךְ טוֹב לְיִשְׂרָאֵל אֱלֹהִים ("Surely God is good to Israel").

4. Some grammars assert that a predicate adjective never has a definite article (GKC §126i,k; Waltke-O'Connor §14.3.2). However, Exod 9:27 has two examples of a definite predicate adjective. In this passage Pharaoh admits that he has sinned because the Lord is the righteous one in contrast with his own wickedness: יהוה הַצַּדִּיק וַאֲנִי וְעַמִּי הָרְשָׁעִים, ("The Lord is the righteous one and I and my people are the wicked ones"; thus also Joüon §137*l*). While examples of the definite article appearing with a simple predicate adjective are admittedly rare, the definite article regularly appears with the predicate adjective when it functions as a superlative (discussed below).

modifies and *always agrees in gender, number, and definiteness* with the noun. If these conditions are not met, the adjective must be predicative. In other words, if an adjective occurs *before* the noun or if an adjective *does not agree in definiteness* with the noun it modifies, then it must be a predicate adjective. Every other case is open to either option, and you must rely on context.

Table 6.1: Distinguishing Adjective Function

1. Adjectives *before* the noun = Predicate adjectives
   טוֹב מֶ֫לֶךְ "a good [one], a king" = "A king is good"

2. Adjectives that *do not match definiteness* = Predicate adjectives
   הַמֶּ֫לֶךְ טוֹב "the king, a good [one]" = "The king is good"

3. *Otherwise rely on context*

While these principles provide helpful guidelines for distinguishing the function of adjectives in a sentence, remember that it is less important to be able to label their function than to understand their meaning in the text. Read adjectives the same every time you come to them (e.g., טוֹב "a good [one]") and understand the Hebrew in its own right instead of trying to force it to follow an English model (as demonstrated at the beginning of this section).

Adjectives Used as Comparatives and Superlatives

One subset of the Hebrew predicate adjective is its use to express comparative or superlative ideas. *Comparative adjectives* are used to "compare" two items (e.g., faster, slower, better, worse). *Superlative adjectives* indicate that someone or something is the *most* or *least* within a group.

Comparative Adjective

The comparative adjective is formed by the combination of an adjective plus the preposition מִן ("from"). For example, to express the idea that "David was better than Saul" we would say דָּוִיד טוֹב מִן שָׁאוּל (lit. "David was good ***from*** Saul"). The word מִן ("from") can express separation between two entities. In other words, the item in focus is separated out from a group and has a certain quality to a greater or lesser degree than the other(s). The objective of a comparative adjective is to show relative scales of comparison rather than to designate one as "the" most or least within a group. Thus a comparative adjective will never have a definite article.

Superlative Adjective

To communicate a superlative idea Hebrew uses an adjective with the definite article.[5] For example, if we wanted to say that "David is *the best* of the men," we would say דָּוִיד הַטּוֹב מִן הָאֲנָשִׁים (lit. "David is ***the*** good [one] ***from*** the men").

The use of the article to denote a superlative makes sense because the article sets the item apart. With nouns, an article indicates that not just any item is referenced, but a specific one (e.g., not "a king" but "the king"). The same is true with adjectives. If someone is "the good [one]," it follows that there is none better, and thus he is the best.

Summary

In the above discussion we have presented attributive adjectives and predicate adjectives and shown how they can also be used to communicate a comparative or superlative idea. Some of you may notice that we have presented you very few "rules" to distinguish between these different functions. When an adjective appears before the noun or when the noun and adjective do not agree in definiteness it is automatically a predicate adjective. But this leaves a wide range of situations where the function of the adjective is clarified by context alone. For example the phrase הַמֶּלֶךְ הַטּוֹב ("the king, the good [one]") can be either attributive, predicative, or superlative. Advanced grammars provide lengthy discussions on the expected features of each. However, the bottom line is that your understanding of the relationship between the noun and adjective is always guided by context.

When you read, get in the habit of provisionally identifying each adjective as describing someone or something (e.g., "David, the small [one]"). Then let context determine the relationship between the noun and adjective. Once you have meaning in your mind, translate that meaning into a smooth English sentence. The following examples demonstrate this approach to reading and show how context clarifies meaning when you encounter a phrase that could have multiple meanings.

5. This discussion is limited to the use of the adjective to express superlative ideas. There are other ways to express superlatives using adverbs with the adjective (e.g., טוֹב מְאֹד = ***very*** good) or using the construct relationships discussed in the next chapter.

אָמַר הַמֶּ֫לֶךְ הַטּוֹב אֶל־הָאִישׁ

The king, the good [one], spoke to the man =

"The good king spoke to the man"

ATTRIBUTIVE ADJECTIVE

הַמֶּ֫לֶךְ הַטּוֹב וְהָעָם הָרָע

The king, the good [one] and the people, the evil [ones]

"The king is the good one and the people are the evil ones"

PREDICATE ADJECTIVE

הַמֶּ֫לֶךְ הַטּוֹב מִן כָּל־הַמְּלָכִים

The king, the good [one] from all the kings

"The king was the best of all the kings"

SUPERLATIVE ADJECTIVE[6]

DEMONSTRATIVE PRONOUNS

While dealing with adjectives it will be helpful to also discuss demonstrative pronouns because they behave similarly. *Demonstrative pronouns* are words that are used in place of nouns to identify precisely which object is being indicated: "*this* one" or "*that* one." It might help you to remember the term demonstrative pronoun if you think of them as "demonstrating" (or pointing out) an object. Hebrew has only a handful of demonstrative pronouns, and these are listed in table 6.2.

Demonstrative pronouns are classically divided into two categories, those identifying things near to the speaker ("this, these") and those identifying something relatively distant ("that, those") in either time or space. They always agree with the noun in gender and number. Thus you will notice that demonstrative pronouns have both singular and plural options ("this, that" and "these, those") and are marked for gender (masculine and feminine).

6. The adjective is superlative here, rather than comparative, because it has the definite article.

Table 6.2: Demonstrative Pronouns

Things close at hand		*Things farther away*	
זֶה	"this" (m. sg.)	הוּא	"that" (m. sg.)
זֹאת	"this" (f. sg.)	הִיא	"that" (f. sg.)
אֵלֶּה	"these" (pl.)	הֵם or הֵמָּה	"those" (m. pl.)
		הֵן or הֵנָּה	"those" (f. pl.)

Like adjectives, demonstratives can be used attributively (e.g., "*this* king"), predicatively (e.g., "*this* is the king"), or serve as a substantive to replace a noun in the sentence (e.g., "The king did *this*"). Unlike adjectives, it is easy to distinguish between attributive and predicative uses of the demonstrative pronoun. Demonstrative pronouns are by nature definite. When functioning attributively, the noun it modifies must also be definite (e.g., "this king" must refer to a specific king). Thus, when a demonstrative pronoun is functioning as an attributive, both the noun and the pronoun take the article (e.g., הַמֶּלֶךְ הַזֶּה). Demonstrative pronouns functioning as a predicate will always be indefinite (e.g., הַמֶּלֶךְ זֶה "This is the king"). Demonstrative pronouns that serve as substantives are evident from context. These basic principles and examples are reviewed in the charts below.

Table 6.3: Determining the Function of Demonstrative Pronouns

1. Demonstrative *with* definite article = Attributive use

הַמֶּלֶךְ הַזֶּה	"the king, the this [one]" = "**this** king"

2. Demonstrative *without* definite article = Predicate use

זֶה הַמֶּלֶךְ	"this [one], the king" = "***This is*** the king"
הַמֶּלֶךְ זֶה	"the king, this [one]" = "***This is*** the king"
מֶלֶךְ זֶה	"a king, this [one]" = "***This is*** a king"

One conceptual difference you will encounter between Hebrew and English is that English maintains a distinction between demonstrative pronouns (e.g., this, that) and independent pronouns (e.g., he, she, it), while Hebrew can use the same word for both concepts (e.g., הוּא "he, it, that"). In Hebrew, both concepts point to a person or object outside the context of your immediate conversation. When you are reading, convert the author's thought into smooth English using the best English word for that context. For example, הוּא בָּא אֶל־יִשְׂרָאֵל might be translated, "***That [one]*** came to Israel" or "***He*** came to Israel" depending upon the circumstances in which it is expressed. A good translation begins with an accurate understanding of meaning and ends with a clear communication of that meaning in English.

Another distinction between Hebrew and English use of demonstrative pronouns involves the way they represent proximity to the speaker. Hebrew prefers to designate objects based on nearness to the speaker while English will opt to convey contrast over proximity. For example, Isaiah 6:3 mentions the seraphim surrounding the throne of God and says that קָרָא זֶה אֶל־זֶה, "***This*** called out to ***this.***" From Isaiah's standpoint each seraph is in close proximity and thus designated by the same demonstrative pronoun "this." The same phrase in English would highlight the contrast and prefer a translation like "*This one* called out to *that one*" or "*One* called out to *another*." Once again your task is to represent the Hebrew meaning in smooth English.

FUNCTION OF HEBREW NOUNS

One focus of this grammar is to teach students how to read with understanding and to translate as a natural expression of that understanding. Many students mistake translation for decoding. By decoding we mean that someone only understands the text once the Hebrew has been converted into some kind of formal English equivalent. The process of translation then requires yet another step where the formal rendering is paraphrased into idiomatic English. ***Understanding should precede translation, not the other way around.*** Moreover, readers who decode find it difficult to remember the details of the story as they move from sentence to sentence. They are overwhelmed trying to keep track of individual words rather than scenes and images.

The following discussion on nouns will help you create a mental picture of what you are reading and appreciate the subtle nuances the author captures in his description. Remember, the goal of interpretation is not to recreate the event that occurred but to understand how the author interprets it for you, including how he focuses your attention. At the same time be careful not to over-interpret when it comes to focus. Focus is not necessarily meant to add emphasis, merely nuance. The art of reading is something you will have to practice.

One way to help you understand the function of nouns (whether in English or Hebrew) is to compare sentences to photographs. Just as a photograph captures an event, so too an author crafts a sentence in order to create a mental picture. Assume for a moment that you are taking pictures at a martial arts event. During a power-breaking demonstration your interest is drawn toward a martial artist attempting to break a stack of cinder blocks. Your camera is focused primarily on the man as you wait to see if he will indeed be successful.

Notice that the subject or focal point of your photo is the martial artist. The blocks are secondary objects receiving the action. If you were to describe this picture in words, you would say that, "The *man* broke the blocks." The man is the grammatical *subject* of the sentence just as he is the subject of the photo. The blocks, which are directly impacted by the action, are of secondary importance in the photo.

Now imagine for a moment that instead of focusing on the man, you are amazed by the thickness and quantity of cinder blocks that he is breaking. As a result, you direct your camera toward the blocks.

This time the blocks are the subject or focal point of the picture, and the man has become an object in the background of the scene. If you were to put this picture into words, you would say that, "*The blocks* were broken by the man." The blocks are the grammatical *subject* of the sentence just as they are the subject of this second photo. The same scene can be captured in different ways. Just as each picture reveals the focus of the photographer's attention, so too each sentence reveals the focus of the author's attention.

When you read Hebrew, allow the text to paint a mental picture. Use the analogy of a photographer to guide your formation of the components of that image—subject, verb, and, where applicable, the object impacted by the action. Other words that you encounter in the sentence add clarity and detail to the scene and help bring the sentence to life. If you read this way, you should be able to remember the scenes more clearly and string them together into a cohesive sequence without losing track of the author's train of thought.

With this anology in mind, let us discuss the terminology used to describe Hebrew nouns and their function. Although Hebrew does not use specific endings to designate the grammatical function of nouns like Greek or Latin do (i.e., case endings), grammars customarily use case-related terms when discussing Hebrew nouns. In this grammar we call attention to these labels but explain the grammatical concepts with terms that are more familiar to English-speaking students. Do not get bogged down with details. Try to understand the concepts and relate them to the process of reading and comprehension. You will have plenty of time to assimilate this material in the days ahead as you translate.

Subject (Nominative)

The *subject (nominative)*[7] of a sentence will always be the person or object that is the focal point of the scene. Remember that the same scene can be captured using different grammatical subjects depending on how the author wants to focus your attention. The subject could be the person or object doing the action (e.g., "*The man* broke the blocks"), the one impacted by some action (e.g., "*The blocks* were broken"), or the one existing in a particular state or condition (e.g., "*The man* was skilled"). Your task is not simply to know what happened but to know how the author wants you to see the event.

Object (Accusative)

The *object (accusative)*[8] is the part of the sentence that receives the action of the verb (e.g., "the man broke *the blocks*"). Grammarians use specific terms to more precisely describe the relationship of the object to the verb. When the person or object is the item most "directly impacted" by the action we refer to it as the *direct object* ("The man broke *the blocks*"). If the person or object is "indirectly impacted" by

7. The subject of a sentence is sometimes referred to as a *nominative* in some grammars (from Latin *nomino*, "to mention, speak about"). You can perhaps remember this by recognizing that the subject is the person or object that is "nominated" or set forth to be considered.

8. The object is often referred to as an *accusative*. This term is used to designate a noun that is associated with the verbal idea.

the action we refer to it as the *indirect object* ("The man showed *the audience* the blocks"). If the person or object is connected to a preposition, it is described as the *object of a preposition* ("The man broke the blocks *with his hand*").[9]

The direct object marker אֵת

When a word is functioning as the direct object of the sentence, Hebrew will often mark that for you by means of the particle אֵת or ־אֶת. This Hebrew particle is itself left untranslated and is only used if the object is definite. In other words, the direct object must be a proper name (e.g., Joseph), a noun with a definite article (e.g., "*the* flock"), or something demarcated by a possessive pronoun (e.g., "*my* flock") so that the object is set apart from other objects. If the direct object is unspecified (e.g., "a flock"), the particle אֵת is not used, and you will have to rely on context to inform you which word is the direct object.[10]

Translating accusatives

Frequently the object of a Hebrew sentence is left unmarked and you will need to rely upon the context to determine how best to incorporate this into the sentence. In addition, Hebrew will use objects (accusatives) in the sentence without additional words to clarify the relationship to the verb. We do this in English as well, although not as frequently as in Hebrew. For example, in the sentence, "He threw *me* the ball," "me" functions as the indirect object and its identification as such is evident from meaning alone. However, we are just as likely to say, "He threw the ball *to me*," where we clarify the relationship of "me" to the verb with the helpful preposition "to." Hebrew can also use prepositions to link an object to a verb, but it frequently does not. You need to use context (and logic) to understand the relationship between the object and the verb. Once you understand that relationship, you are free to translate it in a way that will make sense to the English reader. The examples below illustrate how your sense of context will guide you as you translate even when a Hebrew object does not match English syntax. Since your Hebrew vocabulary is limited, the examples have

9. A preposition is a word that is "positioned before" (pre-positioned) a noun to describes its relationship to another word in the sentence. English examples of prepositions are words such as "at, by, over, under, in, on, from, like."

10. The use of אֵת for definite direct objects but not indefinite ones is probably designed to help the reader distinguish between the direct object and the subject (which often tends to be definite).

been presented in English using a hyperliteral translation so that you can get a feel for what you might encounter in the Hebrew text. You will be surprised how easy it is to capture the sense of each sentence.[11]

- "They cried out *you*" *[to] you*
- "All the land was weeping *a loud voice*" *[with] a loud voice*
- "He was sitting *the entrance* of the tent" *[at] the entrance*

Sometimes Hebrew uses two objects with the same verb. One corresponds to the English direct object and a secondary object will be variously translated depending on the context (grammarians refer to this as a *double accusative*.) Again, if you seek meaning before smooth translation, you should have no problem interpreting them in context.[12]

- "And the Lord God formed *the man dust*" *the man [from] dust*
- "He built *the stones an altar*" *stones [into] an altar*
- "God anointed *you oil*" *you [with] oil*

Occasionally you will also find Hebrew direct objects that are from the same root as the verb (called a *cognate*).[13] You will thus find sentences like those listed below.[14]

- "They feared a fear"
- "Jerusalem sinned a sin"
- "They will dream dreams"

You should not assume that the use of an object from the same root as the verb implies that the author is trying to intensify the meaning. This is just a Hebrew idiom and should be expressed with simple English sentences. For example, the Hebrew sentence "They feared a fear" (Ps 14:5) should be translated into English simply as "They were afraid."

11. The following examples are taken Neh 9:28, 2 Sam 15:23, and Gen 18:1 respectively.

12. The following examples are taken Gen 2:7, 1 Kgs 18:32, and Ps 45:8 [Eng 45:7] respectively.

13. The term "cognate" means these words have the same root. Since an object is called an accusative in some grammars these constructions are also referred to as *cognate accusatives*.

14. The following examples are taken Ps 14:5, Lam 1:8, and Joel 3:1 [Eng 2:28] respectively.

Predicate Noun Some sentences contain one noun that serves as the subject (usually the more specific of the two) and another noun that serves as the verbal side of the sentence (i.e., the predicate). This second noun, called a *predicate noun*, further identifies the subject (e.g., "David is *a king*").[15] Predicate nouns act in the same manner as the predicate adjective discussed earlier in the chapter (e.g., "the Lord is *good*"). Thus, the connection between the two parts of the sentence is created by some form of the verb "to be" (e.g., is, are, was, were). English requires that this verb be explicitly stated. However, Hebrew can leave the verb implied. As a result, a Hebrew sentence or clause can be comprised only of nouns, and you must supply the verb.[16]

With a stated verb	הָיָה דָוִד מֶ֫לֶךְ׃ "David was king"	(2 Sam 2:11)
With an implied verb	יְהוָה הָאֱלֹהִים "YHWH is God"	(Josh 22:34)

Both of these examples present the subject and then the predicate. However, the word order can present the predicate first. You must rely on the context to determine how the sentence should be translated into English.

Object of a Preposition A noun can also be connected to a sentence by means of a preposition. For example, "The man broke the blocks *with his hand.*" You have already learned some prepositions in your vocabulary—e.g., אֶל ("to, toward"), בְּ ("in, on, with"), and לְ ("to, toward"). The noun associated with a preposition is called the *object of a preposition* and together they comprise a *prepositional phrase.*

When it comes to translation there is some overlap between prepositional phrases and direct or indirect objects. Some Hebrew verbs mark their object with a preposition and some do not. We encounter the

15. The predicate noun cannot be described as an object because it is not impacted by the action of any verb. Since the predicate noun is essentially a restatement of the subject, grammars that refer to the subject of the sentence as a nominative will refer to the predicate noun as a *predicate nominative*.

16. Grammars thus refer to this as a *nominal clause* (a noun clause).

same phenomenon in English. For example, the English words "hear" and "listen" both mark their objects differently. We would say "Hear *me*" but "Listen *to me*." Thus, you may translate a prepositional phrase as a direct object or the reverse depending on the Hebrew verb you encounter and the English equivalent you choose. Doing so does not jeopardize the accuracy of your translation. For example:

שָׁמַע לְדָוִיד	"He listened *to David*" or "He heard *David*"

Direct Address (Vocative)

At times a noun such as a proper name or title is used to address a person. This is called *direct address (vocative)*.[17] In such cases, the name or title corresponds to the person to whom one is speaking. English translations typically use the word "O" to alert the reader to direct address. For example, "Me, *O King*, you restored to my office."

Hebrew frequently uses the definite article to mark a direct address. In the example above, the word "king" appears with the article—"Me, *O King* (הַמֶּלֶךְ), you restored to my office." The article will not appear on vocatives that are proper names because proper names are definite by nature—e.g., "Reuben (רְאוּבֵן), you are my firstborn" (Gen 49:3). The presence of the definite article is a Hebrew idiom that seems awkward in English, and you will leave the article untranslated. Sensitivity to the context will guide you to correctly identify such words as direct address.

Restatement (Apposition)

The terms above refer to the grammatical function of nouns in a sentence (subject, object, object of a preposition, direct address). Within these grammatical functions an author can use *apposition* to restate or rename a person or object already mentioned in the sentence. Words in apposition usually appear side-by-side and always stand in the same grammatical slot in the sentence. For example, "Abram took <u>Sarai</u> <u>his wife</u>" (Gen 12:5). Apposition is different than a compound subject or object (e.g., "Abraham took *flocks and herds*" Gen 21:27). It is also different than providing an explicit subject for the embedded pronoun in

17. Words used in direct address are referred to as a *vocative* in some grammars (a term derived from the Latin *vocare*, "to call").

a verb (e.g., שָׁמַר יוֹסֵף אֶת־הַצֹּאן "*he* kept, [namely] *Joseph*, the flock"). Apposition renames a noun already in the sentence and provides greater clarity for the reader. When constructing your mental picture, be aware that you can fit two or more nouns into the same grammatical slot with the same referent (e.g., "*Potiphar*, *Pharaoh's official*, *captain of the guard*, *an Egyptian* purchased him" Gen 39:1).

EXERCISE FOR CHAPTER 6 Complete the translation exercise for chapter 6 that appears in the workbook.

CHAPTER 7

Constructs, Directional Ending, Prepositions, and Interrogatives

In the previous lessons we covered the endings that mark gender and number together with the definite article and conjunction. We are now going to further our discussion of gender and number endings by introducing you to a feature called the Hebrew construct. You will also learn about other supplemental elements such as the directional ending, prepositions, and interrogatives. The construct, directional ending, and prepositions demonstrate the relationship of words or phrases to the rest of the sentence. The interrogative marker transforms statements into questions.

CONSTRUCT ENDINGS

What Is a "Construct"? (Function)

Hebrew has a grammatical feature known as the *construct*. The Hebrew construct is used to bind two or more words together with the implied word "of" to create a single idea or "construction" (e.g., מֶ֫לֶךְ יִשְׂרָאֵל "the king [of] Israel"). The first word in the construct chain identifies the central idea (the topic) that is then clarified by one or more additional words. Because construct phrases are not a feature of English, you may have to translate a Hebrew construct into English in a variety of ways—using a preposition, possessive, or adjective. This range of English translation is a reflection of the fact that Hebrew uses the construct phrase to compensate for its lack of a possessive ending (e.g., king's throne) and its relatively limited use of adjectives and prepositions. For example, in Exod 4:10 Moses complains that he is not אִישׁ־דְּבָרִים ("a man *of words*"), meaning he is not an *eloquent* man.

How Do You Translate a Construct?

When words are in construct with one another, you can translate them by inserting the English word "of." For example, independently the word

מֶ֫לֶךְ means "king" and אֶ֫רֶץ means "land." But when they are placed in construct, the phrase מֶ֫לֶךְ אֶ֫רֶץ means "a king *of* a land" (i.e., "a land's king"). A construct chain can consist of any number of nouns. For example, when the words בֵּן ("son"), מֶ֫לֶךְ ("king"), and אֶ֫רֶץ ("land") appear in construct, the phrase can be understood by inserting the word "of" between each constituent (i.e., בֶּן מֶ֫לֶךְ אֶ֫רֶץ = "a son of a king of a land").

מֶ֫לֶךְ אֶ֫רֶץ "a king **of** a land"

בֶּן מֶ֫לֶךְ אֶ֫רֶץ "a son **of** a king **of** a land"

Note that in the first example, a "king" is identified as the topic and is further clarified by his relationship to a particular land. Likewise, in the second example, a "son" is identified as the topic and is clarified by his relationship to a king of some unspecified country.

Do not assume that just because you have translated a construct phrase you understand what it is conveying. You have merely decoded the words. You still have to determine meaning based on context.[1] Hebrew uses construct phrases to convey a number of different ideas (e.g., possession, relationship, location—see the list below). All of these nuances of meaning are determined by context, as Hebrew does not have visual indicators to distinguish one use of the construct from another.

The following examples give you an idea of the types of meanings that construct phrases can communicate. Note that in each example you can instinctively understand the nuance simply through the word "of." So begin to unpack the meaning of the construct using the word "of" and then choose English expressions that better communicate the author's message. Again, notice that context is always the determining factor for meaning.[2] You do not need to memorize the list of potential meanings as long as you learn to recognize and convey what the author is saying.

1. E.g., the phrase "the love *of* God" could mean that God loves you or that you love God. Or it could simply indicate a category of love (e.g., "love of God" rather than "love of possessions"). Context indicates whether a noun is responsible for an action (implied subject) or receives action (implied object).

2. When you encounter biblical resources that identify construct phrases as having one particular meaning, remember that they are simply arguing from context. Weigh that particular interpretation based on its merits.

Sample Constructs

- **Possession**: Jer 7:4 "the temple *of the Lord*" = the Lord's temple
- **Agent**: Isa 53:4 "stricken *of God*" = stricken by God
- **Instrument or Means**: Isa 1:7 "burned *of fire*" = burned with fire
- **Action to/by/with someone**: 1 Kgs 2:43 "oath *of the Lord*" = oath to the Lord
- **Cause or Effect**: Gen 3:24 "tree *of life*" = life-giving tree
- **Purpose or Result**: Ps 44:23 [E.T. 44:22] "sheep *of slaughter*" = sheep to be slaughtered
- **Advantage or Disadvantage**: Jer 50:28 "vengeance *of his temple*" = vengeance on behalf of his temple
- **Relationship**: Jonah 1:1 "Jonah, the son *of Amittai*"
- **Attribute**: Isa 11:9 "the mountain *of my holiness*" = my holy mountain
- **Sphere ("with respect to")**: Isa 6:5 "unclean *of lips*" = unclean lips[3]
- **Personal characteristics**: Gen 21:5 "a son *of 100 years*" = 100 years old
- **Classification**: Deut 24:1 "indecency *of a thing*" = any kind of indecency
- **Composition**: Exod 20:24 "an altar *of earth*" = an altar made of earth
- **Content**: Judg 6:19 "an ephah *of grain*"
- **Topic**: Isa 13:1 "the oracle *of Babylon*" = prophecy about Babylon
- **Superlative (best)**: Exod 26:34 "the holy *of holies*" = the holiest place

3. Technically "unclean with respect to lips." The focus of the construct chain is always on the first word of the sequence (uncleanness), even though it may be difficult to capture in English.

- **Location**: Gen 22:17 "stars *of heaven*" = stars in heaven
- **With respect to**: Isa 38:18 "those going down *of the pit*" = to the pit
- **Measure**: Ezek 47:3 "water *of ankles*" = water up to the ankles

Ultimately, the meaning of a construct phrase is determined by context. Use the English equivalent "of" and carefully evaluate what the author seems to mean by that expression.

How Do You Recognize a Construct? (Form)

Hebrew constructs are marked by a separate set of gender and number endings from those you learned in chapter 4. In addition, Hebrew constructs are accented differently than when these same nouns stand alone, and the adjustment in accent usually results in vowel changes. The complete chart of gender and number endings below includes both sets of endings: the *absolute* endings you learned (when words stand "absolutely" alone) and the new *construct* endings (when linked words "construct" a single unit). Memorize these new endings. In construct, Hebrew no longer distinguishes between plural and dual.

Table 7.1: Gender, Number, and Construct Endings

	Masculine		Feminine	
	Absolute	*Construct*	*Absolute*	*Construct*
Singular	□□□	□□□־֫	□□□ָה	□□□ַת־֫
Plural	□□□ִים	□□□ֵי־֫	□□□וֹת	□□□וֹת־֫
Dual	□□ַ֫יִם	*Same as pl. cst.*	□□□ָתַ֫יִם	*Same as pl. cst.*

Memorize the construct forms exactly as they appear in the chart—including the *maqqeph* (hyphen) and accent marker (e.g., ˂ ־□□□). The Hebrew text does not always include a *maqqeph* with construct forms. However, memorizing the *maqqeph* as part of the construct forms reminds you that a word in construct cannot be separated from the following word(s). Likewise, the accent sign (˂) reminds you that the whole construct chain is governed by the accent on the final word; thus all the vowels in a construct word follow the rules for unaccented syllables. While the *maqqeph* is a helpful memory device, remember from chapter 3 that the *maqqeph* does not affect meaning and is not exclusive to the construct.[4]

Theoretically only the last word of a construct chain is accented, and all the preceding words follow the vowel rules for *unaccented* syllables. This means that sometimes the words in construct may have undergone vowel changes that are different than those in the absolute form. As a result, even though the absolute and construct forms of a noun may have the same endings (i.e., m. sg. and f. pl.), words in construct *may be* vocalized differently than absolute forms.[5]

סוּס	a horse (abs.)	Absolute and construct forms are the same
סוּס־מֶ֫לֶךְ	a horse (cst.) of a king	

Historic long vowel does not change

אָדוֹן	a lord (abs.)	Absolute and construct forms are different
אֲדוֹן־אֶ֫רֶץ	a lord (cst.) of a land	

Distant open syllable reduces

Historic long vowel does not change

4. The *maqqeph* is used to link many word combinations and signals only that there is a tight bond between the words. For example, it is also used to link prepositions to nouns (אֶל־הַמֶּ֫לֶךְ = *to the king*).

5. In the examples with אָדוֹן ("lord"), both the absolute form (אָדוֹן) and construct form (אֲדוֹן) are based on the historic אַדוֹן*. In the absolute form the first vowel lengthens in a near open syllable. In the construct form the first vowel reduces because the construct chain places it in a distant open syllable.

Because constructs are always vocalized as if they lose their accent to become part of the following word, remember to look for these vowel changes as an important indicator that words are in construct. For example, the dictionary form of the word "mountain" is הָר (with a long vowel), but in construct the word appears with a short vowel, הַר קֹדֶשׁ ("mountain of holiness") because the vowel theoretically stands in a closed unaccented syllable. Similarly, the dictionary form of "son" is בֵּן, but in construct we find בֶּן דָּוִיד ("the son of David"). Such changes also happen with longer words. A word like דָּבָר ("word") will change in construct to produce דְּבַר דָּוִיד ("the word of David") based on the vowel rules you learned in chapter 5.[6]

absolute	construct
הָר	הַר קֹדֶשׁ
בֵּן	בֶּן דָּוִיד
דָּבָר	דְּבַר דָּוִיד

Again, the vowel changes we have been discussing are a means of signaling that the words of the construct phrase belong together. How you *pronounce* constructs depends upon whether or not they are joined with a *maqqeph*. With a *maqqeph,* words are pronounced together as a single word, and only the final word is accented in the Hebrew text. Without a *maqqeph,* words are accented separately in the Hebrew text, despite the vowel changes that resulted from the shift of accent to the final word. The presence or absence of *maqqeph* does not affect meaning and is more a product of cadence and rhythm of the language.

דְּבַר דָּוִיד	d^{e}-***var***´ dā-***vīd***´
דְּבַר־דָּוִיד	d^{e}-var-dā-***vīd***´

6. Remember, the vowel changes do not reflect a shift from the absolute form to the construct form. Rather, the historic form has adjusted in each setting based on the placement of the accent and the vowel rules.

What Rules Govern a Construct? (Syntax)

The fact that words in a construct phrase are linked not only affects vocalization and pronunciation but also how construct phrases function as a unit (syntax).[7] First, because Hebrew treats the construct as a single unit, the whole unit is either definite (e.g., "*the* house of *the* man") or indefinite (e.g., "*a* house of *a* man"). Hebrew does not allow construct phrases to communicate mixed definiteness (e.g., NOT "*a* house of *the* man"). Second, because Hebrew views the construct as a single unit, most secondary grammatical elements appear before or after the construct phrase (i.e., conjunction, preposition, adjective, possessive pronoun). For the most part, this principle will be relatively obvious to an English reader. On the other hand, the definite article and the directional ending (discussed later in this chapter) can appear within the construct phrase.

Construct Chain Is Entirely Definite or Entirely Indefinite

The definiteness of a construct chain is determined by the final word in the sequence, the only word in the construct sequence that can take the article. The final word determines whether every word in the phrase is definite or indefinite. If the final word is indefinite, then every word in the construct phrase is indefinite. If the final word is definite, then every word in the construct phrase is definite, even though it does not have a definite article.

בֵּית אִישׁ	"**a** house of **a** man"
בֵּית הָאִישׁ	"**the** house of **the** man"
קוֹל־שְׁמוּאֵל	"**the** voice of ***Samuel***"

When Hebrew wishes to express a concept with mixed definiteness, it cannot use a construct phrase. For example, a construct chain cannot be used to express "**a** psalm of David" because the proper name *David*

7. Syntax refers to the relationships between words and the rules that govern how words are put together.

would automatically make the word "psalm" definite, thus implying that David wrote only one psalm (i.e., "*the* psalm of David"). Hebrew must use another means of expressing possession. The preposition לְ ("to, for") can be used for this purpose to indicate that the psalm in question *"belongs to"* David. The Hebrew Bible thus introduces many psalms with the heading מִזְמוֹר לְדָוִד ("*a* psalm *belonging to* David"). Prepositions are introduced more fully later in this chapter.

Construct Chain with Adjectives

Construct chains do not allow anything to interrupt the unit except the definite article or directional ending (discussed later in the chapter). As a result, Hebrew adjectives that modify nouns within a construct phrase must appear either before or after the construct chain. Adjectives can be part of a construct chain if they are used in place of a noun (e.g., קְדוֹשׁ־יִשְׂרָאֵל "the ***Holy One*** of Israel"), but you will never see an adjective interrupt a construct chain.

When an *attributive adjective* is used, the adjective must *follow* the construct chain (just as it would when modifying a single word), regardless of which word in the construct chain that adjective describes. Remember that attributive adjectives must agree with the noun they modify in gender, number, and definiteness. If the gender or number of the words in construct does not match, you will be able to match the adjective to the intended noun by means of gender-number agreement. For example, the plural adjective must modify the plural noun in the phrase בְּנֵי־דָוִיד הַצַּדִּיקִים ("the *righteous sons* of David"). Conversely, the singular adjective in בְּנֵי־דָוִיד הַצַּדִּיק ("the sons of *righteous David*") clearly describes David. When there is no distinction in gender and number, context will have to determine which association is intended. For example, the phrase בֶּן־דָּוִיד הַצַּדִּיק can mean either "the *righteous son* of David" or "the son of *righteous David*."

When a *predicative adjective* is used, the adjective can be positioned on either side of the unit just as it is when an adjective is used with a single noun. For example, the expression "the king of Israel is great" can be expressed either as מֶלֶךְ־הָאָרֶץ גָּדוֹל or as גָּדוֹל מֶלֶךְ־הָאָרֶץ. In this example, the adjective "great" is indefinite, but each word in the construct chain is definite because the final word is definite. Therefore, the adjective can only be a predicative adjective.

As you might expect, you can encounter passages where context is the only guide. For example, the phrase שֵׁם־אִישׁ טוֹב follows the criteria for both attributive adjectives and predicative adjectives. The adjective "good" (טוֹב) appears after the construct phrase, is not definite, and agrees with both nouns. Context should help you decide whether this phrase is best translated as "a *good reputation* of a man," "a reputation of a *good man*," or "a reputation of a man *is a good thing*."[8]

Attributive adjective

בְּנֵי־דָוִיד הַצַּדִּיק	"the sons of ***righteous David***"
בְּנֵי־דָוִיד הַצַּדִּיקִים	"the ***righteous sons*** of David"

Predicative adjective

מֶלֶךְ־הָאָרֶץ גָּדוֹל גָּדוֹל מֶלֶךְ־הָאָרֶץ	"the king of the land ***is great***"

Ambiguous

שֵׁם־אִישׁ טוֹב	"a ***good reputation*** of a man" "a reputation of a ***good man***" "a reputation of a man ***is a good***

DIRECTIONAL ENDING

Hebrew has another type of ending that it can add to nouns. The *directional ending* ◌ָ◌֫◌ה is added to the end of a word (after it has been formed for gender and number) to signify direction *toward* the noun to which it is attached (e.g., מִצְרַ֫יְמָה = "*to* Egypt").

מִצְרַ֫יְמָה "**to** Egypt"

The significance of this Hebrew particle is essentially the same as that of the prepositions אֶל ("to, towards") and לְ ("to").[9] You will see the

8. While the standard practice in Biblical Hebrew marks definiteness only on the final word of a construct chain, you will find rare exceptions (e.g., Ezek 45:16 כֹּל הָעָם הָאָ֫רֶץ "all of the people of the land").

9. The directional ending is considered by grammarians to be the remnant of an old accusative case ending. While the directional meaning accounts for most occurrences of final unaccented ◌ָ◌֫◌ה, on rare occasions it does not seem to convey directional movement and is not reflected in translation. Cf. Job 37:12 "on the face of the inhabited *world*" (אַ֫רְצָה) (Joüon §93i).

directional ending and prepositions used interchangeably for both motion toward an object or location and for movement in time.[10]

While the directional ending may look similar to the feminine singular noun ending, the two can always be distinguished based on the accent. The feminine singular ending takes the accent (e.g., סוּסָה "a *female* horse"), and the directional ending never takes the accent (e.g., הַבַּיְתָה "*to* the house"). Because it never takes the accent, the directional ending has a minimal effect on vowel changes, allowing you to recognize both the noun and ending.[11] When applied to a feminine noun, the directional ending attaches to the construct ending (e.g., תִּרְצָה "Tirzah" vs. תִּרְצָתָה "to Tirzah").

While most grammatical elements appear either before or after the construct chain, the directional ending can appear in the middle of the chain. Thus, Hebrew can say אַרְצָה מִצְרַיִם ("*to* the land of Egypt").

אַרְצָה מִצְרַיִם "***to*** the land of Egypt"

PREPOSITIONS

Hebrew also uses *prepositions* to demonstrate the relationship of nominal forms (i.e., noun, pronoun, etc.) to the rest of the sentence. For example, הָלַךְ אֶל־הַשָּׂדֶה means "He walked *to* the field." The function of the preposition and construct overlap, as does the function of the preposition and directional ending. For example, cities (f.) are described as "burned with fire" by means of a construct שְׂרֻפוֹת אֵשׁ (Isa 1:7 "burned *of* fire") or by means of a preposition שְׂרוּפָה בָּאֵשׁ (1 Sam 30:3 "burned *with* fire"). Likewise, the phrase "to the house" can be expressed with a directional ending הַבַּיְתָה (Gen 39:11) or a preposition אֶל־הַבַּיִת (Lev 14:46).[12]

Inseparable Prepositions

Some Hebrew prepositions stand alone as separate words (e.g., אֶל and עַל), just as in English. However, other Hebrew prepositions are attached directly to the noun. These prepositions are called *inseparable prepositions* because they are always attached to the following

10. E.g., מִיָּמִים יָמִימָה "from year to year" (lit. "from days to days").

11. The vowel reduction rules apply with the directional ending, but you will not notice vowel changes because the accent usually remains on the same syllable as when the word stands alone.

12. Word choice may have been influenced by cadence, rhythm, or colloquialisms that a natural speaker would more readily recognize.

word (מֶ֫לֶךְ + לְ = לְמֶ֫לֶךְ). These inseparable prepositions are בְּ ("in, on, with, at"), כְּ ("like, as, according to"), and לְ ("to, for"). The preposition מִן ("from") is unique in that it can appear either as a separable or inseparable preposition. The preposition מִן will be discussed separately because, unlike vowelless כְּ, בְּ, and לְ, the preposition מִן has its own vowel.

While you will readily recognize both the preposition and its noun, understanding how these prepositions attach will help you later when you are exposed to grammatical features with similar appearance. You memorized the three primary inseparable prepositions with *shewa* (בְּ, כְּ, and לְ) to remind you that they have no vowel of their own. When inseparable prepositions are attached to a word, they are vocalized according to the environment of the syllables they create. Since you have already learned how to attach the conjunction (also a vowelless prefix) and the definite article, most of the following discussion reviews familiar concepts.

1) Prepositions do not carry their own vowel

The inseparable prepositions do not have their own vowel. Whenever possible the inseparable preposition is added to the front of a word with a simple *shewa* marking the absence of a vowel. Hebrew words can begin with a vocal *shewa* if the following consonant has its own vowel, thus beginning its own syllable (see table 2.4, rule 1).

אֶ֫רֶץ + ל	→	לְאֶ֫רֶץ
"land" + "to"		preposition attached with *shewa*

2) Hebrew words cannot begin with two shewas

Remember from chapter 2 that a Hebrew word cannot begin with two *shewas* in a row. If a preposition is attached to a noun beginning with a *shewa*, a vowel must be provided for the vowelless preposition to avoid having to pronounce three consonants with no intervening vowel (e.g., לְשְׁמוּאֵל*). Because **a *shewa* is a *shewa* is a *shewa*,** the same principle applies even if the word begins with a composite *shewa* (e.g., כְּאֲשֶׁר*). To avoid this type of awkward consonant cluster, the preposition requires a short vowel.

Before simple shewa—ḥireq added

If the noun to which the preposition is attached begins with a simple *shewa*, Hebrew prepositions are usually vocalized with a *ḥireq*.

שְׁמוּאֵל + ל → *לְשְׁמוּאֵל → לִשְׁמוּאֵל

"Samuel" + "to" — *consonant cluster cannot be pronounced* — ḥireq *added for pronunciation*

A *ḥireq* is used because it is a short vowel that forms a stable, closed unaccented syllable and helps avoids confusion with the definite article (often a *pataḥ*).

When the first letter of the noun is a vowelless *yod*, the word formation involves an additional step. The *yod* will coalesce (merge) with the *ḥireq* (/i/) to produce a long vowel (*ḥireq yod*). As a result, the *shewa* under the *yod* is dropped because the *yod* now functions as a vowel marker rather than as a true consonant.

יְהוּדָה + ל → *לְיְהוּדָה → *לִיְהוּדָה → לִיהוּדָה

"Judah" + "to" — *consonant cluster cannot be pronounced* — yod *coalesces*

While the steps may seem complex, recognizing לִיהוּדָה as "to Judah" will be relatively straightforward, especially given context.

Before a composite shewa—vowels match

If the noun to which the preposition is attached begins with a composite *shewa*, the preposition will take on the vowel reflected by the composite *shewa*. Chapter 4 introduced this "matching rule" in the discussion of the conjunction.[13]

Some words beginning with *aleph* + composite *shewa* experience additional modification identical to the vocalization taught in chapter 4.

אֲשֶׁר + כּ → *כְּאֲשֶׁר → כַּאֲשֶׁר

"which" + "like"

אֱדוֹם + בּ → *בְּאֱדוֹם → בֶּאֱדוֹם

"Edom" + "in"

חֳלִי + ל → *לְחֳלִי → לָחֳלִי

"illness" + "for"

consonant cluster cannot be pronounced — *use matching vowels*

When the inseparable prepositions are added to אֱלֹהִים and אֲדֹנָי one might expect *לֶאֱלֹהִים and *לַאֲדֹנָי based on the "matching principle" described above. Yet, because a vowelless *aleph* quiesces (i.e., loses its consonantal value), the composite *shewa* drops and the vowel under the preposition is left in an open unaccented syllable (e.g., *לַאֲדֹנָי → לַאדֹנָי). In the case of לַאדֹנָי there is no further change (despite the fact that open syllables require long vowels). However, the vowel under the preposition before אֱלֹהִים lengthens to adjust for the open syllable (e.g., *לֶאֱלֹהִים → *לֶאלֹהִים → לֵאלֹהִים).

*לַאֲדֹנָי → לַאדֹנָי

(לַיהוָה)

*לֶאֱלֹהִים → *לֶאלֹהִים → לֵאלֹהִים

expected form — aleph *quiesces* — *vowel lengthens in open syllable*

The Tetragrammaton (יהוה) is also affected by this phenomenon because the Hebrew reading tradition typically substitutes אֲדֹנָי in place of pronouncing God's personal name.[14] As a result, ל + יהוה will reflect the vowels adopted from לַאדֹנָי (i.e., לַיהוָה) to remind you of the preferred reading tradition.[15]

13. Technically, the environment of the word determines the vowel class of the composite *shewa*, which in turn determines the selection of a vowel for the preposition.

14. See the discussion in exercise 3A.

15. Although God's personal name is usually vocalized using אֲדֹנָי (i.e., יְהוָה or יְהֹוָה), it is sometimes vocalized using אֱלֹהִים (i.e., יֱהוִה or יֱהֹוִה). However, there are no occurrences of a preposition with the second vocalization.

3) Prepositions with the definite article—vowels are usurped

When the vowelless preposition is attached to a word with the definite article, the preposition is added after the definite article has been applied (e.g., לְהַמֶּ֫לֶךְ). On rare occasions the fully spelled form is preserved (see 2 Chr 10:7 לְהָעָם "to the people"), but normally the *heh* is overpowered by the preposition and drops out of the word. Though the *heh* drops, the vowel and *dagesh* remain to preserve the presence of the definite article (e.g., לַמֶּ֫לֶךְ). The preposition takes whatever vowel is required by the vocalization of the definite article (see table 4.3).

To recognize these forms either remember that the preposition "covers up" the *heh* and takes over the vowels of the definite article, or understand that the *heh* simply gets lost in the process of rapid pronunciation (e.g., in לְהַמֶּ֫לֶךְ *l*ᵉ*ham* easily slurs to *lam*).

הַמֶּ֫לֶךְ + ל → לְהַמֶּ֫לֶךְ → לַמֶּ֫לֶךְ

4) Preposition in a near open syllable—qamets possible

When a preposition is added to a word that is accented on the first syllable, the preposition normally takes a *shewa* as outlined above (e.g., לְמֶ֫לֶךְ). However, in certain cases Hebrew will use the *qamets* instead (long /ā/). The vocalization of the preposition with *qamets* has no effect on meaning and merely reflects the Hebrew preference for vocalizing with *qamets* before accented syllables. The use of *qamets* with the preposition is infrequent in nouns but common with pronouns (e.g., לָזֶה), words used in close combination (e.g., Gen 1:6: מַ֫יִם לָמָ֫יִם), and certain forms of the pronominal suffixes addressed in the following chapter (e.g., לָכֶם). When you encounter *qamets* with the preposition, do not let your lack of familiarity with the definite article lead you to automatically assume that the article is present. Check the form against the principles for forming the definite article (see ch. 4) and recognize that Hebrew has an affinity for *qamets* in prefixes immediately before the accent.

The following table highlights the similarity between the inseparable preposition and the conjunction you have already learned. Ideally these recurring discussions about Hebrew syllables will increase your familiarity with their behavior and minimize the need to memorize specific rules or examples.

Table 7.2: Summary Comparison of Prepositions and Conjunctions

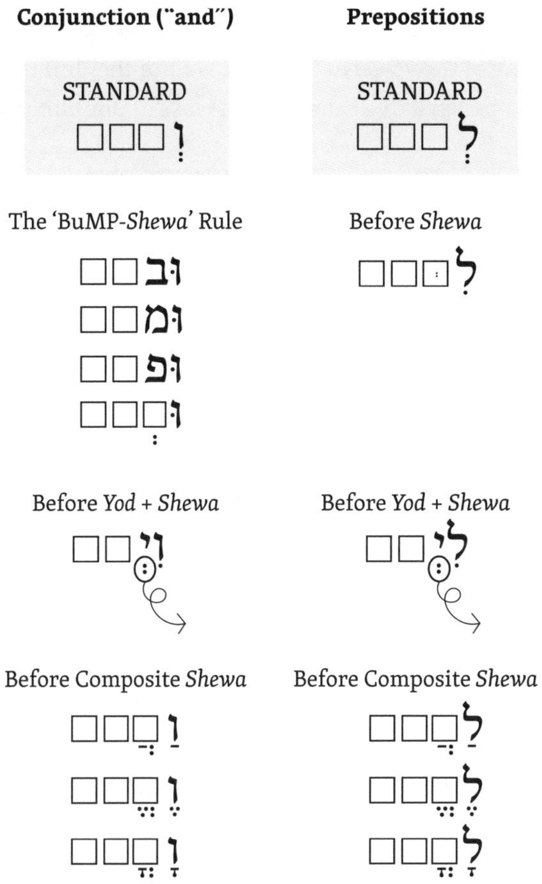

The Preposition מִן ("from")

The preposition מִן ("from") is unique in that it can either stand alone or behave like an inseparable preposition. The preposition מִן can stand alone (e.g., מִן שָׂדֶה "*from* a field").[16] When it is attached directly to the word as an inseparable preposition, the form of מִן changes slightly because of the *nun*. Hebrew does not typically like a vowelless *nun* at the end of a syllable. The *nun* will change to match the following consonant in a process called *assimilation* (e.g., מִנְשָׂדֶה* → מִשְׂשָׂדֶה*).[17] The assimilated *nun* appears as a *dagesh forte* in the following letter, thus preserving each component of the preposition מִן (e.g., מִשָּׂדֶה). If the following consonant is a guttural or *resh*, that consonant cannot take a *dagesh forte* (i.e., cannot double). In such cases, the absence of a *dagesh forte* leaves the syllable open, and the short i-class vowel must lengthen (e.g., מִנְאָדָם* → מֵאָדָם). Grammars use the term *compensatory lengthening* to describe the lengthening of the vowel to "compensate" for the shift from a closed syllable to an open syllable caused by the loss of doubling.

מִן שָׂדֶה	*from a field*	**Separate preposition**
מִנְשָׂדֶה* → מִשְׂשָׂדֶה* → מִשָּׂדֶה	*from a field*	**Assimilation**
מִנְאָדָם* → מִנאָדָם* → מֵאָדָם	*from a man*	**Compensatory lengthening**

When מִן is joined to a word with the definite article, it cannot take on the vowels of the definite article and displace the *heh* because מִן already has its own vowel. The *heh* of the definite article will remain and be treated like any other guttural (e.g., מֵהַשָּׂדֶה "from the field").

Every time an inseparable preposition is attached to a word, the newly formed word follows predictable patterns that are driven by preferences of sound and speech. As you learn these preferences and patterns you will begin to recognize the "personality" of the Hebrew language, and the memorization of rules will become less and less important.

Compound Prepositions

One feature of Hebrew prepositions that students find unfamiliar is the compounding of prepositions. It is common to see two, three, or even four prepositions joined together. For example, in Exod 9:18 God threatens to send hail unlike anything Egypt has seen "*from* the day" it was founded (lit. לְמִן־הַיּוֹם "to-from the day").[18] While English has

16. As a separable preposition, מִן can also appear with *maqqeph* so that the words are pronounced as a single unit (e.g., מִן־שָׂדֶה). Meaning is unaffected by the form that מִן takes.

17. Assimilation of vowelless *nun* is driven by pronunciation. The /n/ sound is not strong enough to hold its own sound when it has no vowel. Assimilation happens in English as well. The /n/ of the Latin prefix *in-* ("not") assimilates when it is prefixed to certain letters (e.g., <u>ir</u>responsible).

compound prepositions as well (e.g, onto, into, within), we generally perceive them as individual words and no longer think of them as compounds. Thus while unfamiliar Hebrew combinations may seem odd, they are not actually a foreign idea.

Recognize that learning Hebrew is a cross-cultural experience in which ideas are communicated differently than in English. When you encounter a compound preposition, pay attention to the context and focus on the preposition that conveys the dominant idea.

INTERROGATIVES

Sentences that ask questions are referred to as *interrogatives*.[19] English denotes questions by means of voice inflection (e.g., "He came from Israel?") and/or modifications in wording (e.g., "Did he come from Israel?" or "He came from Israel, didn't he?"). In written English every question is marked with punctuation ("?"). Written Hebrew does not have punctuation, but it does have ways of indicating that a question is being asked. Hebrew questions can be signaled by means of an interrogative marker (הֲ), interrogative pronouns (e.g., מָה "what?" or "how"?), or by context. The first two are helpful because they appear at the beginning of the clause and alert the reader to expect a question. However, sometimes context will be the only signal that a question is being expressed, as is the case in 2 Sam 18:29 שָׁלוֹם לַנַּעַר "Is it well with the boy?" (lit. "peace to the boy").

Interrogative Marker (הֲ)

The Hebrew interrogative marker (הֲ) stands at the beginning of a Hebrew clause and is used to mark a yes or no question. Since the Hebrew interrogative visually marks the presence of a question, it can be compared to the English question mark. However, like the direct object marker אֵת the interrogative הֲ is spoken but not translated and has no English word to represent it.

Function of the interrogative הֲ

The Hebrew interrogative is used to introduce a broad range of yes or no questions: (1) Questions that expect a response (e.g., Gen 27:24 "Are you indeed my son Esau?"), (2) rhetorical questions to which one expects no answer (e.g., Gen 4:9 "Am I my brother's keeper?"), and

18. Similarly, 1 Kgs 7:32 mentions the wheels "*beneath*" (-לְמִתַּחַת לְ *to-from-below-to*) the washbasins in the temple.

19. You can remember this term by thinking of how we interchangeably refer to being "questioned" by the police and facing "interrogation."

(3) questions that are asked indirectly. In English we typically express indirect questions as assertions. For example, "he sent off the dove to see whether [הֲ] the waters had receded" (Gen 8:8). But in Hebrew indirect questions are still marked as questions. The interrogative הֲ is sometimes used with אִם ("if") to express an "either ... or" question. For example, Gen 27:21 "[הֲ] *Are* you really my son Esau [אִם] *or* not?"

Form of the interrogative הֲ

The interrogative heh (הֲ) attaches directly to the beginning of the first word of the question. The vocalization is fairly straightforward and adjusts according to patterns you have already seen. (1) With most words the interrogative takes a composite *shewa* (i.e., הֲ□□□). (2) If the word begins with *shewa*, the interrogative upgrades from composite *shewa* to *pataḥ* in order to avoid two *shewas* at the start of a word (i.e., הֲ□ְ□□ → הַ□ְ□□). (3) If the word begins with a guttural, the interrogative takes *pataḥ* (e.g., הַ[G]□□) unless (4) the guttural is paired with *qamets* resulting in the use of *segol* (e.g., הֶ[G]ָ□□).[20]

Table 7.3: Interrogative Particle

הֲ□	STANDARD FORM
הַ□ְ	Before *shewa*
הַ[G]	Before gutturals
הֶ[G]ָ	Before gutturals with *qamets*

The vocalization of the interrogative may at times overlap with the definite article. In instances when the forms are identical, context will help you determine the sense. Though it would appear that the room for overlap between the interrogative and article is great, in reality, the interrogative is predominantly seen as הֲ□□□ or הַ□□□, while the definite article most frequently occurs as הַ□ּ□□ and הָ[G]□□. The following table provides a comparison of

20. The boxed "G" represents the gutturals and the letter *resh* that responds in a manner similar to gutturals.

the vocalization patterns for the definite article and interrogative. The red highlighting emphasizes the conditions in which the two forms are indistinguishable.

Table 7.4: Comparison of Interrogative Particle & Definite Article

Interrogative Particle		Definite Article	
הֲ□	STANDARD FORM	הַ□·	STANDARD FORM
הַ□ְ	Before *shewa*	הָ[G]	Before א, ע, ר
הַ[G]	Before gutturals	הַ[G]	Before ה, ח
הֶ[G]ָ	Before gutturals with *qamets*	הֶ[G]ָ	Before הָ, חָ, עָ

Interrogative Pronouns

Hebrew can also introduce a question using interrogative pronouns such as מִי ("who?), מָה ("what? how?"), and לָמָה/לָ֫מָּה ("why?").[21] Most of these interrogative pronouns appear in the sentence exactly as they appear in the lexicon, and translation is fairly straightforward. However, the interrogative מָה undergoes slight adjustments in vocalization based on the the first syllable of the following word. This particle either stands alone or attaches to the following word with *maqqeph*. Either way, the interrogative מָה is vocalized using the same patterns you learned for the definite article.

Table 7.5: The Pointing of Interrogative מַה

מַה־מֶּלֶךְ	STANDARD	
מָה־אָדָם	Before	ע, א, ר
מַה־הוּא	Before	ח, ה
מֶה־עָשָׂה	Before	ע, ח, ה + *qamets*

21. Note the joined components לְ + מָה ("for what").

Translation of Interrogatives

Most students have no problem translating questions introduced with an interrogative pronoun (i.e., what? when? who?). Questions introduced with the interrogative הֲ can be more difficult because the particle does not have a translation equivalent and the following words seem to form a statement.

To translate a question introduced by interrogative *heh* (הֲ): (1) interpret the הֲ as indicating a yes or no question, (2) translate the following clause as an assertion, and (3) reframe the statement as a yes/no question. While you should seek to understand Hebrew words without first giving them an English equivalent, at this stage you inevitably need to follow a process of decoding, inflecting, and translating. The following examples illustrate this process for questions identified by the interrogative marker (הֲ), an interrogative pronoun (מָה), and context. The final example illustrates a rhetorical question that is best conveyed in English by an assertion.[22]

Table 7.6: Translating Interrogatives

הֲלֹא הוּא אָמַר	Decode:	(?) not he said
	Inflect:	He did not say?
	Translate:	Did he not say?
מֶה־עָשָׂה הָעָם	Decode:	What(?) did the-people
	Inflect:	What the people did?
	Translate:	What did the people do?
(context) שָׁלוֹם לַנַּעַר	Decode:	Well-being to the boy
	Inflect:	Well-being to the boy?
	Translate:	Is the boy well?
מַה־הִיא	Decode:	What(?) it
	Inflect:	What is it?
	Translate:	It is nothing. *(referring to land worth 400 shekels of silver)*

22. The examples in table 7.6 are adapted from Gen 20:5 (הֲלֹא הוּא אָמַר־לִי אֲחֹתִי הִוא), Exod 32:21 (מֶה־עָשָׂה לְךָ הָעָם הַזֶּה), 2 Sam 18:29, and Gen 23:15.

EXERCISE FOR CHAPTER 7

The workbook includes an exercise that enables you to practice adding construct endings to nouns and adjectives. Skim back through the principles of vowel reduction in chapter 5 and then complete the exercise on "Vowel Changes with Construct Nouns" (Exercise 7). In addition, complete the translation exercise for chapter 7.

CHAPTER 8

Pronominal Suffixes and Review of Definiteness

In the previous lessons you were introduced to various components that can be attached to Hebrew nouns and adjectives. The final component to discuss is the pronominal suffix. Pronominal suffixes are pronouns that attach directly to the end of Hebrew words (e.g., *his* horse = סוּסוֹ). Because pronominal suffixes are attached to words, they require more explanation than pronouns that stand alone.

PRONOMINAL SUFFIXES

A pronoun is a word that stands in place of a person, place, thing, or idea. Hebrew pronouns reflect gender, number, and person. The concepts of *gender* (m./f.) and *number* (sg./pl.) were introduced in the earlier discussion on nouns. *Person* identifies the pronoun from the frame of reference of the speaker. The easiest way to understand "person" is to picture yourself as the center of the conversation; you are number one. Thus first person pronouns involve concepts like "I/me" or "we/us." The second person pronouns refer to anyone to whom you are directly speaking ("you/yours"). The third person pronouns include concepts of "he/she/it/they." Any people, objects, or ideas that you might refer to outside your immediate conversation are technically considered third person.

	Singular	**Plural**
First Person	I, me, my	we, us, our
Second Person	you, your	you, your
Third Person	he, him, his she, her, hers it, its	they, them, their

To simplify grammatical discussion, a shorthand system is used for person, gender, and number. The numbers 1, 2, and 3 designate first, second, and third person. Masculine and feminine are designated by "m" and "f." When the same form is used for both masculine and feminine, the letter "c" is used to designate a "common" form. The letters "s" and "p" indicate singular and plural.[1] For example, "me" is designated grammatically as 1cs (first person common singular).

What Do Pronominal Suffixes Do? (Function)

The English pronouns give you a frame of reference for understanding Hebrew pronominal suffixes. However, the overlap between English and Hebrew is not exact. English uses different types of pronouns depending on their function in the sentence. For example, English first person includes "*I* went" (subject pronoun), "to *me*" (object pronoun), and "*my* house" (possessive pronoun). Hebrew uses a single set of pronominal suffixes to fill any one of these functions.[2] Thus the English expressions "*my* horse" and "to *me*" have identical endings in Hebrew (e.g., סוּסִי and לִי). When you encounter a pronominal suffix in your reading, focus on gender, number, and person and translate according to the needs of the sentence. For example, the word סוּסִי is a combination of "horse" and a first person pronoun. In English your options are "*I* horse," "*me* horse," or "*my* horse." As you translate into English, your selection of the correct pronoun is intuitive. Obviously, "*my* horse" is the only option that makes sense. Likewise, the word לִי is a combination of the preposition "to" (לְ) and a first person pronoun. The obvious choice here is "to *me*" (NOT "to *I*" or "to *my*").

סוּסִי	"***my*** horse"	(NOT "*I* horse" or "*me* horse")
לִי	"to ***me***"	(NOT "to *I*" or "to *my*")

You will be able to accurately translate pronominal suffixes using your intuition of proper English. However, those familiar with principles

1. For suffixes, the dual does not apply. The abbreviation for dual is usually du. (though "dual" is often simply written out).

2. Hebrew uses one basic set of suffixes with numerous parts of speech. We will revisit the suffixes again when dealing with pronominal suffixes on verbs (ch. 22).

of grammar may find additional explanation helpful. In Hebrew, all pronominal suffixes are technically *object suffixes*. When pronominal suffixes are attached to a preposition, the suffix functions as the object of a preposition (לִי = "to *me*"). When attached to nouns and adjectives, the pronominal suffixes function like the construct sequences discussed in the previous chapter. Just as "David's house" is expressed in Hebrew as "the house *of* David" (בֵּית דָּוִד) so too the English phrase "my house" is expressed in Hebrew as "the house *of* me" (בֵּיתִי), as the object of the implied preposition "of." Later when you learn to spot suffixes on verbs, the suffix will usually function as the object ("killed *him*").[3]

What Do Pronominal Suffixes Look Like? (Form)

Pronominal suffixes attach directly to the end of a word. Therefore, you will need to learn both the form of the suffix itself and how that suffix affects the word to which it is attached.

The Basic Set of Pronominal Suffixes

The suffixes themselves are fairly straightforward. Table 8.1 below presents the suffixes both by themselves and attached to the simple word סוּס ("horse"). The parentheses contain historic forms that also appear in the biblical text.[4] Most of these forms are used when the more popular ending cannot be used because it would result in two consecutive vowels (e.g., "his father" = אָבִ֫יהוּ NOT אֲבִי + וֹ). The historic 2ms form (the one with a dagger † in table 8.1) is also common, appearing at major points of pause in a sentence (e.g., סוּסְךָ vs. the form as it appears in pause סוּסֶ֫ךָ).[5] The shift in accent helps to slow down the sentence and bring the reader to a stop. The historic 2fs ending (כִי) appears in gray because it is extremely rare and is presented here only to alert you to its existence.[6]

3. Even when infinitives use the suffixes to indicate the subject of the action, it does so using an infinitive *construct* with an object suffix (e.g., in the ruling of *him* = "when he ruled"). See ch. 16.

4. Most of the examples with historic forms developed because of the loss of *heh*: the 3ms (ֵ֫הוּ → ו ָ → וֹ), 3mp (ֵהֶם → ם), and 3fp (ֵהֶן → ן). The 3fs suffix retained the *heh* but lost the final vowel (e.g., 3fs ַ֫הָ → ָ֫הּ) and used *mappiq* to indicate that the *heh* is a true consonant.

5. Pausal forms in Hebrew reflect a pause in speech or a break in thought. In many cases these are places where we might insert punctuation in English.

6. See Jer 11:15 רָעָ֫תֵכִי ("your evil").

Table 8.1: Pronominal Suffixes (with Singular Nouns)

3ms	him/his	◌וֹ (הוּ)	סוּסוֹ	"his horse"
3fs	her	◌ָהּ (הָ)	סוּסָהּ	"her horse"
2ms	you/your	◌ְךָ (→ ◌ֶ֫ךָ)†	סוּסְךָ	"your (m.s.) horse"
2fs	you/your	◌ֵךְ (כִי)	סוּסֵךְ	"your (f.s.) horse"
1cs	me/my	◌ִי	סוּסִי	"my horse"
3mp	them/their	◌ָם‡ (הֶם)	סוּסָם	"their (m.p.) horse"
3fp	them/their	◌ָן (הֶן)	סוּסָן	"their (f.p.) horse"
2mp	you/your	◌ְכֶם	סוּסְכֶם	"your (m.p.) horse"
2fp	you/your	◌ְכֶן	סוּסְכֶן	"your (f.p.) horse"
1cp	us/our	◌ֵ֫נוּ	סוּסֵ֫נוּ	"our horse"

† Pausal form ‡ Also has poetic form ◌ָמוֹ

Suffixes Attach to the Construct Form

The pronominal suffixes attach to the construct endings. Remember to think of the "construct" form as the form that is used for "construction" (building onto a word). Thus if the feminine singular word "mare" stands alone (absolute form), it appears with the feminine singular ending as סוּסָה. Yet when you attach a suffix to the word, it appears on the construct form סוּסַתְכֶם ("your [m.p.] mare"). Since you already learned the construct forms (ch. 6), you will be able to recognize the base word even when it differs from the vocabulary form.

	Absolute form	Construct form		Words with 2mp pronominal suffix
m. sg.	□□□	□□□	→	□□□ְכֶם
f. sg.	□□□ָה	□□□ַת	→	□□□ַתְכֶם
m. pl.	□□□ִים	□□□ֵי	→	□□□ֵיכֶם
f. pl.	□□□וֹת	□□□וֹת	→	□□□וֹתֵיכֶם†

† Feminine plural words always add the m. pl. cst. ֵי to וֹת when attaching suffixes.

The suffix endings presented in table 8.1 attach to singular construct endings without difficulty. When these same suffixes attach to the plural construct (ֵי), the form is slightly altered. Since the historic changes are complex for beginning students, it is easier to memorize the forms resulting from the masculine plural construct ending ֵי + suffix, rather than to remember how and why these changes occurred.[7] The forms of the suffixes when they are attached to plural nouns are presented in table 8.2 below.

The *yod* from the construct ֵי is present in every plural form, identifying the noun as plural. Thus there is a visible distinction between singular and plural nouns even when they have a suffix ending. Note that the first person singular suffix ends in *yod* on both singular and plural nouns. To distinguish them you need to pay attention to the vowels.

סוּסִי "***my*** horse"

סוּסַי "***my*** horse***s***"

7. Though you learn the m. pl. construct as ֵי (alternatively expressed as ֶי), originally it was ַי. The historic ַי contracted into long /ē/ before consonantal sufformatives (e.g., ַיְנוּ → ֵינוּ or ַיְךָ → ֶיךָ). What appear as variations from the familiar ֵי construct form reflect the historic a-class vowel: 1cs (ַיִי slurred to ַי), 2fs (ַיִךְ), and 3ms (ָיו pronounced /av/). The contraction from ַי to long /ē/ is discussed more fully in ch. 24.

Table 8.2: Chart of Pronominal Suffixes

		Suffixes (on sg. nouns)	Suffix + mp cst. (on pl. nouns)
3ms	his	□□□וֹ (הוּ)	□□□ָיו‡
3fs	her	□□□ָהּ (הָ)	□□□ֶ֫יהָ
2ms	your (m.)	□□□ְךָ (ךָ ֶ֫ →)†	□□□ֶ֫יךָ
2fs	your (f.)	□□□ֵךְ (כִי)	□□□ַ֫יִךְ
1cs	my	□□□ִי	□□□ַי
3mp	their (m.)	□□□ָם❖ (הֶם)	□□□ֵיהֶם
3fp	their (f.)	□□□ָן (הֶן)	□□□ֵיהֶן
2mp	your (m.)	□□□ְכֶם	□□□ֵיכֶם
2fp	your (f.)	□□□ְכֶן	□□□ֵיכֶן
1cp	our	□□□ֵ֫נוּ	□□□ֵ֫ינוּ

† Pausal form ‡ Pronounced *"av"* ❖ Poetic form ָמוֹ

The chart below illustrates the various suffixes attached to the noun סוּס (*horse*) so that you can see what nouns of each gender and number look like with suffixes.[8] Since the noun סוּס has no changeable vowels, it will let you focus on the endings without having to face modifications in form to distract you from the suffix itself. By way of reminder, note that: (1) Each suffix attaches to the construct form of the word, (2) the vowel of the feminine singular construct (ַת) lengthens in near open syllables (e.g., סוּסָתוֹ), and (3) the masculine plural construct ending is reflected in all plurals.

8. While listing the pronominal suffixes from 3rd–1st person is backwards from what you are accustomed to in English, this matches the standard order of the Hebrew verb paradigms.

Table 8.3: Pronominal Suffixes on סוס

	horse (m. sg.)	mare (f. sg.)	horse**s** (m. pl.)	mare**s** (f. pl.)
his	סוּסוֹ	סוּסָתוֹ	סוּסָיו	סוּסוֹתָיו
her	סוּסָהּ	סוּסָתָהּ	סוּסֶיהָ	סוּסוֹתֶיהָ
your (m. sg.)	סוּסְךָ	סוּסָתְךָ	סוּסֶיךָ	סוּסוֹתֶיךָ
your (f. sg.)	סוּסֵךְ	סוּסָתֵךְ	סוּסַיִךְ	סוּסוֹתַיִךְ
my	סוּסִי	סוּסָתִי	סוּסַי	סוּסוֹתַי
their (m.)	סוּסָם	סוּסָתָם	סוּסֵיהֶם	סוּסוֹתֵיהֶם
their (f.)	סוּסָן	סוּסָתָן	סוּסֵיהֶן	סוּסוֹתֵיהֶן
your (m. pl.)	סוּסְכֶם	סוּסַתְכֶם	סוּסֵיכֶם	סוּסוֹתֵיכֶם
your (f. pl.)	סוּסְכֶן	סוּסַתְכֶן	סוּסֵיכֶן	סוּסוֹתֵיכֶן
our	סוּסֵנוּ	סוּסָתֵנוּ	סוּסֵינוּ	סוּסוֹתֵינוּ

In summary, to translate you need to accurately identify the base word and the suffix. In the beginning you will have to rely heavily on memorization, but faithful practice will result in the suffix endings becoming intuitive. It also helps to be able to discuss a word according to its grammatical elements. To grammatically describe any suffixed nouns, identify the base word and suffix separately.

סוּסוֹתֵינוּ = fem. pl. סוּס ("mares") + 1cp suffix ("our")
"our mares"

The Syntax of Pronominal Suffixes

Pronominal Suffixes Impart Definiteness

Words with a pronominal suffix are considered definite, even though they never have the definite article. Pronominal suffixes indicate that the author is referring to a specific object. For instance, "horse" can refer to any horse, but "my horse" indicates one particular horse. Thus nouns or adjectives with a suffix are implicitly definite and do not take a definite article (i.e., NOT "the my horse").[9]

Pronominal Suffixes on Construct Chains

Since pronominal suffixes impart definiteness and only the last word of a construct chain is marked for definiteness, pronominal suffixes in a construct chain always appear on the final word.[10] When a construct chain has a pronominal suffix, the entire construct chain is definite. In Hebrew the construct chain is seen as one single idea and the pronominal suffix modifies the whole chain. When conveying the idea in English, the pronominal suffix may be associated with either noun. For example, הַר־קָדְשִׁי ("the mountain of the holiness of me") could be translated as *"the mountain of my holiness"* or *"my holy mountain."*[11]

הַר־קָדְשִׁי — "the mountain of ***my holiness***" *or* "***my holy*** mountain"

NOT

~~הָרִי־קֹ֫דֶשׁ~~

SUFFIXES WITH PREPOSITIONS

When pronominal suffixes appear on prepositions, rely on your knowledge of English to translate them correctly. For example, בְּ + 1cs suffix is translated "in *me*" because neither "in *I*" or "in *my*" makes sense in English. This translational approach will always work for prepositions.

One translational nuance that you will frequently encounter is that Hebrew can use the preposition לְ to convey possession. If you start with לְ as "to/for" and add the pronoun, context will help you determine when "to me" is being used to convey "belonging to me" (i.e., I have). Thus כֹּל אֲשֶׁר לִי "all which is to me" = "all I have" (1 Kgs 20:4). When לְ

9. Like every Hebrew "rule," you will find rare exceptions (e.g., Josh 7:21 הָאָהֳלִי "my tent").

10. See ch. 7.

11. The question of how you translate הַר־קָדְשִׁי to best capture the nuance intended by the author is important and will be guided by context. But avoid the common error of suggesting grammatical priority of one interpretation over another when the Hebrew is syntactically ambiguous.

expresses possession it is often preceded by a particle of existence (יֵשׁ "there is"/אֵין "there is not") or the "to be" verb (הָיָה).

כֹּל אֲשֶׁר לִי	"all which *is to me*"	=	"all ***I have***"
יֵשׁ לִי בֵן	"*there is to me* a son"	=	"***I have*** a son"
הָיָה לִי בֵן	"*there was to me* a son"	=	"***I had*** a son"

Special Forms of the Prepositions

The short introduction above is sufficient for you to translate prepositions with suffixes. All other considerations regarding prepositions with pronominal suffixes concern only form and do not affect translation.

Suffix Endings on Prepositions

Certain prepositions consistently prefer to use the suffixes that appear with singular nouns (e.g., לוֹ, לָהּ; "to *him*," "to *her*,") and others consistently prefer the suffixes used with plural nouns (e.g., עָלָיו, עָלֶיהָ; "on account of *him*," "on account of *her*"). Since prepositions have no sense of singular of plural, do not worry about what type of pronominal suffix a preposition utilizes. The choice of suffix endings on a preposition has no effect on meaning and is merely a matter of Hebrew preference.

Compound Forms (כָּמוֹ- and מִמֶּנ-)

Two prepositions appear in alternate forms when they attach to certain suffixes. The preposition כְּ ("like") often appears as כָּמוֹ and the preposition מִן ("from") as מִמֶּנ (reduplication of מִן + מִן with assimilation of *nun*).

כָּמוֹ or כְּ	=	"like, as"
מִמֶּנ or מִן	=	"from"

Besides recognizing these alternate forms as synonymous, you must also know how these forms affect the suffix endings. First, the 1cs suffix takes an alternate form on these prepositions. Instead of ִי you will see נִי (i.e., כָּמוֹנִי "like *me*" and מִמֶּנִּי "from *me*").[12] Second, the tendencies of the *nun* and the *heh* to assimilate or drop create a situation where

12. Both forms of the suffix are related to the independent pronoun אֲנִי ("I") that you will learn in ch. 13.

the 1cs and 3ms suffixes appear identical when attached to מִמֶּנּ. Thus, מִמֶּנּוּ can mean either "from *him*" or "from *us*" depending on context.

מִמֶּנְהוּ → מִמֶּנּוּ = "from him"

מִמֶּנְנוּ → מִמֶּנּוּ = "from us"

Because Hebrew uses these prepositions with high frequency, they will become familiar without a great deal of memorization.

Table 8.4: Special Forms of the Preposition with Suffixes

	"like___"	"from___"
him	כָּמוֹהוּ	מִמֶּנּוּ (=מִמֶּנְהוּ)
her	כָּמוֹהָ	מִמֶּנָּה (=מִמֶּנְהָ)
you (m. sg.)	כָּמוֹךָ	מִמְּךָ or מִמֶּךָּ (=מִמֶּנְךָ)
you (f. sg.)	כָּמוֹךְ	מִמֵּךְ
me	כָּמוֹנִי	מִמֶּנִּי
them (m.)	כָּהֶם	מֵהֶם ,מֵהֵמָּה
them (f.)	כָּהֶן	מֵהֶן ,מֵהֵנָּה
you (m. pl.)	כָּכֶם	מִכֶּם
you (f. pl.)	כָּכֶן	מִכֶּן
us	כָּמוֹנוּ	מִמֶּנּוּ (=מִמֶּנְנוּ)

SUFFIXES ON THE DIRECT OBJECT MARKER (אֶת־ / אֵת)

Suffixes can also attach to the direct object marker אֵת (אֶת־), which looks identical to the preposition "with." When אֵת stands alone the direct object and preposition are indistinguishable apart from context. Fortunately, the difference between them is visible when pronominal suffixes are attached. You will recognize these forms but may struggle to remember which is which. It will help if you can remember that when אֵת occurs **with** *dagesh* it is the preposition "**with**," but the "**o**" vowel indicates it is the **object** (e.g., אִתּוֹ "***with*** him" vs. אוֹתוֹ direct *object* "him").[13]

Table 8.5: Suffixes on the Direct Object Marker and Preposition אֵת

אֶת־ / אֵת

Direct Object (Think: "O" = Object)		"With" (Think: "with" a dot)	
אוֹתוֹ	"him"	אִתּוֹ	"with him"
אוֹתָהּ	"her"	אִתָּהּ	"with her"
(אוֹתָךְ or) אוֹתְךָ	"you" (ms)	(אִתָּךְ or) אִתְּךָ	"with you" (ms)
אוֹתָךְ	"you" (fs)	אִתָּךְ	"with you" (fs)
אוֹתִי	"me"	אִתִּי	"with me"
(אֶתְהֶם or) אוֹתָם	"them"	אִתָּם	"with them"
(אֶתְהֶן or) אוֹתָן	"them"	אִתָּן	"with them"
אֶתְכֶם	"you" (mp)	אִתְּכֶם	"with you" (mp)
אֶתְכֶן	"you" (fp)	אִתְּכֶן	"with you" (fp)
אוֹתָנוּ	"us"	אִתָּנוּ	"with us"

At times the form in the text does not match context. Do not panic. Remember that languages are messy. Languages are living entities that flex with local usage and reflect the leveling and confusion that sometimes happens with similar forms. As a result, there are cases where

13. Note that the forms אוֹתָךְ and אִתָּךְ listed in table 8.5 are used at points in the sentence when there is a major pause (e.g., at the end of a verse).

the preposition is clearly intended, but you will find the direct object form. The reverse is also the case. As always, let context guide you.

REVIEW OF DEFINITENESS

The introduction of the pronominal suffixes completes the list of options for communicating definiteness in Hebrew. In Hebrew a word is definite if it: (1) Bears the definite article (הַ□), (2) is a proper noun (e.g., Samuel), (3) contains a pronominal suffix (e.g., *my* house), or (4) appears in a construct where the final noun is definite, thus imparting definiteness to the whole sequence (סוּס הַמֶּ֫לֶךְ "*the* horse of *the* king").

Table 8.6: Marks of Definiteness

(1) Definite article	הַמֶּ֫לֶךְ	"**the** king"
(2) Proper name	שְׁמוּאֵל	"***Samuel***"
(3) Possessive suffix	קוֹלִי	"***my*** voice"
(4) Construct with definite noun	סוּס הַמֶּ֫לֶךְ	"**the** horse of my **the** king"

EXERCISE FOR CHAPTER 8

Exercise 8 in the workbook ("Pronominal Suffixes") will give you practice identifying pronominal suffixes and recognizing the vocabulary form of nouns and adjectives. You should also complete the translation exercise for chapter 8 in the workbook.

CHAPTER 9

Learning to Read Intuitively: Common Patterns in Hebrew Nouns

Up to this point our study of nouns and adjectives has looked only at the components that are added *after* the noun or adjective is already formed. This chapter discusses the formation of the nouns and adjectives themselves. The more you read, the more you will encounter unfamiliar words that you must either look up in the lexicon or deduce from context. If you know the meaning of a verbal root, you can often anticipate the meaning of an unfamiliar word from that same root simply because you know the significance of the formation patterns. Conversely, your familiarity with the common patterns can help you isolate and identify an unknown root so that you can more efficiently use your Hebrew lexicon.

A number of predictable patterns are especially helpful for recognizing nouns and adjectives. The following groups of words are by no means the only noun and adjective formations available, but they do illustrate some of the most common patterns you will encounter in the biblical text.[1] In some cases these patterns may have functions beyond those noted in this chapter, but the ones outlined here are the most prominent.

PREFORMATIVE MEM

One of the most common patterns in Hebrew is the addition of a preformative *mem* to create a noun indicating: (1) A place, (2) instrument, or (3) abstraction (a concept derived from the verb).[2] Based on the context surrounding a given word, you should be able to use the meaning of the verbal root as a starting point and then see which one of these

1. For a more extensive discussion of noun and adjective patterns, see Waltke-O'Connor, 85–94.

2. Some verb forms use the preformative *mem* as well, but the verb paradigms enable you to distinguish between verbs and the nouns discussed here.

concepts best fits the sentence. For example, notice the following nouns that commonly appear in the Hebrew Bible.

Place

מָקוֹם	*standing place* (קום)	→	place
מִשְׁכָּב	*lying place* (שׁכב)	→	bed
מִגְדָּל	*tall place* (גדל)	→	tower
מַמְלָכָה	*ruling place* (מלך)	→	kingdom
מוֹצָא	*going out place* (יצא)	→	exit
מוֹשָׁב	*sitting/dwelling place* (ישׁב)	→	seat, dwelling

Instrument

מַאֲכֶלֶת	*eating instrument* (אכל)	→	knife
מַרְאָה	*seeing instrument* (ראה)	→	mirror
מַפְתֵּחַ	*opening instrument* (פתח)	→	key

Abstraction

מַאֲכָל	*thing eaten* (אכל)	→	food
מִלְחָמָה	*thing fought* (לחם)	→	battle
מִסְפָּר	*thing counted* (ספר)	→	number
מִצְוָה	*thing commanded* (צוה)	→	commandment
מַעֲשֶׂה	*thing done* (עשׂה)	→	work, deed
מַרְאֶה	*thing seen* (ראה)	→	appearance
מוֹצָא	*thing going out* (יצא)	→	utterance (see "exit" above)

This noun pattern is common and helps in learning vocabulary and intuitively assessing the meaning of words when you sight-read. Later in the Joseph narrative you will find that the translation exercises encourage you to rely on these patterns without giving you glosses for vocabulary that you should be able to deduce.

NATIONALITIES

Designations of nationality are another category of formation that you may encounter with some level of frequency. Just as English adds an ending like "ite" to specify a person's nationality (e.g, Israelite), so too Hebrew uses a *ḥireq yod* to form an adjective describing one's country of origin. Unlike the 1cs suffix added to the end of a complete word, the *ḥireq yod* of the gentilic ending is part of the vocabulary word itself. Look for the simple *ḥireq yod* of the masculine adjective (ִי) and the same *ḥireq yod* with final *tav* to mark the feminine form (ִית).

עִבְרִי	Hebrew (man)	עִבְרִית	Hebrew (woman)
מִצְרִי	Egyptian (man)	מִצְרִית	Egyptian (woman)
מוֹאָבִי	Moabite (man)	מוֹאָבִית	Moabite (woman)

TRAITS OR PROFESSIONS

Another helpful noun pattern identifies people who are characterized by a particular trait or profession. These nouns are characterized by an internal *pataḥ-dagesh-qamets* pattern (e.g., גַּנָּב "thief").

גַּנָּב	thief	(גנב to steal)
דַּיָּן	judge	(דין to judge)
חַטָּא	sinner	(חטא to sin)
פָּרָשׁ	horseman	(פרשׁ horse)

The word פָּרָשׁ may seem out of place in this list, but it has been included to illustrate an important point. It is the historic structure that identifies words sharing a common origin, not the actual vowels that eventually appear in Biblical Hebrew. Because the letter *resh* cannot be doubled, the historic closed unaccented syllable at the beginning of this word has lengthened in the now open unaccented syllable (*פַּרַּשׁ → פָּרָשׁ). The word פָּרָשׁ thus has the same historic base as all the other examples listed above. As evident in this example, be alert for consonants that may affect the appearance of historic patterns.[3]

ABSTRACT NOUNS / ADJECTIVES Most words ending in וֹן, ִית, or וּת are abstract nouns or adjectives. Think of abstracts as things that exist but are difficult to touch, to draw, or to hold in the hand (e.g., hope). Note the following examples.

רֵאשִׁית	beginning (ראשׁ head)	Abstracts
אַחֲרִית	end, outcome (אַחַר behind, after)	
יַלְדוּת	childhood (ילד to give birth)	
מַלְכוּת	royalty, reign (מלך to rule)	
זִכָּרוֹן	commemoration (זכר to remember)	
בִּזָּיוֹן	contempt (בזה to despise)	
פִּתְרוֹן	interpretation (פתר to interpret)	
אַחֲרוֹן	later; west (אַחַר behind, after)	Adjectives
רִאשׁוֹן	first, former (ראשׁ head)	

GEMINATE PATTERNS The last group of words mentioned in this brief overview does not necessarily have one dominant meaning. Instead, they bear mentioning so that you can recognize where to find these words in the Hebrew lexicon. This pattern is common with roots that have the same second and third consonants (called geminates). The pattern consists of a תְּ at the beginning of the word, doubling that reflects the doubled letter of the root, and a feminine ending. Use the *dagesh* to remind you of the geminate root.

תְּפִלָּה	prayer	(פלל to pray)
תְּהִלָּה	praise	(הלל to praise)
תְּחִלָּה	beginning	(חלל to begin)
תְּחִנָּה	supplication, request for grace	(חנן to petition)

3. The word for *horse* and *horseman* actually look identical in the lexical form פָּרָשׁ. But once endings are added it quickly becomes apparent that *horse* comes from the historic base פַּרַשׁ* while the word *horseman* comes from the pattern outlined above (פַּרַּשׁ*). Because of the underlying historic structure, vowel reductions behave differently with each word. The plural *horses* is פְּרָשִׁים (distant open syllable reduces) while the plural *horsemen* will be פָּרָשִׁים. The first vowel in פָּרָשִׁים must remain long in order to preserve the historic structure of the word (i.e., a hypothetical פַּרְשִׁים*). Note: Vowels that result from compensatory lengthening never reduce because the long vowel preserves an originally closed unaccented syllable.

SUMMARY

Recognizing basic noun and adjective patterns will help you intuitively identify the meaning of unfamiliar words. These familiar patterns can also help you identify the root you need to look up in the lexicon. Remember that these are not comprehensive lists. Learn to look for structural patterns and associations with verbal roots so that you can read with greater ease.

CHAPTER 10

Numbers

This chapter covers the use of numbers in Biblical Hebrew. You do not need to learn all the forms now as you will be introduced to the numbers in the vocabulary lists. The discussion here presents the various types of Hebrew numbers, how they are formed, and how they are used.

HEBREW NUMBERS

In English we use two different sets of numbers, one set for counting (e.g., one, two, three) and another to convey order or sequence (e.g., first, second, third). We refer to the numbers used for counting as *cardinal numbers* (think "c̲" for c̲ounting) and numbers that reflect order as *ordinal numbers* (think "o̲" for o̲rder). In both cases we represent these numbers either by using numeric symbols (e.g., 1 or 1st) called Arabic numerals, or by expressing these quantities in word form (e.g., one or first). In practice, we tend to rely upon symbols more frequently than words. Our use of numbers in word form is usually limited to writing out a personal check or composing a formal paper.

Hebrew uses both cardinal and ordinal numbers, and these numbers can be expressed by means of words or symbols (e.g., אֶחָד "one" or א "1"). You will not see numeric symbols in the biblical text itself, though symbols are used in certain editions of the Hebrew Bible for identifying chapter and verse numbers. This chapter focuses primarily on words for Hebrew numbers and how they are used. The end of the chapter provides a short introduction to the system of symbols.

English and Hebrew write out numbers in different sequences. In English we place numbers in descending order: thousands + hundreds + tens + ones. For example, the number 147 is written in English as "one hundred forty-seven." Conversely, in Hebrew large numbers are typically constructed from smallest to largest: ones + tens + hundreds + thousands. As a result, Hebrew records the number 147 as "seven and forty and one hundred."

Another difference between Hebrew and English is the way that numbered items are designated. In English, if you have twenty-seven of something, the referent is listed as a plural (e.g., 27 items, NOT 27 item). Hebrew does not always bother placing the item in question in a plural form. In Hebrew, the numbers two through nineteen are typically associated with nouns in the plural, while numbers higher than this are simply followed by nouns in the singular. Both styles appear in the sequence in Gen 47:28, שֶׁ֫בַע שָׁנִים וְאַרְבָּעִים וּמְאַת שָׁנָה (7 *years* and 40 and 100 year = "one hundred forty-seven years"). Remember that your translation is not about representing the form of the word, but rather its meaning. When confronted with a large number paired with a singular noun, English requires that you translate that noun in the plural according to English convention.

FORMATION OF HEBREW NUMBERS

The table below presents the numbers one through ten in the Hebrew cardinal and ordinal system. Familiarize yourself with the basic patterns that create the distinctions between cardinal and ordinal numbers and that serve to mark gender and construct.

Cardinal Numbers (Gender Reversed)

The first thing you need to get used to is the fact that most cardinal numbers use gender endings that are opposite of what you would normally expect. The masculine cardinal numbers look like feminine forms (e.g., שְׁלֹשָׁה m. and שְׁלֹשֶׁת m. cst. "three"),[1] and the feminine cardinal numbers look like masculine forms (e.g., שָׁלֹשׁ f. "three"). Remember, the gender of a number matches the gender of the object it is describing.

1. With certain numbers the feminine construct ending *tav* is added without a vowel and the resulting consonant cluster at the end of the word is broken up by the addition of a helping vowel (e.g., שְׁלוֹשְׁת → שְׁלוֹשֶׁת or אַרְבַּעְת → אַרְבַּ֫עַת).

Feminine	Masculine	
אַחַת	אֶחָד	"one"
שְׁתַּ֫יִם	שְׁנַ֫יִם	"two"
שָׁלֹשׁ	שְׁלֹשָׁה	"three"
אַרְבַּע	אַרְבָּעָה	"four"
	etc.	

Most numbers appear to be reversed in form

The only exceptions to this inverted gender marking are the numbers one and two, which follow the regular pattern.[2] In most cases the gender issue should not cause much problem because you are reading Hebrew sentences, not composing them. However, you should log this reversed gender pattern into your mind and get accustomed to it through exposure to the text.

The construct forms of the Hebrew numbers reflect the same vowel changes as Hebrew nouns. Numbers appearing in construct reflect the vowel changes that result from a shift in accent. For example, the word שָׁלֹשׁ (f. "three") is the result of a lengthened historic short a-class vowel in the near open syllable (i.e., שַׁ|לוֹשׁ* → שָׁלוֹשׁ). The construct שְׁלֹשׁ, on the other hand, is joined to the following word as a single unit so that the historic a-class vowel stands in a distant open syllable and must reduce (e.g., ׳-שַׁ|לוֹשׁ* → ׳-שְׁ|לוֹשׁ).[3]

The final item to notice about cardinal numbers is that Hebrew has an alternate construct form for the number one (עַשְׁתֵּי). The variation in construct form has no affect upon meaning. Memorize this form when it is listed in your vocabulary.[3]

2. The feminine form of the number one (אַחַת) can be recognized by associating this form with the old feminine ending now preserved in the feminine construct ending you learned in ch. 7 (e.g., ַת). The feminine form of the number two (שְׁתַּ֫יִם) can be recognized by making a connection with the feminine dual you learned in ch. 4 (e.g., ָתַ֫יִם).

3. The word עַשְׁתֵּי appears in some Assyrian-Babylonian inscriptions in the form *ištin* or *ištên* and was probably imported into Hebrew from those languages. Constructions with עַשְׁתֵּי appear predominantly in exilic and postexilic passages (2 Kgs 25:2; Jer 39:2; 52:5; Ezek 26:1; 40:49; Zech 1:7; 1 Chron 12:14; 24:12; 25:18; 27:14) and in a handful of verses in the Pentateuch (Exod 26:7–8; 36:14–15; Num 7:72; 29:20; Deut 1:3).

Table 10.1: The Numbers One through Ten

Ordinal Numbers			Cardinal Numbers				
f.	m.		f. cst.	f.	m. cst.	*m.*	
רִאשׁוֹנָה	רִאשׁוֹן	first	אַחַת (or עַשְׁתֵּי)	אַחַת	אַחַד (or עַשְׁתֵּי)	אֶחָד	one
שֵׁנִית	שֵׁנִי	second	שְׁתֵּי	שְׁתַּ֫יִם	שְׁנֵי	שְׁנַ֫יִם	two
שְׁלִישִׁית	שְׁלִישִׁי	third	שְׁלֹשׁ	שָׁלֹשׁ	שְׁלֹ֫שֶׁת	שְׁלֹשָׁה	three
רְבִיעִית	רְבִיעִי	fourth	אַרְבַּע	אַרְבָּע	אַרְבַּ֫עַת	אַרְבָּעָה	four
חֲמִישִׁית	חֲמִישִׁי	fifth	חֲמֵשׁ	חָמֵשׁ	חֲמֵ֫שֶׁת	חֲמִשָּׁה	five
שִׁשִּׁית	שִׁשִּׁי	sixth	שֵׁשׁ	שֵׁשׁ	שֵׁ֫שֶׁת	שִׁשָּׁה	six
שְׁבִיעִית	שְׁבִיעִי	seventh	שְׁבַע	שֶׁ֫בַע	שִׁבְעַת	שִׁבְעָה	seven
שְׁמִינִית	שְׁמִינִי	eighth	שְׁמֹנֵה	שְׁמֹנֶה	שְׁמֹנַת	שְׁמֹנָה	eight
תְּשִׁיעִית	תְּשִׁיעִי	ninth	תְּשַׁע	תֵּ֫שַׁע	תִּשְׁעַת	תִּשְׁעָה	nine
עֲשִׂירִית	עֲשִׂירִי	tenth	עֶ֫שֶׂר	עֶ֫שֶׂר	עֲשֶׂ֫רֶת	עֲשָׂרָה	ten

Ordinal Numbers (Regular Gender with Double Ḥireq Yod)

The recognizable feature of ordinal numbers is the *ḥireq yod* in the final two syllables (e.g., שְׁלִישִׁי), though short *ḥireq* is used with "sixth" because a closed unaccented syllable requires a short vowel (e.g., שִׁשִּׁי). The feminine ordinal numbers attach a *tav* to the end of that same pattern (i.e., שְׁלִישִׁית).

Ordinal (f.)		**Ordinal (m.)**	
שְׁלִישִׁית	←	שְׁלִישִׁי	*"third"*

This double *ḥireq yod* pattern is present in most ordinal numbers. The numbers one and two are again the exceptions. Here you see either a slight variation of the regular pattern (i.e., שֵׁנִי NOT שִׁינִי) or the use of an entirely different term (e.g., אֶחָד "one" vs. רִאשׁוֹן "first").

Multiples of Ten (10, 20, 30, . . . , 100, 1000, 10,000)

The tens digits (i.e., 30, 40, 50, etc.) are constructed by adding a masculine plural ending to the singles digits (e.g., שְׁלוֹשִׁים "thirty"). This is true for all the numbers from thirty to ninety. The number twenty, on the other hand, is created by adding a plural ending to the number ten. (i.e., עֶשְׂרִים)

The numbers for one hundred and above are represented by separate terms that you must simply memorize. If an author wishes to express multiples of a hundred (מֵאָה), thousand (אֶלֶף), or ten thousand (רִבּוֹ or רִבּוֹא), he will usually use a construct form of the numbers one through nine before these terms (e.g., שְׁלשׁ מֵאוֹת = "three of hundreds" or 300). However, when there are only two of the unit in question, you will sometimes see a dual ending (e.g., מָאתַ֫יִם "two hundred").

Table 10.2: Multiples of Tens, Hundreds, and Thousands

Tens

twenty	עֶשְׂרִים	←		עֶ֫שֶׂר	ten
thirty	שְׁלוֹשִׁים	←		שָׁלֹשׁ	three
forty	אַרְבָּעִים	←		אַרְבַּע	four
fifty	חֲמִשִּׁים	←	+ □ִים (pl.)	חָמֵשׁ	five
sixty	שִׁשִּׁים	←		שֵׁשׁ	six
seventy	שִׁבְעִים	←		שֶׁ֫בַע	seven
eighty	שְׁמֹנִים	←		שְׁמֹנֶה	eight
ninety	תִּשְׁעִים	←		תֵּ֫שַׁע	nine

Ten Thousands		*Thousands*		*Hundreds*	
רִבּוֹא	10,000	אֶ֫לֶף	1000	מֵאָה	100
שְׁנֵי רִבּוֹא	20,000	אַלְפַּ֫יִם *(dual)*	2000	מָאתַ֫יִם *(dual)*	200
שְׁלֹשׁ רִבּוֹא	30,000	שְׁלֹשׁ אֲלָפִים	3000	שְׁלֹשׁ מֵאוֹת	300

COMBINING NUMBERS TOGETHER

The numbers introduced above comprise the framework for the entire numbering system. All other numbers are written as a combination of these numbers. The numbers 11-19 are noteworthy in that they use a unique form of the number ten (m. עָשָׂר instead of עֲשָׂרָה and f. עֶשְׂרֵה instead of עֶ֫שֶׂר). Thus the number thirteen appears as שְׁלֹשָׁה עָשָׂר (3+10) Likewise, the number twenty-three appears as עֶשְׂרִים וְשָׁלוֹשׁ (20 and 3). Keep in mind that Hebrew usually (though not always) constructs large numbers opposite of the way English does. As a result,

Hebrew writes the number 123 as שָׁלֹשׁ וְעֶשְׂרִים וּמֵאָה (3 + 20 + 100). However, you will also find numbers arranged just like in English.

ALPHABET USED FOR HEBREW NUMERALS

Most modern editions of the Hebrew Bible and reference works related to its use are printed with the Arabic numerals you are familiar with in English (1, 2, 3, etc.). However, on occasion you will run across Hebrew numbers represented by symbols (especially with chapter and verse references). Hebrew uses the letters of the alphabet to represent the various units that make up the numbering system. The letters א-ט stand for 1-9, י-צ represent the multiples of ten from 10-90, and the letters ק-ת represent 100-400. The table below illustrates the correspondence between the Hebrew alphabet and numbering system.

Table 10.3: The Alphabet Used to Represent Numbers

א	1	י	10	ק	100
ב	2	כ	20	ר	200
ג	3	ל	30	ש	300
ד	4	מ	40	ת	400
ה	5	נ	50	ך	500
ו	6	ס	60	ם	600
ז	7	ע	70	ן	700
ח	8	פ	80	ף	800
ט	9	צ	90	ץ	900

To identify the number you simply add the figures together (e.g., קלד = ק 100 + ל 30 + ד 4 = 134). The only special rule you should be aware of is the unique presentation of the numbers fifteen and sixteen. Following the normal application of these numerical symbols, the numbers fifteen and sixteen would appear as יה and יו respectively, both of which are abbreviations of God's personal name (יהוה). As a result, the number fifteen is written טו (9 + 6) and sixteen is written as טז (9 + 7) to avoid an association with God's sacred name. In both cases the numerical symbol is still a matter of simple addition.

EXERCISE FOR CHAPTER 10

An optional translation exercise provided for chapter 10 adapts various passages from Genesis for the specific purpose of working with numbers. Even if you skip this translation exercise, the numbers are covered in subsequent lessons. Whenever numbers are relevant to the translation exercises, they are included as vocabulary items without assuming that you already know them and are accompanied by a notation that refers you back to the discussion in this chapter.

CHAPTER 11

Introduction to Hebrew Verbs

INTRODUCTORY CONCEPTS

In chapter 4 you were shown a few basic verb forms that allowed you to begin translation exercises that are fairly close to how these stories appear in the Hebrew Bible. This chapter provides a more detailed discussion of those verb forms to fill in the gaps that are missing in each paradigm and to explain the other verb forms to which you have not yet been exposed.

In any language a complete expression of thought is comprised of a subject and a verb (e.g., *he heard*). Additional information can be supplied (e.g., he heard *a loud noise*), but the subject and verb convey the core of each thought. Since Hebrew generally has a subject embedded in each verb, the Hebrew verb itself is central to any sentence.

Active, Passive, Reflexive

Each Hebrew verb also reflects the relationship between that verb and its embedded subject. Hebrew verbs can be active, passive, or reflexive. To explain these concepts it is helpful to think of each verb as a verbal picture. Building on the illustration of the camera in chapter 6, the question to ask is: Who or what is the camera focused on, and how is the focal point of the picture connected to the action? The three photographs below all capture the same event, although with different points of focus.

1

2

3

1. The man *kicked* the target.
2. The target *was kicked* by the man.
3. The man *vaulted himself* into the air.

In the first photograph (sentence 1) the focal point of the action is the man, and the action generates outward from him toward the object he is kicking. When the subject is portrayed as *doing an action,* the verb is identified as an *active verb.*

In the second photograph (sentence 2) the focal point of the action is the target and the action, kicking, is directed into the center of the picture toward the target. The target, which is the subject of this photo, is a passive participant in the action. Because the subject *receives the action,* the verb is identified as a *passive verb.*

In the third photograph (sentence 3) the focal point of the action is once again the martial artist. However, this photograph is focused solely upon the action of the man. In this case the photographer may have been focused upon the man's ability to jump or the way the action affects the martial artist himself. Any sentence focused upon *an action generated upon or for oneself* is said to have a *reflexive verb* because the verb directs the action back onto the subject that generated that action.

Preformatives and Sufformatives

Like nouns, Hebrew verbs are created by changing the vowel patterns and by applying additions to the front and end of a Hebrew *root* (the three-consonant base, e.g., גדל "to be great"). These additions are called *preformatives* and *sufformatives* because they are part of the "form" of the verb. When combined together, the vowel patterns, preformatives, and sufformatives distinguish the verb *stem,* the *conjugation,* and the *person*, *gender*, and *number* of person(s) involved. The following discussion presents the basic components of the Hebrew verb: (1) root, (2) stem, (3) conjugation, (4) person, (5) gender, and (6) number.

HEBREW ROOTS

As with nouns, Hebrew verbs are formed from triconsonantal roots that convey the base meaning. So the idea, *"he made himself great,"* begins with the selection of a root that conveys the verbal idea of "being great" (גדל). The root forms the core meaning of the verb. Identifying the root will help you accurately spot the addition of preformatives and sufformatives. For example, our phrase "he made himself great" would appear as הִתְגַּדֵּל as a form of the root גדל with an added preformative.

VERB STEMS

In Hebrew there are seven basic verb stems: *qal*, *niphal*, *piel*, *pual*, *hithpael*, *hiphil*, and *hophal*. With the exception of the term *qal* (from קַל, meaning *simple* or *basic*), these names reflect the sound of the vowel patterns and preformatives used to create each verb stem. Early Hebrew grammarians used the root פעל ("to make, do") for their verb paradigms with the result that the verb stems took their names from the simplest form in each verb stem: *niphal* (נִפְעַל), *piel* (פִּעֵל), *pual* (פֻּעַל), *hithpael* (הִתְפַּעֵל), *hiphil* (הִפְעִיל), and *hophal* (הָפְעַל). Thus, as odd as these names sound, they are especially helpful in remembering the form and structure of the various verb paradigms.

The following table depicts the relationships between the verb stems. We will systematically explain each of these verb stems as we progress through the chapters on the Hebrew verb. For now, familiarize yourself with the placement of each stem within the verbal system.

<table>
<tr><th></th><th>Basic Meaning</th><th>Cause a State†
Look It Up!</th><th>Cause an Action
Look it Up!</th></tr>
<tr><td>Active / Stative†</td><td>QAL
he was great
HE HEARD</td><td>PIEL
he caused [someone] to be great</td><td>HIPHIL
HE CAUSED TO HEAR</td></tr>
<tr><td>Passive</td><td rowspan="2">HE WAS HEARD
NIPHAL
HE HEARD HIMSELF</td><td>PUAL
he was caused to be great</td><td>HOPHAL
HE WAS CAUSED TO HEAR</td></tr>
<tr><td>Reflexive</td><td>HITHPAEL
[he caused himself to be great]</td><td></td></tr>
</table>

† Statives will be discussed at a later point.

Notice that vertically the verb stems shift from active to passive to reflexive. For example, the root שׁמע means "he heard" in the *qal*, but in the *niphal* it means "he *was heard*" (passive) or "he *heard himself*" (reflexive), depending on context. Horizontally the columns can be loosely categorized in the following fashion: 1) Simple action or basic meaning, 2) causing a state of being, and 3) causing an action. For example, "he heard" in the *qal* becomes "he caused to hear" (i.e, "he proclaimed") in the *hiphil*. Other times the relationship is more obscure, and one must look up the word in a lexicon.

VERB CONJUGATIONS

Another important component of the verb is the verb *conjugation*. This term is used to describe the modifications made within each verb stem to indicate things such as when the action is being done (past, present, or future) and whether the action is stated as a fact, a command, a request, or used with some other special sense.

You have already been introduced to several of these conjugations. In chapter 4 you learned basic forms of the perfect (e.g., שָׁמַר), the imperfect (e.g., יִשְׁמֹר), the *waw* consecutive perfect (e.g., וְשָׁמַר), and the *waw* consecutive imperfect (e.g., וַיִּשְׁמֹר). Other conjugations are familiar to you from English grammar. Imperatives (i.e., commands), participles, and infinitives are concepts that you employ every day, even if you do not know exactly what they mean. We will reintroduce these concepts in the coming chapters and help you understand how to translate them.

The verbal conjugations are subcategories of the verb stems. Imagine that you are working on a computer and have a screen in front of you that represents the Hebrew verbal system in a grid as presented below.

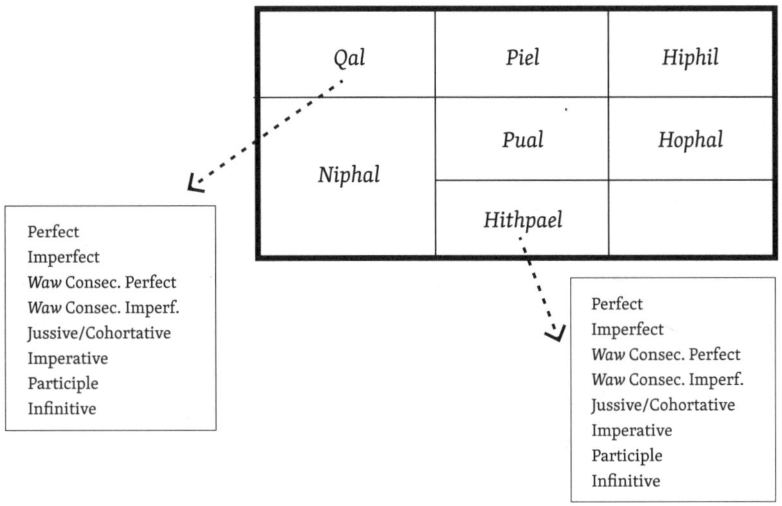

If you click to open the *qal* verb, you would find a number of different verb conjugations to choose from—perfect, imperfect, etc. If you were to open any other stems, you would find those same verb options. This means that as we progress through each conjugation of the basic *qal* verb, you will be learning the concepts that apply to all Hebrew stems.

PERSON, GENDER, NUMBER

The concepts of person, gender, and number were introduced in the previous discussion about possessive suffixes on nouns. These concepts apply to verbs because the inherent subject is marked for person, gender, and number. Gender is limited to masculine or feminine and refers to grammatical gender. A masculine verb could refer to a man ("he") or to an object ("it"). Grammatical number indicates whether a subject is viewed as singular or plural. However, like English, Hebrew uses some singular words to identify a group as a single entity (e.g., "the class stands" vs. "the students stand").

When grammars talk about the *person* of a verb, they are describing the person or thing doing the action as viewed from the speaker's own vantage point.

	Singular	**Plural**
First Person	I	we
Second Person	you	you
Third Person	he or she	they

The easiest way to become familiar with these labels is to imagine yourself in a conversation with a friend and to describe the things you talk about on the basis of their relationship to your own point of view. From your perspective, you are the primary participant in the conversation. As a result, verbs referring to *I* or *we* are described as being *first person* verbs. The person or group that you are speaking to is the secondary partner in the conversation (i.e., *you*) and are called *second person* verbs. People and objects that you talk about make up the third group of constituents. As a result, verbs that express what *he, she, it,* or *they* did are described as being *third person* verbs.

BASIC TERMINOLOGY

The verb stem, conjugation, person, gender, and number of a verb are conveyed by components that are added to the front and back of the root and by its vocalization. Familiarity with the following terminology will help you understand the descriptions of how verbs are formed.

The elements added to the front and back of verbs fall into two categories: (1) Those that "form" an essential part of the verb itself, and (2) those that are added to a verb after it is formed. Of these, each type of ending is further divided based on whether that ending (3) begins with a vowel or (4) begins with a consonant. Finally, the vowels within a verb are labeled based on whether they appear (5) as part of the preformative or (6) within the verbal root.

1. Preformatives and Sufformatives

Preformatives are elements added to the front of verbs that are an essential part of the verb itself (i.e., part of their *form*), elements added to the back are called *sufformatives*. Note, for example, the preformative and sufformative on this familiar verb form יִשְׁמְרוּ ("***they*** will keep").

Sufformative יִשְׁמְרוּ Preformative

"***they*** will keep"

2. Prefixes and Suffixes

Prefixes are components added onto the front of a word after it is fully formed. Components added to the back of a fully formed word are called *suffixes* (e.g., הֲיִשְׁמְר֫וּנוּ "**will** they keep **us?**"). When prefixes and suffixes are removed the word is still intact.

Suffix הֲיִשְׁמְר֫וּנוּ Prefix

"will they keep ***us?"***

3. Vocalic Sufformative or Vocalic Suffix

A *vocalic* ending is any ending that *begins with a vowel.* For example, the verb שָׁמְרוּ has a sufformative that begins with a vowel. In this case, the sufformative is only a vowel, but the main point is that it attaches to the verb by means of that vowel. Another example is the verb שְׁמָרָ֫נוּ, which has an attached suffix that begins with a long /ā/ (ָנוּ).

Vocalic sufformative שָׁמְרוּ

4. Consonantal Sufformative or Consonantal Suffix

On the other hand, a *consonantal* ending is one that *begins with a consonant.* For example, the verb שָׁמַ֫רְתָּ ("***you*** kept") has a sufformative that begins with a *tav* (תָּ). Likewise, the verb שְׁמַרְכֶם ("he kept ***you***") has a suffix that begins with a *kaph* (כֶם).

Consonantal sufformative שָׁמַ֫רְתָּ

5. Preformative Vowel

The vowel that stands under the preformative of a noun or verb is called a preformative vowel (e.g., יִשְׁמֹר).

preformative vowel יִשְׁמֹר

6. Theme Vowel

Theme vowel is a designation for the characteristic vowel of a verb that helps to distinguish it from related forms. In the verb paradigms this vowel is usually associated the second consonant of the root.

Theme vowel יִשְׁמֹר

BREAKING SENTENCES INTO MANAGEABLE UNITS

Verbs are the backbone of a Hebrew sentence. As you learn the Hebrew verbal system you will be able to appreciate the rich nuances of the Hebrew language. Verbs also provide important guideposts for breaking sentences into smaller units of thought. Beginning students struggle to translate, in large part because they have difficulty knowing how to group the Hebrew words together so that they make sense. Knowing the verbs will help you break a text down into manageable units so that you can deal with one unit of thought before moving on to the next.

Sentences, clauses, and phrases

Grammarians use the terms *sentence, clause,* and *phrase* to identify the clusters of words that create units of thought. A *sentence* includes *a subject, a verbal idea, and expresses a complete thought.* In English, every sentence must have a written verb. The subject, though usually written, can be implicit. For example, "She stayed" is a complete sentence. It tells who the sentence is about ("she" = subject), what was done ("stayed" = verb) and expresses an idea that can stand alone as a complete thought. English sentences can also have an implied subject. Thus, the command to "Stay!" is technically a sentence, though only the verb is written. The subject ("you") is implied. Since Hebrew verbs have built-in subjects (שָׁמַר = "*he* guarded"), many Hebrew sentences automatically have both a subject and a verb. However, unlike English, Hebrew allows a sentence to have an implied verb. Thus, the words יהוה אֱלֹהֵינוּ ("The Lord [is] our God") is a complete sentence in Hebrew even though it has no written verb.

Though sentences are familiar, a more fundamental unit of thought is the *clause.* A clause *must contain a subject and a verbal idea,* but unlike a sentence, it does not need to be a complete thought. For example, "because he went" has a subject ("he") and a verb ("went") but cannot stand alone as a complete thought. (Thus, sentences are clauses, but clauses are not necessarily sentences.) Like sentences, Hebrew clauses can have implied verbs. Grammarians refer to these as *verbless clauses* or *nominal clauses* (i.e., noun clauses). Nominal clauses are translated by supplying a form of the verb "to be." Since clauses are the most basic unit of thought that contain a verb, and verbs carry the action through the text, clauses are considered the primary units of thought in Hebrew.

In addition to a subject and verbal idea, a clause may also include *phrases* that provide supplemental information. A phrase *provides a unit of thought that complements the clause* and does not need a subject-verb component. For example, "he went" can be further clarified by the phrase *"to the temple."* The terms sentence, clause, and phrase are sometimes used interchangeably because of the measure of overlap in definition.

Hebrew clauses can be expressed independently, or they can be linked together in such a way that one or more clauses explain the main idea. For example, each of the following clauses stands alone.

> He arrived.
>
> He proclaimed the prophecy to the people.
>
> He received the prophecy from God.

However, those same clauses can be reconfigured to say:

> When he arrived,
>
> he proclaimed the prophecy to the people
>
> that he had received from God.

The central clause serves as the main idea and could stand alone. This is called the *main clause.* The other clauses are worded in such a way that they do not make sense on their own (i.e., "when he arrived"). Clauses that rely upon the main clause and convey supporting material are referred to as *subordinate clauses.*

Identifying Clauses Identifying clauses helps you identify the words that belong together when translating. Rather than finding a verb and putting it with any noun in the sentence that might fit (a typical beginner approach), seeing the larger structure of the sentence (syntax) allows the author to guide your grouping of ideas. Because clauses contain both a subject and verbal idea, each clause provides information with which the reader can paint a mental picture. When you allow the author's words to paint an image clause-by-clause, the passage will flow more smoothly, and you will be able to retain the concepts you just read—even after you have moved on to the next verse. Helpful guidelines for determining which Hebrew words belong together include:

- Every verb stands in its own clause. This includes places where the verb "to be" (e.g., am, is, are) is implied rather than stated.
- Verbs preceded by the conjunction begin a new clause (וְשָׁמְרָה "and she will guard"). This includes places where the negative particle לֹא intervenes between the conjunction and verb (וְלֹא שָׁמְרָה "and she did not guard").
- Some words consistently mark the presence of subordinate clauses—e.g. אֲשֶׁר ("who, which"), כִּי ("because, that"), לְמַעַן ("so that"), and פֶּן ("lest"). Each of these words begins a new clause that includes the words that immediately follow.
- Accents. The Masoretes used a system of accents to mark the rhythm and flow of the text. The accents serve several functions simultaneously, one of which is to show how the scribes grouped the words within each verse.

Notice the application of these principles to a passage you translated in chapter 7 (a modified versions of Gen 38:22). In the narrative below Judah has just sent his friend, Hirah, back to pay the harlot that Judah met along the road as they were going to shear their flocks. The text then states:

וַיֵּלֶךְ אֶל־יְהוּדָה וַיֹּאמֶר כִּי לֹא מָצָא אֶת־הַזּוֹנָה...

harlot — p.n. — (הלך)

The verse begins with a verb + conjunction that signals the start of a new clause ("and he went" circled above). The words "to Judah" fit naturally with this verb, a connection confirmed when the next verb + conjunction signals the start of a second clause ("and he said" circled above). The new clause will not draw from the words of the preceding clause. Immediately following the second verb you encounter the particle כִּי ("because, that") that signals the beginning of a third clause. Since כִּי introduces a subordinate clause, you can anticipate that this clause provides supporting information. Further, because every clause includes a subject and verb, you must continue reading as long as it takes to find the associated verb (in this case מָצָא circled above). The presence of a convenient direct object אֶת־הַזּוֹנָה serves as a natural conclusion to the verb מָצָא ("he found"), but even this would need to be confirmed by the next clause break in the narrative.

Another aid to identifying phrases and clauses is the accent marks added by early Hebrew scholars (called Masoretes) as an aid for reading. The translation exercises you have encountered thus far have not included these accents.[1] But from this point on, they do. These accents are discussed more fully in appendix 2, but for the sake of the present discussion, note that the accents appear as markings that do not match the vowels you learned. The text of Gen 1:1 is provided here to illustrate a biblical text with accents.

בְּרֵאשִׁ֖ית בָּרָ֣א אֱלֹהִ֑ים אֵ֥ת הַשָּׁמַ֖יִם וְאֵ֥ת הָאָֽרֶץ׃ Gen 1:1

While you should learn to recognize the clause breakdowns for yourself, these accents give you a reference point and may prove helpful in difficult passages. Accents fall into two main categories, those that intentionally group words together (*conjunctive*, think "conjoin") and those that mark a break in thought (*disjunctive*, think "disjoin"). The disjunctive accents are especially helpful for identifying clauses. The

1. All text taken directly from the Hebrew Bible contains the Masoretic accents; words without accents indicate portions that have been modified for the sake of the reader's skill level.

main accents to look for are the *atnaḥ* that marks the center point of the verse (֑) and the accents *zaqeph* (֔ or ֕) and *revia* (֗) that subdivide each half into smaller units. The end of the verse is marked with an accent called *silluq* and the "end-of-verse" symbol (: ֽ). If masoretic accents are applied to the previous example from the graded reader, one would find that the disjunctive accents correspond to the clause breaks.

↓ ↓ ↓

וַיֵּ֫לֶךְ אֶל־יְהוּדָ֔ה וַ֕יֹּאמֶר כִּי לֹא מָצָא אֶת־הַזּוֹנָ֑ה..

Recognizing individual clauses allows you to focus on a limited number of words at a time and provides boundaries for connecting ideas within the verse. Try to keep these clause division markers in mind as you read and translate.

Translating Units Within a Clause

Standard Word Order in Verbal Clauses

Word order can also provide clues for putting together sentences when translating. Since many sentences begin with a verb, the pronoun embedded in the verb serves as your first introduction to the subject. If a subject is specifically mentioned, it usually follows the verb. Any object (direct object, indirect object, or object of a preposition) typically follows the pattern Verb + Subject + Object.

זָכְרוּ אֶת־יהוה

"***They*** remembered the LORD"

זָכְרוּ הָאֲנָשִׁים אֶת־יהוה

"***The men*** remembered the LORD"

When the object of a sentence appears as a pronoun, word order often shifts. The pronoun usually appears between the verb and subject. This type of shift in word order is frequent, and you should learn to anticipate it. The same thing applies to pronouns in prepositional phrases.

וַיֹּאמֶר אַבְרָהָם אֶל־יהָאֱלֹהִים "And Abraham said ***to God***"	זָכְרוּ הָאֲנָשִׁים אֶת־יהוה "The men remembered ***the LORD***"	Noun as object
וַיֹּאמֶר אֵלָיו אַבְרָהָם "And Abraham said ***to him***"	זָכְרוּ אֹתוֹ הָאֲנָשִׁים "The men remembered ***him***"	Pronoun as object

Agreement within the Clause

Since the interrelationship of words within the clause is very important, related words should agree in gender and number. This agreement can help you make the appropriate word associations in a sentence. For example, in the phrase וַתִּקְרָא שְׁמוֹ יְהוּדָה, neither "his name" nor "Judah" can be the subject of a feminine verb, and one must translate "and ***she called*** his name Judah." However, grammatical agreement does not always occur like you would expect. Instead of thinking of exceptions as errors, remember that, as a living language, Hebrew reflects the idiosyncrasies of actual dialogue. When you read enough Hebrew, you will notice that the apparent inconsistencies often follow similar patterns. For example, the verb sometimes does not agree with the subject of the clause because a masculine verb is used as the default gender, because a singular subject like "seed" is actually a collective noun signifying many, or because the verb agrees with only the first in a list of stated subjects.

Indefinite or Impersonal Subjects

Sometimes a verb is used in such a way that no specific subject is intended but rather reflects an indefinite "someone" or impersonal "it." English also uses impersonal subjects with an active verb. For example, "they say the movie is great" is more colloquial than "the movie is said to be great." A speaker may have no specific individuals in mind, but an active verb is a common default. In such instances the verb may be translated like a passive. For example:

קָרָא שְׁמָהּ בָּבֶל	"its name *was called* Babel" (Gen 11:9) *lit. one called its name Babel*

Coordination of Clauses (Joining Clauses Together)

Most Hebrew clauses are joined together by the conjunction *waw*. This conjunction can be translated "and," but the *waw* is more appropriately described as a link between related words or phrases. Context determines the nature of that relationship. To create a smooth translation you need to determine the best way to express that relationship in English. For example, *waw* can express contrast ("but"), succession ("so then"), purpose ("so that" or "in order that"), a break in thought with a new idea ("Now"), or the second half of an "if" clause ("if . . . then"). Your task as a translator is to determine what the author is trying to say and then bring this out in your translation. Again, translation is not about decoding. One should not simply insert English equivalents for Hebrew words. You must comprehend what you are reading and then determine how best to convey that thought in English.

Increasing Your Reading Comprehension

Students who are learning to read Hebrew often find that they are so intently focused on the sentence they are trying to decipher that once they move on to the next sentence they have difficulty remembering what they just read. Moreover, students sometimes try to compensate for the differences between Hebrew and English word order by hunting for each successive part of an English sentence (first subject, then verb, etc.) in an attempt to create a sentence. Instead, when you read Hebrew, try to create a picture of the action in your mind in the order that the Hebrew author presents it. Allow the sentence to present a visual image that slowly comes into focus as each part of the sentence is presented.

The subject of the sentence should always be in the center of your mental image, and verbal action is always closely associated with the subject. Pay attention to the idea conveyed by the verbal root and to the active-passive-reflexive orientation of the verb. If the verb is active, anticipate that the character is generating the action (i.e., the action is moving out from the subject). If the verb is passive, anticipate that the action is flowing toward the subject. If the verb is reflexive, picture the individual doing that action to/for himself or herself.

Additional words or phrases add detail and dimension to your image. Prepositional phrases like "in the land" provide the backdrop or scene in which the action is taking place. Direct objects receive whatever action is being directed toward or against them. In this way you can reconstruct each part of the scene as it is presented in the sentence. You do not have to dissect the word order. Accept the sentence as it is presented, and allow the information to fill in your mental picture.

Your ability to quickly visualize the action will be the key to understanding the Hebrew text *while you read*. It is much easier to trace a series of visual images or scenes than to remember a string of Hebrew words. In fact, you will eventually find that if you can remember the images the author creates for you, you can reconstruct how the author worded it. After all, his presentation shapes your perception of the event—an event that could have been described in different ways.

CHAPTER 12

Vowel Changes in Verbs

Now that you have received an introduction to the Hebrew verbal system, it is time to focus on each verb stem and memorize the verbs that make up each paradigm. This chapter focuses on supplementing your understanding of vowel reductions in Hebrew verbs and outlining the methodology for learning verbs that is applied in the subsequent chapters.

VOWEL CHANGES IN VERBS

In chapter 5 you learned three rules that govern vowel changes in Hebrew words. These vowel rules were as follows:

Table 12.1: Rules for Vowel Change

1. **Closed unaccented syllables** require short vowels.
2. Near **open** syllables (1 syllable before the accent):
   a. Lengthen for Nouns.
   b. Reduce for Verbs—but lengthen a-class vowels and preformative vowels.
3. Distant **open** syllables (2+ before the accent).

(modified from Manuel, "Notes")

At the time we encouraged you to simply focus on the implications for nouns until we began learning the Hebrew verbs. It is now time to expand your understanding of the rules governing vowel change.

In all Hebrew words we find that closed unaccented syllables take short vowels and distant open syllables reduce. But in near open syllables nouns and adjectives lengthen historic short vowels, while verbs have a *tendency* to reduce them. The only exception to this principle is that verbs will not reduce the near open syllable if it contains an a-class vowel or if that vowel is part of the preformative. These principles of vowel reduction are applied throughout the entire verbal system.

As we begin discussing the Hebrew verbal system it is imperative that you reinforce your awareness of these rules for vowel change. Do not feel like you have to fully understand them at this time. We will reinforce these principles over and over again as we tackle each set of verbs. The key is to take advantage of how these rules might help you remember the shape and structure of the various Hebrew verbs.

The way that vowels react in verbs is driven by a desire to achieve clarity in communication by reducing the chance of overlap between similar forms. The fact that *near open syllables lengthen in nouns and reduce in verbs* maintains a distinction between parts of speech that would otherwise look identical (e.g., adj. חֲכָמָה "wise woman" vs. verb חָכְמָה "she was wise"). By preserving near open preformative vowels, Hebrew found a way to distinguish similar verb forms (e.g., *hiphil* pf. הֵקִים vs. *hiphil* impv. הָקִים). Likewise, verb forms that might otherwise be identical are made distinct by treating near open i-class and u-class vowels differently than near open a-class vowels (e.g., inf. cst. קְטוֹל vs. inf. abs. קָטוֹל).

DO NOT WORRY ABOUT EXCEPTIONS

Although the vowel rules are very important for understanding the changes that take place in most verbs, you will occasionally run across anomalous forms that do not seem to follow the rules you have learned. For example, in the familiar 3fs perfect קָֽטְלָה (derived from original קַטַל*) the near open a-class vowel does not lengthen like you would expect, and the distant open syllable does not reduce to match the vowel rules.

N D

קַ|טַ|לָ֫ה → קָֽטְלָה (but expect קְטָלָה*)

Anomalies such as this one are all due to the fact that the strong verb paradigms have undergone secondary modifications that sometimes obscure the original vowel changes. Remember that we are teaching you advanced concepts in order to ease in your mastery of Hebrew word formation. Where this information is useful we will call attention to its relevance. Where the development of the Hebrew language is complicated by multiple influences, we will encourage you to simply memorize forms.

The discussions on the *qal* verb in chapters 13–17 are foundational to all other discussions about the Hebrew verb. Using the *qal* verb as a template for the formation of the other verb stems (chs. 18–21) simplifies the process of learning the Hebrew strong verb. The strong verb together with the vowel rules will in turn help you identify verb forms that depart from the strong verb patterns because of the addition of direct object suffixes (chs. 22–23) or the presence of weak root letters (chs. 24–33).

USING THE QAL AS A TEMPLATE

As noted in the previous chapter, the Hebrew verbal system is comprised of seven basic verb stems that affect how the action of the verbal root is portrayed. Within each of these verb stems there is also a full set of paradigms that further modify the meaning of the verb.

<table>
<tr><th></th><th>Basic Meaning</th><th>Cause a State Look it up!</th><th>Cause an Action Look it up!</th></tr>
<tr><td>Active / Stative</td><td>QAL</td><td>PIEL</td><td>HIPHIL</td></tr>
<tr><td>Passive</td><td rowspan="2">NIPHAL</td><td>PUAL</td><td>HOPHAL</td></tr>
<tr><td>Reflexive</td><td>HITHPAEL</td><td></td></tr>
</table>

Perfect
Imperfect
Waw Consec. Perfect
Waw Consec. Imperf.
Jussive/Cohortative
Imperative
Participle
Infinitive

Because the various verb paradigms are replicated in each verb stem, the best way to master the Hebrew verbal system is to use the *qal* verb as a template for learning the preformatives and sufformatives that make up each verb conjugation (e.g., perfect, imperfect). In chapters 13–17 we will systematically deal with each conjugation of the *qal* verb so that you have time to memorize how they are formed and fully appreciate their meaning and significance. By chapter 16 you will be able to produce the verb forms in the following table.

Table 12.2: Using the Qal as a Template

	Ch. 16	
	Inf. Cst.	*Inf. Abs.*
	קְטֹל	קָטוֹל

	Ch. 13	**Ch. 14**	**Ch. 15**			**Ch. 16**
	Perfect	*Impf.*	*Jussive*		*Impv.*	*Active Ptc.*
he (3ms)	קָטַל	יִקְטֹל	יִקְטֹל			קֹטֵל
she (3fs)	קָטְלָה	תִּקְטֹל	תִּקְטֹל		(קָטְלָה)	קֹטְלָה
you (2ms)	קָטַלְתָּ	תִּקְטֹל	תִּקְטֹל	→	קְטֹל	(קֹטֶלֶת)
you (2fs)	קָטַלְתְּ	תִּקְטְלִי	תִּקְטְלִי	→	קִטְלִי	קֹטְלִים
I (1cs)	קָטַלְתִּי	אֶקְטֹל	אֶקְטְלָה			קֹטְלוֹת
						Passive Ptc.
they (3mp)	קָטְלוּ	יִקְטְלוּ	יִקְטְלוּ			קָטוּל
they (3fp)		תִּקְטֹלְנָה	תִּקְטֹלְנָה			קְטוּלָה
you (2mp)	קְטַלְתֶּם	תִּקְטְלוּ	תִּקְטְלוּ	→	קִטְלוּ	קְטוּלִים
you (2fp)	קְטַלְתֶּן	תִּקְטֹלְנָה	תִּקְטֹלְנָה	→	קְטֹלְנָה	קְטוּלוֹת
we (1cp)	קָטַלְנוּ	נִקְטֹל	נִקְטְלָה			

If you master the *qal* verb so that you can produce each form, the paradigms for the remaining verb stems, *niphal-hophal* (chs. 18–20), can be mastered by memorizing only four forms for each stem. For example, in the *niphal* you need only memorize the four forms highlighted in the chart below. The representative *niphal* perfect gives you the basic form to which the endings you of the *qal* perfect are added to create the *niphal* perfect. The representative *niphal* participle gives you the form to which the same endings are added that learn for in the *qal*. The infinitive construct gives you the base to which the same preformatives and sufformatives you observe in the *qal* will be added to create the imperfects, jussives, and imperatives. The infinitive absolute is included for memorization because it often has a unique form.

Table 12.3: Generating Stems From Four Key Forms

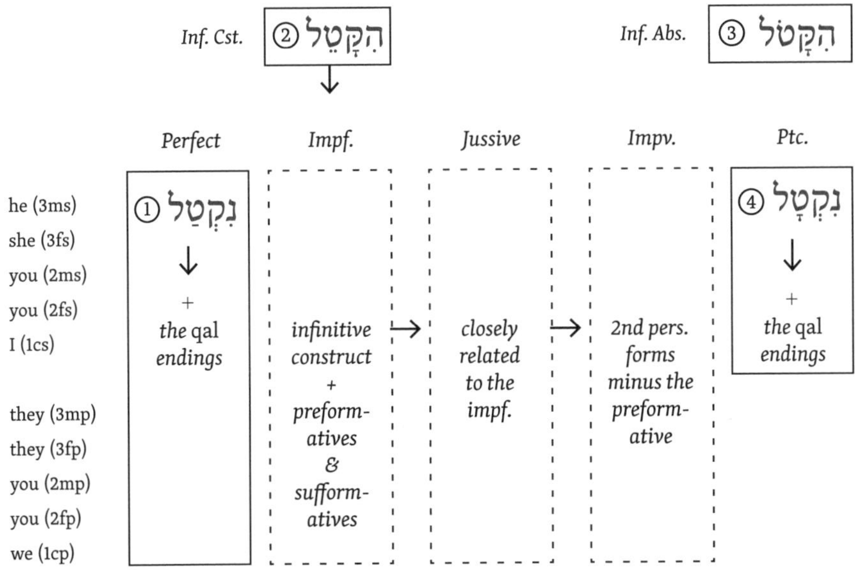

This same process is repeated for each of the verb stems—*niphal, piel, pual, hithpael, hiphil,* and *hophal*—with each new set only requiring four new forms to learn. As a result, while we cover the *qal* systematically in five chapters, giving you time to practice using it and memorizing it. The remaining verb stems can be learned with minimal memorization.

EXERCISE FOR CHAPTER 12

Complete the translation exercise for chapters 11–12.

CHAPTER 13

Qal Perfects

As briefly introduced in chapter 11, the *qal* (קַל "simple") is the most basic verb stem. The *qal* presents the subject doing or exhibiting the root idea (e.g., קָטַל "he kills" or גָּדַל "he is great"). Because it has a limited number of characteristic features, the *qal* provides a template for the other stems. The first of the *qal* conjugations that we will examine is the *qal* perfect. You have already become familiar with these verbs by using the third person forms קָטַל, קָטְלָה, and קָטְלוּ in the translation exercises.

MEANING OF THE QAL PERFECT

The term *perfect* is used to describe this verb conjugation because it is commonly understood to denote "complete action" in the mind of the speaker.[1] In other words, the speaker is looking at the whole act as a complete package. The perfect conjugation is used to communicate the following:

1. Complete action as past tense

Since these verbs look at the action as a complete package, perfect verbs are often used for the past tense. Past events are, after all, concluded and thus viewed as complete.

2. Complete action as present/future

Sometimes perfect verbs will be translated by an English present or future tense. Words that deal with thinking, knowing, and perceiving

1. The view represented here reflects the commonly accepted analysis of the Hebrew perfect. Scholars have suggested other portraits of the development and function of the perfect. Since these theories will be easier to follow in a discussion of advanced grammar after you have learned the fundamentals, they are not discussed here. For one of the more recent discussions see Elizabeth Robar, *The Verb and the Paragraph in Biblical Hebrew* (Leiden: Brill, 2015).

are frequently translated as a present. For example, a verb like יָדְעָה can mean "she knew" (past tense), but knowledge gained is not usually lost. As a result, יָדְעָה can be translated in some contexts as a present tense "she knows" (i.e., *she came to know*). The perfect is also used of future events when an event is viewed as certain in the mind of the speaker. This happens most frequently in prophetic and poetic texts.

3. Waw consecutive perfect

Another prominent use of the perfect is the *waw consecutive perfect* that you have been exposed to since the beginning of your translation exercises. We will discuss the *waw* consecutive perfects in more detail in a subsequent chapter. Until then, continue to assume that any perfects that appear in the translation exercises with a conjunction ("and") are *waw* consecutive perfects conveying a present/future tense.

Perfect	*Waw* Consecutive Perfect
שָׁמַר "he kept"	וְשָׁמַר "**and** he **will keep**"
שָֽׁמְרָה "she kept"	וְשָֽׁמְרָה "**and** she **will keep**"
שָֽׁמְרוּ "they kept"	וְשָֽׁמְרוּ "**and** they **will keep**"

The sense and meaning of the Hebrew perfect can be summarized in the following manner.

Perfect is COMPLETE ACTION in the mind of the speaker.

Perfect is generally *past* but can be *present/future*.

SUFFORMATIVES ON PERFECTS

The Hebrew perfect conjugation is formed by adding sufformatives to the end of the verb to designate the subject. Sufformatives refer to the endings that are attached to the end of the verbal root and are part of the "form" of the word itself. You have already learned the endings for the third person. The remainder of the perfects are usually formed by adding a sufformative adapted directly from the independent pronouns.[2] The following diagram outlines the various endings and corresponding independent pronouns.

Table 13.1: The Perfect Conjugation

	Singular			Plural	
	Sufformatives	*Pronouns*		*Sufformatives*	*Pronouns*
he (3ms)	□□□		they (3cp)	□□□וּ	
she (3fs)	□□□ָה				
you (2ms)	□□□ְתָּ†	אַתָּה	you (2mp)	□□□ְתֶּם	אַתֶּם
you (2fs)	□□□ְתְּ	אַתְּ	you (2fp)	□□□ְתֶּן	אַתֶּן
I (1cs)‡	□□□ְתִּי	(אָנֹכִי)❖	we (1cp)	□□□ְנוּ	אֲנַחְנוּ

† The 2ms sufformative sometimes appears with a vowel marker as in the pronoun (תָּה).

‡ The "c" in 1cs and 1cp stands for "common" and indicates that the form is used both for masculine and feminine.

❖ The 1cs pronoun is related to the ending on the verb. The shift from כ to ת was probably due to harmonization with the other verb forms.

A number of helpful observations can be made about these new perfect endings. First, the second person sufformatives have a close affinity with the second person suffixes you already learned. Note that ת endings indicate that you are dealing with a *verb sufformative* while כ endings indicate that you are dealing with a *pronoun suffix* (highlighted by the box in the diagram below).

2. Scholars speculate that the perfect may have started out as a noun clause made up of an adjective describing a state of being and a personal pronoun (e.g., כָּבֵד אַתָּה = *you are heavy*). This would then have later merged into a verb form applicable to all active verbs as well.

	Singular *sufformatives*	*pronoun suff.*		Plural *sufformatives*	*pronoun suff.*
you (2ms)	□□□ְתָּ	□ְךָ	you (2mp)	□□□ְתֶּם	□ְכֶם
you (2fs)	□□□ְתְּ	□ֵךְ	you (2fp)	□□□ְתֶּן	□ְכֶן
I (1cs)	□□□ְתִּי	□ִי	we (1cp)	□□□ְנוּ	□ֵ֫נוּ

Also be sure to distinguish between the first person sufformatives and suffixes. The first person singular perfect has a *tav* sufformative similar to the majority of forms in the verb paradigm. The first person plural may be more easily confused. However, you will often find an accented connecting vowel alerting you to the presence of the pronoun suffix. Context and vowel patterns will tell you whether you are looking at a noun or a verb.

Second, make sure that you maintain a clear distinction between the endings וּ ("they" 3cp) and נוּ ("we" 1cp). Students have a tendency to miss the *nun* and identify both endings as 3cp. Be alert for both options. Do not mistake *nun* as part of the root when it is actually part of the sufformative (בָּאנוּ "we came"). Likewise, do not assume that a *nun* is part of the sufformative when in fact it is part of the root (e.g., נָתְנוּ "they gave").

Finally, do not be surprised by the fact that the third feminine singular form is so similar to nouns. The Hebrew language is formed this way because the association between feminine forms is helpful. Moreover, the chance of confusing nouns and verbs is minimized by the context of the sentence and by differences in vowel reduction that distinguish nouns and verbs. Remember, nouns and adjectives lengthen near open syllables (e.g., חֲכָמָה "a wise woman") while verbs have a general tendency to reduce near open syllables (e.g.,חָֽכְמָה).

The table presented at the beginning of this section (table 13.1) presents the perfect endings using boxes in place of actual Hebrew roots in order to highlight the endings themselves. *Memorize these endings.* It is important that these endings jump off the page as you read so that you can quickly tell who is doing the action. These same endings are used for the perfect conjugation in every verb stem that you learn (e.g., the *qal, niphal, piel*) regardless of their unique vowel patterns. This means that the front of the word may look different depending on the type of verb stem, but the sufformative identifies it as a perfect and tells you who is doing the action.

FORMATION OF THE QAL PERFECT

You have already been exposed to the basic forms of the *qal* perfect from the introduction to the verb in chapter 4. The verbs שָׁמַר, שָׁמְרָה, and שָׁמְרוּ that are used as examples in that lesson give you a great start toward mastering the *qal* perfect. The only difference is that you will learn the strong verb patterns using the verb קָטַל ("he killed"), the standard in many Hebrew grammars.

Most of the *qal* perfect is created by attaching sufformatives directly to the verb you learned on your vocabulary card. Thus, the verb קָטַל ("he killed") produces קָטַלְתָּ (you m.sg.), קָטַלְתְּ (you f. sg.), קָטַלְתִּי (I), קָטַלְנוּ (we), and so on. Remember that every consonant in a word except the final consonant must have vowel pointing, the final root letter appears with *shewa* when the addition of an ending leaves that letter without some kind of vowel notation (e.g., תָּ + קָטַל → קָטַלְתָּ).

The second person plural verbs have heavy endings, so named because they always require the accent. This naturally results in a reduction of the distant open syllable, following the vowel rules. Thus you find a shift from *קָטַלְתֶּם → קְטַלְתֶּם and *קָטַלְתֶּן → קְטַלְתֶּן. When the verb adds a vocalic sufformative (one that starts with a vowel), the perfects have a *shewa* in the near open syllable (e.g., קָטְלָה and קָטְלוּ). A more precise explanation for the vocalization of קָטְלָה and קָטְלוּ is presented at the end of this lesson, but some students find it easier to simply memorize the form without worrying about how it developed.

The *Qal* Perfect

	Active
he (3ms)	קָטַל
she (3fs)	קָֽטְלָה
you (2ms)	קָטַ֫לְתָּ
you (2fs)	קָטַ֫לְתְּ
I (1cs)	קָטַ֫לְתִּי
they (3mp)†	קָֽטְלוּ
they (3fp)	*same*
you (2mp)	קְטַלְתֶּם
you (2fp)	קְטַלְתֶּן
we (1cp)	קָטַ֫לְנוּ

† The 3mp form serves for both genders and can be labeled 3cp. However, it is easiest to keep the 3fp slot in the table because other conjugations have a distinct 3fp form.

ACTIVE AND STATIVE PATTERNS OF THE QAL PERFECT

Memorize the *qal* perfect according to the forms above, but be aware that the vowel pattern can vary slightly. In the *qal,* Hebrew distinguishes between *active verbs* where the subject is doing the action and *stative verbs* where the subject is described by that verb. Active and stative patterns are sometimes distinguished by their vowel patterns. For example, the active verb קָטַל ("he killed") and the stative verbs גָּדַל ("he was great"), כָּבֵד ("he was heavy"), and קָטֹן ("he was small") are all *qal* perfects. The vowel in the second syllable of these *qal* verbs is called the *theme vowel* because it helps differentiate these verbs.

The *qal* perfect is characterized by an a-class vowel in the first syllable. *Qal* perfects in which the subject is performing an action (active verbs) always have an a-class theme vowel in the second syllable (e.g., קָטַל "he killed"). However, *qal* perfects that are used to describe qualities or states of being (called *stative verbs*) can have any vowel class in the second syllable (כָּבֵד "he was great," גָּדַל "he was heavy," קָטֹן "he was small"), though the a-class pattern will still be the most prevalent.

Because the a-class theme vowel is so prevalent, you will have to rely upon your familiarity with the vocabulary and upon the context to determine whether most *qal* perfects are active or stative. However, a perfect with an i-class or u-class theme vowel is immediately flagged as stative.

Active perfects	Stative perfects
קָטַל	גָּדַל כָּבֵד קָטֹן

You have already seen evidence of this important distinction in theme vowels in the translation exercises, though you did not recognize it at the time. For example, if a verb loses one of its root letters so that it ends up having only one syllable instead of two, the theme vowel is the one that is preserved because it gives you the most information about the verb. The verb בָּא ("he came" from בוא) has an a-class vowel because it is an active verb. The verb מֵת ("he died" from מות) has an i-class vowel because it is a stative verb (i.e., "he is dead").

The a-class theme vowel is the most dominant pattern in the verb paradigm, being used for all the active verbs and for most of the stative verbs. In fact, the i-class stative preserves its distinctive vowel only in the third masculine singular כָּבֵד. The u-class pattern is the only one that maintains a unique vowel pattern throughout the entire paradigm. The original short u-class vowel either lengthens under the accent (e.g., קָטֹנְתָּ "you [ms] were small"), remains short in a closed unaccented syllable (e.g., קְטָנְתֶּם = *qetontem* "you [mp] were small"), or reduces in a near open syllable (e.g., קָטְנוּ "they were small").[3] Since most of the *qal* perfects are going to follow the a-class pattern, concentrate on memorizing the paradigm for קָטַל and the three representative stative verbs (גָּדַל, כָּבֵד, קָטֹן). The latter will help you recognize the alternate

3. Most verbs are recognized as active or stative based on your familiarity with vocabulary. However, when you are reading an unfamiliar passage and run across a verb you do not know, an i-class or u-class *qal* perfect can help at least give you a frame of reference. You can recognize it is a stative verb and perhaps have a good sense from the passage what the meaning of the verb is.

theme vowels that can appear in the text. The following table shows how the *qal* perfect for stative verbs compares to the standard *qal* perfect you must memorize.[4]

Table 13.2: The *Qal* Perfects

	Active	Stative		
	(a-class)	(a-class)	(i-class)	(u-class)
he (3ms)	קָטַל	גָּדַל	כָּבֵד	קָטֹן
she (3fs)	קָטְלָה	גָּדְלָה	כָּבְדָה	קָטְנָה
you (2ms)	קָטַלְתָּ	גָּדַלְתָּ	כָּבַדְתָּ	קָטֹנְתָּ
you (2fs)	קָטַלְתְּ	גָּדַלְתְּ	כָּבַדְתְּ	קָטֹנְתְּ
I (1cs)	קָטַלְתִּי	גָּדַלְתִּי	כָּבַדְתִּי	קָטֹנְתִּי
they (3mp)	קָטְלוּ	גָּדְלוּ	כָּבְדוּ	קָטְנוּ
they (3fp)				
you (2mp)	קְטַלְתֶּם	גְּדַלְתֶּם	כְּבַדְתֶּם	קְטָנְתֶּם
you (2fp)	קְטַלְתֶּן	גְּדַלְתֶּן	כְּבַדְתֶּן	קְטָנְתֶּן
we (1cp)	קָטַלְנוּ	גָּדַלְנוּ	כָּבַדְנוּ	קָטֹנּוּ

DISTINGUISHING BETWEEN QAL PERFECT AND NOUNS

The *qal* perfect has a historic a-class vowel in the first syllable, for example, קָטְלָה (pronounced *qā-tᵉ-lā*). Noun patterns with a similar appearance have a different syllable structure and vowel. For example, the verb חָכְמָה ("she was wise") is pronounced חָ|כְ|מָה (*ḥā-kᵉ-mā*) following the paradigm קָטְלָה (*qā-tᵉ-lā*). You also know from your vocabulary that the noun חָכְמָה ("wisdom") is pronounced חָכְ|מָה (*ḥok-mā*). This distinction in word formation is particularly helpful for determining the correct pronunciation of ambiguous words. Since the first vowel could be equally identified as a long /ā/ or short /o/, context determines which vowel you must use.

4. In table 13.2, note again that the 3mp form serves for both genders. In the 1cp form of קָטֹן, notice that the vowelless *nun* at the end of the syllable has assimilated just like it does with the preposition מִן (i.e., קָטֹנְנוּ → קָטֹנּוּ).

Nouns	***Qal* verbs**
(*'ok-lā*) אָכְ|לָה	(*'ā-kᵉ-lā*) אָ|כְ|לָה
(*ḥok-mā*) חָכְ|מָה	(*ḥā-kᵉ-mā*) חָ|כְ|מָה

If you understand the text you are reading and know whether you are approaching a verb or a noun, you will know how to pronounce the word.

In cases like the examples above, when syllable division might be confusing, the Masoretes occasionally inserted a short vertical line called a *metheg* ("bridle") to aid you in pronunciation.

Nouns	**Verbs**
(*'ok-lā*) אָכְ|לָה	(*'ā-kᵉ-lā*) אָֽ|כְ|לָה
(*ḥok-mā*) חָכְ|מָה	(*ḥā-kᵉ-mā*) חָֽ|כְ|מָה

It may be helpful to think of the *metheg* like the "bridle" on a horse. The *metheg* holds you back and keeps you from rushing forward to the next consonant. As a result, it forces you to draw out the vowel and make the *shewa* vocal. The *metheg* can alert you to the presence of a long /ā/.

Unfortunately, the *metheg* is not consistently applied in these contexts and slows down pronunciation in contexts other than just long /ā/ before *shewa*.[5] Though the *metheg* occasionally proves helpful for distinguishing long /ā/ and short /o/, you will find that your familiarity with the structural patterns of words is more reliable.

ANOMALIES IN THE VOWELS OF THE QAL PERFECT

Some verbs in the *qal* perfect paradigm do not seem to follow the rules for vowel change. In the 3fs קָטְלָה and the 3cp קָטְלוּ the near open syllable is not lengthened and the distant open syllable is not reduced. Though the vowel rules were in fact faithfully applied, the words have gone through additional changes. The discussion below explains these apparent anomalies. You are not expected to master this material. It serves only to expose you to the issues so that you will have a framework for more advanced discussions later in your study. Moreover, it

5. See Yeivin, *Introduction*, 240–64.

reiterates that the general principles are reliable and form an important frame of reference for understanding the whole language. For now you should simply memorize the *qal* perfects as a template for all the verb paradigms and try to follow the discussion below. These concepts are revisited in later lessons.

Most of the verbs in the biblical text follow the vowel rules as you would expect. However, a handful of forms (e.g., *qal* perfect 3fs קָטְלָה and 3cp קָטְלוּ) now appear with the accent at the end of the word, and the vowel where the accent once stood has been replaced with a *shewa*. These altered forms seem to depart from the standard vowel rules by creating the impression that they have reduced near open a-class vowels (that should lengthen) and have lengthened distant open syllables (that should reduce). In actuality the vowel rules were consistently applied, but a secondary accent shift obscures the original form. The original forms of these verbs are preserved when words appear in a major pause like at the end of a verse (compare קָטְלָה with pausal form קָטָ֫לָה).

Biblical Hebrew provides evidence of further development in Hebrew verbs. The rules for vowel change (table 12.1) were consistently applied to all Hebrew verbs throughout all the paradigms. However, years later the accent shifted to the final syllable of verbs with vocalic sufformatives.[6] When this shift in accent took place, people no longer reacted to short vowels like they had centuries before. (Otherwise, the short vowel in a near open syllable would have lengthened according to Rule 2, and the distant open syllable would have reduced according to Rule 3). Those changes in pronunciation had long been forgotten. Instead, when the accent shifted on verbs with vocalic sufformatives, the short vowel in this newly created near open syllable reduced to *shewa*, regardless of vowel class.

a-class (קָטַל)	*קָטַ֫לוּ	→	קָטְל֫וּ
i-class (כָּבֵד)	*כָּבִ֫דוּ	→	כָּבְד֫וּ
u-class (קָטֹן)	*קָטֻ֫נוּ	→	קָטְנ֫וּ

Since the rules for vowel change were no longer in operation, no additional changes were made to the rest of the syllables in the verb. As a result, the current verb paradigms exhibit anomalies in only a handful of forms with vocalic sufformatives. The illustration below provides a step-by-step explanation of the development of verbs with vocalic sufformatives.

		Initial vowel changes	*Later adaptations*	
	Original form	Rule 2: Near open /a/ lengthens	Accent shifts with vocalic sufformatives	Reduction of near open syll. (all vowel classes)
Qal perf.	קַטַ֫לוּ →	קָטַ֫לוּ →	קָטַלוּ֫ →	קָטְלוּ

At this later date, the vowel rules were no longer applied. The distant open qamets remained.

The rules for vowel changes in verbs that you have learned are applicable to all verbs. They become most pertinent in later lessons (1) when we are dealing with infinitives and participles, (2) when attaching direct object suffixes to the end of the verb, and (3) when you are introduced to weak verbs. At this stage of your training, learn the forms by memorizing the *qal* paradigm. Use the rules for vowel change to the fullest extent that they can help you. When you run across a verb with slight anomalies in vowel pattern, remember that it is the result of accent shifts that occurred after the vowel rules were applied.

DEALING WITH IRREGULAR ROOTS

By now you have become accustomed to dealing with irregular verb forms in your translations because we taught you to focus on the structural components at the beginning and ending of each verb. Thus a root with a sufformative but no preformative must be a perfect, regardless

6. Remember that a vocalic sufformative is a sufformative that begins with a vowel.

of its form (e.g., קָטְלוּ and בָּאוּ). Similarly, a root with a preformative must be an imperfect, regardless of its form (e.g., יִקְטֹל and יָבוֹא).

Irregular forms (weak verbs) are discussed in more detail later in the grammar so that you understand why they have a different shape and pronunciation. For now, rest assured that the translations include only the verb forms you know (perfect, imperfect, and *waw* consecutives), and that irregular roots are glossed to ensure proper identification. You should be able to recognize a *qal* perfect of the irregular verbs using your skills of deductive reasoning. While you may find that the shape and vocalization of some verbs differs from the קָטַל paradigm you are memorizing, the characteristic sufformatives equip you to identify and translate the *qal* perfect (e.g., קָטַ֫לְתָּ "you killed," בָּ֫אתָ "you came," חָטָ֫אתָ "you sinned," עָנִ֫יתָ "you answered").

EXERCISE FOR CHAPTER 13 Memorize the *qal* perfect paradigm in the chart below and then complete the exercise and translation for chapter 13 in the workbook.

QAL PERFECTS VERB CHART

			Inf. Cst.		*Inf. Abs.*	
	Pf.	*Impf.*	*Juss.*	*Impv.*		*Active Ptc.*
he (3ms)	קָטַל					
she (3fs)	קָֽטְלָה					
you (2ms)	קָטַ֫לְתָּ					
you (2fs)	קָטַ֫לְתְּ					
I (1cs)	קָטַ֫לְתִּי					
they (3mp)						*Passive Ptc.*
they (3fp)	קָֽטְלוּ					
you (2mp)	קְטַלְתֶּם					
you (2fp)	קְטַלְתֶּן					
we (1cp)	קָטַ֫לְנוּ					

CHAPTER 14

Qal Imperfects

You are already familiar with some of the *qal* imperfects because you have used third person imperfects in the translation exercises (e.g., יִקְטֹל, תִּקְטֹל, and יִקְטְלוּ). This chapter reviews the meaning of the imperfect verb and discusses the preformatives and sufformatives that are used to create the entire imperfect paradigm.

MEANING OF THE IMPERFECT

The term *imperfect* is used to describe this verb conjugation because it denotes "incomplete action" in the mind of the speaker.[1] In other words, the speaker is envisioning the action in his mind as an ongoing event. Because of this outlook you will see the imperfect conjugation used in the following ways:

1. Incomplete action as present/future

Since the imperfect denotes incomplete action in the mind of the speaker, it is primarily used to describe actions that correspond to our present or future tense. After all, events that are incomplete and ongoing are usually taking place in the present or will take place in the future. Imperfects are used regardless of whether the future event is actual or hypothetical (e.g., "he will go" vs. "he would go"). In English this distinction is expressed by the addition of words like "would" or "should." You will need to rely on the immediate context to determine what sense to use with a Hebrew imperfect.

1. The view represented here reflects the commonly accepted analysis of the Hebrew imperfect. Scholars have suggested other theories about the development and function of the imperfect. Since these theories will be easier to follow in a discussion of advanced grammar after you have learned the fundamentals, they are not discussed here. For one of the more recent discussions see Robar, *Verb and the Paragraph*.

2. Incomplete action as continuous past

Imperfects are sometimes used to emphasize continuous action in the past. Such uses of the imperfect reflect the ongoing, incomplete nature of the activity or vividly express the event as if it were just happening. For example:

כָּ֣כָה יַעֲשֶׂה אִיּוֹב כָּל־הַיָּמִים	Thus Job ***used to do*** all the time (Job 1:5)
אָז יָשִׁיר־מֹשֶׁה וּבְנֵי יִשְׂרָאֵל אֶת־הַשִּׁירָה הַזֹּאת ליהוה	Then Moses and the sons of Israel ***were singing*** this song to the LORD (Exod 15:1)

With this range of possible meanings, it is important to rely upon the context to get some kind of sense for what the Hebrew imperfect conveys. Remember that the imperfect denotes "incomplete action" in the mind of the speaker (i.e., how he views the action he is narrating) and is often translated with an English present or future tense. However, it is occasionally used for past events to emphasize ongoing action or vivid narration.

Imperfect is INCOMPLETE ACTION in the mind of the speaker.
Imperfect is generally *present/future* but can be *continuous past*.

FORMATION OF THE IMPERFECT

The Hebrew imperfect conjugation identifies the subject of the verb primarily by means of preformatives (e.g., י□□□ = 3ms "he"). This is the opposite of what we saw with the *qal* perfects where the subject of the verb is identified by means of sufformatives. A few imperfect forms also have a sufformative element in order to help distinguish gender and number.

The table below illustrates the imperfect preformatives and sufformatives using boxes instead of actual Hebrew roots in order to highlight the identifying markers themselves. Learn to quickly spot these indicators of person, gender, and number. In an effort to focus your attention on the formation of the imperfect and to underscore the fact that these same forms are used with all verbs stems (*qal, niphal, piel,* etc.), this initial diagram presents only preformatives and sufformatives.

Table 14.1: The Imperfect Conjugation

	Singular		Plural
he (3ms)	י□□□	they (3mp)	י□□□וּ
she (3fs)	ת□□□	they (3fp)	ת□□□ְנָה
you (2ms)	ת□□□	you (2mp)	ת□□□וּ
you (2fs)	ת□□□ִי	you (2fp)	ת□□□ְנָה
I (1cs)	א□□□ (cf. אָנֹכִי)	we (1cp)	נ□□□ (cf. אֲנַחְנוּ)

The preformatives and sufformatives evidence some helpful patterns. First, plurals are usually distinguished from singulars by the sufformatives וּ (all masculine plural)and נָה (all feminine plural). A sufformative is not required in the first person plural "we" because of the unique preformative (נ) that distinguishes it from all the others. Second, the preformatives of the imperfect exhibit patterns that revolve around one's frame of reference or place in a conversation. Third person imperfects are related in form, second person forms also share similar features, and first person forms both have unique preformatives reminiscent of the first person pronouns.

Patterns for the Third Person Imperfect

Those about whom you are talking (third person) are described using verbs with *yod* or *tav* pattern depending on gender. Any imperfect with a *yod* preformative (e.g., יִקְטֹל and יִקְטְלוּ) designates masculine gender, regardless of whether it refers to an individual (sg.) or a group (pl.). The distinction in number is conveyed using the וּ sufformative for masculine plural. In English we would use the pronouns *he, it, they* to represent these verbs.

	Singular		Plural	
he (3ms)	י□□□	they (3mp)	י□□□וּ	*third person*
she (3fs)	תּ□□□	they (3fp)	תּ□□□ְנָה	
you (2ms)	תּ□□□	you (2mp)	תּ□□□וּ	*second person*
you (2fs)	תּ□□□ִי	you (2fp)	תּ□□□ְנָה	
I (1cs)	א□□□	we (1cp)	נ□□□	*first person*

Feminine verbs describing the actions of those outside the scope of your conversation (third person) are represented by verbs that begin with the preformative *tav* (e.g., תִּקְטֹל and תִּקְטֹלְנָה). You know from the feminine construct ending (e.g., סוּסַת "mare of" that ת is often associated with feminine forms). The *tav* preformative is used for third person feminine regardless of whether it is an individual (sg.) or a group (pl.). The distinction in number is conveyed by the נָה sufformative for feminine plural. These third person feminine subjects are translated into English using the pronouns *she, it, they.*

Patterns for the Second Person Imperfect

Those to whom you are directly speaking (second person) are always designated by verbs that begin with the letter *tav* (ת), regardless of their gender (e.g., תִּקְטֹל, תִּקְטְלִי, תִּקְטְלוּ, and תִּקְטֹלְנָה). This is similar to the use of *tav* in the second person perfects that you learned in the last chapter (i.e., קָטַלְתָּ, קָטַלְתְּ, קְטַלְתֶּם, קְטַלְתֶּן).

Because the second person imperfects all begin with the *tav* preformative, sufformatives are needed to differentiate each of these forms. The וּ (m. pl.) and נָה (f. pl.) endings clearly identify the gender and number of the plural second person verbs. Another ending was required to distinguish when you are talking directly to a woman (תִּקְטְלִי "you" f.) and when you are talking to a man (e.g., תִּקְטֹל ("you" m.).

	Singular		Plural	
he (3ms)	י□□□	they (3mp)	י□□□וּ	*third person*
she (3fs)	תּ□□□	they (3fp)	תּ□□□ְנָה	
you (2ms)	תּ□□□	you (2mp)	תּ□□□וּ	*second person*
you (2fs)	תּ□□□ִי	you (2fp)	תּ□□□ְנָה	
I (1cs)	א□□□	we (1cp)	נ□□□	*first person*

It may initially seem a bit disconcerting that the second feminine singular ending is just like the first person singular pronoun suffix that you saw on nouns (e.g., סוּסִי "***my*** horse"), but there are a limited number of options available for creating new combinations, so some overlap in form is inevitable. Nouns and verbs serve distinct roles and the context usually dictates when you are dealing with a verb and when you are dealing with a noun.

Another observation about the second person imperfects is that two forms overlap with third person forms.

	Singular		Plural	
he (3ms)	י□□□	they (3mp)	י□□□וּ	*third person*
she (3fs)	תּ□□□	they (3fp)	תּ□□□ְנָה	
you (2ms)	תּ□□□	you (2mp)	תּ□□□וּ	*second person*
you (2fs)	תּ□□□ִי	you (2fp)	תּ□□□ְנָה	

The verb תִּקְטֹל could refer to the actions of a woman outside of the immediate conversation ("she will kill") or serve as a direct address to an individual man ("you will kill"). Similarly, the verb תִּקְטֹלְנָה could refer to a group of women outside your conversation ("they will kill") or a group of women to whom you are speaking ("y'all will kill"). In each case context determines whether a second or third person verb is most appropriate.

Patterns for the First Person Imperfect

The first person endings are easily distinguished from the other forms because of their unique preformatives. The first person singular is marked with an *aleph*, perhaps drawing upon the initial consonant of the pronoun אָנֹכִי ("I"). The first person plural is introduced with a *nun* that is probably derived from the personal pronoun אֲנַחְנוּ ("we").

ACTIVE AND STATIVE PATTERNS OF THE QAL IMPERFECT

Like the *qal* perfect, the *qal* imperfect has vowel patterns that distinguish between active and stative verbs. As you may recall, the *qal* perfect has a fixed a-class theme vowel in the active (e.g., קָטַל) and a variable theme vowel in the stative (e.g., גָּדַל, כָּבֵד, or קָטֹן). In the *qal* imperfect this pattern is reversed. The actives have a variable theme vowel (e.g., a-class יִלְמַד, i-class יִתֵּן, or u-class יִקְטֹל)[2] and the statives have a fixed a-class theme vowel (e.g., יִכְבַּד).

	Qal actives	*Qal* statives
Perfects	קָטַל	קָטֹן כָּבֵד גָּדַל
Imperfects	יִקְטֹל (יִתֵּן) יִלְמַד	יִכְבַּד

Historically, the *qal* imperfects were also distinguished by preformative vowels. The *qal* actives had a historic a-class preformative vowel and the *qal* statives had a historic i-class preformative vowel (e.g., יַקְטֹל* vs. יִכְבַּד). The *qal* imperfects that you are currently learning have lost this distinction and were harmonized so that they have an i-class preformative vowel regardless of whether they are active (e.g., יִלְמַד, יִקְטֹל) or

2. There is no suitable example of a strong verb with i-class theme vowel. The i-class pattern is common in weak verbs. While you have not yet been formally introduced to these weak verbs, many of them you have encountered glossed in your translation exercises. e.g., יָשִׂים (from שׂים), יִתֵּן (from נתן), and יֵשֵׁב (from ישׁב).

stative (e.g., יִכְבַּד). The original a-class preformative vowel of the active is now seen only in certain irregular verb forms. You have already run across irregular *qal* verbs with this a-class preformative vowel in your translations, for example, יָבוֹא ("he will come"), יַעֲשֶׂה ("he will do"), and יָשִׂים ("he will put"). Though you are able to identify them using your basic understanding of preformatives and sufformatives, you can now see that these are not truly exceptions. They preserve the historic a-class preformative vowel of the *qal* imperfect.

These vowel variations are the reason we stressed that you spot the basic perfect and imperfect structures rather than worrying about the vowels. The *qal* has the most variation of all the Hebrew verbs. Just because a verb does not match the vowel pattern you memorized for the קָטַל paradigm does not mean it is not a *qal*. At this point you can assume that most of the imperfects in your translations are *qal* verbs. As you learn new verb stems (stems that are relatively fixed in comparison with the *qal*), you will be able to confirm the identity of a troublesome *qal* verb by virtue of the fact that it is *not* one of the other verb stems.

The table below summarizes historic features of the *qal* verb.

Table 14.2: Historic Patterns of the *Qal* Verb

	Qal actives	*Qal* statives
Perfects	קָטַל **(a + a)**	כָבד (? under ב) **(a + ?)**
Imperfects	*יַקְטל (? under ט) **(a + ?)**	יִכְבַּד **(i + a)**

? = any vowel class

In this table the roots קטל and כבד are used only as representative forms. The root קטל is used to represent all active *qal* verbs and the root כבד is used to represent all stative *qal* verbs. The question mark (?) shows where the vowel class is variable. The highlighted vowels under the preformative of the imperfect remind us that the historic preformative vowel was once an a-class vowel in the active verbs and an i-class vowel in the stative verbs. Consistent with the יִקְטֹל paradigm, many *qal* imperfects have an i-class preformative vowel. However, do not be surprised when some *qal* imperfects preserve the historic a-class preformative.

Memorize the paradigm for the *qal* imperfect of קטל (see column in bold in table 14.3) and be able to write it out with the appropriate vowels and accent. Since the *qal* imperfects take the same preformatives and sufformatives regardless of which theme vowel is used, recognize other theme vowels as simple variations of the *qal* imperfect. Start with the basic form יִקְטֹל and use it to generate the rest of the paradigm. Most of the verbs in this paradigm reflect this same verbal core. Note, for example, how יִקְטֹל ("he will kill") can be used to produce תִּקְטֹל (she/you), אֶקְטֹל (I), תִּקְטֹ֫לְנָה (they or y'all), and נִקְטֹל (we). Every consonant in a word except the final consonant must have some vowel notation. When the addition of a sufformative leaves the final root letter without a vowel notation, a *shewa* is added (e.g., תִּקְטֹל + נָה → תִּקְטֹ֫לְנָה). When the verb takes a vocalic sufformative (one that starts with a vowel) it follows the *general tendency* of verbs to reduce near open syllables (e.g., *תִּקְטֹלִי → תִּקְטְלִי and *תִּקְטֹלוּ → תִּקְטְלוּ). Imperfects with a-class theme vowels also reduce to shewa in a manner that seems contrary to Vowel Rule 2 (near open a-class vowels lengthen in verbs). However, the reduction to *shewa* in these forms results from a later shift in accent (i.e., the same phenomenon seen in the *qal* perfect described in ch. 13).

Table 14.3: The *Qal* Imperfects

	Actives			Statives
	(a-class)	(i-class)	(u-class)	(a-class)
he (3ms)	יִלְמַד	(יִתֵּן)	יִקְטֹל	יִכְבַּד
she (3fs)	תִּלְמַד		תִּקְטֹל	תִּכְבַּד
you (2ms)	תִּלְמַד		תִּקְטֹל	תִּכְבַּד
you (2fs)	תִּלְמְדִי		תִּקְטְלִי	תִּכְבְּדִי
I (1cs)	אֶלְמַד		אֶקְטֹל	אֶכְבַּד
they (3mp)	יִלְמְדוּ		יִקְטְלוּ	יִכְבְּדוּ
they (3fp)	תִּלְמַ֫דְנָה		תִּקְטֹ֫לְנָה	תִּכְבַּ֫דְנָה
you (2mp)	תִּלְמְדוּ		תִּקְטְלוּ	תִּכְבְּדוּ
you (2fp)	תִּלְמַ֫דְנָה		תִּקְטֹ֫לְנָה	תִּכְבַּ֫דְנָה
we (1cp)	נִלְמַד		נִקְטֹל	נִכְבַּד

Learn to spot preformatives and sufformatives on the *qal* imperfect, despite variable theme vowels, and to recognize historic preformative vowels. Those skills prepare you to identify *qal* imperfects in irregular verbs. Irregular roots, often called weak roots, are systematically discussed in chapters 24–33. For now, if you run across a weak verb like יָבוֹא ("he will come") from the root בוֹא, you can identify it as a *qal* imperfect because of the *yod* preformative. In fact, the whole paradigm bears a striking resemblance to the imperfect forms you memorize. Thus you will see יָבוֹא (he), תָּבוֹא (she), תָּבוֹא and תָּב֫וֹאִי (you), אָבוֹא (I), יָב֫וֹאוּ (they), and so on.

EXERCISE FOR CHAPTER 14

Memorize the *qal* imperfect paradigm in the chart below and then complete the exercise and translation for chapter 14 in the workbook.

QAL IMPERFECTS VERB CHART

Inf. Cst.

Inf. Abs.

	Pf.	*Impf.*	*Juss.*	*Impv.*	*Active Ptc.*
he (3ms)	קָטַל	יִקְטֹל			
she (3fs)	קָֽטְלָה	תִּקְטֹל			
you (2ms)	קָטַ֫לְתָּ	תִּקְטֹל			
you (2fs)	קָטַ֫לְתְּ	תִּקְטְלִי			
I (1cs)	קָטַ֫לְתִּי	אֶקְטֹל			
					Passive Ptc.
they (3mp)	קָֽטְלוּ	יִקְטְלוּ			
they (3fp)		תִּקְטֹ֫לְנָה			
you (2mp)	קְטַלְתֶּם	תִּקְטְלוּ			
you (2fp)	קְטַלְתֶּן	תִּקְטֹ֫לְנָה			
we (1cp)	קָטַ֫לְנוּ	נִקְטֹל			

CHAPTER 15

Qal Volitionals

Now that you have learned to create the full paradigms for the verb forms you learned at the beginning of your study of Hebrew, it is time to address some new types of verbs. The *qal* perfect and imperfect are what grammarians refer to as *indicatives*. The significance of this term can best be remembered by noting that such verbs "indicate" facts that occur in past, present, or future time. *Volitional verbs* (or *volitives*) are not statements of fact but rather require some kind of response on the part of an individual before these actions can be realized. The outcome of these verbs is thus "voluntary," regardless of how mildly or forcefully these requests are made. The meaning of these verbs is similar to ideas we express in English. The formation of these verbs is similar to the *qal* imperfect that you just learned.

MEANING OF THE VOLITIONAL VERBS

Hebrew has two kinds of volitional verbs: the jussive/cohortative and the imperative. Together these two types of verbs allow a person to voice intentions, requests, and commands in first, second, and third person.

Imperative

The term *imperative* is another word for a command. The label for these verbs is derived from an awareness that when you are given a command it is "imperative" (necessary) that you do as you are told. There are three things to remember about Hebrew imperatives. First, in both English and Hebrew a command is always spoken directly to the person with whom you are speaking. We do not give commands to someone outside our immediate conversation. Thus, Hebrew imperatives appear only in second person "you."[1] Second, an imperative is a request used by anyone, regardless of position or authority. The force of that request is determined by implied tone and the identity of the one who makes the request, not by the use of the verb form itself. In Hebrew, people making a request to God or to a king use imperatives. Third, Hebrew imperatives cannot be expressed with the negative particle. For example, you can tell a friend "Go!" But Hebrew does not use an imperative to express "Do *not* go." Negative commands must use the jussive verbs discussed below.

Jussive/Cohortative

Since imperatives are only used for positive commands expressed directly to the person in question (i.e., second person), another verb paradigm is needed to express commands or requests not covered by the imperative. These verbs are called *jussives.* An additional term, *cohortative,* is used to describe the first person forms of this jussive paradigm.[2] The jussive/cohortative usually conveys a request for someone to allow something to happen—e.g., "*let* him go" and "*let* her go." When making a request for yourself, you would use a cohortative in the same manner—e.g., "*let* me go" or "*may* I go." You can usually use the English equivalents "may" or "let" when translating jussives and cohortatives.

The cohortative is also used to express intent—e.g., "I *intend* to go." An expression of intent is a logical extension of a request for permission. The difference between intent and request is that, instead of directing the request toward another person, the cohortative is voiced to oneself as an expression of what one desires to do. A good example of this use of the cohortative is found in Exod 3:3 where Moses sees the burning bush and says, "*I will turn aside* and see this great sight, why the bush is not consumed." The first verb is a cohortative. Since Moses is not actually requesting permission to do this, we translate the cohortative as an expression of intent.

1. This comment may seem superfluous, but languages like Greek have third person imperatives (e.g., "let him go" or "let her go").

2. The term *cohortative* (derived from the word cohort, i.e., a group) applies only to the first person forms that are distinguished by their unique ending and that convey a request to the group of which the speaker is a part ("let me" or "let us").

As noted above, the jussive/cohortative is used in contexts where an imperative cannot be used. Since the imperative is only used when speaking directly to an individual (second person), these verbs are needed for making requests pertaining to oneself or to someone outside your conversation (first person and third person). Moreover, since imperatives cannot be negated, these verbs are used for expressing prohibitions or negative commands for all persons (first, second, and third person). The following list clarifies the range of uses of the jussive/cohortative:

1) Third Person Jussives

The third person jussive expresses a *request or mild command* to encourage a certain behavior in a person outside of direct conversation. Jussives are translated using the English equivalents of "may" and "let" (e.g., "may he," "let him").

2) Second Person Jussives

Second person jussives are not as common because second person commands use the imperative. However, since Hebrew imperatives cannot be negated, the second person jussives are crucial for expressing *prohibitions or requests that someone **not** do something*. Jussives are negated using אַל (NOT לֹא).

3) First Person Cohortatives

The first person cohortative expresses *personal requests* ("may I . . ." or "let me . . .") or *personal intent* (e.g., "I intend to . . ." or simply, "I will . . .").

The combined use of the imperatives (limited to second person and never negated) and the jussives/cohortatives (all persons and can be negated) allows for the expression of commands and requests in all contexts. If we could represent this visually it would look something like the following diagram.

Table 15.1: The Use of Volitional Verbs

	JUSSIVES AND COHORTATIVES		*Emphatic*
First person	אֶשְׁמְרָה "Let me keep"	אַל־אֶשְׁמְרָה "Do **not** let me keep"	
Second person	IMPERATIVE שְׁמֹר "Keep!"	אַל־תִּשְׁמֹר "Do **not** keep"	IMPERFECT לֹא־תִשְׁמֹר "You shall **not** keep"
Third person	יִשְׁמֹר "Let him keep"	אַל־יִשְׁמֹר "Do **not** let him keep"	

Occasionally, the imperfect + לֹא ("not") is used as a more forceful way of asserting that an action *must not* take place (dashed box above). When expressed in this manner the listener is presented with a demand. This nuance is intrinsic to the nature of these verbs: the jussive as a volitional verb (dependent on the compliance of the individual) and the imperfect as an indicative verb (indicating facts). By stating that an action *will not take place* (indicative), obedience is assumed and demanded. As a result, the imperfect + לֹא is a more forceful manner of expression and is especially apparent in certain forms of divine legislation, including the Ten Commandments. Using a negated imperfect to "indicate" that an action is absolutely not allowed does not mean it will not happen. Consider the rhetoric of a parent emphatically saying to a child, "You will not talk back to me."

The imperative, jussive, and cohortative verbs used in the Hebrew Bible are sometimes followed by the particle נָא, for example, שְׁמַע־נָא ("Hear!") and אַל־נָא תִּשְׁמַע ("Do not listen!"). Grammars and lexicons often suggest translation equivalents for this particle of entreaty like *please, I pray, surely,* and *now*. However, נָא does not appear to indicate additional elements of either entreaty (*please, I pray*) or ugency (*surely, now*) beyond what is already conveyed by the jussive or imperative. In most cases it should be left untranslated.

FORMATION OF THE VOLITIONAL VERBS

The volitional verbs in Hebrew are easy to remember because they look like the imperfects. As illustrated in the table below, the jussives are almost identical to the imperfects, and the imperatives can be formed by removing the preformative of the jussive.

Table 15.2: The *Qal* Jussives, Cohortatives, and Imperatives

	Imperfects	Jussives		Imperatives
he (3ms)	יִקְטֹל	יִקְטֹל		
she (3fs)	תִּקְטֹל	תִּקְטֹל		
you (2ms)	תִּקְטֹל	תִּקְטֹל	→	קְטֹל (קָטְלָה)
you (2fs)	תִּקְטְלִי	תִּקְטְלִי	→	קִטְלִי
I (1cs)	אֶקְטֹל	אֶקְטְלָה		
he (3mp)	יִקְטְלוּ	יִקְטְלוּ		
she (3fp)	תִּקְטֹלְנָה	תִּקְטֹלְנָה		
you (2mp)	תִּקְטְלוּ	תִּקְטְלוּ	→	קִטְלוּ
you (2fp)	תִּקְטֹלְנָה	תִּקְטֹלְנָה	→	קְטֹלְנָה
I (1cp)	נִקְטֹל	נִקְטְלָה		

3. Rarely, a verb will have a cohortative meaning without the cohorative ending (cf. Joüon 6114b[1]). Although the cohortatives now appear only for the first person, some scholars believe that the jussives and cohortatives were once separate verb paradigms. In Biblical Hebrew these paradigms have merged so that the jussives are used exclusively for second and third person and the cohortatives are used only for first person (Waltke-O'Connor § 34.1a–b; 34.2.1b).

Formation of Jussives and Cohortatives

The *qal* jussives are identical to the imperfect in most forms. Only the cohortatives (1cs and 1cp) vary in that they have an additional ending (e.g., אֶקְטְלָה and נִקְטְלָה).[3] The jussive/cohortative forms mirror the imperfect including their use of variable theme vowels. Thus the forms יִלְמַד, יִתֵּן, and יִקְטֹל could be imperfects or jussives. The jussive/cohortative is negated using the negative particle אַל (unlike the imperfect, which is negated by לֹא).

Formation of Imperatives

In English, commands omit the subject of a statement; thus "you will go" becomes "go!" In Hebrew, imperatives are formed similarly. The singular jussive תִּקְטֹל ("may you kill") can be stripped of its preformative to produce קְטֹל ("kill!"). The plural תִּקְטֹלְנָה can be similarly modified to create קְטֹלְנָה ("kill!"). Whenever stripping off the preformative would result in a form with two vocal *shewas* in a row, then the first *shewa* is replaced with a vowel to create a stable closed unaccented syllable (תִּקְטְלוּ → קְטְלוּ → קִטְלוּ). The vowel that is used is usually a short /i/.[4] You can remember this shift if you imagine dropping one of the dots in the first *shewa* to leave only one dot under the first consonant.

Imperfect		Imperative			
תִּקְטֹל	→	קְטֹל			Preformative drops (no changes needed)
תִּקְטְלִי	→	קְטְלִי	→	קִטְלִי	Preformative drops (double *shewa* adjusted)

The *qal* imperative paradigm includes an alternate second masculine singular imperative form (קָטְלָה, pronounced *qotlā*).[5] Since the imperatives are formed off the jussive paradigm, it should not be surprising that this verb is formed by analogy with the *cohortative* (e.g., אֶקְטְלָה), which is an essential part of that paradigm.

4. Imperatives with the initial i-class vowel are the most common. However, on rare occasions you will see forms with a short u-class vowel just like the alternative 2ms imperative קָטְלָה (*qotlā*). This u-class vowel is the historic vowel of the imperative. See Judg 9:10, 12, where you find מָלְכִי *molkī* ("rule") instead of מִלְכִי.

5. Notice that the imperative קָטְלָה (*qotlā*) is pronounced differently than the *qal* perfect קָטְלָה (*qāt^{e}lā*).

2ms impv.	(alternate)	
קְטֹל	קָטְלָה	"kill!"

Notice also that vowels matter! At the beginning of your study of Hebrew you learned the *qal* perfect קָטַל ("he killed"). Now you must learn to recognize קְטֹל ("kill!"). You cannot simply rely upon the absence of preformatives and sufformatives to help you recognize forms. You must pay attention to the vowel patterns. Vowel patterns offer important clues regarding the identification of meaning. You should memorize these.

The number of new forms that you need to learn for this lesson is quite limited: two cohortatives and four imperative forms. As much as you can, try to understand how these verbs are formed so that you can figure out what they ought to be instead of just relying on rote memory for the entire verb conjugation.

DISTINGUISHING JUSSIVES FROM IMPERFECTS

As noted earlier, the cohortative is distinguished from other verbs by its characteristic ending and the fact that it appears only in the first person (אֶקְטְלָה and נִקְטְלָה). However, the jussive looks identical to the imperfect. Moreover, a few weak verbs do not use the final ָה sufformative when conveying a cohortative meaning. So how can we tell the difference between the imperfect and the jussive or cohortative? Three features will help distinguish between these similar forms.

1. Context
2. Distinct negation לֹא תִשְׁמֹר imperfect
   אַל תִּשְׁמֹר jussive
3. Short form jussives (*hiphil* and weak verbs)

1) Context

Context is often the only way to tell the difference between the imperfect and jussive. Since these forms are often identical in appearance, you must be sensitive to where the dialogue is headed and learn to anticipate the meaning that is required by the context.

2) Distinct negation (אַל vs. לֹא)

The forms of negation provide a clear distinction between the imperfect and jussive. The indicative verbs (pf. and impf.) are always negated by the word לֹא ("not"), while the volitional verbs (juss./cohort.) are negated by אַל ("not"). These distinct negations eliminate any ambiguity between negated forms of the imperfect and jussive.

3) Short forms

Later you will learn that it is typical for jussives to exhibit short forms whenever possible. By this we mean that jussives evidence the presence of historic short vowels rather than pure long vowels. In the strong verb this only happens in the *hiphil,* and in the weak verbs it happens only with certain types of roots, though in weak verbs it occurs across all verb stems (*qal–hophal*). For example, when we get to the *hiphil* verb stem you will find the jussive written with a *short /i/* lengthened to *long /e/* (יַקְטֵל) instead of the *historic long /i/* of the *hiphil* imperfect (יַקְטִיל). This feature is discussed more fully in the chapters dealing with the *hiphil* and appropriate weak verb stems. For now, remember that, wherever possible, jussives use a shorter form than the imperfect.

EXERCISE FOR CHAPTER 15

Memorize the paradigms for the *qal* jussive, cohortative, and imperative in the chart on the following page and then complete the exercise and translation for chapter 15 in the workbook.

QAL VOLITIONALS VERB CHART

	Pf.	Impf.	Juss.		Impv.		Inf. Cst. / Inf. Abs. / Active Ptc.
he (3ms)	קָטַל	יִקְטֹל	יִקְטֹל				
she (3fs)	קָֽטְלָה	תִּקְטֹל	תִּקְטֹל				
you (2ms)	קָטַ֫לְתָּ	תִּקְטֹל	תִּקְטֹל	→	קְטֹל	(קָטְלָה)	
you (2fs)	קָטַ֫לְתְּ	תִּקְטְלִי	תִּקְטְלִי	→	קִטְלִי		
I (1cs)	קָטַ֫לְתִּי	אֶקְטֹל	אֶקְטְלָה				
							Passive Ptc.
they (3mp)	קָֽטְלוּ	יִקְטְלוּ	יִקְטְלוּ				
they (3fp)		תִּקְטֹ֫לְנָה	תִּקְטֹ֫לְנָה				
you (2mp)	קְטַלְתֶּם	תִּקְטְלוּ	תִּקְטְלוּ	→	קִטְלוּ		
you (2fp)	קְטַלְתֶּן	תִּקְטֹ֫לְנָה	קְטֹ֫לְנָה	→	קְטֹ֫לְנָה		
we (1cp)	קָטַ֫לְנוּ	נִקְטֹל	נִקְטְלָה				

CHAPTER 16

Qal Participles and Infinitives

In this chapter we discuss participles and infinitives. You may recall from the introduction to Hebrew verbs in chapter 11 that participles are verbal adjectives and infinitives are verbal nouns. As a result, the number of forms included in these conjugations is quite limited in comparison to the others you have learned. The participles have four forms because they reflect only gender and number like nouns and adjectives. They do not reflect person like other verbs (first, second, and third person). Infinitives are not conjugated at all and exist in only two forms, the infinitive construct and infinitive absolute.

MEANING OF THE PARTICIPLE (-ING VERBAL ADJECTIVE)

A participle can best be described as an *-ing verbal adjective*. While more precise definitions are available, conceptualizing the participle in this fashion is extremely helpful for understanding its function and effectively translating it. By identifying the participle as an *-ing verbal adjective* we mean that the participle is used just like any other adjective and yet it also captures some kind of verbal idea. The verbal component of a participle can be generated by first converting the verbal root into an *-ing* form (e.g., to walk → *walking*). The adjective component is conveyed by converting the verbal idea into the description of a person, place, or thing (e.g., walking → *walking one*). The following discussion reviews the function of Hebrew adjectives and explains the verbal nature of the participle.

In chapter 6 you learned that adjectives are used to express an attribute of a noun (e.g., "a *good* king"), to convey the predicate (e.g., "the king is *good*"), or to stand in place of a noun ("a *good* [man] is king").[1] Chapter 6 outlines the principles for distinguishing these functions as follows, although you will usually be able to tell from context. To review:

Review of Adjective Function

Attributive Adjectives

הַמֶּ֫לֶךְ הַטּוֹב "the king, the good [one]"= "the good king"

Predicate Adjectives

הַמֶּ֫לֶךְ טוֹב "the king, a good [one]" = "the king is good"

Substantival Adjectives (in place of a noun)

הַטּוֹב אָמַר "the good [one] said"

In addition to recognizing the adjectival function of the participle, it is important to appreciate its verbal character. A participle *describes a person, place, or thing* (adjective) *by what it is doing* (a verbal concept). Think of every Hebrew participle as an ***-ing verbal description***—e.g., *walk**ing one***. When viewed in this way, every usage of the participle is consistent with its essential character as a verbal adjective. Moreover, since a participle is a verbal *adjective*, no sense of tense (past, present, or future) is ever intrinsic to the participle itself. Tense must rather be determined by the context in which the participle is used.

Participle = "(verb)*ing one*"

Students are often confused by participles because their inclusion within the verb paradigm gives the impression that a participle functions primarily as a verb (e.g., I am *walking* to town). Because Hebrew uses participles more frequently than English, they translate into English as verbs, adjectives, or nouns (substantival adjectives). This

1. The word "man" is simply an English equivalent for the masculine singular gender of the adjective.

type of variation is confusing unless you learn to think of the participle as a verbal adjective. Regardless of how a participle is used, begin by thinking of it as an *-ing* form of the verbal root. Understand the participle in Hebrew first, then figure out how to reflect this in English.

Participle as Attributive Adjective

Sometimes a participle is used like an attributive adjective to describe some attribute or quality of a person, place, or thing. Like all attributive adjectives, this type of expression requires that the adjective follow the noun it modifies and agree with that noun in gender, number, and definiteness. When studying adjectives we saw how a phrase like הַמֶּ֫לֶךְ הַטּוֹב essentially states the identity of the individual twice—once as "the king" and a second time as "the good one" or "the good person." Although Hebrew expresses הַמֶּ֫לֶךְ הַטּוֹב as "the king, the good one," we capture this in proper English as "the good king." This is exactly how you should respond to a participle. Since the participle is an *-ing* verbal adjective, an expression like הַמֶּ֫לֶךְ הָהֹלֵךְ means "the king, the walking one." Once you understand that the author is merely honing the identity of this man—once as "the king" and again as "the walking one"—you can then translate this into smooth English. In this case you could use either "the walking king" or "the king who walks," depending on what is most appropriate for the context.[2]

הַמֶּ֫לֶךְ הָהֹלֵךְ

(think: "the king, the walking one")

"the king who walks"

Participle as Predicate Adjective

A participle can also act as the predicate or verbal component of a clause just like a predicate adjective. Predicate adjectives are clearly evident when the adjective is placed *before* the noun or when the adjective and noun do not agree in definiteness. If neither the noun nor adjective is definite, you must rely on context. For example, the adjective in הַמֶּ֫לֶךְ טוֹב does not agree with the noun in definiteness and thus functions as the verbal portion of the sentence, that is, "the king [is] a good one." We would translate this into proper English as "the king is good." While "is good" sounds like a verb, it would be improper to

2. It does not matter that you have used "who" when the word אֲשֶׁר is not present in the Hebrew text. The point is to capture the meaning of the Hebrew text in good English, not to decode words.

identify the adjective "good" as a verb just because of how it sounds in English. The same is true with participles. By thinking of the participle as an *-ing* verbal adjective (i.e., *walking one*), the clause הַמֶּ֫לֶךְ הֹלֵךְ translates to "the king [is] a walking one." While this is an accurate reflection of the Hebrew text, it is an awkward expression in English. We could translate this better as "the king is walking." Do not be concerned that your final translation makes the participle sound like a verb; Hebrew and English sometimes convey ideas differently. Your task is to convey the same idea, not replicate grammatical forms.

הַמֶּ֫לֶךְ הֹלֵךְ

(think: "the king [is] a walking one")
"the king is walking"

The predicate use of the participle is especially common when you encounter independent pronouns (e.g., אַתֶּם הֹלְכִים "you [are] walking") or pronouns attached to the end of the word הִנֵּה (e.g., הִנְּנוּ הֹלְכִים "behold, we [are] walking"). When you see independent pronouns or the word הִנֵּה, anticipate that you may soon encounter a participle.

Participle as Substantive

Adjectives can also be used in place of a noun, with the gender and number indicating the person or object to which the adjective is referring. For example, the statement הַטּוֹבִים אָמְרוּ ("the good [men] said ") uses the adjective in place of a masculine plural noun, e.g., men, people, or elders. Participles can function in the same manner. Once again the function of the participle will be readily apparent if you first understand the participle as a verbal adjective. The clause הָהֹלְכִים אָמְרוּ means that "the walking ones said." This should be translated into smooth English as "those who were walking said." Sometimes English will have an available noun that provides a smoother translation. For example, if the above phrase read הַשֹּׁמְרִים אָמְרוּ, "the guarding ones said" could be translated "the *guards* said."

הָהֹלְכִים אָמְרוּ

(think: "the walking ones said")
"those who were walking said"

In all the examples given above, the participle is being used in a manner consistent with its true character, regardless of what the translation ends up looking like in English. Begin by thinking of a participle as an *-ing* verbal adjective, and then convert it into a smoother English equivalent to fit the context.

Because of its relationship to adjectives, a participle takes the gender and number endings of the nouns and adjectives. It has no true tense. A participle depends on context for tense and person. Thus, the phrase אַתֶּם הֹלְכִים could be translated as "you *were* walking" or "you *are* walking" or "you *will be* walking." The participle likewise has no person. The same participle form can be used to designate any group of persons: אֲנַחְנוּ הֹלְכִים ("we are walking"), אַתֶּם הֹלְכִים ("you are walking"), or הָאֲנָשִׁים הֹלְכִים ("the men are walking"). Participles are labeled only on the basis of gender and number and never include additional information. For example, the participle in the clause אַתֶּם הֹלְכִים ("you are walking") is simply a *qal masculine plural* (NOT 2nd person).

MEANING OF INFINITIVES (-ING VERBAL NOUNS)

Hebrew infinitives are another verbal hybrid that can be understood as *-ing* words. Infinitives are actions being referred to as nouns. They are used where syntax requires a noun. In other words, while participles function as *-ing* verbal adjectives (e.g., "walking one"), the infinitives function as *-ing verbal nouns* (e.g., the act of "walking"). While participles only reflect gender and number (not person or tense), the infinitives reflect none of these items. Hebrew infinitives appear in two forms. The infinitive construct functions as a verbal noun that is attached or joined ("constructed") with other words. The infinitive absolute functions as an unattached verbal noun (that stands "absolutely" alone).

Infinitive Construct

An infinitive construct is a *verbal noun* that is linked to other words in the sentence. As with participles, it is easiest to grasp the meaning of infinitive constructs if you begin by understanding them as *-ing* verbal nouns and then adjust your translation to the context. Since an infinitive conveys no tense on its own, context determines whether the action is past, present, or future. In the following examples, the infinitive construct שְׁפֹט ("judging") is used to illustrate the types of components that can be joined to the infinitive construct.

1) Joined to a Noun

An infinitive construct can appear in construct with a noun. Take the statement that "God condemns *judging [of] a man*" (שְׁפֹט אִישׁ). In this clause the noun joined to the infinitive can function as either the subject or object of the underlying verbal idea. In other words, the phrase could indicate that God condemns how a man is judging others (אִישׁ = subject) or that God condemns how other people are judging some man (אִישׁ = direct object). Context is the only way to determine which is correct.

שְׁפֹט אִישׁ

(think: "judging of a man")
"a man judging" (אִישׁ = subject)
"judging a man" (אִישׁ = direct object)

2) Joined with Pronoun Suffixes

The infinitive construct can also have pronoun suffixes attached to it just like regular nouns. Like the example above, the suffix on an infinitive construct can indicate either the subject or object of the verbal idea. Perhaps it would be helpful to think of the suffix as the "possessor" of the action. The question is whether the person possesses the action because they have done it or because it was done *to* them.[3] As a result, an expression like שְׁפָטְכֶם literally translates as "the judging of ***you***."[4] Context determines whether the suffix indicates "you judging" other people (suffix = subject) or other people "judging you" (suffix = direct object).

שְׁפָטְכֶם

(think: "judging of you")
"you judging" (pronoun = subject)
"judging you" (pronoun = direct object)

3. This will be discussed more fully in ch. 22, which deals specifically with suffixes on verbs.

4. The second vowel of the infinitive construct שְׁפֹט has reduced here to a short /o/ in a closed unaccented syllable.

3) Joined with the Preposition ל (Expresses Purpose)

The infinitive construct frequently appears together with the preposition ל ("to, for") to indicate the purpose for some other action. For example, the statement "God came down *for judging* (לִשְׁפֹּט) the people," would translate more idiomatically into English as "God came down *to judge.*" For many Hebrew students this use of the infinitive seems most natural because English infinitives are expressed as "to judge." Like every other use of the infinitive construct, the infinitive is an *-ing* verbal noun expressing the abstract idea conveyed by the verbal root.

לִשְׁפֹּט

(*think: "for judging"*)
"to judge"

4) Joined with the Prepositions ב or כ (Expresses Time)

When the infinitive construct is joined to the prepositions בְּ and כְּ it indicates *when* something happens. For example, בִּשְׁפֹּט שְׁמוּאֵל ("***in*** the judging of Samuel") and כִּשְׁפֹּט שְׁמוּאֵל ("***according to*** the judging of Samuel") both convey the idea "when Samuel judged." Since infinitives have no tense, tense is always derived from context. As a result, the use of the infinitive construct in expressions of time (temporal clauses) often is preceded by some form of the verb היה ("is, was") to clearly express when this action took place. For example, in the following clauses the form of the verb "to be" signals how the infinitive is to be translated—וַיְהִי כִּשְׁפֹּט שְׁמוּאֵל (= "***And it happened*** when Samuel ***judged***") or וְהָיָה כִּשְׁפֹּט שְׁמוּאֵל (= "***And it will come about*** when Samuel ***judges***").

וַיְהִי בִּשְׁפֹּט שְׁמוּאֵל

(*think: "**in** the judging of Samuel"*)
"and **when** Samuel judged"

When Hebrew uses היה to establish a temporal reference for the infinitive construct, the larger sentence structure can feel awkward to translate. Note the example from Isa 37:1.

"***And it happened*** when the king *heard*... ***that he tore*** his garments" OR "When the king heard..., he tore his garments"	וַיְהִי כִּשְׁמֹעַ הַמֶּ֫לֶךְ ... וַיִּקְרַע אֶת־בְּגָדָיו

In English, joining these phrases with "and" implies that whatever happened occurred "when he heard *and* tore." However, the Hebrew conjunction does not mean "and" but joins two words or phrases together. The nature of the link is inferred from context. In the context of Isa 37:1, the link is one of temporal setting ("when he heard") and event ("he tore"). In the example above, there are actually two assertions. The text says *something happened* when the king heard AND that what happened was that *the king tore his clothes.* In English, these ideas are best expressed either as "And it happened when he heard ..., that he tore ..." or, more smoothly, "When he heard ..., he tore...."

Infinitive Absolute

The infinitive absolute is also a verbal noun, but unlike the infinitive construct it will never be linked to other words, either directly attached or in a construct phrase. Instead the infinitive absolute stands "absolutely" alone. This infinitive serves as an *-ing verbal noun* that modifies the meaning of a verb (adverbial) or stands in place of a regular verb or noun. Because the infinitive absolute functions in the place of an adverb, verb, or noun, think of it as a wild card. Usually the infinitive absolute is used as an adverb to clarify the meaning of another verb. For example, Hebrew might use an expression like "*dying* you will die" to convey the English concept "you will *surely* die." Although the infinitive absolute occasionally functions in a manner other than as an adverb, any use of the infinitive absolute can be understood by thinking of the infinitive absolute as an *-ing* verbal noun (e.g., to go → *going*). The functions of the infinitive absolute are summarized as follows:

1) Highlights Main Verb (Most Common Usage)

An infinitive absolute often appears alongside a regular verb to highlight or emphasize the action. Most of the time the infinitive and verb are from the same verbal root (grammarians refer to this infinitive as a cognate accusative), but not always. Context always determines the nuance of meaning conveyed by the infinitive absolute. The following examples summarize the most common nuances of the infinitive absolute when it is used to enhance the meaning of another verb in the sentence.

- **Adds emphasis** ("surely")—An infinitive absolute can be used alongside a regular verb to express certainty. For example, the expression הָלֹךְ הָלַכְתָּ in Gen 31:30 literally says "*going* you have gone." In context, the verse reads, "Now you have *certainly* gone because you longed for your father's house."

- **Indicates continual or progressive action** ("continually")—The infinitive absolute can be used alongside a regular verb to express the ongoing or continual nature of an action. A common example is seen when הלך, often in combination with another infinitive absolute, is used to modify a regular verb. For example, the phrase in Gen 26:13, וַיִּגְדַּל הָאִישׁ וַיֵּלֶךְ הָלוֹךְ וְגָדֵל (lit. "the man became great; and he went, *going and growing*") says of Isaac that "he became great and *continued to increase* until he became very great."

- **Indicates manner**—An infinitive absolute can also be used alongside a regular verb to reflect how an action is carried out. For example, the expression in Gen 43:7, שָׁאוֹל שָׁאַל (lit. "*asking* he asked"), suggests in the context that "the man questioned us *carefully* about ourselves and our relatives."

It is not necessary to memorize English equivalents to use when the infinitive absolute modifies the meaning of another verb. If you begin by thinking of the infinitive as an *-ing* verbal abstraction of the root idea, as demonstrated above, you should be able to envision what the author is trying to say and convert it into a proper English sentence.

2) Substitute for a Regular Verb

In some instances the infinitive absolute is used in place of a main verb. When this happens, it can represent any kind of verb (e.g., perfect, imperfect, imperative). Elements like person, number, and tense must all be determined from context. One familiar example of this use of the infinitive absolute is found in the Ten Commandments: "*Remember* [זָכוֹר] the Sabbath day to keep it holy" (Exod 20:8). Here the infinitive absolute (*remembering*) serves as a substitute for the second person imperative that one expects in this list of commands. Although a variety of theories seek to explain why the infinitive absolute is used this way, at this point in your study you should simply recognize that the infinitive absolute can be used in place of a regular verb.

3) Stands in Place of a Noun

Sometimes when a person is talking about an abstract verbal idea, they may use an infinitive absolute as the subject or object of the sentence instead of a noun. For example, Isa 1:17 uses an infinitive absolute in a manner identical to the following clause that uses a noun—"Learn ***doing-good*** (inf. abs.); seek *justice* (n.)" The infinitive absolute is used because the slot in the sentence requires a noun, more specifically a noun that refers to or labels an action.

FORMATION OF THE QAL PARTICIPLE

Qal Active/stative Participles

The *qal* active participle takes the form קֹטֵל (occasionally קוֹטֵל) with a characteristic long /ō/ in the first syllable. This long /ō/ is an unchangeable long vowel that consistently appears in all forms of the active *qal* participle. The *tsere* reduces when endings are attached (following the vowel rules for verbs). The full range of *qal* participles is created by adding the familiar noun and adjective endings to indicate gender and number (e.g., קֹטֵל, קֹטְלָה, קֹטְלִים, קֹטְלוֹת). The feminine singular has an alternate form based on a segolate pattern (e.g., קֹטֶלֶת).[5] Construct endings are applied to participles just as they are with nouns. The feminine singular construct uses the alternate feminine singular form above (e.g., קֹטֵל, קֹטֶלֶת, קֹטְלֵי, קֹטְלוֹת).

The *qal* participles of stative verbs (verbs that express a state of being rather than an action) appear in a variety of forms. The i-class

5. This form is essentially the masculine perfect with a *tav* added to it (קֹטֵל+ת → *קֹטֶלְת → קֹטֶלֶת)

and u-class statives (e.g. כָּבֵד and קָטֹן) take the same form as the stative perfect. Some a-class statives adopt these forms as well. These stative participles follow the vowel rules for nouns and adjectives and lengthen near open syllables (e.g., כָּבֵד, כְּבֵדָה, כְּבֵדִים, כְּבֵדוֹת). As a result, the theme vowel of stative participles is always visible to help you recognize them. The remaining a-class statives take the active קֹטֵל pattern. Since stative participles borrow from forms you already know, there is no need to memorize special forms as long as you are aware of the similarity between the stative perfect and stative participle. Table 16.1 visually captures the formation of both active and stative participles.

Qal Passive Participles

The *qal* is unique in having both an active/stative participle and a passive participle. The active participle is consistent with the basic meaning of the *qal* verb (e.g., "the killing [one]"), while the passive participle reflects the passive meaning of the *qal* (e.g., "the being killed [one]"). The *qal* passive participles takes the form קָטוּל with an unchangeable long /ū/ in the second syllable. Though the *qamets* reduces in distant open syllables, the long /ū/ remains in every form (e.g., קָטוּל, קְטוּלָה, קְטוּלִים, קְטוּלוֹת). Stative verbs do not have a passive participle since stative cannot be made passive (e.g., "being heavy" cannot become "being heavied").

Memorize the forms for the active and passive participles of קטל highlighted by the bold boxes in table 16.1. Pay close attention to the ō-ē pattern characteristic of the *qal* active participle (קֹטֵל) and the characteristic long /ū/ theme vowel of the passive participle (קָטוּל). The remaining forms in each paradigm are created by adding the noun endings.

Table 16.1: The *Qal* Participles

	Qal actives	*Qal* statives (a-class)	*Qal* statives (i-class)	*Qal* statives (u-class)
Qal perfects	קָטַל	גָּדַל†	כָּבֵד	קָטֹן
	Active participles			
m. sg.	קֹטֵל		כָּבֵד	קָטֹן
f. sg.	קֹטְלָה (קֹטֶ֫לֶת)		כְּבֵדָה	קְטֹנָה
m. pl.	קֹטְלִים		כְּבֵדִים	קְטֹנִים
f. pl.	קֹטְלוֹת		כְּבֵדוֹת	קְטֹנוֹת
	Passive participles			
m. sg.	קָטוּל			
f. sg.	קְטוּלָה			
m. pl.	קְטוּלִים			
f. pl.	קְטוּלוֹת			

† Although a-class participles can adopt either form, each root follows one pattern or the other.

FORMATION OF THE QAL INFINITIVES The *qal* infinitive absolute and infinitive construct forms are presented in table 16.2. The infinitive absolute takes only one form, although it is written with both full and defective spelling (קָטוֹל and קָטֹל). Since the infinitive absolute is never attached to other words, this one form is all you need to know. The infinitive construct, on the other hand, can have the same theme vowel variation seen in the *qal* imperfects that you learned earlier in chapter 14. Though *qal* infinitive constructs can take a-class or i-class theme vowels (e.g., שְׁמַע), the u-class pattern קְטֹל is predominant.

Table 16.2: The *Qal* Infinitives

Infinitive Absolute	קָטוֹל
Infinitive Construct	קְטֹל

The *qal* infinitive construct adjusts in form depending on the relationship of the syllables to the accent. Because these adjustments to the infinitive construct follow the vowel rules for verbs, it is unnecessary to memorize its different forms. The key to recognizing apparently disparate forms is to understand that each form comes from the historic root קֻטֻל. Observe how this historic form explains two of the simplest forms of the infinitive construct קְטֹל.

Historic form		Vowel rules applied	
קֻ|טֻל*	→	קְ|טֹל	*Accented vowel lengthens; near open reduces*
(N D) □́-קֻ|טֻל*	→	□́-קְ|טָל	*Closed unaccented takes short vowel; distant open reduces*

The same historic form also explains the forms you encounter when suffixes are added. Samples of the various forms resulting from the historic קֻטֻל are represented in table 16.3.

Tale 16.3: The Historic *Qal* Infinitive Construct

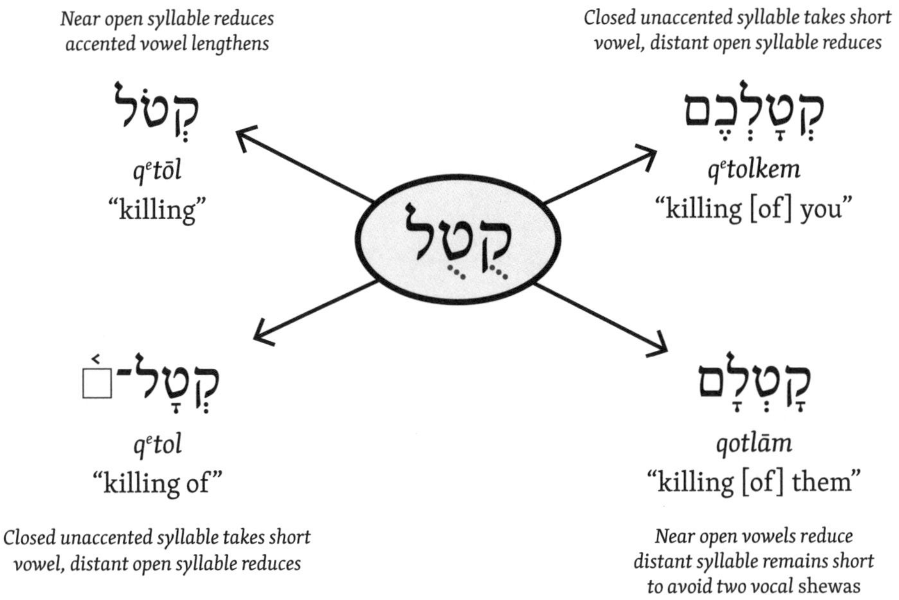

Notice the importance of vowel patterns in verbs. Though preformatives and sufformatives help distinguish some verb forms, many *qal* verbs are distinguishable only by their vowel patterns—*qal* perfect קָטַל ("he killed"), *qal* imperative or infinitive construct קְטֹל ("kill!" or "killing," respectively), *qal* active participle קֹטֵל ("killing one"), *qal* passive participle קָטוּל ("one being killed"), and *qal* infinitive absolute קָטוֹל. Learn the *qal* verb forms well!

EXERCISE FOR CHAPTER 16 Memorize the paradigms for the *qal* participles and infinitives in the chart on the following page and then complete the exercise and translation for chapter 16 in the workbook.

קְטֹל	*Inf. Cst.*	קָטוֹל	*Inf. Abs.*

↓

	Pf.	*Impf.*	*Juss.*		*Impv.*	*Active Ptc.*
he (3ms)	קָטַל	יִקְטֹל	יִקְטֹל			קֹטֵל
she (3fs)	קָֽטְלָה	תִּקְטֹל	תִּקְטֹל			קֹטְלָה (קֹטֶ֫לֶת)
you (2ms)	קָטַ֫לְתָּ	תִּקְטֹל	תִּקְטֹל	→	קְטֹל (קָטְלָה)	קֹטְלִים
you (2fs)	קָטַ֫לְתְּ	תִּקְטְלִי	תִּקְטְלִי	→	קִטְלִי	קֹטְלוֹת
I (1cs)	קָטַ֫לְתִּי	אֶקְטֹל	אֶקְטְלָה			
						Passive Ptc.
they (3mp)	קָֽטְלוּ	יִקְטְלוּ	יִקְטְלוּ			קָטוּל
they (3fp)		תִּקְטֹ֫לְנָה	תִּקְטֹ֫לְנָה			קְטוּלָה
you (2mp)	קְטַלְתֶּם	תִּקְטְלוּ	תִּקְטְלוּ	→	קִטְלוּ	קְטוּלִים
you (2fp)	קְטַלְתֶּן	תִּקְטֹ֫לְנָה	תִּקְטֹ֫לְנָה	→	קְטֹ֫לְנָה	קְטוּלוֹת
we (1cp)	קָטַ֫לְנוּ	נִקְטֹל	נִקְטְלָה			

CHAPTER 17

Qal Waw Consecutives

There are two more sets of verbs to cover before we complete our introduction to the verb conjugations: the *waw consecutive imperfect* and the *waw consecutive perfect*. Because you have already been using basic forms of these *waw* consecutives in your translation exercises, this chapter refines and consolidates familiar material.

INTRODUCTION TO THE WAW CONSECUTIVE IMPERFECT

In chapter 4 you were briefly introduced to the *waw consecutive imperfect* as one of the basic verb forms necessary for getting started in your translation of the Joseph narrative. You learned to translate both the imperfect and the imperfect with a simple conjunction as present/future tense (e.g., יִשְׁמֹר "he will keep" and וְיִשְׁמֹר "and he will keep"). You also were introduced to the *waw* consecutive imperfect that takes a special form of the conjunction and is translated the opposite of the imperfect (e.g., וַיִּשְׁמֹר "and he kept").

Imperfect	Simple Conjunction Imperfect	*Waw* Consecutive Imperfect
יִשְׁמֹר "he will keep"	וְיִשְׁמֹר "and he will keep"	וַיִּשְׁמֹר "and he ***kept***"
תִּשְׁמֹר "she will keep"	וְתִשְׁמֹר "and she will keep"	וַתִּשְׁמֹר "and she ***kept***"
יִשְׁמְרוּ "they will keep"	וְיִשְׁמְרוּ "and they will keep"	וַיִּשְׁמְרוּ "and they ***kept***"

In chapter 14 you learned that the imperfect communicates incomplete action in the mind of the speaker, a perspective that is naturally most pertinent for the present and future. However, it can also be used of the past when the author is describing events as if they are ongoing.

Despite the similarity in form between the imperfect and the *waw* consecutive imperfect, the latter seems to be a distinct conjugation devoted to conveying past tense. It serves as the standard verb form for past tense narrative.[1] Because it is not truly related to the imperfect and is in fact a true past tense conjugation, modern scholars prefer to use the term *preterite* ("past tense") to describe these verbs rather than the term *waw* consecutive imperfect.[2] However, beginning students find it helpful to use the term *waw* consecutive imperfect because this label highlights all three prominent features of this conjugation: (1) The presence of the unique conjunction ◌ּ◻ַוַ; (2) its use as the standard form in past tense narration; and (3) the similarity in form to the imperfect. Understand that in function this conjugation is a preterite (past tense) though we predominantly refer to it as a *waw* consecutive imperfect.

As you can see from the chart below, the *waw* consecutive imperfects are easy to identify once you know the imperfects. They are marked by a special form of the conjunction composed of *waw* + short /a/ + doubling of the preformative consonant (וַיִּקְטֹל). When the preformative is a guttural (i.e., first person singular), the guttural cannot double. Thus the *pataḥ* naturally lengthens to compensate for the absence of doubling and creates a new stable syllable (וָאֶקְטֹל). Remember, open unaccented syllables take long vowels.

Pay close attention to this special conjunction (e.g., וַיִּקְטֹל and וָאֶקְטֹל) because it will always help you isolate the beginning of the verbal root. The consonant that is doubled by the conjunction, or that forces the compensatory lengthening of the vowel under the conjunction,

1. The view represented here reflects the common understanding of the Hebrew *waw* consecutive imperfect. Scholars have suggested other portraits of the development and function of the imperfect but these are better reserved for advanced discussions.

2. Early grammars referred to these verbs as waw *conversive imperfects,* as if the conjunction "converted" the regular meaning of the imperfect from future tense to past tense. Later it became customary to refer to them as waw *consecutive imperfects* because they perpetuate the tense initiated by the past tense narrative. But sometimes these verbs are used even at the start of the narrative (e.g., Josh 1:1: וַיְהִי אַחֲרֵי מוֹת מֹשֶׁה "Now it happened after the death of Moses"). Scholarly opinion now leans toward identifying these verbs as an original past tense form that is not related to the imperfects at all. Another reason scholars prefer the term *preterite* is that in rare instances the conjugation appears without the special conjunction; e.g., Hos 6:1, "Come, let us return to the LORD; for he has torn [pf.], but he will heal us, he has struck [יַךְ] but he will bind us."

is always the preformative (e.g., וַיִּקְטֹל and וָאֶקְטֹל). It is never part of the root. The root must begin after the preformative (e.g., וַיִּקְטֹל). This will be especially important to remember when working with weak verbs like some that you have already seen in the Joseph narratives. For example, וַיָּשֶׂם cannot be from ישׂם but must be from שִׂים ("put, place") because the וַ⊡ only attaches to a preformative.

The *waw* consecutive imperfects often mirror the form of the imperfect but occasionally they take a form that is historically shorter than the imperfect. Thus the *waw* consecutives look just like the jussives (see ch. 15). While jussives and *waw* consecutive imperfects are independent verb conjugations, recognize the similarity between these forms. In the strong verb you will see no difference in form until we get to the *hiphil*, but in certain weak verbs, you can see this difference in length throughout the verb stems (*qal–hophal*).

Table 17.1: The *Qal Waw* Consecutive Imperfects

	Imperfects	Jussives	*Waw* Consec. Impf.
he (3ms)	יִקְטֹל	יִקְטֹל	וַיִּקְטֹל
she (3fs)	תִּקְטֹל	תִּקְטֹל	וַתִּקְטֹל
you (2ms)	תִּקְטֹל	תִּקְטֹל	וַתִּקְטֹל
you (2fs)	תִּקְטְלִי	תִּקְטְלִי	וַתִּקְטְלִי
I (1cs)	אֶקְטֹל	אֶקְטְלָה	וָאֶקְטֹל or וָאֶקְטְלָה
he (3mp)	יִקְטְלוּ	יִקְטְלוּ	וַיִּקְטְלוּ
she (3fp)	תִּקְטֹלְנָה	תִּקְטֹלְנָה	וַתִּקְטֹלְנָה
you (2mp)	תִּקְטְלוּ	תִּקְטְלוּ	וַתִּקְטְלוּ
you (2fp)	תִּקְטֹלְנָה	תִּקְטֹלְנָה	וַתִּקְטֹלְנָה
I (1cp)	נִקְטֹל	נִקְטְלָה	וַנִּקְטֹל or וַנִּקְטְלָה

We will discuss these distinctions when we reach the chapters dealing with the *hiphil* and appropriate weak verb stems. Already in your reading of the Joseph narrative you have seen some of these short-form *waw* consecutive imperfects. For example, the *waw* consecutive imperfect וַיָּשֶׂם ("and he put") does not take the *historic long i-class vowel* of the imperfect יָשִׂים ("he will see"). You have also run across verbs like וַיַּרְא, which drops the final letter of the root ראה ("and he saw"), used in passages along with the imperfect יִרְאֶה ("he will see") where the root is fully visible. For now, simply remember that **waw *consecutive imperfects exhibit short forms whenever possible*.**

The fact that the short forms are common to both the jussive and *waw* consecutive imperfect may help you remember that the first person *waw* consecutive sometimes follows the pattern of the cohortative (part of the jussive paradigm). Some first person *waw* consecutives have the simple short form (e.g., וָאֶקְטֹל "and I killed"). Other *waw* consecutive forms look like a cohortative (e.g., וָאֶקְטְלָה "and I killed"). There is no difference in meaning between these two forms.

MEANING OF THE WAW CONSECUTIVE IMPERFECT

As noted earlier, the *waw* consecutive imperfect is a true past tense verb form. It is a simple past tense and relates events without stressing anything about the duration of time in which they occurred. The *waw* consecutive imperfect is the standard verb used in past tense narrative and presents narrative as a succession of events. Because Hebrew does not use subordination of clauses or nuanced conjunctions (e.g., *but, or, then, because*) to the extent we do in English, events are presented as grammatically parallel ideas. The conjunction is part of the fixed form of the conjugation and marks the verb as a new clause. The precise relationship between clauses must be supplied by the reader from context. In some cases the conjunction is represented in translation; in others it is not.[3]

Whenever a *waw* consecutive imperfect is used, it always appears as the first word in the clause. If context demands that another word appear at the beginning of the clause (e.g., לֹא "not") and separates the conjunction from the verb, then a different verb form must be used to

3. The use of the *waw* consecutive imperfect as the standard verb for narrative explains why this verb appears even at the beginning of a story. For example, the presence of the conjunction at the beginning of Lev 1:1, וַיִּקְרָא אֶל־מֹשֶׁה ("And he called to Moses"), might seem awkward to English readers, but the *waw* consecutive is simply setting the tense for the following narrative.

communicate the past tense (usually a perfect). However, the author reverts back to the *waw* consecutive imperfect in the following clauses because it is the standard way to recount past events in Hebrew.

The placement of the *waw* consecutive imperfect in first position is illustrated in the passage below. In order to heighten your awareness of this grammatical structure, each clause begins at the far right margin and each *waw* consecutive imperfect is highlighted in red. Note that the placement of another word at the front of the clause results in the use of a different verb form (see underlining).

Genesis 1:1–5

1 ***In the beginning*** God created (pf.)	בְּרֵאשִׁית בָּרָא אֱלֹהִים
the heavens and the earth.	אֵת הַשָּׁמַיִם וְאֵת הָאָרֶץ׃
2 And ***the earth*** was (pf.) formless and void	וְהָאָרֶץ הָיְתָה תֹהוּ וָבֹהוּ
and ***darkness*** was over the face of the deep	וְחֹשֶׁךְ עַל־פְּנֵי תְהוֹם
and ***the breath of God*** was hovering (ptc.)	וְרוּחַ אֱלֹהִים מְרַחֶפֶת
over the surface of the waters.	עַל־פְּנֵי הַמָּיִם׃
3 And God said, "Let there be light."	וַיֹּאמֶר אֱלֹהִים יְהִי אוֹר
And there was light.	וַיְהִי־אוֹר׃
4 And God saw that the light was good	וַיַּרְא אֱלֹהִים אֶת־הָאוֹר כִּי־טוֹב
and God separated between light and darkness.	וַיַּבְדֵּל אֱלֹהִים בֵּין הָאוֹר וּבֵין הַחֹשֶׁךְ׃
5 And God called the light day	וַיִּקְרָא אֱלֹהִים לָאוֹר יוֹם
and ***the darkness*** he called (pf.) night.	וְלַחֹשֶׁךְ קָרָא לָיְלָה
And there was evening	וַיְהִי־עֶרֶב
and there was morning—day one.	וַיְהִי־בֹקֶר יוֹם אֶחָד׃

INTRODUCTION TO THE WAW CONSECUTIVE PERFECT

Chapter 4 also introduced you to the *waw consecutive perfect*. You were instructed to translate any perfect verb with a conjunction as if it were opposite of the perfect, namely as a present or future (e.g., וְשָׁמַר "***and*** he ***will keep***"). Perfects can also appear with a simple conjunction that does not affect how you translate the verb (e.g., וְשָׁמַר "***and*** he kept"). The difficulty is that there is usually no visual distinction between *waw* consecutive perfects and perfects with a simple conjunction (e.g., וְשָׁמַר can mean either "and he will keep" or "and he kept").

The translation exercises thus far have only incorporated the *waw* consecutive perfect, so you have not had to deal with any simple conjunctions on the perfect. The following discussion explains the function of the *waw* consecutive perfect more thoroughly so that you can tell the difference and can recognize all uses of the perfects.

Perfect	Simple Conjunction Perfect	*Waw* Consecutive Perfect
שָׁמַר "he kept"	וְשָׁמַר "and he kept"	וְשָׁמַר "and he ***will keep***"
שָׁמְרָה "she kept"	וְשָׁמְרָה "and she kept"	וְשָׁמְרָה "and she ***will keep***"
שָׁמְרוּ "they kept"	וְשָׁמְרוּ "and they kept"	וְשָׁמְרוּ "and they ***will keep***"

MEANING OF THE WAW CONSECUTIVE PERFECT

The *waw* consecutive perfect is essentially the reverse of the *waw* consecutive imperfect. It is prefixed by the conjunction (hence the *waw* in the title) and must appear as the first word in the clause. It conveys a time frame that is opposite of what you expect from the perfect, namely present/future (e.g., שָׁמַר "he kept" becomes וְשָׁמַר "he will keep").

The *waw* consecutive perfect is a true "consecutive" verb.[4] Unlike the *waw* consecutive imperfect, which is a true past tense (preterite) and does not need another verb to establish tense, the *waw* consecutive perfect requires an initial verb to introduce the present/future time frame of the dialogue or narrative before it can be used. This can be accomplished by means of an imperfect, an imperative, or even a participle. Once the present/future time frame has been established, the subsequent clauses use the *waw* consecutive perfect to continue the sequence of ideas. In these situations the *waw* consecutive perfect can have the same translation value as the initial verb in the sequence or it can convey some other present/future nuance. The best way to appreciate this is in the process of translating a passage like the familiar verses below.

The earlier example from Gen 1:1–5 emphasized the placement of the *waw* consecutive imperfect at the beginning of the clause. The following example from Deut 6:4–9 shows that the same is true for the *waw* consecutive perfect. A second feature is also illustrated, namely the dependence of the *waw* consecutive perfect upon another verb to establish the present/future time frame. If for some reason the verb is separated from the conjunction, then the perfect cannot be utilized and some other means of expressing the present/future tense must be used. The dialogue reverts back to using the *waw* consecutive perfect as soon as conditions allow. In the following examples the verb that establishes the present/future time frame has been highlighted by means of a box and the subsequent *waw* consecutive perfects are highlighted in red. The lead verb שְׁמַע is an imperative, which by virtue of being a command assumes *future* fulfillment.

Deuteronomy 6:4–9

4 Hear, O Israel!	(imperative) שְׁמַע יִשְׂרָאֵל
The LORD is our God.	יְהוָה אֱלֹהֵינוּ
The LORD is one.	יְהוָה אֶחָד׃
5 and you will love the LORD your God	וְאָהַבְתָּ אֵת יְהוָה אֱלֹהֶיךָ
with all your heart,	בְּכָל לְבָבְךָ
and all your soul,	וּבְכָל־נַפְשְׁךָ

4. Scholars suggest that the current use of *waw* consecutive perfect may have originated from the use of a perfect in the second half of a conditional sentence ("if . . . , then . . ."). In such instances the second clause would be the logical outflow or certain result of the previous condition. In that context a "complete action" perfect would have been an appropriate verb to use. The *waw* consecutive perfect could also have been influenced by a tendency to replicate the perceived relationship between the *waw* consecutive imperfect by creating a corresponding *waw* consecutive perfect pattern (Waltke-O'Connor, 522).

and all your strength.	וּבְכָל־מְאֹדֶֽךָ׃
6 and they will be (namely, these words	וְהָיוּ הַדְּבָרִים הָאֵלֶּה
which I am commanding you today)	אֲשֶׁר אָנֹכִי מְצַוְּךָ הַיּוֹם
upon your heart	עַל־לְבָבֶֽךָ
7 and you will teach them to your children	וְשִׁנַּנְתָּם לְבָנֶיךָ
and you will speak about them	וְדִבַּרְתָּ בָּם
in your sitting in your house,	בְּשִׁבְתְּךָ בְּבֵיתֶךָ
and in your walking on the road,	וּבְלֶכְתְּךָ בַדֶּרֶךְ
and in your lying down	וּבְשָׁכְבְּךָ
and in your rising up.	וּבְקוּמֶֽךָ׃
8 And you will bind them as signs on your hand.	וּקְשַׁרְתָּם לְאוֹת עַל יָדֶךָ
And they will be as frontlets between your eyes.	וְהָיוּ לְטֹטָפֹת בֵּין עֵינֶֽיךָ׃
9 And you will write them	וּכְתַבְתָּם
upon the doorposts of your house	עַל מְזוּזֹת בֵּיתֶךָ
and upon your gates.	וּבִשְׁעָרֶֽיךָ׃

RECOGNIZING THE WAW CONSECUTIVE PERFECT

In light of the discussion above, you can see that context is the primary means of distinguishing between *waw* consecutive perfects and simple conjunction perfects. *Waw* consecutive perfects follow a verb that establishes a present/future time frame, while simple conjunction perfects follow another expression of the past. Context is extremely important, and you must learn to follow the Hebrew narrative closely to recognize the significance of the verb.

Three forms of the *waw* consecutive perfect can be distinguished from the simple conjunction perfect. The 2ms, 1cs, and 1cp shift the accent to the final syllable of the word, while simple conjunction perfects keep the accent in its typical place. The verbs with this shift in accent are highlighted in table 17.2.

Table 17.2: Accent Shifts in *Waw* Consecutive Perfects

Perfect	Simple Conjunction Perfect	*Waw* Consecutive Perfect
קָטַל	וְקָטַל	וְקָטַל
קָטְלָה	וְקָטְלָה	וְקָטְלָה
קָטַ֫לְתָּ	וְקָטַ֫לְתָּ	וְקָטַלְתָּ֫
קָטַ֫לְתְּ	וְקָטַ֫לְתְּ	וְקָטַ֫לְתְּ
קָטַ֫לְתִּי	וְקָטַ֫לְתִּי	וְקָטַלְתִּ֫י
קָטְלוּ	וְקָטְלוּ	וְקָטְלוּ
קְטַלְתֶּם	וּקְטַלְתֶּם	וּקְטַלְתֶּם
קְטַלְתֶּן	וּקְטַלְתֶּן	וּקְטַלְתֶּן
קָטַ֫לְנוּ	וְקָטַ֫לְנוּ	וְקָטַלְנ֫וּ

This shift in accent occurs in forms with consonantal sufformatives that can receive the accent.[5] This shift in accent provides immediate confirmation that you are reading about a present/future event. If you reexamine the passage from Deut 6:4–9 presented above, you will see that the accented final syllable of several *waw* consecutive perfects has been marked (e.g., וְאָהַבְתָּ֫) to call attention to this shift in accent.[6]

5. The sufformative on the perfect 2fs (וְקָטַ֫לְתְּ) cannot take the accent and the second person plural forms (וּקְטַלְתֶּ֫ם and וּקְטַלְתֶּ֫ן) cannot be distinguished because these sufformatives always have the accent.

6. Other forms like וְשִׁנַּנְתָּם (v. 7), וּקְשַׁרְתָּם (v. 8), and וּכְתַבְתָּם (v. 9) are accented on the final syllable because of the additional suffix and would be accented this way regardless of whether they were simple conjunction perfects or *waw* consecutive perfects. We will be studying suffixes on verbs later in ch. 22.

WAW CONSECUTIVE FORMS OF היה ("TO BE")

The *waw* consecutive forms of the verb היה ("to be") merit special attention for two reasons. First, the *waw* consecutive imperfect is vocalized quite differently than the imperfect (i.e., וַיְהִי 3ms *waw* consec. impf. vs. יִהְיֶה 3ms impf.). Second, the *waw* consecutive perfect has become a frozen form that functions independently as a future tense.

וַיְהִי

The *waw* consecutive imperfect is vocalized quite differently from the regular imperfect due to its shortened form (i.e., וַיְהִי vs. יִהְיֶה). While it looks a little odd at first, it is extremely common. You may have already gotten used to it from its many occurrences in your translation exercises (for example, וַיְהִי "and he/it was" and וַתְּהִי "and she was"). A more detailed discussion of how the unique forms of the verb היה originate can be found in chapter 25.

וְהָיָה

When you encounter the word וְהָיָה, you should anticipate that it is probably a frozen form of the *waw* consecutive perfect. In other words, it is so frequently used that it becomes the default meaning. While Hebrew generally requires a clear present/future context before introducing the *waw* consecutive perfect, וְהָיָה does not need one. This verb can appear even at the beginning of a narrative unit with the meaning "and there will be" or "and it will come about."

EXERCISE FOR CHAPTER 17

Review the discussion of the *waw* consecutive paradigms in this chapter and then complete the translation exercise for chapter 17 that appears in the workbook.

CHAPTER 18

Niphal

The *niphal* is the primary verb stem for expressing the passive and reflexive meaning of the *qal* verb. Hebrew does on rare occasion show evidence of a historic verb stem devoted exclusively to expressing a *qal* passive.[1] However, the *niphal* almost completely displaced this *qal* passive and is used for both the passive voice and reflexive meaning in Biblical Hebrew.

MEANING OF THE NIPHAL

As the counterpart to the *qal* verb the *niphal* takes the core idea of the *qal* and expresses it in a passive voice (e.g., the action is done to the subject) or a reflexive meaning (i.e., one is doing the action to or for oneself). As you can see from the sample expressions included in the chart below, the *niphal* is only useful for active verbs. Stative verbs (red print below) cannot be converted as there is no action for the subject to receive.

	Basic Meaning		
Active Stative	**QAL** *HE HEARD* ***he was great***		
Passive	*IT WAS HEARD*		
	NIPHAL		
Reflexive	*HE HEARD HIMSELF*		

1. This will be discussed more fully in ch. 21, which deals with rare verb stems.

The shift from active to passive does not change the nature of the action being described. It merely adjusts the reader's perspective or focus. The active construction focuses on the individual(s) doing the action while the passive voice shifts the reader's attention to the person or object to which the action is done.

In most cases you will find that it is easiest to decipher the meaning of a *niphal* verb by starting with the meaning of the *qal* you learned in your vocabulary and then transforming the verb into a passive or reflexive sense. For example, the following sentences reflect the relationship between the *qal* and *niphal* and the kind of meanings you will see in the *niphal*.

Qal	He heard (שָׁמַע).	Active
Niphal	He was heard (נִשְׁמַע).	Passive
	He heard himself (נִשְׁמַע).	Reflexive

Whenever you encounter a *niphal* you will have to rely on context to determine whether passive or reflexive best suits the passage.

Keep in mind that some verbs are reflexive by nature. This may not come out in translation because of how English expresses the same ideas. For example, the verb לחם ("to fight") is rarely used in the *qal* and appears mostly in the *niphal*. Though it does not usually come across explicitly in the English word "fight," the reflexive *niphal* sense is integral to conflict between two parties. Likewise, the verb שׁבע ("to swear an oath") rarely occurs in the *qal* and is commonly used in the *niphal*. The reflexive sense of placing oneself under an oath is implicit in the act of swearing an oath.

SYNTAX OF THE NIPHAL

Niphal and the direct object marker

In English, direct objects are reserved for transitive verbs—verbs that "transfer" action from the subject *to another object*. A passive or reflexive verb does not take a direct object because the action of the verb is directed *towards the subject*. Likewise, the passive/reflexive *niphal* does not normally take a direct object. However, on occasion you will find the *niphal* appearing with the direct object marker אֵת even when it functions as a true passive. For example, in Exod 21:28 the text states, וְלֹא יֵאָכֵל אֶת־בְּשָׂרוֹ ("***it, its flesh,*** will not be eaten").

The use of the direct object marker with a passive *niphal* makes sense if you recognize that אֵת is used to mark the recipient of the action. In an active verb the recipient of the action is an object other than the subject. In a passive verb the recipient of the action is the subject. When the *niphal* takes the direct object marker, it marks the subject as the recipient of the action, thus restating the subject.

This use of the direct object marker is seen with other passive verb stems as well. However, now that you have been exposed to this feature of the passive voice, the next two chapters will not return to this topic. Make sure that you take note of this unique use of the direct object marker with passive verbs.[2]

Niphal and the imperative

The passive qualities of the *niphal* also affect its relationship to the imperative. Passive ideas cannot be commanded. Commands assume a response, and as soon as a person responds, he or she has "acted." However, since the *niphal* is also used for reflexive ideas (actions that one does to oneself), *niphal* verbs do have an imperative form.

FORMATION OF THE NIPHAL

If you remember the name and correct spelling of a verb stem, you already know what the perfect looks like. In this case the name *niphal* reminds you that the perfect must be represented in the strong verb as נִקְטַל.[3] The name of the stem also helps you to remember that the characteristic feature of the *niphal* is the presence of a *nun* in every form (*nun* for niphal). As you will see below, the *nun* is always visible in the perfects and the participles (נִקְטַל and נִקְטָל). In the remaining conjugations, the *nun* has assimilated into the first consonant of the root (הִנְקָטֵל → הִקָּטֵל) and is visible in the sense that the *dagesh forte* (doubling dot) represents the assimilation of a vowelless *nun*.

2. For examples with the passives in other stems (*pual* and *hophal*), see Jer 50:20 יְבֻקַּשׁ אֶת־עֲוֹן יִשְׂרָאֵל ("the iniquity of Israel will be searched out") and Exod 10:8 וַיּוּשַׁב אֶת־מֹשֶׁה וְאֶת־אַהֲרֹן אֶל־פַּרְעֹה ("And Moses and Aaron were brought back to Pharaoh"). The particle אֵת marks the subject in only twenty occurrences of the *niphal*, one occurrence of the *pual*, and fourteen occurrences of the *hophal*.

3. Remember that the verb stems originally got their names from a time when grammars used the root פעל for the paradigms. The *niphal* was thus derived from the 3ms perfect נִפְעַל.

Table 18.1: Creating the *Niphal* Strong Verb Paradigm

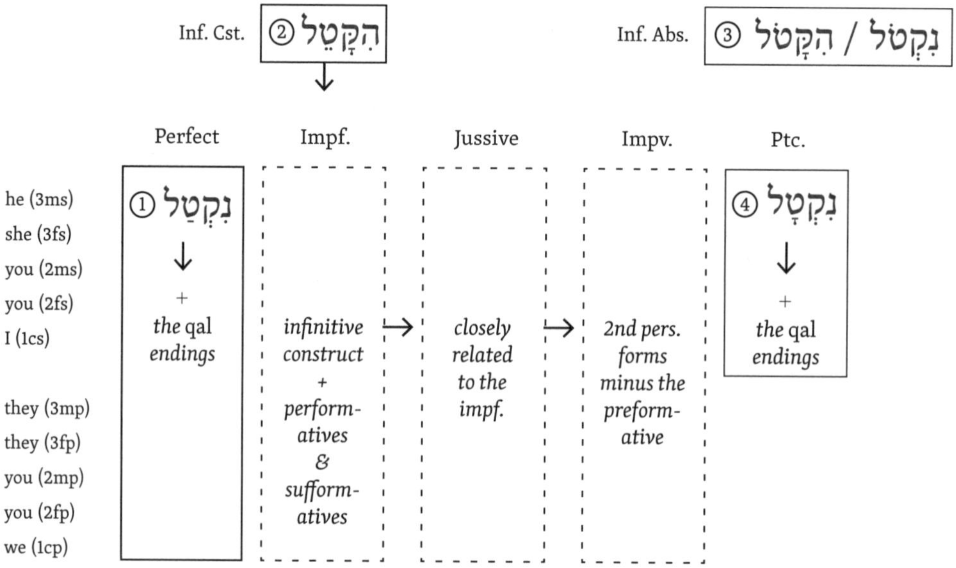

As pointed out in chapter 12, once you have mastered the formation of the *qal* verb, you can learn another entire verb stem by concentrating only on four verb forms: (1) the third masculine singular perfect, (2) the infinitive construct, (3) the infinitive absolute, and (4) the masculine singular participle. These four forms give you the structural patterns and vowel combinations unique to the *niphal*. The remaining forms in each paradigm can be generated by adding the appropriate preformatives and sufformatives that you learned in the *qal*.

1) Niphal Perfects (נִקְטַל)

The representative form of the *niphal* perfect (נִקְטַל) is used to generate the remainder of the perfect paradigm. To do this you will take the representative *niphal* perfect and add the endings you learned for the *qal* paradigm (e.g., נִקְטַל, נִקְטְלָה, נִקְטַלְתָּ).

נִקְטַל + קָטְלָה = נִקְטְלָה "and she was killed"

Niphal perfect — *Qal* perfect ending — Conjugated *niphal* perfect

2) Derivatives of the Niphal Infinitive Construct (הִקָּטֵל)

The infinitive construct can be used to produce most conjugations of the strong verb paradigms. Let's review how this works with the *qal* infinitive construct you learned in chapter 16. The *qal* infinitive construct קְטֹל serves as the base to which preformatives and sufformatives are added to create the imperfect (e.g., קְטֹל → יִקְטֹל). The imperfect in turn serves as a base for the jussive, cohortative, and *waw* consecutive imperfect. The jussives are generally identical to the imperfect (יִקְטֹל → יִקְטֹל), while the cohortatives add a characteristic ending to the first person imperfect forms (e.g., אֶקְטֹל → אֶקְטְלָה). The *waw* consecutive imperfects are formed off the jussive and cohortative by adding their unique form of the conjunction (e.g., יִקְטֹל → וַיִּקְטֹל). The imperatives are created by chopping off the front of the imperfect (e.g., תִּקְטֹל → קְטֹל). Thus the imperative is identical to the infinitive construct with which you started.

Imperfect: The pattern observed in the *qal* applies to each of the strong verb stems (*qal* to *hophal*). Thus the *niphal* infinitive construct (הִקָּטֵל) can be used to generate the imperfects, jussives/cohortatives, and imperatives. The imperfect is created by adding the appropriate preformatives and sufformatives to the infinitive construct form. In doing so, the preformative that marks the imperfect for person and gender "covers up" the preformative ה that is present in the infinitive construct (הִקָּטֵל + י = יִקָּטֵל).[4] From the initial 3ms imperfect you can produce the rest of the *niphal* imperfect paradigm using the patterns you memorized for the *qal* imperfect (see below). One oddity is that the *niphal* 3fp and 2fp imperfects do not keep the *tsere* theme vowel and instead have a *pataḥ* (compare יִקָּטֵל and תִּקָּטַלְנָה)

Jussive/Cohortative: The imperfects enable you to generate the conjugations related in form to the imperfect. Like the *qal,* the jussives of the *niphal* are identical to the imperfects. The cohortatives are formed by adding the extra ending to the first person imperfect forms (e.g., אֶקָּטֵל → אֶקָּטְלָה). The *waw* consecutive imperfects are then created by adding the special conjunction (e.g., יִקָּטֵל → וַיִּקָּטֵל). It will

4. This is similar to the way prepositions take over the definite article (e.g., הַמֶּלֶךְ + לְ → לַמֶּלֶךְ). See ch. 7.

be helpful if you get in the habit of associating the *waw* consecutive imperfects with the jussives and cohortatives rather than the imperfects. One reason for this is that the first person *waw* consecutive forms tend to utilize a form identical to the cohortative (e.g., וָאֶקָּטְלָה).[5]

Imperative: Like the *qal*, the imperatives of the *niphal* are produced by removing the preformatives from the second person imperfect forms. Remember that the preformative of the imperfect "covers up" the preformative of the infinitive. When the preformative is removed, the ה will reappear (תִּקָּטֵל minus תּ = הִקָּטֵל).

Inf. Cst.		Imperfects		Imperatives
הִקָּטֵל	+ י =	יִקָּטֵל		
		תִּקָּטֵל		
		תִּקָּטֵל	minus ת =	הִקָּטֵל
		תִּקָּטְלִי	minus ת =	הִקָּטְלִי
		אֶקָּטֵל		

Please note that all forms derived from the infinitive construct contain evidence of the *nun* that is characteristic of the *niphal*. Although the *nun* is not visible like it is with the *niphal* perfect and participle, it is still implicit in the *dagesh forte* (doubling dot) that represents the assimilation of the vowelless *nun* (compare נִקְטַל and הִקָּטֵל).

3) Niphal Infinitive Absolute

The *niphal* infinitive absolute appears as either הִקָּטֹל or נִקְטֹל . Both of these forms exhibit the characteristic long /ō/ theme vowel typical of the infinitive absolute. The variation in form reflects the familiar *niphal* patterns, one of them formed with the assimilated *nun* and the other formed with the visible *nun* (compare הִקָּטֹל and נִקְטֹל).

5. Remember that in the *hiphil* strong verb and many weak verb stems the jussives and *waw* consecutive imperfects both exhibit short forms in contrast with the imperfect (i.e., historic short theme vowels where the imperfect takes historic or contracted long vowels). For a review of that discussion see the end of ch. 15.

4) Niphal Participles (נִקְטָל)

The representative *niphal* participle (נִקְטָל) is the base to which you will add the noun endings to create the rest of the participles. Note that the representative form of the *niphal* participle has a long /ā/ theme vowel (נִקְטָל), that distinguishes it from the *niphal* perfect (נִקְטַל). The *niphal* participle keeps this long /ā/ throughout the paradigm. The reason it keeps the long /ā/ is that the noun endings that are attached to participles always carry the accent. The vowel rules apply normally with the near open a-class vowel lengthening (rule #2). As a result, there will always be a distinction between the *niphal* perfect and *niphal* participle that helps you differentiate these two forms.

	Niphal perfect		*Niphal* participle
he (3ms)	נִקְטַל	ms	נִקְטָל
she (3fs)	נִקְטְלָה	fs	נִקְטָלָה
you (2ms)	נִקְטַלְתָּ	mp	נִקְטָלִים
you (2fs)	נִקְטַלְתְּ	fp	נִקְטָלוֹת
I (1cs)	נִקְטַלְתִּי		

This long /ā/ theme vowel (ָ) is characteristic of all participles in the passive stems (*niphal, pual,* and *hophal*).

IMPORTANCE OF USING THE QAL AS A TEMPLATE

The full *niphal* paradigm can be created using the four representative forms of the *niphal* and the structural patterns of the *qal* strong verb. Certain forms of the *niphal* do not seem to follow the vowel rules you learned.[6]

As in the *qal*, these anomalies exist because finite verb forms (i.e., verbs other than participles and infinitives) were subjected to an accent

6. In some cases near open a-class vowels do not lengthen as the vowel rules anticipate (i.e., perfect נִקְטְלָה and נִקְטְלוּ). In other cases distant open syllables do not reduce as prescribed (i.e., imperfect יִקָּטְלוּ, תִּקָּטְלִי, תִּקָּטְלוּ). We encountered these same anomalies in the *qal* paradigm. For a discussion of these anomalous verb forms see the end of ch. 13 (on the *qal* perfects).

shift *after* the vowel rules were applied. Using the *qal* strong verb as a template allows you to create the *niphal* paradigms without worrying about secondary vowel changes.

SUMMARY

The *niphal* conveys the passive or reflexive sense of the meaning of the *qal* verb. Whenever you have difficulty translating a *niphal* verb, start with the *qal* meaning and then shift the focus to the passive or reflexive sense. The shift in focus between active and passive is an important feature of storytelling. Even though the active and passive could both accurately capture what took place, the author uses each type of verb to focus the reader's perception of what occurred. In the active *qal* he focuses on the individual doing the action and presents the direct object as supporting information. In the passive voice the author draws the reader's attention to the object impacted by the action by making it the focus of discussion (i.e., the subject of the verb).

Although the passive voice does not take a direct object, you will occasionally find the *niphal* accompanied by the direct object marker אֵת. In these cases, the direct object restates the subject of the passive verb.

To learn the *niphal*, carefully memorize the four representative forms and then apply the patterns you learned with the *qal* strong verb to form the rest of the paradigm. Learning the paradigms in this way eliminates the need for massive amounts of rote memorization and internalizes these forms more solidly because they are based on understanding. Whenever possible try to understand the concepts behind what you are learning rather than just trying to keep track of details.

EXERCISE FOR CHAPTER 18

Review the *niphal* paradigm on the following page, memorize the four representative forms, and then complete the exercise and translation for chapter 18 in the workbook.

NIPHAL VERB CHART

② הִקָּטֵל *Inf. Cst.* ↓

③ נִקְטֹל / הִקָּטֹל *Inf. Abs.*

	Pf.	*Impf.*	*Juss.*		*Impv.*	*Ptc.*
he (3ms)	① נִקְטַל	יִקָּטֵל	יִקָּטֵל			④ נִקְטָל
she (3fs)	נִקְטְלָה	תִּקָּטֵל	תִּקָּטֵל			נִקְטָלָה
you (2ms)	נִקְטַ֫לְתָּ	תִּקָּטֵל	תִּקָּטֵל	→	הִקָּטֵל	נִקְטָלִים
you (2fs)	נִקְטַ֫לְתְּ	תִּקָּטְלִי	תִּקָּטְלִי	→	הִקָּטְלִי	נִקְטָלוֹת
I (1cs)	נִקְטַ֫לְתִּי	אֶקָּטֵל	אֶקָּטְלָה			
they (3mp)	נִקְטְלוּ	יִקָּטְלוּ	יִקָּטְלוּ			
they (3fp)		תִּקָּטַ֫לְנָה	תִּקָּטַ֫לְנָה			
you (2mp)	נִקְטַלְתֶּם	תִּקָּטְלוּ	תִּקָּטְלוּ	→	הִקָּטְלוּ	
you (2fp)	נִקְטַלְתֶּן	תִּקָּטַ֫לְנָה	תִּקָּטַ֫לְנָה	→	הִקָּטַ֫לְנָה	
we (1cp)	נִקְטַ֫לְנוּ	נִקָּטֵל	נִקָּטְלָה			

CHAPTER 19

Piel, *Pual*, and *Hithpael*

The *piel*, *pual*, and *hithpael* make up the second family of verb stems. These verb stems got their names from the use of פעל in the verb paradigms of early Hebrew grammars. As a result, the first verb in each paradigm appeared as פִּעֵל, פֻּעַל, הִתְפַּעֵל. The disadvantage of this root was that the guttural ע could not reflect one of the key features of these stems—the doubling of the second consonant of the root. So now grammars use the root קטל to represent these stems (e.g., קִטֵּל, קֻטַּל, הִתְקַטֵּל). This does not mean that you will actually see these forms of קטל in the Hebrew Bible. Grammars simply use one standard root throughout the verb charts so that you see the characteristic features of each stem without being distracted by an unfamiliar root.

MEANING OF THE PIEL, PUAL, AND HITHPAEL

Cause a State of Being

The functions of the *piel*, *pual*, and *hithpael* stems can be captured by the two phrases "cause a state" and "look it up." The first phrase, "cause a state," expresses the tendency of the *piel* and related stems to take the basic sense of the *qal* stative and adjust it to express the idea of *causing a state of being*. For example, the *qal* verb גָּדַל is a stative verb meaning "he was great." When used in the *piel* it means "he caused to be great" (i.e., to magnify). In a particular context this causation may imply that someone is directly *causing* this state, *allowing* it to happen, or *declaring* it to be so (e.g., to declare someone to be holy).[1] Context determines which of these nuances is intended. Because these verbs express causation resulting in a state of being, it will come as no

1. Many grammars thus refer to this as a *declarative-factitive*. By this they mean that these verbs express how you "declare or cause [something] to be a fact." However, it will be easier to remember the simple phrase "cause a state" and then rely on context to determine how this causation is carried out.

surprise that the *piel, pual,* and *hithpael* are most common with verbs that have a stative meaning in the *qal*.

	Basic Meaning	Cause a State Look It Up!	
Active / Stative	QAL ***he was great***	**PIEL** ***he caused [someone] to be great***	
Passive	NIPHAL	**PUAL** ***he was caused to be great***	
Reflexive		**HITHPAEL** ***he caused himself to be great***	

Look It Up! The second type of *piel, pual,* and *hithpael* verbs is captured by the phrase "look it up!" The meaning of these verbs cannot be anticipated from the *qal* and you must *look them up in the lexicon.* This is why some of the vocabulary words you learn have separate entries for the *piel*. For example, the definition of סָפַר is "to count; *piel:* to recount, tell." This definition indicates that the verb has one meaning in the *qal* (and related *niphal*), but in the *piel* (and potentially the related stems)[2] it has a specialized meaning that must be memorized or looked up in the lexicon.[3] The "look it up!" category is primarily applicable to verbs that cannot have the *stative → cause a state of being* relationship found between the *qal* and *piel.*

The relationship between the *piel, pual,* and *hithpael* is like that of the *qal* and *niphal*. The *pual* and *hithpael* express the passive and reflexive meanings of the *piel* (e.g., *piel* "he magnified" → *pual* "he was magnified" and *hithpael* "he magnified himself"). The *hithpael* may also have a passive sense on occasion, similar to the dual function of the *niphal.*

Translating a Piel, Pual, or Hithpael When you encounter a *piel* verb form, convert the basic meaning of the root that you learned for the *qal* (i.e., your vocabulary definition) into an image of someone causing a state of being. The context must

2. The verb ספר appears in both *piel* and *pual* but never in the *hithpael.*

3. The *qal* "to count" refers to the numbering of items and the *piel* "to recount" refers to the retelling of an event.

guide you as to how the subject is causing this state. Are they directly causing it? Are they implicitly causing it by allowing it to happen? Or are they making it so by declaring it to be a fact? When the concept "cause a state" does not make sense, then you will need to look it up.

If the verb you encounter in the text is a *pual* or *hithpael*, you will find it easiest to make the initial conversion from *qal* to *piel* or "look it up" and then convert the active meaning you have ascribed to the *piel* into a passive or reflexive idea. Eventually you will be able to visualize the meaning of a *pual* or *hithpael* without recourse to the *piel*. But for now you will find it easiest to convert from *qal* to *piel*, and then from *piel* to either the *pual* or *hithpael*.

גָּדַל
to be great

CAUSE A STATE or **LOOK IT UP**

Piel	He made [someone] great (גִּדֵּל).	*Active*
Pual	He was made great (גֻּדַּל).	*Passive*
Hithpael	He made himself great (הִתְגַּדֵּל).	*Reflexive*

FORMATION OF THE PIEL, PUAL, AND HITHPAEL

Once you master the preformatives and sufformatives for each of the *qal* verb conjugations, you can learn an entirely new verb stem by concentrating on four forms: (1) the third person masculine singular perfect, (2) the infinitive construct, (3) the infinitive absolute, and (4) the masculine singular participle. These forms give you the structural patterns and vowel combinations unique to the verb stem. The remaining forms in the paradigm are generated by adding the appropriate preformatives and sufformatives from the *qal* verb. The verb forms you need to memorize for the *piel*, *pual*, and *hithpael* are presented in the following illustration.

Representative Forms for the *Piel–Hithpael*

	pf.	inf. cst.	inf. abs.	ptc.
Piel	קִטֵּל	קַטֵּל	קַטֵּל (קַטֹּל)†	מְקַטֵּל
Pual	קֻטַּל	קֻטַּל	קֻטֹּל	מְקֻטָּל
Hithpael	הִתְקַטֵּל	הִתְקַטֵּל	הִתְקַטֵּל	מִתְקַטֵּל

† The *piel* infinitive absolute קַטֵּל is the predominant form.

Characteristic Doubling

The primary characteristic of the *piel, pual,* and *hithpael* is the doubling of the second root consonant. Think: "The middle column takes a dot in the middle of each form." This *dagesh forte* not only helps identify these stems, it also ensures that the first vowel is in a stable closed unaccented syllable and is consistently visible.

The characteristic doubling dot is a helpful feature for identifying these stems. Unfortunately, it is sometimes omitted. Remember that the "Skin 'em Levi" consonants ("s" sounds ס, צ, שׂ, שׁ and the consonants (י, ו, ל, מ, נ, ק) can drop the *dagesh forte* when they appear with a vocal *shewa*. When the vowel under the second root letter reduces to *shewa* because of a vocalic sufformative, a "Skin 'em Levi" consonant may omit the *dagesh* (e.g., יְקַטְּלוּ vs. יְבַקְשׁוּ). The rest of the word remains unchanged and allows you to use the vowel pattern to identify the verb stem.

יְקַטְּלוּ	or	יְבַקְשׁוּ	*piel* 3mp impf.
"they will kill"		"they will seek"	

Vowel Patterns

As indicated by its name, the *piel* takes an i-class vowel in the perfect. This i-class pattern is distinct from the a-class vowel used in the other three representative forms of the *piel* (e.g., קִטֵּל vs. קַטֵּל, קַטֹּל, and מְקַטֵּל), and creates a distinction between *piel* perfects and all other *piel* conjugations.

	Perfects (i-class)	Other forms (a-class)
Piel	קִטֵּל	קַטֵּל קַטֵּל מְקַטֵּל

The *pual* and *hithpael* have a more consistent vowel pattern throughout. The *pual* has the same vowel under the first consonant of the root throughout. The *hithpael* has the same vowel pattern in every form.

Perfects

The representative forms of the perfect are used to generate the rest of the paradigm by adding the same endings you learned for the *qal* perfect.[4] Moreover, the *qal* will accurately help you vocalize verb forms that you might otherwise wrongly anticipate. For example, you might expect the *piel* perfect קִטֵּל to produce a form like קִטֵּ֫לְתָּ*. But this is incorrect. The form is קִטַּ֫לְתָּ, just like you see in the *qal* verb קָטַ֫לְתָּ. As a result, the easiest way to learn the perfects for any strong verb paradigm is to use the *qal* verb as a template and simply apply the same endings.

Infinitive Construct and Related Forms

As you learned in the last chapter, the infinitive construct form is the basis for most of the conjugations in each verb stem. The imperfect is formed by adding a preformative, such as *yod*, directly onto the infinitive construct (e.g., קַטֵּל + י). In the *piel* and *pual* this preformative is added directly onto the word with a *shewa* (e.g., קַטֵּל + י = יְקַטֵּל).[5] In the *hithpael* the imperfect is formed by "covering up" the preformative *heh* that already appears on the infinitive construct (הִתְקַטֵּל + י = יִתְקַטֵּל). This is just like what you saw with the *niphal*.

Once you have the initial imperfect form, you can easily produce the remainder of the imperfects for each verb stem. These in turn will enable you to produce the jussives, cohortatives, and *waw* consecutive imperfects. By removing the preformative of the second person imperfects you are able to create the imperatives. Remember that the preformatives in the *hithpael* imperfect merely "cover up" the preformative on the infinitive construct, so when the preformative is removed to create the imperative, the *heh* will reappear (e.g., תִּתְקַטֵּל → הִתְקַטֵּל).

4. The *qal* template helps you create even anomalous forms. E.g., קִטְּלָה and קִטְּלוּ seem to *reduce* a near open a-class vowel. See the discussion in ch. 13.

5. The *qal* verb naturally requires a preformative vowel because adding a preformative without a vowel would result in a cluster of vowelless consonants at the front of the word (e.g., the impossible יְקְטֵל*).

The *pual* does not take jussives or imperatives. A passive command makes no sense because you only have control over what you do, not what happens to you. As a result, you will only see imperatives in the *piel* and *hithpael*.

Participles Another convenient aspect of these verb stems is that the participle is also formed off the infinitive construct. This is a characteristic of all the strong verb stems other than the *qal* and *niphal*. All you need to create the participle is to add a *mem* onto the front of the infinitive construct (e.g., קַטֵּל + מ → מְקַטֵּל).

As usual, the participles follow the standard rules for vowel change in verbs. Once the endings are added, the near open i-class vowel of the *piel* and *hithpael* reduces (e.g., מְקַטֵּל, מְקַטְּלָה, מְקַטְּלִים, מְקַטְּלוֹת), and the near open a-class vowel of the *pual* lengthens (e.g., מְקֻטָּל, מְקֻטָּלָה, מְקֻטָּלִים, מְקֻטָּלוֹת). This long a-class vowel is charactistic of all the passive participles (*niphal, pual, hophal*). The *piel* feminine singular participle predominantly follows the segolate pattern (מְקַטֶּ֫לֶת) instead of simply adding the feminine ending (מְקַטְּלָה). You may recall that you learned this type of feminine segolate ending as an alternate form in the *qal* (e.g., קֹטְלָה and קֹטֶ֫לֶת). Remember that all participles outside of the *qal* and *niphal* are created by adding a *mem* to the front of the infinitive construct.

METATHESIS AND ASSIMILATION IN THE HITHPAEL

The *hithpael* is one of the easiest verb forms to recognize because of its consistency in form and its two-consonant preformative. The following discussion may sound complicated, but the idiosyncrasies of the *hithpael* are natural adjustments for the sake of pronunciation.

Metathesis The *hithpael* sometimes transposes or switches the order of the letters in the verb. This is due to the fact that Hebrew does not like to have a vowelless *tav* (with silent *shewa*) immediately before an "s" sound (called *sibilants*). So whenever the *hithpael* preformative (הִתְ) appears before the consonants ס, צ, שׂ, or שׁ, the "t" and "s" sounds will switch places while retaining the original placement of the vowels (e.g., *הִתְשַׁמֵּר → הִשְׁתַּמֵּר).[6] This phenomenon is called *metathesis*. It might

6. The *tav* in the second form has a *dagesh lene* because it now follows a silent *shewa*.

be helpful for you to remember that children do something similar in English when they are trying to learn the word "spaghetti." You can call this the "p-sghetti" rule.

הִתְשַׁמֵּר* → הִשְׁתַּמֵּר   *metathesis ("ts" → "st")*

If you relax and concentrate on the principles you have learned, metathesis in a word like הִשְׁתַּמֵּר need not trouble you. You know that while the ה could be a preformative (הִשְׁתַּמֵּר), the שׁ and ר are not the kind of letters added to the front or back of Hebrew words, so they must be part of the root. But this seems to leave you with a root containing four root consonants (i.e., הִשְׁתַּמֵּר). When you have a root that seems too long, remember that you might have a word with a two-consonant preformative. Also check for the "st" combination indicative of metathesis.

Metathesis and Partial Assimilation

In some instances the appearance of the *hithpael* is impacted not only by metathesis but also by partial assimilation of the consonants. This happens frequently with verbal roots that start with a צ. For example, when the verb צדק ("be righteous") occurs in the *hithpael*, the צ and ת switch places (e.g., הִתְצַדֵּק*→ הִצְתַּדֵּק*). But there is a second change that occurs as well. The hard "s" sound of the צ causes the ת to to switch to a ט, which historically was also a hard sound distinct from ת (i.e., הִצְתַּדֵּק* → הִצְטַדֵּק).[7] This is called partial assimilation because the ת takes on only part of the features of the צ.[8]

metathesis + partial assimilation

הִתְצַדֵּק* → הִצְתַּדֵּק* → הִצְטַדֵּק

This assimilation of consonants is important to keep in mind when trying to determine the verbal root of irregular verb forms. For example, when you encounter the verb הִצְטַדֵּק you again know that the consonant ה is a common preformative for adding onto verbs (הִצְטַדֵּק). But

7. The *tav* has a *dagesh lene* because it follows a silent *shewa*. The *tet* of the final form does not take the *dagesh lene* because it is not a *BeGaD KePhaT* letter.

8. Partial assimilation occurs in English as well. For example, the Latin prefix *in*- means "not." This prefix fully assimilates the "n" to the following letter in the word irresponsible, but only partially assimilates in the word impossible. The historic distinction in pronunciation between ת and ט is no longer apparent, but the historical distinction is still evident in verbs like this.

you need a three consonant root and removing the ה still leaves you with four consonants. Neither the צ nor ק is an acceptable preformative or sufformative. But the "st" (צט) combination alerts you to the potential for metathesis and helps you spot the actual root צדק.

Metathesis and Full Assimilation

In other instances you may even see full assimilation when the *hithpael* preformative (הִתְ) appears before consonants like ד or ט. This is because the ד, ט, and ת are all pronounced in the same place in the mouth.[9] For example, the root דבר ("to speak") appears several times as a *hithpael* participle. When it does you will find that the ת has fully assimilated to the following ד (e.g., the participle מִתְדַבֵּר* → מִדְדַבֵּר* → מִדַּבֵּר).[10] A similar phenomenon happens with the root טמא ("be unclean"). In the *hithpael* it will shift from מִתְטַמֵּא* → מִטְטַמֵּא* → מִטַּמֵּא.

Full Assimilation

מִתְדַבֵּר* → מִדְדַבֵּר* → מִדַּבֵּר

מִתְטַמֵּא* → מִטְטַמֵּא* → מִטַּמֵּא

HISHTAPHEL OF חוה

The verb הִשְׁתַּחֲוָה, meaning "worship, prostrate oneself" (i.e., bow with one's face to the ground), is a rare verb stem that used to be confused with the *hithpael*. Older lexicons assumed הִשְׁתַּחֲוָה (impf. יִשְׁתַּחֲוֶה) was a *hithpael* from the root שחו* that metathesized like the forms above (i.e., הִתְשַׁחֲוָה* → הִשְׁתַּחֲוָה).[11] Scholars now recognize this word as a *hishtaphel* stem of the root חוה (i.e., הִשְׁתַּחֲוָה) The *hishtaphel* stem is comprised of a reflexive *hit-* preformative (like the *hithpael*) plus the *shaphel* stem that appears only in other Semitic languages (i.e., הִתְשַׁחֲוָה* → הִשְׁתַּחֲוָה after metathesis). This word appears frequently in the Hebrew Bible, but חוה is the only root that occurs in the *hishtaphel* stem.

9. These sounds are referred to as *dentals* because they are articulated with the tongue placed right behind the teeth.

10. The first form should have a *dagesh lene* in the ד, but it has been left out in order to heighten the contrast with the *dagesh forte* in the second form.

11. See, for example, the lexicon by Brown-Driver-Briggs (BDB).

הִשְׁתַּחֲוָה *Hishtaphel* of חוה
"to worship"

EXERCISE FOR CHAPTER 19

Review the paradigms for the *piel*, *pual*, and *hithpael* on the following pages, memorize the representative forms for each stem, and then complete the exercise and translation for chapter 19 in the workbook.

PIEL VERB CHART

Inf. Cst. ② קַטֵּל ↓

Inf. Abs. קַטֵּל (קַטֹּל) ③

	Pf.	*Impf.*	*Juss.*		*Impv.*	*Ptc.*
he (3ms)	① קִטֵּל	יְקַטֵּל	יְקַטֵּל			④ מְקַטֵּל
she (3fs)	קִטְּלָה	תְּקַטֵּל	תְּקַטֵּל			מְקַטֶּ֫לֶת
you (2ms)	קִטַּ֫לְתָּ	תְּקַטֵּל	תְּקַטֵּל	→	קַטֵּל	מְקַטְּלִים
you (2fs)	קִטַּ֫לְתְּ	תְּקַטְּלִי	תְּקַטְּלִי	→	קַטְּלִי	מְקַטְּלוֹת
I (1cs)	קִטַּ֫לְתִּי	אֲקַטֵּל	אֲקַטְּלָה			
they (3mp)	קִטְּלוּ	יְקַטְּלוּ	יְקַטְּלוּ			
they (3fp)		תְּקַטֵּ֫לְנָה	תְּקַטֵּ֫לְנָה			
you (2mp)	קִטַּלְתֶּם	תְּקַטְּלוּ	תְּקַטְּלוּ	→	קַטְּלוּ	
you (2fp)	קִטַּלְתֶּן	תְּקַטֵּ֫לְנָה	תְּקַטֵּ֫לְנָה	→	קַטֵּ֫לְנָה	
we (1cp)	קִטַּ֫לְנוּ	נְקַטֵּל	נְקַטְּלָה			

PUAL VERB CHART

② קֻטַּל *Inf. Cst.* ↓

③ קֻטֹּל *Inf. Abs.*

	Pf.	*Impf.*	*Ptc.*
he (3ms)	① קֻטַּל	יְקֻטַּל	④ מְקֻטָּל
she (3fs)	קֻטְּלָה	תְּקֻטַּל	מְקֻטָּלָה
you (2ms)	קֻטַּלְתָּ	תְּקֻטַּל	מְקֻטָּלִים
you (2fs)	קֻטַּלְתְּ	תְּקֻטְּלִי	מְקֻטָּלוֹת
I (1cs)	קֻטַּלְתִּי	אֲקֻטַּל	
they (3mp)	קֻטְּלוּ	יְקֻטְּלוּ	
they (3fp)		תְּקֻטַּלְנָה	
you (2mp)	קֻטַּלְתֶּם	תְּקֻטְּלוּ	
you (2fp)	קֻטַּלְתֶּן	תְּקֻטַּלְנָה	
we (1cp)	קֻטַּלְנוּ	נְקֻטַּל	

② הִתְקַטֵּל ***Inf. Cst.***

↓

③ הִתְקַטֵּל ***Inf. Abs.***

	Pf.	*Impf.*	*Juss.*		*Impv.*	*Ptc.*
he (3ms)	① הִתְקַטֵּל	יִתְקַטֵּל	יִתְקַטֵּל			④ מִתְקַטֵּל
she (3fs)	הִתְקַטְּלָה	תִּתְקַטֵּל	תִּתְקַטֵּל			מִתְקַטְּלָה
you (2ms)	הִתְקַטַּ֫לְתָּ	תִּתְקַטֵּל	תִּתְקַטֵּל	→	הִתְקַטֵּל	מִתְקַטְּלִים
you (2fs)	הִתְקַטַּ֫לְתְּ	תִּתְקַטְּלִי	תִּתְקַטְּלִי	→	הִתְקַטְּלִי	מִתְקַטְּלוֹת
I (1cs)	הִתְקַטַּ֫לְתִּי	אֶתְקַטֵּל	אֶתְקַטְּלָה			
they (3mp)	הִתְקַטְּלוּ	יִתְקַטְּלוּ	יִתְקַטְּלוּ			
they (3fp)		תִּתְקַטֵּ֫לְנָה	תִּתְקַטֵּ֫לְנָה			
you (2mp)	הִתְקַטַּלְתֶּם	תִּתְקַטְּלוּ	תִּתְקַטְּלוּ	→	הִתְקַטְּלוּ	
you (2fp)	הִתְקַטַּלְתֶּן	תִּתְקַטֵּ֫לְנָה	תִּתְקַטֵּ֫לְנָה	→	הִתְקַטֵּ֫לְנָה	
we (1cp)	הִתְקַטַּ֫לְנוּ	נִתְקַטֵּל	נִתְקַטְּלָה			

CHAPTER 20

Hiphil and *Hophal*

The *hiphil* and *hophal* make up the third family of verb stems. These verb stems got their names from the use of פעל in the early Hebrew grammars, so rely upon the names of the stems themselves to help you remember the sound and form of the verbs in each paradigm.

MEANING OF THE HIPHIL AND HOPHAL

Like the other stem families in the Hebrew verbal system, the *hiphil* and *hophal* carry a special nuance of meaning. The *qal* and *niphal* convey simple actions or states of being. The *piel-pual-hithpael* family expresses the notion of causing a state of being (*cause a state*) or carries an independent meaning that requires you to *look it up*. The *hiphil* and *hophal* are used to describe someone causing another person or object to perform the action of the *qal* (*cause an action*). However, the *hiphil* and *hophal* sometimes have a meaning that is not causative, and you will need to *look it up*.

<table>
<tr><th></th><th>Basic Meaning</th><th>Cause a State
Look It Up!</th><th>Cause an Action
Look It Up!</th></tr>
<tr><td>Active / Stative</td><td>QAL
HE HEARD</td><td>PIEL</td><td>HIPHIL
HE CAUSED TO HEAR</td></tr>
<tr><td>Passive</td><td rowspan="2">NIPHAL</td><td>PUAL</td><td>HOPHAL
HE WAS CAUSED TO HEAR</td></tr>
<tr><td>Reflexive</td><td>HITHPAEL</td><td></td></tr>
</table>

As you recall, the *piel*, *pual*, and *hithpael* verbs have a causative function. The difference is that the *piel* expresses causing a state of being (e.g., "cause someone/something *to BE x*") while the *hiphil* tends to convey the idea of causing an action (e.g., "causing someone/something *to DO x*"). Thus *qal* verbs with stative meanings often appear in the *piel* to express causation, while *qal* roots with active meanings appear in the *hiphil*. The *hophal* is naturally a passive expression of the *hiphil*. For example:

שָׁמַע to hear	**CAUSE A STATE** or **LOOK IT UP**		*Active*
Hiphil	He caused to hear (הִשְׁמִיעַ).	CAUSE AN ACTION	*Active*
Hophal	He was caused to hear (הָשְׁמַע).		*Passive*

The causative meaning of the *hiphil* and *hophal* is fairly consistent, so you should have little trouble translating most of these verbs. Keep in mind that the core idea of causing an action may not always strictly come across as *making* something happen. In some cases it could also imply the notion of *allowing* it to occur (e.g., Prov 10:3 "The LORD *will not allow* the righteous *to hunger*"). Moreover, in many cases your English translation may use entirely different words that express the element of causation and the core meaning of the root. For example, a concept like "cause to hear" is best captured with something like "proclaim." Similarly, "cause to come" is expressed in English as "bring."

Sometimes the *hiphil* seems to lose this causative focus. Scholars label this use of the *hiphil* as an *internal hiphil*. In other words, the action is generated with respect to oneself rather than causing another person to do it. For example, Psalm 113:5–6 declares, "Who is like the LORD our God, who sits on high and *stoops* to look upon the heavens and earth."[1] Although this verb is in the *hiphil*, the context makes it quite apparent that God is doing it himself. This also explains why Zeph 3:17 is translated differently by the various English translations. Some state that God "*will quiet [you]* with his love" (NIV, ESV), while others suggest that God "*will be quiet* in his love" (KJV, NASB). The first translation presupposes the typical causal meaning of the *hiphil* and

1. The simple sense of the *hiphil* is also seen in Job 39:27 where the text states, "Is it at your command that the eagle *takes flight*?" (יַגְבִּיהַּ נָשֶׁר). The eagle is not causing something else to fly, nor in this context is God causing the eagle to fly. In English we see this action as a simple active verb.

the second translation assumes that the context demands that God is acting in reference to himself—both viable meanings of the *hiphil*.

FORMATION OF THE HIPHIL AND HOPHAL

The full paradigms for the *hiphil* and *hophal* are found in the charts at the end of this chapter. The discussion below will guide you through those charts. The representative forms that you need to remember for the *hiphil* and *hophal* are as follows:

Representative Forms of the *Hiphil*-*Hophal*

	Pf.	Inf. Cst.	Inf. Abs.	Ptc.
Hiphil	הִקְטִיל	הַקְטִיל	הַקְטֵל	מַקְטִיל
Hophal	הָקְטַל	הָקְטַל	הָקְטֵל	מָקְטָל

Characteristic Features

The representative forms of the *hiphil* and *hophal* reveal a number of characteristic features.

1) The Hiphil is characterized by ḥireq-yod

One of the dominant features of the *hiphil* is the *ḥireq-yod* theme vowel (e.g., הִקְטִיל). Although the *ḥireq-yod* does not appear in all *hiphil* verb forms, it is one of the most striking features of the *hiphil*. You should anticipate the *ḥireq-yod* in most forms as a helpful key for recognizing the *hiphil*. Since the *ḥireq-yod* does not always appear, it is also helpful to understand the principles dictating when *ḥireq-yod* is used or not used so that you can confirm that a verb without this feature is indeed a *hiphil*. The principles governing the use of *ḥireq-yod* in the *hiphil* are discussed below.

2) Hiphil preformatives: i-class perfect / a-class everywhere else

A second observation about these representative forms is that the *hiphil* perfect has an initial i-class preformative vowel (הִקְטִיל pf.) while all the other *hiphil* forms take an a-class preformative vowel (הַקְטִיל inf. cst.). We saw this same distinction in the *piel* (e.g., perfect קִטֵּל vs. others מְקַטֵּל, יְקַטֵּל, קַטֵּל). The difference is that while the *piel* has these vowels under the *first consonant* of the root (e.g., קִטֵּל, קַטֵּל, מְקַטֵּל), the *hiphil* has these vowels before that consonant under the *preformative* (e.g., הִקְטִיל, יַקְטִיל, הַקְטִיל). Think: "i-class in the perfect; a-class everywhere else."

	Perfects (i-class)	Other forms (a-class)		
Piel	קִטֵּל	קַטֵּל	קַטֵּל	מְקַטֵּל
Hiphil	הִקְטִיל	הַקְטִיל	הַקְטֵל	מַקְטִיל

3) Hiphil/Hophal participles take mem

A third feature of *hiphil* and *hophal* is the *mem* preformative used in the participles. This *mem* preformative is seen in the *piel* (מְקַטֵּל), *pual* (מְקֻטָּל), *hithpael* (מִתְקַטֵּל), *hiphil* (מַקְטִיל), and *hophal* (מָקְטָל). The only strong verb stems that lack this pattern are the *qal* and *niphal* that you learned first (e.g., *qal* active קֹטֵל / passive קָטוּל, and *niphal* נִקְטָל). So be on the lookout for this telltale sign of the participle as you read Hebrew texts.

Participles

קָטוּל/קֹטֵל *Qal*	מְקַטֵּל *Piel*	מַקְטִיל *Hiphil*
נִקְטָל *Niphal*	מְקֻטָּל *Pual*	מָקְטָל *Hophal*
	מִתְקַטֵּל *Hithpael*	

4) Hiphil/Hophal infinitive absolutes have matching theme vowels

The last thing you should note about these representative forms is that there is a close affinity between the *hiphil* and *hophal* infinitive absolutes. All the other passive infinitive absolutes are formed with a characteristic long /ō/ vowel. The *niphal* infinitive absolute is הִקָּטֹל (or נִקְטֹל) and the *pual* infinitive absolute is קֻטֹּל. But the *hiphil* and *hophal* infinitive absolutes both exhibit a long /ē/ theme vowel (e.g., הַקְטֵל and הָקְטֵל). This vowel is quite natural for the *hiphil* with its recurring i-class theme vowels. The *hophal*, which otherwise has a-class theme vowels, is apparently borrowing the vowel pattern of the *hiphil* to which it is most closely related in meaning.

Formation of the Hiphil

While the representative forms are foundational to generating the full *hiphil* paradigm, two additional principles are necessary to help you anticipate the seemingly sporadic presence of the characteristic *ḥireq-yod* theme vowel (e.g., הִקְטִיל). A consistent pattern governs when this *ḥireq-yod* is used and when it is not. The use of *ḥireq-yod* is related to the type of sufformative—namely, no ending, vocalic sufformative, and consonantal sufformative.

No ending	Vocalic sufformatives	Consonantal sufformatives
קָטַל	קָטְלָה	קָטַלְתָּ

Because the *ḥireq-yod* is a key feature of the *hiphil*, it helps to think of the *ḥireq-yod* as the default form for the *hiphil* (e.g., pf. הִקְטִיל, הִקְטִילָה). It is then only necessary to recognize when the *ḥireq-yod* is *not* used. The *ḥireq-yod* does not appear with any consonantal sufformatives or short forms with no endings.

Ḥireq-yod Not Used with Consonantal Sufformatives

Throughout all the *hiphil* paradigms, including the short forms (jussives and imperatives), any *hiphil* that has a consonantal sufformative does not have the characteristic *ḥireq-yod.* A "consonantal sufformative" is a sufformative that begins with a consonant (e.g., הִקְטַלְתָּ). The *hiphil* perfects with consonantal sufformatives follow the *qal* template (e.g., *qal* קָטַלְתָּ and *hiphil* הִקְטַלְתָּ), just like all the other perfects you have learned (e.g., *niphal* נִקְטַלְתָּ, *piel* קִטַּלְתָּ, *pual* קֻטַּלְתָּ, *hithpael* הִתְקַטַּלְתָּ). *Hiphil* imperfects that appear with consonantal sufformatives take a *tsere* (e.g., תַּקְטִיל → תַּקְטֵלְנָה).

Ḥireq-yod Not Used in Short Forms With No Endings

The second context in which *ḥireq-yod* is not used is with *hiphil* short forms that have no ending. This grammar has repeatedly stressed the fact that the imperfects and jussives are distinct verb forms despite their similarity in appearance. Moreover, the grammar has also asked you to think about generating the imperatives and *waw* consecutive imperfects off the jussive (rather than the imperfect). The reason for the insistence upon this distinction is that the jussives, imperatives, and *waw* consecutive imperfects all display a tendency toward forms that are historically shorter than the forms of the imperfect. For this reason, we refer to these types of verbs as *short forms*.

In the strong verb this distinction in length is seen only in the *hiphil*. The *hiphil* jussives, imperatives, and *waw* consecutive imperfects include forms that are distinct from the historic long vowel of the imperfects (e.g., imperfect תַּקְטִיל, but jussive תַּקְטֵל). In addition to the forms with consonantal sufformatives that do not take the *ḥireq-yod* in any *hiphil* conjugation, the *hiphil* short forms with no ending also appear without the characteristic *ḥireq-yod*.

Table 20.1: Principles Governing the Use of *Ḥireq-yod* in the *Hiphil*

הִקְטִיל	Characteristic *ḥireq-yod*	
הִקְטַלְתָּ תַּקְטֵלְנָה	1) Consonantal endings = no *ḥireq-yod* • Perfects use a-class (like *qal*), • others use i-class	
יַקְטֵל	2) No-ending short forms = no *ḥireq-yod* (i.e., *tsere* in juss., impv., *waw* cons. impf.)	

Using the Qal as a Template

Apart from the special guidelines for the *ḥireq-yod* discussed above, the formation of the *hiphil* verb stem matches what you have done to learn the other verb stems.

Perfect: The representative form of the *hiphil* perfect (הִקְטִיל) is used to produce the rest of the perfect paradigm. Remember to look for the i-class preformative vowel that identifies the *hiphil* perfect (הִקְטִיל) in contrast with the a-class preformative vowel used in all the rest of the *hiphil* paradigms. Since the perfects are formed predominantly with consonantal sufformatives, the characteristic *ḥireq-yod* of the *hiphil* only appears in the third person forms. Fortunately, these are the forms most often encountered in the narrative you are currently reading. However, you need to become accustomed to all the *hiphil* forms and remember that all forms with consonantal sufformatives follow the *qal* template (e.g., *qal* קָטַ֫לְתָּ, *hiphil* הִקְטַ֫לְתָּ).

Hiphil Perfects

he (3ms)	הִקְטִיל	they (3mp)	הִקְטִ֫ילוּ
she (3fs)	הִקְטִ֫ילָה	they (3fp)	
you (2ms)	הִקְטַ֫לְתָּ	you (2mp)	הִקְטַלְתֶּם
you (2fs)	הִקְטַ֫לְתְּ	you (2fp)	הִקְטַלְתֶּן
I (1cs)	הִקְטַ֫לְתִּי	we (1cp)	הִקְטַ֫לְנוּ

Imperfect: With the exception of the infinitive absolute (הַקְטֵל), all the rest of the *hiphil* verbs can be generated off the infinitive construct (הַקְטִיל). In the imperfect the preformative letter covers up the *heh* preformative of the infinitive construct (e.g., יַקְטִיל = י + הַקְטִיל), though in rare cases the imperfect preformative is added without displacing the *heh* (e.g., יְהוֹשִׁיעַ and יוֹשִׁיעַ "he will save"). The *hiphil* imperfect is affected by the additions of sufformatives as well. Remember that the *ḥireq-yod* will not be present if the verb takes a consonantal sufformative (e.g., יַקְטִיל, תַּקְטִיל, תַּקְטִיל, תַּקְטִ֫ילִי, . . . תַּקְטֵ֫לְנָה). Forms with a consonantal sufformative reflect a historic short i-class vowel (lengthened to *tsere*) in place of the characteristic *ḥireq-yod*.

Jussive/Cohortative and Waw Consecutive: From the imperfects you can predict the jussives and cohortatives, which in turn help you form the imperatives and *waw* consecutives. However, the *hiphil* maintains a distinction between the imperfects and the short form jussives, imperatives, and *waw* consecutives. Jussives and imperatives without sufformatives take short forms so that the *hiphil* imperfect תַּקְטִיל is distinct from the corresponding forms in the jussive תַּקְטֵל and imperative הַקְטֵל. The *waw* consecutives look just like the jussive/cohortative paradigm with the special conjunction added (וַיַּקְטֵל, וַתַּקְטֵל, וַתַּקְטֵל, וַתַּקְטִ֫ילִי, וָאַקְטִ֫ילָה, etc.).

Imperative: When forming the imperatives remember that removing the second person preformative (ת) causes the *heh* ה preformative of the *hiphil* to reappear (תַּקְטֵל to הַקְטֵל). Though both the *hiphil* perfect and imperative appear with a *heh* preformative, the distinctive i-class preformative of the perfect allows you to tell the two forms apart (cf. pf. הִקְטִ֫ילוּ and impv. הַקְטִ֫ילוּ).

Participle: The *hiphil* participles take the a-class preformative vowel like most of the *hiphil* paradigm (מַקְטִיל). Since none of the noun endings attached to the participle begin with a consonant, all

Hiphil Inf. Cst.	הַקְטִיל	→	*Hiphil* Ptc.		מַקְטִיל
	↓				
	Hiphil Impf.		*Hiphil* Juss.		*Hiphil* Imp.
he (3ms)	יַקְטִיל	→	‡יַקְטֵל		
she (3fs)	תַּקְטִיל		תַּקְטֵל		
you (2ms)	תַּקְטִיל		תַּקְטֵל	→	הַקְטֵל
you (2fs)	תַּקְטִ֫ילִי		תַּקְטִ֫ילִי	→	הַקְטִ֫ילִי
I (1cs)	אַקְטִיל		אַקְטִ֫ילָה		
he (3ms)	יַקְטִ֫ילוּ		יַקְטִ֫ילוּ		
she (3fs)	†תַּקְטֵ֫לְנָה		תַּקְטֵ֫לְנָה		
you (2ms)	תַּקְטִ֫ילוּ		תַּקְטִ֫ילוּ	→	הַקְטִ֫ילוּ
you (2fs)	תַּקְטֵ֫לְנָה		תַּקְטֵ֫לְנָה	→	הַקְטֵ֫לְנָה
I (1cp)	נַקְטִיל		נַקְטִ֫ילָה		

† *Hiphil* forms with consonantal sufformatives do not take *ḥireq-yod*
†† Short forms with no ending do not take *ḥireq-yod*

these participles will evidence the characteristic *ḥireq-yod* of the *hiphil* (e.g., מַקְטִיל, מַקְטִילָה, מַקְטִילִים, מַקְטִילוֹת).

Formation of the Hophal

The formation of the *hophal* can be created from the representative forms. Remember that the *hophal* (like the *pual*) will have no imperatives. A passive imperative makes no sense because the passive expresses what happens to you, not what you do.

Inf. Cst. ② הָקְטַל ↓ (to Impf.)

Inf. Abs. ③ הָקְטֵל

	Perfect	Impf.	Jussive	Impv.	Ptc.
he (3ms) she (3fs) you (2ms) you (2fs) I (1cs) they (3mp) they (3fp) you (2mp) you (2fp) we (1cp)	① הָקְטַל ↓ + *the* qal *endings*	*infinitive construct* + *performatives* & *sufformatives*	***N/A***	***N/A***	④ מָקְטָל ↓ + *the* qal *endings*

While you are learning the *hophal* הָקְטַל, note that the historic form is הֻקְטַל*. The *hophal* typically uses the short /o/ to represent the u-class vowel in this verb because *qibbuts* (ֻ) is used almost exclusively before doubled consonants. However, you will see forms with the *qibbuts* הֻשְׁכַּב (*hophal* pf. "he has been laid down"). Moreover, an awareness of this historic form will prepare you for adjustments you encounter when learning the Hebrew weak verbs (chs. 24–33).

EXERCISE FOR CHAPTER 20

Review the paradigms for the *hiphil* and *hophal* on the following pages and complete the exercise on representative forms in the workbook. Read the "Introduction to Hebrew Poetry" before completing the translation exercise for chapter 20.

HIPHIL VERB CHART

Inf. Cst.	②הַקְטִיל ↓		Inf. Abs.	③הַקְטֵל

	Pf.	Impf.	Juss.		Impv.	Ptc.
he (3ms)	①הִקְטִיל	יַקְטִיל	יַקְטֵל			④מַקְטִיל
she (3fs)	הִקְטִילָה	תַּקְטִיל	תַּקְטֵל			מַקְטִילָה
you (2ms)	הִקְטַלְתָּ	תַּקְטִיל	תַּקְטֵל	→	הַקְטֵל	מַקְטִילִים
you (2fs)	הִקְטַלְתְּ	תַּקְטִילִי	תַּקְטִילִי	→	הַקְטִילִי	מַקְטִילוֹת
I (1cs)	הִקְטַלְתִּי	אַקְטִיל	אַקְטִילָה			
they (3mp)	הִקְטִילוּ	יַקְטִילוּ	יַקְטִילוּ			
they (3fp)		תַּקְטֵלְנָה	תַּקְטֵלְנָה			
you (2mp)	הִקְטַלְתֶּם	תַּקְטִילוּ	תַּקְטִילוּ	→	הַקְטִילוּ	
you (2fp)	הִקְטַלְתֶּן	תַּקְטֵלְנָה	תַּקְטֵלְנָה	→	הַקְטֵלְנָה	
we (1cp)	הִקְטַלְנוּ	נַקְטִיל	נַקְטִילָה			

Remember: The *hiphil* has a characteristic *ḥireq-yod* except when: (1) forms with consonantal sufformatives take short /a/ in the perfect (like the *qal*) and *tsere* everywhere else, and (2) short forms with no ending take *tsere*.

HOPHAL VERB CHART

Inf. Cst.	Inf. Abs.
② הָקְטַל ↓	③ הָקְטֵל *matches Hiphil*

	Pf.	*Impf.*	*Ptc.*
he (3ms)	① הָקְטַל	יָקְטַל	④ מָקְטָל
she (3fs)	הָקְטְלָה	תָּקְטַל	מָקְטָלָה
you (2ms)	הָקְטַ֫לְתָּ	תָּקְטַל	מָקְטָלִים
you (2fs)	הָקְטַ֫לְתְּ	תָּקְטְלִי	מָקְטָלוֹת
I (1cs)	הָקְטַ֫לְתִּי	אָקְטַל	
they (3mp)	הָקְטְלוּ	יָקְטְלוּ	
they (3fp)		תָּקְטַ֫לְנָה	
you (2mp)	הָקְטַלְתֶּם	תָּקְטְלוּ	
you (2fp)	הָקְטַלְתֶּן	תָּקְטַ֫לְנָה	
we (1cp)	הָקְטַ֫לְנוּ	נָקְטַל	

CHAPTER 21

Rare Verb Stems

In addition to the common verb stems that you have already learned, there are additional formations that appear from time to time. While these other stems are relatively rare in comparison with the strong verb stems, some of them are frequent enough to merit discussion. You have already been introduced to the *hishtaphel* הִשְׁתַּחֲוָה (imperfect יִשְׁתַּחֲוֶה) from the root חוה ("to worship").[1] A few of the other rare stems are discussed below. You need not memorize specific forms, but you should memorize the names of these stems. The labels given to them by scholars match their form and thus will make parsing them rather intuitive.

REDUPLICATED STEMS

In many cases the less common verb stems serve as substitutes for the standard *piel, pual,* and *hithpael.* One set of irregular verbs reduplicates one of the root consonants. The names of these stems suggest their structure, thus the *polel, polal,* and *hithpolel* appear as קוֹמֵם, קוֹמַם, הִתְקוֹמֵם (from קום). In another set of stems, two consonants reduplicate to create the *pilpel, polpal,* and *hithpalpel* series (e.g., כִּלְכֵּל and כָּלְכַּל from כול and הִתְמַהְמֵהַּ from מהה).[2] To these forms are added the same endings used for

1. See the discussion of this verb in ch. 19. The *hishtaphel* הִשְׁתַּחֲוָה occurs 164 times in the Hebrew Bible.

2. The *polel-hithpolel* stems together occur almost 300 times and the *pilpel-hithpalpel* stems occur about 70 times. As noted in previous chapters, the early Hebrew grammars generated the verb paradigms using the root פעל. In their system the letter *pe* represented the first consonant of any root, the letter *ayin* represented the second consonant of any root, and the letter *lamed* represented the third consonant of any root. The names of these irregular stems (like the names of the strong verb) are all based off פעל in an attempt to convey something about the structure and vocalization of the verb. For example, the *polpal* tells you that the verb reduplicates using only the first and last consonants of the root (e.g., פלפל with no ע or second root letter).

all the other verb stems: perfects with perfect endings, imperfects with imperfect preformatives and sufformatives, and so on.

	Strong verb	Reduplication (one consonant)	Reduplication (two consonants)
Active	*Piel* קִטֵּל	*Polel* קוֹמֵם	*Pilpel* כִּלְכֵּל
Passive	*Pual* קֻטַּל	*Polal* קוֹמַם	*Polpal* כָּלְכַּל
Reflexive	*Hithpael* הִתְקַטֵּל	*Hithpolel* הִתְקוֹמֵם	*Hithpalpel* הִתְמַהְמֵהַּ

Some weak verb stems use the *polel–hithpolel* as a substitute for the standard *piel–hithpael*. In other words, a *polel* can be used with the same meaning as a *piel*. Other times both related forms are utilized with different nuances of meaning. For example, the root קום appears in the *piel* meaning "to confirm, ratify," while the *polel* means "to raise up" (e.g., *to cause ruins to rise*) and *hithpolel* "to rise up" (i.e., *to raise yourself against in rebellion*). While all these ideas are linked to the basic sense of causing something to stand, each stem conveys a unique nuance of the root.

The conceptual similarity between the *piel–hithpael* and *polel–hithpolel* allows you to anticipate the translation of these rare stems based on your knowledge of the strong verb. When the expected meaning of a simple *piel-polel* substitution does not fit the context, consult the lexicon to see if that *polel* form is used to convey a distinct nuance.

THE QAL PASSIVE

The *qal* verb appears to have once had a dedicated passive stem related to the *qal* in a manner similar to the relationship of the *piel* and *pual* and the *hiphil* and *hophal*. Scholars usually refer to this simply as a *qal passive*. When we speak of the *qal* passive we are not referring to the *qal* passive participles (e.g., קָטוּל). Based on the evidence, we know that the *qal* passive stem once had its own unique participle form (distinct from קָטוּל) and likewise had perfects and imperfects.

The History of the Qal Passive (Where did they go?)

Scholars know that *qal* passives had the same *u-a* vowel pattern as the other passive stems: *qal* passive קֻטַל*, *pual* קֻטַּל, and *hophal* הֻקְטַל.[3] For some reason the *qal* passive was eventually forgotten, probably due to similarity in sound between the *qal* passive and certain forms of the *pual* and *hophal.*

The *qal* passive perfect and participle (both קֻטַל*) would easily be confused with the similar sounding *pual* (קֻטַּל). Likewise, the *qal* passive imperfect (יֻקְטַל*) would have become identical to the *hophal* once the *hophal* began to displace the *heh* preformative when conjugating the imperfect (e.g., יְהֻקְטַל* → יֻקְטַל or יָקְטַל). Thus historic *qal* passive forms were easily mistaken for either *pual* or *hophal* imperfects. The *niphal,* which perhaps originally served a more reflexive function, took over the function of the passive in order to compensate.[4]

	Historic		Biblical Hebrew	
Qal Pass. (pf. / ptc.)	קֻטַל*	→	קֻטַּל	*Pual* in form
Pual (pf.)	קֻטַּל			

Qal Pass. (impf.)	יֻקְטַל*	→	יֻקְטַל	*Hophal* in form
Hophal (impf.)	יְהֻקְטַל*			

3. In Biblical Hebrew the short u-class vowels are most often represented by the *qamets qaton* (short /o/), with *qibbuts* reserved for use before doubled consonants (e.g., *pual* קֻטַּל). However, there are verbs in Biblical Hebrew that still exhibit the historic vowels (e.g., *hophal* הֻשְׁלַךְ). The historic short /u/ preformative is used here to show the continuity between the various passive stems and to highlight the development that precipitated the loss of the *qal* passive.

4. Waltke-O'Connor, §22.6; Ronald J. Williams, "The Passive *Qal* Theme in Hebrew," in *Essays on the Ancient Semitic World,* ed. John W. Wevers and D. B. Redford (Toronto: University of Toronto Press, 1970), 43–50.

Recognizing the Qal Passive

In the biblical text *qal* passives now appear as *pual* or *hophal* verbs, but there are ways you can recognize them.

1) The *pual* or *hophal* form is not syntactically appropriate.
2) The *pual* or *hophal* has no comparable *piel-hithpael* or *hiphil.*
3) The simple passive meaning is the best fit in context.

In most cases a combination of these signs alerts you to the presence of a *qal* passive. For example, Exod 3:2b states that Moses looked "and behold, the bush was burning (בֹּעֵר) with fire, but the bush was not *being consumed* (אֵינֶנּוּ אֻכָּל)." The Hebrew text of this verse is provided below along with a footnote containing the vocabulary that is unfamiliar to you.[5]

? *anticipates a participle* *participle*

וְהִנֵּ֤ה הַסְּנֶה֙ בֹּעֵ֣ר בָּאֵ֔שׁ וְהַסְּנֶ֖ה אֵינֶ֥נּוּ אֻכָּֽל׃

1) The pual or hophal form is not syntactically appropriate

Hints from within this verse suggest that the form in Exod 3:2 should be a participle. The word אֻכָּל (pausal אֻכַּל) is parallel to the participle בֹּעֵר in the first half of the verse; it follows the negative particle אַיִן (appearing here with a 3ms suffix אֵינֶנּוּ, "it is not") which is predominantly used with participles. Therefore, a *pual* perfect is out of place, and a *pual* participle would have a *mem* preformative. Though it looks like a *pual* perfect, syntax leads us to identify אֻכַּל as a vestige of the *qal* passive participle.

2) The pual or hophal has no comparable piel-hithpael or hiphil

The verb אֻכַּל in Exod 3:2 would be the only occurrence of אכל in a *piel, pual,* or *hithpael* in the Hebrew Bible, providing further evidence that this verb is not a *pual.*

5. The vocabulary words you have not yet learned are סְנֶה ("bush"), בָּעַר ("to burn"), and אֵשׁ ("fire").

3) The simple passive meaning is the best fit in context

A simple passive meaning of the root אכל is the most natural translation for אֻכָּל in Exod 3:2. The passive of the *qal* ("to be eaten/consumed") aligns with the parallel idea from the first half of the verse, בֹּעֵר ("burning"), and offers a smooth translation, "the bush was not consumed."

Common Qal Passive (לקח)

One of the more common *qal* passives is found with the root לקח.[6] This root merits special attention in the discussion of the *qal* passive because the root is also affected by the assimilation of *lamed* when that *lamed* is vowelless. The assimilation of the *lamed* is discussed in later chapters. In Biblical Hebrew the passive forms of לקח appear in the perfect with the pointing of a *pual* (לֻקַּח) and in the imperfect with the pointing of a *hophal* (i.e., יֻלְקַח* → יֻקַּח).

The indicators of a *qal* passive noted above suggest that the passive forms of the verb לקח are *qal* passives. First, passives of לקח occur in only in the *pual* perfect and *hophal* imperfect. These two verb forms match the structure of the historic *qal* passive. Second, neither לֻקַּח or יֻקַּח have the meanings of a *pual* or *hophal* in the contexts where they are used. They instead have a simple passive sense consistent with a basic *qal* meaning ("to take" → "to be taken"). Finally, of more than 950 occurrences of the verb לקח, there are no comparable *piel* or *hiphil* forms.[7] This root appears overwhelmingly in the *qal*. Collectively these factors indicate that the passive forms of לקח are remnants of the *qal* passive.

SUMMARY

This chapter is intended as background information to fill out your understanding of the Hebrew language. You do not need to memorize these elements, but we do not want you to be blindsided when you encounter them in the biblical text.

6. Of the approximately seventy remnants of the *qal* passive that are preserved in the Hebrew Bible, most appear with the verbs לקח ("to take"), נתן ("to give"), and ילד ("to give birth").

7. The verb לקח does occur twice in the *hithpael*, but only in a specialized sense of lightening *flashing back and forth*.

CHAPTER 22

Verbs with Object Suffixes

In this chapter you will learn how the Hebrew language attaches direct object pronouns onto the Hebrew verb. Up to this point the translation exercises have used direct objects that are either fully expressed (שָׁמַע קוֹל "he heard ***a sound***") or that are conveyed by means of pronominal suffixes attached to the direct object marker (e.g., שָׁמַע אֹתָנוּ "he heard ***us***").[1] You will continue to see direct object pronouns expressed this way throughout the Hebrew Bible. However, Hebrew also attaches the direct object pronoun directly to the verb (e.g. שְׁמָעָנוּ "he heard ***us***"). There is no difference in meaning or significance between these two expressions. The use of שָׁמַע אֹתָנוּ versus שְׁמָעָנוּ is merely stylistic. The only difference is seen in how the suffix affects the vocalization of the verb.

שָׁמַע אֹתָנוּ	"he heard ***us***"
שְׁמָעָנוּ	"he heard ***us***"

BACKGROUND INFORMATION ON SUFFIXES

Translating direct object suffixes that are attached directly to the verb is similar to translating pronominal suffixes attached to the direct object marker אֵת. However, to become comfortable with direct object

1. As we learned earlier, when the direct object is indefinite it is placed in the sentence without any marking (שָׁמַע קוֹל "he heard *a sound*"). When it is definite, it is accompanied by the direct object marker (שָׁמַע אֶת־הַקּוֹל "he heard *the sound*").

suffixes on verbs: (1) You need to know what the suffixes look like, and (2) you need to know how the suffixes affect the accents.

What Do the Direct Object Suffixes Look Like?

The suffixes used to mark direct objects on verbs are similar in form to the pronominal suffixes you already learned for use with nouns.

Table 22.1: Pronominal Suffixes on Nouns and Verbs

	Suffixes on singular nouns	Suffixes on verbs
he (3ms)	□□□וֹ (הוּ)	□□□֫הוּ (וֹ)
she (3fs)	□□□ָה (ָהּ)	□□□֫הָ (ָהּ)
you (2ms)	□□□ְךָ	□□□֫ךָ
you (2fs)	□□□ֵךְ	□□□֫ךְ
me (1cs)	□□□ִי	□□□֫נִי
them (3mp)	□□□ָם	□□□֫ם
them (3fp)	□□□ָן	□□□֫ן
you (2mp)	□□□ְכֶ֫ם	□□□כֶ֫ם
you (2fp)	□□□ְכֶ֫ן	□□□כֶ֫ן
us (1cp)	□□□ֵ֫נוּ	□□□֫נוּ

The suffixes for nouns and verbs are identical in form with only two exceptions. Although nouns and verbs use the same two suffixes for the third person singular, nouns tend to prefer one form (וֹ and ָה) while verbs prefer the other (הוּ and הָ). The other distinction is that the first person singular suffix has one form when attached to nouns (ִי) and another form when it serves as the direct object suffix for a verb (נִי). Otherwise, the forms are just like you learned before.

How Do the Suffixes Affect the Accent?

Understanding how direct object suffixes affect the accent is not a formality reserved for those who wish to compose sentences or stories in Hebrew. It is one of the main clues to help you distinguish between the verb and its suffix. The accent on a suffixed verb generally falls on the final syllable of the verb, namely the syllable that links the verb and suffix together.

Linking syllables are accented—Except כֶּם, כֶּן and usually ךָ.

1) Normal pattern

When direct object suffixes are added to verbs, the accent is normally placed on the final syllable, namely the syllable that links the verb and suffix together. This will help you distinguish between the verb and the suffix.

קִדַּשְׁתָּ + נוּ → קִדַּשְׁתָּנוּ

יְקַדְּשׁוּ + הָ → יְקַדְּשׁוּהָ

2) Suffixes כֶּם and כֶּן

The suffixes כֶּם and כֶּן will always take the accent rather than letting the accent fall to the linking syllable. This is why grammarians call these *heavy endings*.[2]

קִדַּשְׁנוּ + כֶם → קִדַּשְׁנוּכֶם

יְקַדֵּשׁ + כֶם → יְקַדֶּשְׁכֶם

2. This happens with other suffixes too; compare the noun suffixes כֶּם, כֶּן, הֶם, and הֶן and the verb sufformatives תֶּם and תֶּן.

3) Suffix ךָ

The suffix ךָ behaves the same as it does with nouns. It does not require the accent when a vowel is already present to link the word to the suffix (e.g., אָבִיךָ). But it does take the accent when the word ends in a vowelless consonant (e.g., דְּבָרְךָ).

ךָ + קִדַּשְׁנוּ → קִדַּשְׁנוּךָ

ךָ + יְקַדֵּשׁ → יְקַדֶּשְׁךָ

ADDING SUFFIXES TO VERBS

Now that you know what the direct object suffixes look like and where to anticipate the accent, adding suffixes to verbs is relatively straightforward.

1) If a Verb Form Ends in a Vowel, Simply Attach the Suffix

Any verb that ends in a vowel simply adds the suffix directly onto the verb and adjusts the accent accordingly. Because all of the suffixes on verbs can begin with a consonant, the vowel at the end of the verb makes a convenient transition from verb to suffix. When attaching these suffixes, the accent is generally placed on the last syllable of the verb (i.e., between the verb and the suffix). This rule applies for any verb stem (e.g., *qal*, *piel*, *hiphil*) and any conjugation (perfect, imperfect, imperative, etc.).

נִי + קִדְּשׁוּ → קִדְּשׁוּנִי standard

כֶם + יְקַדְּשׁוּ → יְקַדְּשׁוּכֶם heavy ending

2) If the Verb Form Ends in a Consonant, Add a Connecting Vowel.

When a verbal form ends in a consonant, some kind of connecting vowel is generally needed to make the transition. These connecting vowels are extremely helpful for parsing verbs. *Perfects* will take an a-class connecting vowel (e.g., קִדְּשָׁם). *Imperfects and related stems* (ptc. and inf. cst. are handled separately) will take an i-class connecting vowel (e.g., יְקַדְּשֵׁם). The exceptions are found in the second person endings, which are always the same regardless of the verb forms to which they are added. The suffix ◌ֵךְ 2fs always takes an i-class vowel, and ◌ְךָ, ◌ְכֶם, ◌ְכֶן do not take connecting vowels. These principles apply to verbs of any stem (*qal, piel, hiphil*).

*1) Perfects take **a-class** connecting vowels*

נִי + קִדֵּשׁ → קִדְּשַׁנִי

ם + קִדֵּשׁ → קִדְּשָׁם

*2) Imperfects and related forms take **i-class** connecting vowels*

נִי + יְקַדֵּשׁ → יְקַדְּשֵׁנִי

ם + יְקַדֵּשׁ → יְקַדְּשֵׁם

3) Second person suffixes have only one form (◌ֵךְ, ◌ְךָ, ◌ְכֶם, ◌ְכֶן)

Table 22.2: Connecting Vowels with Suffixes

	Perfect (a-class)	Rest (i-class)	Perfect (a-class)	Rest (i-class)	
3ms	□□□ָהוּ	□□□ֵהוּ	□□□ָם	□□□ֵם	3mp
3fs	□□□ָהּ		□□□ָן	□□□ֵן	3fp
2ms	□□□ְךָ		□□□ְכֶם		2mp
2fs	□□□ֵךְ		□□□ְכֶן		2fp
1cs	□□□ַנִי	□□□ֵנִי	□□□ָנוּ	□□□ֵנוּ	1cp

These principles for connecting vowels are not simply technical details. They offer you important information so that you can correctly identify the verb form. Whenever you see an a-class connecting vowel, the verb cannot be an imperative or imperfect. An a-class connecting vowel signals the presence of a perfect. If the verb has an i-class connecting vowel (other than ךְ ֵ֫, which is unchangeable), then it cannot be a perfect.

SPECIAL CONSIDERATIONS FOR PARTICIPLES AND INFINITIVES

Because participles and infinitives are verbal adjectives and verbal nouns, they have greater affinity with nouns than with verbs. They are used in sentences where you would normally find nouns and adjectives, and they generally take pronominal suffixes used on nouns rather than the direct object suffixes used on verbs. For example, you might run across a phrase like אֲנִי יהוה מְקַדְּשָׁם ("I, the LORD, am the one sanctifying ***them***" Lev 21:23). The a-class connecting vowel in מְקַדְּשָׁם follows the pattern for pronominal suffixes on nouns. The literal meaning "the sanctifying one of them" could designate either the one in their midst who has the role of sanctifying or the one who sanctifies them.

ם ָ + מְקַדֵּשׁ → מְקַדְּשָׁם

"the one sanctifying ***them***"
OR
"the one ***of them*** sanctifying"

In the context of this verse, the latter is the correct interpretation. As a result, אֲנִי יהוה מְקַדְּשָׁם can be appropriately translated as "I, the LORD, am the one who sanctifies them." Only rarely will you see the direct object suffix (used with verbs) on a participle.[3]

Infinitives likewise have no embedded subject and take the pronominal suffixes typically used with nouns rather than the direct object suffixes used with verbs. Therefore, infinitives use the possessive pronoun suffixes to express either the subject or direct object of the action. In other words, the suffix on an infinitive indicates the "possessor" of the action (e.g., לְקַדְּשָׁם "for the sanctifying ***of them***"). The question

3. Cf. Joüon §66.

is whether they are the possessor of the action because it was done *by them* or because it was done *to them*. If the action is being done *by them*, then the suffix is the equivalent of expressing the subject of the verbal idea, for example, לְקַדְּשָׁם = "for them to sanctify." If the context implies that the action was done *to them*, then the suffix conveys the same idea as a true direct object suffix, for example, לְקַדְּשָׁם = "for sanctifying them."

לְקַדְּשָׁם	"for ***them*** to sanctify" *OR* "for sanctifying ***them***"

Although infinitives generally take only the pronominal suffixes used on nouns, they do take advantage of one particular direct object suffix. Infinitives make a clear distinction between the subject and object suffixes in the first person singular. The infinitive uses the noun suffix (ִ י) to indicate the subject of the infinitive and the direct object suffix (נִי) to indicate the direct object (the person to whom the action was done).

לְקַדְּשִׁי	"for **me** to sanctify"
לְקַדְּשֵׁנִי	"for sanctifying **me**"

As a result, the phrase לְקַדְּשֵׁנִי (lit. "for sanctifying me") means that someone else is sanctifying **me** (direct object). But לְקַדְּשִׁי (lit. "for me sanctifying") means that I am the possessor or agent of the action (i.e., subject) and should be translated "for **me** to sanctify." With all other suffixes, context is the only way to determine if the suffix is being used as the subject or object of the action.

SUFFIXES ARE ADDED TO ACTIVE STEMS (QAL, PIEL, AND HIPHIL)

Direct objects are only used with verbs that have an active meaning: typically the *qal*, *piel*, and *hiphil*. This knowledge will significantly narrow the options for parsing difficult verbs. Passive and reflexive meanings do not take direct objects.[4] Verbs with passive constructions shift the reader's focus so that the direct object of an active sentence

4. *Hithpael* verbs with an active sense can also take suffixes. Remember also that passives like the *niphal* may on rare occasions appear with a direct object suffix that restates the subject as the recipient of the action (see ch. 18).

becomes the subject and focus of the passive sentence (e.g., he sanctified *us* → *we* were sanctified). In reflexive verbs the subject of the sentence is the same individual directly impacted by the action (e.g., *we* sanctified *ourselves*).

*Direct Object (**ACTIVE**)*	He sanctified ***us***.
No Direct Object (stative verb)	We were sanctified.
(reflexive verb)	We sanctified ourselves.

As a result, only active verbs take direct objects. When you encounter a difficult verb with a direct object suffix, in general your options for parsing this verb narrow to *qal*, *piel*, and *hiphil*.

You should also pay close attention to the vocabulary definitions you learned. Direct objects are only added to verbs that allow for a "transfer" (*transitive verbs*) of action between the subject and another person or object (e.g., he struck the rock). Verbs where action is "not transferred" (*intransitive verbs*) to another person or object do not take direct objects (e.g., he stood). Verbs that express states of being (*stative verbs*) also do not take a direct object (e.g., he was great). Since the verbs עָמַד ("to stand") and גָּדַל ("to be great") cannot take a direct object when used according to basic sense (*qal*), if either of these verbs appears with a direct object, it must be in one of the causative stems (*piel* or *hiphil*). The causative stems allow these actions to be imposed on another person or object.

No Direct Object (intransitive)	The man stood.
(stative verb)	The man was great.
*With Direct Object (**PIEL - CAUSATIVE**)*	He made ***the man*** great.
*(**HIPH. - CAUSATIVE**)*	He made ***the man*** stand.

SUMMARY

1. Direct object suffixes are already familiar to you. Direct object suffixes look virtually the same as the pronominal suffixes used on nouns.

2. Accent helps you distinguish between the verb and suffix. Verb suffixes accent the linking syllable—except כֶם, כֶן and generally ךָ.

   קִדְּשָׁנוּ

3. Participles and infinitive constructs use noun suffixes. Context distinguishes subject and object suffixes in every form except the first person singular suffix on the infinitive construct.

לְקַדְּשָׁם	"for ***them*** to sanctify" (subj.) *OR* "for sanctifying ***them***" (dir. obj.)
לְקַדְּשִׁי	"for ***me*** to sanctify" (subj.)
לְקַדְּשֵׁנִי	"for sanctifying ***me***" (dir. obj.)

4. Connecting vowels can help distinguish perfects from other verb forms.

   - Perfects take a-class connecting vowels. קִדְּשַׁנִי
   - Other verb forms take i-class connecting vowels. יְקַדְּשֵׁנִי
   - Second person suffixes are always ְ כֶן , ְ כֶם , ְ ךָ , ֵ ךְ .

5. Direct object suffixes go on active verbs (*qal*, *piel*, and *hiphil* to express the transfer of action).

EXERCISE FOR CHAPTER 22

Complete the translation exercise for chapter 22 in the workbook.

CHAPTER 23

Irregular Features with Object Suffixes

Although you should be able to recognize the direct object suffixes on most verbs because of your familiarity with the verb paradigms, historical developments result in a few irregular features. First, the imperfects sometimes take direct object suffixes with an infixed *nun*. This feature can change the appearance of the verb enough to cause some confusion if you are unaware of this construction. Second, a few verbs in the perfect paradigm attach suffixes to a historic form that replaces the standard form you learned for the strong verb. Third, the historic vowel patterns for the *qal* perfect and for the *qal* infinitive or imperative affect verbs with direct object suffixes.

ALTERNATIVE SUFFIX FORMS (WITH INFIXED NUN)

Sometimes Hebrew uses an infixed *nun* to link the verb and suffix. Neither meaning nor what you have learned about connecting vowels and accents are affected by these alternate forms. You simply need to be able to recognize these forms so that the infixed *nun* does not confuse you as you try to identify the verbal root.

The dotted column in the suffix chart below presents the alternative forms that are sometimes seen in the Hebrew text. These suffix forms all have an infixed *nun* (for example, יְקַדְּשֶׁנְהוּ = יְקַדְּשֶׁנּוּ) in place of the simple form יְקַדְּשֵׁהוּ.[1] These infixed suffixes are relatively infrequent compared to the regular suffix endings, but you should be familiar with them. When they do appear, they are used almost exclusively with

1. Prefixes go on the front of words. Suffixes appear at the end of words. Infixes are placed *inside* of words.

the imperfect, suggesting that these forms were probably the original suffix form for the imperfect.[2]

Table 23.1: Direct Object Suffixes (Standard and with Infixed *Nun*)

	Suffixes on singular nouns	Suffixes on verbs	Imperfects with infixed *nun*
he (3ms)	□□□וֹ (הוּ)	□□□הוּ (וֹ)	(for □ֶנְהוּ) □□□ֶנּוּ
she (3fs)	□□□ָה (הָ)	□□□ָהּ (ָה)	(for □ֶנְהָ) □□□ֶנָּה
you (2ms)	□□□ְךָ	□□□ךָ	(for □ֶנְךָ) □□□ֶךָּ*
you (2fs)	□□□ֵךְ	□□□ךְ	*Sometimes written as □□□ֶכָּה (with a vowel marker).
me (1cs)	□□□ִי	□□□נִי	(for □ֶנְנִי) □□□ֶנִּי
them (3mp)	□□□ָם	□□□ם	
them (3fp)	□□□ָן	□□□ן	
you (2mp)	□□□ְכֶם	□□□כֶם	
you (2fp)	□□□ְכֶן	□□□כֶן	
us (1cp)	□□□ֵנוּ	□□□נוּ	(for □□□ֶנְנוּ) □□□ֶנּוּ

Table 23.2 below demonstrates what these infixed forms look like on the *piel* of קדשׁ. *Piel* verbs are used to illustrate endings throughout this chapter because the vowels remain fairly constant and allow you to focus on the suffixes. The table illustrates how the historic form (with infix fully visible) transitioned into the form that you now see

2. See Anson F. Rainey, "The Ancient Hebrew Prefix Conjugation in the Light of Amarnah Canaanite," *HS* 27 (1986): 10–12. The suffixes with infixed *nun* are used only rarely with forms other than the imperfect. Cf. Deut 4:36 with the infinitive and Deut 24:13 with the perfect.

in the biblical text. The third person singular suffixes assimilate the first letter of the suffix (ה) back into the infixed *nun*. The other suffixes assimilate the vowelless *nun* of the infix forwards into the suffix.

Table 23.2: Assimilatio with Infixed *Nun*

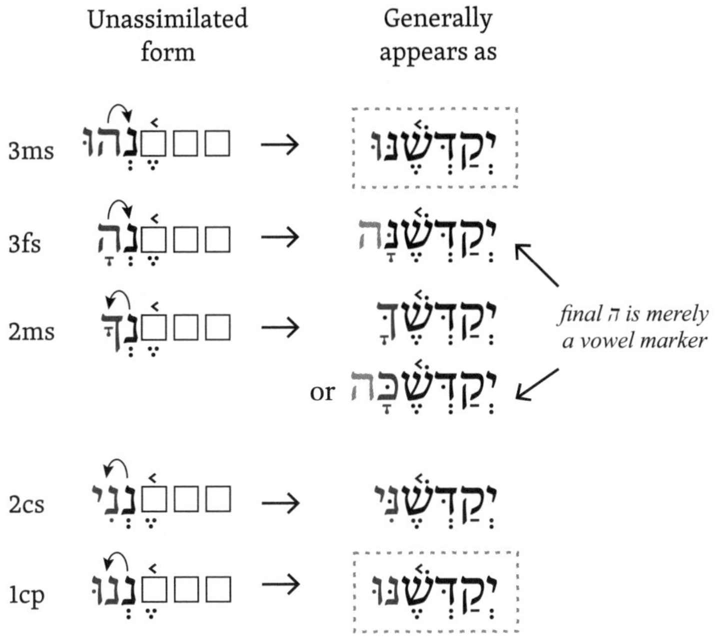

As noted by the dashed boxes in the diagram above, it is important to remember that a verb like יְקַדְּשֶׁנּוּ could have developed from either יְקַדְּשֶׁנְנוּ (1cp suff.) or יְקַדְּשֶׁנְהוּ (3ms suff.). You must rely on context to determine the appropriate meaning.

HISTORIC ENDINGS USED WITH SUFFIXES

Most of the time, suffixes are added onto the strong verb forms you memorized. However, a handful of verbs use historic forms as the base to which the suffixes are added. Historic forms are used in four forms in the perfect conjugation of all stems (3fs, 2fs, 2mp, 2fp) and in the *qal* infinitive construct and masculine singular imperative.

Historic Forms of the Perfect

A handful of verb forms within the perfect conjugation use historic forms when adding direct object suffixes. These special forms of the verb are seen in the 3fs, 2fs, 2mp, and 2fp. These historic forms are slightly different from the forms you learned in the strong paradigm.[3]

Table 23.3: Historic Forms of the Perfect Used with Suffixes

Historic form	(Alone and with suffix)	Biblical Hebrew	
קִטְלַת (pf. 3fs)	→ קִטְלַת	קִטְלָה	
	→ קִטְלַתְנוּ	קִטְלַתְנוּ	
קְטַלְתִּי (pf. 2fs)	→ קְטַלְתִּי	קְטַלְתְּ	
	→ קְטַלְתִּינוּ	קְטַלְתִּינוּ	
קְטַלְתֻּם (pf. 2p)	→ קְטַלְתֻּם	קְטַלְתֶּם	(2mp)
קְטַלְתֶּן	קְטַלְתֶּן	קְטַלְתֶּן	(2fp)
	→ קְטַלְתּוּנוּ	קְטַלְתּוּנוּ	(2mp/2fp)

Over the centuries the historic forms that stood alone were altered to become the verbs you memorized for the strong verb paradigm.[4] However, when suffixes were attached to these historic forms, the suffixes protected the verb and did not permit them to change. As a result, you can still see the historic forms when suffixes are attached.

Be alert for the historic 3fs ◌◌◌ַת, the historic 2fs ◌◌◌ְתִּי, and the historic 2mp/2fp ◌◌◌ְתוּ. These historic forms will appear with direct object suffixes in any of the verb stems (e.g., *qal*, *piel*, *hiphil*).

3. This 3fs historic form is presented in a simplified form in that the development of the 3fs pf. also includes an accent shift and secondary dropping of the theme vowel as described at the end of ch. 13 (e.g., קְטָלַת → קָטְלַת). Since this step in the development of the form is not central to depicting the development of the sufformative, the diagram above leaves that step out so that all the verbs are depicted in the same way.

4. The historic 3fs ◌◌◌ַת dropped the *tav*, lengthened the final vowel, and added *heh* as a vowel marker to produce the strong form (e.g., קָטְלַת → קָטְלָה). The historic ending ◌◌◌ְתִּי (from אַתִּי "you") probably shifted in order to distinguish it from the first person קָטַלְתִּי. Based on studies with other Semitic languages it appears that the 2nd pl. forms were originally ◌◌◌ְתֻּם and ◌◌◌ְתֶּן. With direct object suffixes both forms used the masculine base minus the final *mem* (i.e., ◌◌◌ְתֻּם → ◌◌◌ְתוּ). In Hebrew the masculine form eventually assimilated its vocalization toward the feminine ending to produce ◌◌◌ְתֶּם and ◌◌◌ְתֶּן that we have today.

Knowledge of the historic forms is important for helping you consider all the potential options when parsing verb forms. For example, the verb קְטַלְתִּ֫ים has two potential solutions.

Familiar Form with Suffix

ם	+	קָטַ֫לְתִּי	→	קְטַלְתִּ֫ים	"I killed them"
3mp suffix		1cs pf.			

Historic Form with Suffix

ם	+	קָטַ֫לְתִּי	→	קְטַלְתִּ֫ים	"You killed them"
3mp suffix		historic 2fs pf.			

You need to be aware of the potential ambiguity of these verbs and rely upon the context to guide you in your translation.

The 3fs perfect קָטְלָה takes the historic ending ◌◌◌ַ֫ת when suffixes are added.[5] This historic 3fs ending requires some additional explanation to ensure that you recognize these forms. The unique features that occur when direct object suffixes are added to the 3fs perfect are: (1) the third person singular suffixes assimilate backward into the verb (e.g., קִדְּשַׁתְהוּ* → קִדְּשַׁ֫תּוּ "she sanctified him"), and (2) suffixes are added without a helping vowel (e.g., קִדְּשַׁ֫תְנוּ "she sanctified us") except to break up awkward consonant clusters (e.g., קִדְּשַׁתְם → קִדְּשָׁ֫תַם "she sanctified them"). Without a helping vowel, the accent does not shift when a 3fs perfect adds a suffix like it does in other verbs (e.g., 3fs קִדְּשַׁ֫תְנוּ vs. 2ms קִדַּשְׁתָּ֫נוּ).

5. Though just an analogy, it might help you understand this development if you consider the final "t" in French words. The "t" is not pronounced in the masculine adjective *vert* ("green"). However, the "t" is pronounced in its feminine form *verte*. In a similar fashion, the historic ending of the Hebrew 3fs perfect ceased to be pronounced (or written) when standing alone. The historic form is preserved when suffixes were attached.

Table 23.4: Suffixes on the 3fs Perfect

	Initial combination	Biblical Hebrew	
she sanctified him (3ms)	קִדְּשַׁתְהוּ	קִדְּשַׁתּוּ	(□□□ַתְהוּ)
she sanctified her (3fs)	קִדְּשַׁתְהָ	קִדְּשַׁתָּה	(□□□ַתְהָה) *This final ה is merely a vowel marker*
she sanctified you (2ms)	קִדְּשַׁתְךָ	קִדְּשַׁתְךָ	
she sanctified you (2fs)	קִדְּשַׁתְךְ	קִדְּשָׁתֶךְ	
she sanctified me (1cs)	קִדְּשַׁתְנִי	קִדְּשַׁתְנִי	
she sanctified them (3mp)	קִדְּשַׁתְם	קִדְּשָׁתַם	
she sanctified them (3fp)	קִדְּשַׁתְן	קִדְּשָׁתַן	
she sanctified you (2mp)	קִדְּשַׁתְכֶם	קִדְּשַׁתְכֶם	
she sanctified you (2fp)	קִדְּשַׁתְכֶן	קִדְּשַׁתְכֶן	
she sanctified us (1cp)	קִדְּשַׁתְנוּ	קִדְּשַׁתְנוּ	

1) Third Person Masculine and Feminine Singular Suffixes Assimilate Back into the Verb

When suffixes are added to a 3fs perfect, the 3ms and 3fs suffixes will assimilate back into the verb. For example, the historic קִדְּשַׁתְהוּ* and קִדְּשַׁתְהָ* both assimilate the *heh* back into the *tav* to produce קִדְּשַׁתּוּ and קִדְּשַׁתָּה ("she sanctified him/her").

	Historic Form	Assimilation	+ vowel marker
3ms suff.	קִדְּשַׁתְהוּ* →	קִדְּשַׁתְתוּ* →	קִדְּשַׁתּוּ
3fs suff.	קִדְּשַׁתְהָ* →	קִדְּשַׁתְתָ* → קִדְּשַׁתָּ* →	קִדְּשַׁתָּה

This assimilation of the suffix back into the verb is identical to the pattern of assimilation seen with the suffixes attached with infixed *nun*. You will need to pay attention to this seemingly out-of-place *dagesh* when trying to decipher verb forms. Do not confuse the *dagesh forte* in this *tav* with the *dagesh lene* seen in the standard strong verb form (e.g., 3fs pf. with suffix קִדְּשַׁתָּה vs. 2ms pf. קִדַּשְׁתָּ). This is especially crucial because the 2ms perfect sometimes appears with a vowel marker, making these words even more similar (e.g., 3fs pf. with suffix קִדְּשַׁתָּה vs. 2ms pf. קִדַּשְׁתָּה). The distinction will be apparent if you pay close attention to the type of *dagesh* in the *tav*: *dagesh forte* (follows a vowel) indicating an assimilated suffix and *dagesh lene* (follows a *shewa*) marking the verb sufformative on the verb.

2) Suffixes Are Added Without Helping Vowels (Except with Consonant Clusters)

The third person feminine singular perfect adds suffixes without a helping vowel (e.g., קִדְּשַׁתְנוּ "she sanctified us"), except where this creates a final consonant cluster (e.g., קִדְּשַׁת|ם → קִדְּשָׁ|תַם). The helping vowel used to break up a consonant cluster follows the same vowel class used when adding suffixes to other verbs: a-class for most perfects (קִדְּשָׁתַם, קִדְּשָׁתַן) and i-class for the 2fs suffix (קִדְּשָׁתֶךְ). When this helping vowel is added, the ת naturally shifts to create a suffix syllable, and the vowel in the accented syllable adjusts by lengthening (e.g., קִדְּשַׁת|ם → קִדְּשָׁ|תַם).

The tendency to avoid helping vowels means the accent of a 3fs perfect will remain constant. The accent does not shift when suffixes are added like it does in other verbs. For example, a suffix attached to the 3fs perfect קִדְּשָׁה results in the form קִדְּשַׁתְנוּ ("she sanctified us"). However, a suffix attached to the 2ms perfect results in a shift from קִדַּשְׁתָּ to קִדַּשְׁתָּנוּ ("you sanctified us").

HISTORIC VOWEL PATTERNS IN THE QAL

When suffixes attach to the *qal* forms you learned, the resulting form sometimes varies from the vowel pattern you memorized. The *piel* and *hiphil* do not have this problem. The initial syllable in both the *piel* and *hiphil* is a stable closed unaccented syllable (e.g., קִטַּ֫לְתִּי and הִקְטַ֫לְתִּי).

Qal Perfect = Qatal (קַטַל)

Conversely the *qal* perfect קָטַל evidences a historic vowel pattern with two short a-class vowels (קַטַל*) that are both subject to change. As a result, the *qal* perfect will appear with more variations in form when you encounter them in the text, for example, נִי + קַטַל* = קְטָלַ֫נִי). The shift in accent naturally affects the length of the vowels when suffixes are attached. The changes in vocalization follow the standard rules for vowel change that you learned.

Qal Infinitive Construct and Imperative = Qutul (קֻטֻל)

The other historic form you need to know is the historic vowel pattern for the *qal* infinitive construct and the *qal* masculine singular imperative. You memorized the strong form for both of these as קְטֹל. However, this form has already been affected by vowel reductions, and you will often see different vowels when suffixes are added. The historic form to which suffixes are added is *qutul* (קֻטֻל*).[6]

Table 23.5: The Historic *Qal* Infinitive Construct and Masculine Singular Imperative

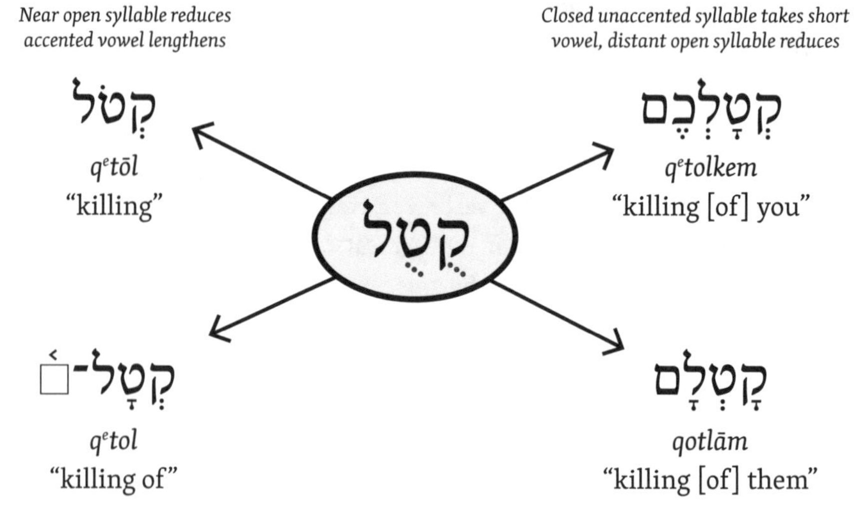

6. The various forms of the *qal* inf. cst. and 2ms impv. in the Hebrew Bible evidence the underlying קֻטֻל* pattern. The form קְטֹל contains a u-class vowel in the accented syllable. The *shewa* reflects a short i/u-class vowel (קֻטֻל) because near open i/u-class vowels *reduce* while historic a-class vowels *lengthen*. From other forms like קָטְלָם we know that this first syllable has a u-class vowel. (The *qamets* in קָטְלָם cannot be an a-class vowel

Although the historic form for both the *qal* infinitive construct and *qal* imperative is the same, you will be able to tell the difference between them by the fact that infinitive constructs take the pronominal suffixes used on nouns while imperatives take true direct object suffixes (with i-class connecting vowels where applicable). Thus, you will see differences like the infinitive קָטְלָם ("killing them") versus the imperative קְטָלֵם ("kill them!"). This was discussed in the previous chapter, and you should review this principle if it is still unclear.

Every vowel change in the *qal* infinitive construct and masculine singular imperative results from the historic form (קֻטֻל*). Once suffixes are attached, the word changes in accordance with the vowel rules you have learned. In order to visually present the suffix at the end of the verb, the following illustration moves from right to left, a pattern we will begin applying consistently now that Hebrew has become more familiar to you. For the first few illustrations, an arrow will be included to remind you of this new orientation.

right to left ←

"keeping"	① ② קְטֹל	←	*קֻ|טֻל	←	*קֻטֻל
"keeping them"	② ③ קָטְלָם	←	*קֻ|טֻ|לָ֫ם	←	*קֻטֻל + ם
"keeping y'all"	④ ⑤ קָטְלְכֶם	←	*קֻ|טֻלְ|כֶ֫ם	←	*קֻטֻל + כֶם

① Accented syllable lengthens.

② Near open i-class and u-class vowels reduce (ֻ → ְ).

③ Distant open syllable would typically reduce, but you cannot have two *shewas* at the beginning of a word. The original u-class vowel is retained and represented as short /o/ because short /u/ is primarily used before doubled consonants.

④ Closed unaccented syllables take short vowels. Short /o/ is present here because short /u/ is reserved for use before doubled consonants.

⑤ Distant open syllables reduce.

because the reduced near open syllable in קְטֹל already rules out this possibility).

The *qal* imperative uses this same historic *qutul* vowel pattern (קֻטֻל*), but only for the masculine singular imperative. The rest of the imperative paradigm attaches suffixes to forms identical to what you learned in the strong verb paradigms.[7] Though this inconsistency may seem to add complexity, you will hardly notice it in the text. The remaining imperative forms occur in the form you expect. The masculine singular imperative is more likely to bring give you pause until you become familiar with the historic base.

הוּ + קֻטֻל* → קָטְלֵהוּ "Kill him!" (you sg.)

הוּ + קִטְלוּ → קִטְלוּהוּ "Kill him!" (y'all)

SUMMARY

1. Imperfects sometimes take suffixes with infixed *nun*.
2. Suffixes use historic forms of the perfect including ◌◌◌ַת (3fs), ◌◌◌ְתִּי (2fs), and ◌◌◌ְתוּ (2mp and 2fp).
3. The 3fs perfect ◌◌◌ַת contains a few irregularities when suffixes are added.
4. The historic *qal* inf. cst. and 2ms impv. is קֻטֻל*.

EXERCISE FOR CHAPTER 23

In the workbook you will find a worksheet designed to help you become more acquainted with how direct object suffixes are added to verbs (exercise 23). Memorize the direct object suffixes and review the principles from these chapters. Then follow the steps given in the workbook for parsing and translating verb forms with suffixes. Do not expect to get every answer right. Instead, use the exercise to test how well you have learned both the endings and the concepts, and use your mistakes to refine your understanding.

7. It appears that the 2ms impv. is based on the original vowel pattern while the rest of the *qal* imperatives are influenced more heavily by the sense that the imperative is a truncated form of the imperfect/jussive (e.g., תִּשְׁפְּטִי → שְׁפְטִי → שִׁפְטִי and תִּשְׁפְּטוּ → שְׁפְטוּ → שִׁפְטוּ).

CHAPTER 24

Hebrew Weak Verbs

In chapters 13–20 you learned the paradigms for the Hebrew strong verb. These paradigms form the basis for understanding all Hebrew verbs. However, some roots contain one or more consonants that obscure the correspondence between the strong verb and the form seen in the text. The resulting changes can make verbs difficult to identify but do not affect meaning. Verbal roots that produce these unique forms are referred to as *weak verbs* or *irregular verbs*.

A weak consonant can occur anywhere in the verbal root. Weak verbs are classified according to the place of the weak consonant and the type of weakness. For example, a I-Guttural root begins with a guttural, a II-Guttural verb has a guttural in the middle, and a III-Guttural ends with a guttural.

		↓	I-Guttural
III	II	I	
ד	מ	ע	"to stand"

You have been exposed to many of these weak verbs in the translation exercises. Until now we have provided assistance in translation by glossing weak verb roots and encouraging you to rely upon the characteristic features of each verb stem. This chapter provides an overview of the principles that govern weak verbs. Each weak verb type is then discussed in detail in later chapters. For now simply concentrate on understanding the general principles, and we will continue to gloss weak verb forms until they are covered more thoroughly in the grammar.

Weak verbs can look very different from strong verbs, yet the basic principles governing weak verbs are really quite simple. For example, the following two words are both examples of the *qal* imperfect second person masculine plural, though they look different in form. The form on the right represents the memorized strong form. The form on the left represents the root with a weak consonant.

Weak Verb		**Strong Verb**
תָּקֹ֫ומוּ		תִּקְטְלוּ
Qal impf. 2mp	=	*Qal* impf. 2mp
"y'all will arise" (קום)		"y'all will kill" (קטל)

Because each weakness results in such different forms, traditionally students have learned Hebrew by memorizing a new paradigm for every weakness. However, if you understand the behavior of the weak consonants (weak verb traits), consider how the weaknesses affect the vowels (vowel rules), and remember the few places where the historical form of the verb differs from the form in the strong verb paradigms (tables 14.2 and 16.3), then you will be able to identify the verbal root and match each weak verb with the strong paradigm. The process takes some getting used to, but overall you will be using features of the Hebrew language that you already know.

WEAK VERB TRAITS

The differences between strong and weak verbs are caused by a handful of consonants that behave in predictable patterns. Native speakers of a language often tend toward efficiency of sound, smoothing over or slurring weaker sounds that are not necessary for meaning. For example, in English we say "dif'rent" for the word spelled "different." At some point English spelling became fixed even though pronunciation continued to change so that what we pronounce does not always match what is written. In Hebrew the words are written as they sound, thus the efficiency of pronunciation (slurring or blending of sounds) is reflected in the form that appears in the text. Hebrew weak verbs are the result of the same historic pattern as the strong verbs. But where certain consonants can be "smoothed out," changes are reflected in the vocalization of the word. Five traits summarize the unique tendencies of weak consonants. Many of these traits are familiar to you already.

As we illustrate the changes that occur in Hebrew spelling and vocalization, note that the illustrations in the remainder of the grammar are read from right to left like the Hebrew text. Now that Hebrew has become more familiar to you, this should be a natural shift. For the first few illustrations, an arrow is included to remind you of this new orientation. Discussions in the body of the chapter will continue to appear from left to right to accommodate the flow of English text.

Trait 1: Vowelless nun likes to assimilate.

In Hebrew it is common for a vowelless *nun* to merge with the next consonant of the word. This process is called assimilation (יִנְסַע* → יִסַּע "he will travel").[1] You can think of assimilation as the vowelless *nun* disappearing into the following consonant and being represented by a *dagesh*. In truth, the vowelless *nun* is pronounced like and takes the shape of the following consonant (יִנְסַע* → יִסְסַע*) so that the *nun* is represented by means of a *dagesh forte* rather than writing the consonant twice (יִנְסַע* → יִסְסַע* → יִסַּע).[2] Because assimilation is motivated by pronunciation, it cannot occur when a *nun* bears its own vowel because the *nun* is then needed to articulate that vowel (e.g., גָּנַבְתָּ "you stole"). You can think of a vowelless *nun* as not being strong enough to stand on its own at the end of a syllable. Assimilation is most common when preformatives are added to roots that begin with a *nun*, that is, roots that have *nun* in first position of the root (called I-*Nun* verbs). However, on rare occasions it can occur at other places in a word.[3] Since not every vowelless *nun* assimilates, it is best to state the principle as vowelless *nun* likes to assimilate.

right to left ←

יִסַּע	←	*יִסְסַע	←	*יִנְסַע	נסע
Written with *dagesh*		Assimilation (נ becomes ס)		*Qal* impf. (expected form)	"to set out, journey"

1. You were exposed to assimilation with מִן ("from"). When מִן is attached to the following word, the vowelless *nun* appears as a *dagesh* in the first letter of the word because it has assimilated (e.g., מֶלֶךְ + מִן → מִמֶּלֶךְ "from a king"). *Nun* is not the only letter that assimilates, and technically consonants can assimilate either toward the following consonant or the preceding consonant. Assimilation toward the following consonant is most common.

2. Assimilation happens in English as well. The /n/ of the Latin prefix *in-* ("not") assimilates when it is prefixed to certain letters (e.g., inseparable vs. irresponsible).

3. Such as נָתַנְתִּי* → נָתַתְתִּי* → נָתַתִּי ("I gave"). In this example the *dagesh lene* is omitted so that the assimilation is clearly evident.

Trait 2: Gutturals do not double, prefer a-class vowels, and often take composite shewa

As we have already learned, the gutturals א, ה, ח, ע, together with the letter ר, share several distinctive features. Because these consonants are produced in the back of the throat, they do not double, prefer a-class vowels, and often take composite *shewa*.

Gutturals do not double

Because gutturals are pronounced in the back of the throat they are difficult to double. (Go ahead, try it!) When the strong verb paradigm calls for doubling, a guttural does not take *dagesh forte*. The preceding vowel will respond in one of two ways:

1. The vowel before the expected *dagesh* can lengthen (compensatory lengthening) to preserve syllable structure. The loss of a *dagesh forte* creates an open unaccented syllable that needs a long vowel. Because this compensatory lengthening preserves evidence of the historic syllable structure, this vowel never changes when vowel rules are applied. The syllable is stable.

right to left ←

בֵּרֵךְ	←	*בִּרֵּךְ	ברך
Piel pf.		Expected *piel* pf.	"to bless"
(open unaccented long vowel)		(closed unaccented short vowel)	

2. The vowel in front of the expected *dagesh* can remain the same as the strong form; in other words, the guttural "pretends" to double. The second option most often occurs with the "h" consonants ה and ח ("honorary" doubling). Once again, vowels reflecting honorary doubling will never shift when vowel rules are applied because they represent historically stable syllables.

right to left ←

בִּעֵר	←	*בִּעֵּר	בער
Piel pf.		Expected *piel* pf.	"to burn"
("honorary" doubling)		(closed unaccented short vowel)	

Gutturals prefer a-class vowels

Gutturals and a-class vowels are both produced in the back of the mouth, making it easier to pronounce them together. Thus verbs with gutturals in their roots may follow one of two patterns:

1. Use an a-class vowel instead of the vowel of the strong verb.

שִׁלַּח	←	*שִׁלֵּח	שלח
Piel pf. (adjusted to /a/)		*Piel* pf. (expected)	"to send"

2. Add an a-class helping vowel (furtive *pataḥ*) before the final consonant.[4]

שֹׁלֵחַ	←	*שֹׁלֵח	שלח
Qal ptc. (with helping vowel)		*Qal* ptc. (expected)	"to send"

In both cases, the a-class vowel helps the speaker transition the sound toward the back of the throat where the guttural is pronounced. While verbs with gutturals have a preference for a-class vowels, they do not necessarily require them. You will see guttural roots that look identical to the strong verb.

Gutturals often take composite shewa

Gutturals can take a simple *shewa*, but they often take a composite *shewa* instead (e.g., יִשְׁאֲלוּ).[5] The composite *shewa* is always voiced and helps to ensure that the weak guttural letters are not lost in pronunciation. As you learned in chapter 3, the composite *shewa* can be used in place of a simple *shewa* regardless of whether you would expect a silent *shewa* (closing a syllable) or vocal *shewa* (opening a syllable).

4. In ch. 3 you learned that furtive *pataḥ* is a helping vowel that is not considered in syllabification and is pronounced before the final consonant. Now you understand that the furtive *pataḥ* is added to help transition from a vowel in the front of the mouth to a guttural in the back of the mouth.

5. As a general rule you will see gutturals with composite *shewas* at the front or middle of verbs (e.g., יַעֲמֹד and יִשְׁאֲלוּ) but not at the end of the verb where the root smoothly transitions into the sufformative (e.g., שָׁמַ֫עְתָּ).

יִשְׁאֲלוּ	←	יִשְׁאְלוּ	שאל
Qal impf. (adjusted)		*Qal* impf. (expected)	"to ask"

Remember, there are only three composite *shewas*, one for each vowel class. Remember also that composite *shewas* usually appear in a matching format. Thus, an i-class preformative with simple *shewa* might be represented in another verb by the i-class composite *shewa* and matching vowel (e.g., יִכְבַּד and יֶחֱזַק). We will review the details in later chapters. For now simply recognize that the presence of a guttural might influence the vocalization of the word.

Trait 3: Aleph likes to quiesce

While *aleph* follows the general traits for gutturals outlined above, it will sometimes quiesce (become "quiet") and lose its consonantal value. You have learned that *aleph* and *ayin* are no longer pronounced (other than stopping air flow). A silent pronunciation is different than quiescing. Though *aleph* and *ayin* are silent, the presence of a vowel or *shewa* indicates their role as consonants. By contrast, a quiescent *aleph* ceases to exist as part of the word. It remains on the page to preserve spelling and help identify the root, but the word is pointed as if the *aleph* were not there. A quiescent *aleph* does not take any vowel pointing or close any syllable, even at the end of a word. Preceding vowels may lengthen. Note, for example, the following forms:

קָטַלְתִּי	קָטַל	Strong verb
↓	↓	
בָּרָאתִי	בָּרָא	*Aleph* quiesces *no vowel notation and preceding vowel lengthens*

When *aleph* loses its consonantal value, it may in rare cases drop out of the word entirely (e.g., בָּרָתִי instead of בָּרָאתִי). However, the *aleph* is usually retained and helps the reader recognize the root.

Trait 4: Waw and yod like to drop or coalesce

The consonants *waw* and *yod* are unique in that they have a close affinity with vowels. The characteristic feature of consonants is that they have a precise point of articulation in the mouth. For example, *dalet* and *tav* are pronounced with the tongue against the back of the teeth. But vowels are created by the flow of air through a constriction of the mouth. The shape of the mouth when pronouncing the /w/ and /y/ sounds of the consonants *waw* and *yod* is similar to how one forms the vowels /ō/ and /ē/. So, unlike vowelless *nun* that likes to react with the following consonant (as discussed above), a vowelless *waw* or *yod* will react with vowels. As a result, you can expect two responses from roots with *waw* and *yod*. *Waw* and *yod* can either drop or coalesce.

1. *Waw* and *yod* like to drop. This means that the *waw* or *yod* is no longer present in the word. For example, a root like בוא ("to come") appears as בָּא ("he came"), but never as *בָּוַא like the strong verb קָטַל. The *waw* in this root has simply dropped, leaving a single syllable that requires only one of the standard vowels of the strong verb.

   בָּא ← בוא *waw/yod* drops

2. *Waw* and *yod* like to coalesce. The term *coalesce* is used to describe the merging of two sounds into one new sound. *Waw* and *yod* can merge with the preceding vowel to create a new long vowel. Memorize these five types of coalescing. Realize that the merger of each vowel with *waw* or *yod* reflects a natural progression of sound. Pronouncing the sequence aloud will help your memorization. You should be able to hear how ַוְ (pronounced /aw/ like ouch!) slurs to וֹ (pronounced /ō/ like oh!).

   יוֹשִׁיב ← *יַוְשִׁיב aw → ō
   יֵיטִיב ← *יַיְטִיב ay → ē (*tsere*)
   תִּגְלֶינָה ← *תִּגְלַיְנָה ay → ē (*segol*)
   יִיטַב ← *יִיְטַב iy → ī
   הוּשַׁב ← *הֻוְשַׁב uw → ū

The dropping and coalescing of *waw* and *yod* can occur at any place in the word. Each type of verb, I-*Waw*/*Yod*, II-*Waw*/*Yod*, and III-*Waw*/*Yod*, will be treated in its own chapter.

Trait 5: Geminates—Hebrew often avoids writing duplicate consonants

Roots that have identical letters in the second and third position are called geminates, a term that means "duplicate" (e.g., סבב "to go around"). These roots frequently use a *dagesh forte* to represent the repeated consonant rather than writing it twice.[6] For example, you will sometimes see סַבּוּ instead of סָבְבוּ (*qal* pf. 3mp, "they went around"). The duplicate consonant may be written only once even at the end of a word where *dagesh forte* cannot appear, resulting in forms like סַב instead of סָבַב (*qal* pf. 3ms, "he went around"). Thus the *dagesh forte* that you have come to associate with the *piel* or *pual* (e.g., קִטֵּל or קֻטַּל) may indicate a geminate root instead.

Geminate סבב "to go around"

סַבּוּ	or	סָבְבוּ	*Qal* pf. 3mp
סַב	or	סָבַב	*Qal* pf. 3ms

Summary

The five traits of weak verbs outlined above apply to the historic forms of the strong verb and are driven by an attempt to smooth out pronunciation. This is great news because it means that you do not need to memorize a new paradigm for each type of weak verb. If you become familiar with these five general principles, you will be able to identify an irregular verb and recognize its relationship to the strong forms you learned. We deal with the specifics of each type of weak verb in the following chapters. Although these traits operate as separate principles, the verbs you encounter in the biblical text may at times exhibit

6. In the treatment of weak stems in ch. 21, you saw that sometimes Hebrew reduplicates the final consonant of a root where one consonant has dropped, e.g, *polel* pf. 3ms of קום = קֹמֵם (written defectively for emphasis). This pattern of writing a single letter twice seems to contradict the pattern in geminate verbs where a verb writes only one of the two duplicate consonants (e.g., *qal* pf. 3ms סָבַב as סַב). Though contradictory on the surface, remember that grammar "rules" are nothing more than an attempt to describe patterns that help students understand and predict how the language behaves. If it helps, consider that the reduplication in weak verbs (e.g., *polel, polal, hithpolel*) occurs only in stems that require doubling of the second root consonant (*piel, pual, hithpael*).

several weak letters (e.g., נסע "to set out, journey"). In such cases the verb exhibits features from each type of weakness. To review:

1. **Vowelless *nun* likes to assimilate (יִנְסַע* → יִסַּע).**
2. **Gutturals do not double, prefer a-class vowels, and often take composite *shewa*.**
3. ***Aleph* likes to quiesce (lose its consonantal value).**
4. ***Waw* and *yod* like to drop (בוא → בָּא) or coalesce (הַוְשַׁב* → הוּשַׁב).**
5. **Geminates: Duplicate consonants can be written once (סַבּוּ instead of סָבְבוּ).**

VOWEL PATTERNS IN WEAK ROOTS

When weak consonants affect the structure of the verb, the vowels are likewise affected. Features of Hebrew already familiar to you will help you recognize the relationship between a weak verb and its strong verb counterpart even when the vowels are different. This section reinforces the importance of considering vowel classes, historic forms, and theme vowels.

Concentrate on Vowel Classes (Not Specific Vowels)

The adjustments that occur in weak verbs can affect the vowels so that they do not match the strong verb you learned. If you rely on the strong verb pattern too rigidly, you may fail to recognize the relationship between the strong verb and weak verb. Remember that Hebrew vowels fall into three vowel classes (a-class, i-class, u-class) and that vowels within each class are sometimes used interchangeably.[7] You must learn to recognize verbs in terms of vowel classes. For example, the *hiphil* imperfect (יַקְטִיל) has an a-class preformative and an i-class theme vowel. In weak verbs this pattern can appear in a variety of ways as long as the essential a + i vowel pattern is preserved.

7. See ch. 5.

	Hiphil impf. 3ms	Preformative vowel and theme vowel
"to kill" קטל	יַקְטִיל	a + i
"to arise" קום	יָקִים	a + i
"to go around" סבב	יָסֵב	a + i
"to sit, dwell" ישׁב	יוֹשִׁיב (from *יַוְשִׁיב aw → ō)	a + i

Each of these verbs represents the a + i vowel combination characteristic of the *hiphil*. Memorizing the strong verb was important for learning the base form common to all Hebrew verbs, but you will discover that the application of that base form will vary. You must shift your perspective from seeing specific vowels to focusing on the underlying structures and vowel patterns of the verbal system.

Historic Preformative Vowels (Qal and Niphal)

You have also seen that the historical development of the Hebrew language occasionally resulted in vowel changes outside of their original vowel class. In the weak verbs such changes are most prominent in the preformatives of the *qal* and *niphal*.[8]

	Qal actives	*Qal* statives
Perfects	קָטַל (a + a)	כ?בָד (a + ?)
Imperfects	*יַקְט?ל (a + ?)	יִכְבַּד (i + a)

The *qal* active and stative imperfects were historically distinguished by a-class preformative vowels for active and i-class preformative vowels for stative (e.g., יַקְטֹל vs. יִכְבַּד). At some point the a-class preformative of the active shifted to i-class, leading to the strong form you memorized. The weak verbs sometimes prevented these historic vowels from

8. Other vowel shifts that harmonize the paradigm will be discussed later when relevant.

changing. As a result, the *qal* imperfect occasionally takes an a-class vowel in the preformative even though you have come to expect a *ḥireq*. Ironically, in these cases the weak verb preserves the historic form better than the so-called strong form. The key piece to integrate into your understanding of verbs is that *qal* imperfects can have an a-class preformative vowel.

For now it is sufficient to know that you can have an a-class or i-class preformative vowel in the *qal* imperfect. But in the long run it will help to understand why. Remember that Hebrew was spoken over thousands of years. Just as English words sound differently now than they did during the days of Chaucer, Hebrew also changed over time. At some point, initial closed unaccented syllables with *pataḥ* shifted to *ḥireq*.[9] This change from /a/ to /i/ was not possible with certain weak roots. For example, gutturals preferred to keep the a-class vowel (e.g., יַעֲמֹד). Some weak consonants drop out of the verb completely, leaving the preformative in an open syllable and preventing the change, which only occurred in closed syllables. When the original a-class vowel was preserved, it followed the standard vowel rules for lengthening and reducing (e.g., *יַסֹב → יָסֹב).[10]

Historic Preformative Shift (/a/ to /i/)

	Biblical Hebrew *qal* impf.		Historic *qal* impf.	
"to kill" קטל	יִקְטֹל	←	*יַקְטֹל	Closed unaccented syllable (/a/ to /i/)
"to stand" עמד	יַעֲמֹד	←	*יַעֲמֹד	Guttural prevents shift (retains /a/)
"to go around" סבב	יָסֹב	←	*יַסֹב	Open syllable prevents shift (retains /a/)

The *niphal* perfects and participles likewise once had a historic a-class preformative vowel. These two verb forms originated as *נַקְטַל *(naqtal)*, not the נִקְטַל form you initially learned. The same principles that applied to the *qal* imperfect affected the *niphal* perfect and participle. A closed

9. A catchy way to remember this is to pronounce the first syllable of the historic *qal* imperfect (*יַקְטֹל) and imagine they heard "yak, yak, yak," and shifted it to /i/.

10. This historic shift from short /a/ to short /i/ in initial closed unaccented syllables (e.g., *יַקְטֹל → יִקְטֹל) occurred in nouns as well. The plural construct of דָּבָר is דִּבְרֵי־ (NOT דַּבְרֵי־).

unaccented a-class preformative shifted to an i-class vowel unless a weak consonant prevented this shift.

Strategic Vowel Choice in Weak Verbs

Finally, when consonants drop so that the verb has only two root letters instead of three, the number of vowels drops as well. Verbs appearing with only two of their root consonants typically keep the vowel that best preserves the information needed to convey meaning. Thus the seemingly random vowels that you see in weak verbs are, in fact, deliberate and offer important clues about meaning. For example, in the *qal* perfect, both the active and the stative begin with a-class vowels but are differentiated by their theme vowel (e.g., קָטַל and כָּבֵד). A verb with only two of its root letters preserves the theme vowel because it conveys meaning.

"he is heavy" כבד	כָּבֵד	Strong verb (*qal* stative)
"he is dead" מות	מֵת	Weak verb (*qal* stative)

APPLYING THE WEAK VERB PRINCIPLES

This chapter has presented the traits of weak consonants and reexamined the importance of vowel classes (rather than specific vowels), historic forms, and theme vowels. Combined, these elements prepare you to recognize irregular verbs.

The Strong-Verb Equation

In order to accurately translate a weak verb, you need to establish a correlation between what you see on the page and the standard strong forms you learned. This process involves identifying features of the weak verb that point to a comparable strong form and accounting for the differences that you observe. In other words, you are essentially positing an equation between the weak verb and strong verb and proving that your equation is correct. This is similar to what you would do in math. For example, 2 + 2 is visually different than 3 + 1. But quantitatively they are identical. In the same way, a weak verb may look different from the strong verb but have the same parsing value. Just as 2 + 2 = 3 + 1 because both equal 4, you will come to recognize that, in regard to parsing, בָּא = קָטַל because both are *qal* perfect 3ms and both are derived from the same underlying historic pattern.

Your ability to read Hebrew results from the interaction between the characteristic features of the Hebrew language and the demands of context. When you parse, allow yourself to be guided by both. Do not be discouraged that it may take you a few tries to correctly identify a verb. Learning to read Hebrew well does not mean you get everything right the first time.

Let's practice identifying a weak verb using both context and form to guide your translation.

עַל־אֹיְבֵיהֶם	בְּנֵי יִשְׂרָאֵל	יָק֫וּמוּ
against their enemies	the sons of Israel	?

The verb at the start of this clause does not match the strong verb forms you learned and is a less familiar root. Context suggests that you are looking for something that the sons of Israel did against their enemies. Thus you suspect that your verb is a third person masculine plural ("they").

Step 1—Initial Identification

The first step in parsing a weak verb is to narrow down what type of verb you think it is—looking for anything you can identify or rule out regarding the root or type of verb. Start with the most obvious choices and then look for other options as needed. A student might assume that יָק֫וּמוּ comes from the root יקם with three strong consonants (i.e., a strong verb). However, the vowels in יָק֫וּמוּ do not match any of the strong verb patterns. Another option is that the *yod* is a preformative, and the verb is an imperfect from the vocabulary word קוּם ("to arise"). The combination of the *yod* and the long /ū/ ending suggest that יָק֫וּמוּ is a third masculine plural imperfect (י□□□וּ), which is consistent with the subject ("sons of Israel").

STEP 1

Isolate the root	יָקוּמוּ	יקם—vowels do not match strong forms קום—familiar vocabulary י could be a preformative
Isolate the form	יָקוּמוּ =	י□□□וּ IMPERFECT 3mp

Step 2—Refine Your Assessment

Now that you know the relevance of the historic forms and the importance of looking at vowel classes rather than individual vowels, you can determine what stem this imperfect comes from. Having identified *yod* as a preformative, you are now looking for a stem with an a-class preformative vowel. In the strong verbs the *hiphil* is the only imperfect that fits this pattern. But the a-class + u-class of יָקוּמוּ cannot be a *hiphil* (a-class + i-class pattern) because it does not have the i-class theme vowel. In weak verbs the a-class preformative vowel can also derive from the historic *qal* imperfect (יַקְטֻל*). By process of elimination, יָקוּמוּ is a *qal* imperfect from the root קום ("to arise"). This root fits the context of the passage: "The sons of Israel will arise against their enemies."

STEP 2

Compare the vowel pattern with verb stems	יָקוּמוּ		Preformative a-class = *hiphil* OR historic *qal*
		≠	*Hiphil* (no i-class theme vowel)
		=	*QAL*

Step 3—Resolve Differences from the Strong Verb

Your final step is to verify your conclusions by explaining each of the differences between the weak verb and corresponding strong form. Each successive chapter will give you the tools to perform this final step, one class of weak verb at a time. For now simply follow the logic of the explanation below.

We have posited that יָקוּמוּ is a *qal* imperfect 3mp ("they will arise"). We know that the basic *qal* imperfect is יִקְטְלוּ (from יִקְטֹל). Obviously the weak verb does not look like the strong verb. But if you can identify the differences between the two verbs and explain how they are related, you can confirm your identification of the verb. The preformative vowels are different (*ḥireq* vs. *pataḥ*) but both represent valid *qal* preformatives (i.e., *qal* יִקְטֹל and historic יַקְטֻל*). The u-class theme vowels (ō vs. ū), are both consistent with the *qal* imperfect (which takes any class theme vowel). The verb is missing one of the root consonants (this *waw* is a vowel marker), but it both matches a root you know (קום) and is consistent with the fact that *waw* and *yod* can *drop or coalesce*. Thus all the differences between יָקוּמוּ and the strong verb יִקְטְלוּ can be explained as variations of the same form.

STEP 3	יָקוּמוּ		יִקְטְלוּ
	Qal impf. 3mp	=	*Qal* impf. 3mp
Resolve differences			
(1)	יָקוּמוּ	✓	*Qal* historic יַקְטֻל*
(2)	יָקוּמוּ	✓	*Qal* יִקְטֹל or historic יַקְטֻל* *Qal* impf. takes any class theme vowel
(3)	יָקוּמוּ	✓	Root is קום (uw → ū) *Waw* and *yod* drop or coalesce

If all the differences can be resolved, it is likely that you have parsed the word correctly.

Multiple Options for Parsing

Because of the changes that occur in Hebrew weak roots, you will find that some verb forms have more than one parsing option. For example, the verb נָסַב could theoretically be a *qal* perfect from נסב* (like קָטַל) or a *niphal* perfect from סבב (from historic *niphal* נַקְטַל* with the duplicate root letters written only once). You are not expected to know these things yet. At this point it is sufficient to keep in mind the general principles that govern weak verbs and anticipate the potential for multiple options. Do not be discouraged that your first choice may not result in a correct identification of a verb. Your familiarity with Hebrew word formation will help you determine which parsing best fits both meaning and context.

EXERCISES FOR CHAPTER 24

In the workbook you will find two exercises that acquaint you with the basic principles of weak verbs. The first worksheet reviews the characteristic features of each type of weak verb (exercise 24A). The second worksheet reinforces your awareness of the original a-class preformative vowel of the *qal* and *niphal* (exercise 24B).

CHAPTER 25

III-*Waw/Yod* Verbs

As you learned in the last chapter, weak verbal roots have one or more consonants that may cause changes in vocalization and structure. It is always possible that weak roots will be formed just like the strong verb. In those cases the strong verb paradigm is sufficient to guide your parsing.[1] More often, however, the weak consonants produce changes in the word to allow for smooth pronunciation. The next three chapters explain how the strong forms are affected by the tendency for *waw* and *yod* to drop or coalesce, depending on the placement of the *waw* or *yod* within the word (I, II, and III-*Waw/Yod*).

When a *waw* or *yod* is in *final position,* as it is in III-*Waw/Yod* verbs, it impacts the verb's connection to the *sufformative* and affects the *end of the word*. The guiding principle for III-*Waw/Yod* verbs is that ***III-Waw/Yod coalesces when followed by consonantal sufformatives and drops everywhere else.***[2] The components at the beginning of the word remain intact to help you recognize the verb stem. This chapter presents and explains the changes that occur at the end of a III-*Waw/Yod* verb so that you can recognize words that look different from the strong paradigm.

1. Examples of historic III-*Waw/Yod* forms appearing in the biblical text include שָׁלַ֫וְתִּי ("I would be at ease" Job 3:26) and חָסָ֫יוּ ("they took refuge" Deut 32:37). Lexicons list these under שׁלה and חסה. In the latter example the accent stands in its historic position like verbs in pause (see ch. 11).

2. In order to help students recognize general patterns, *waws* and *yods* are described here as behaving the same way because the resulting forms are identical regardless of whether they originated with historic *waw* or *yod*. In form, III-*Waw/Yod* verbs all reflect from the coalescing of *yod*.

Sufformative +	↓ III	II	I		
תִ י	לְ	טַ	קָ	קָטַלְתִּי	Strong
תִ י	י	לְ	גָ	גָּלִיתִי	Coalesced†
וּ		לּ	גָ	גָּלוּ	Dropped

† Coalescing occurs when a *waw/yod* combines with a compatible vowel to become a pure long vowel, and dropping is when the *waw/yod* falls completely out of the word.

WHAT IS A III-WAW/YOD VERB?

The III-*Waw/Yod* designation signifies that the third consonant of a root was historically a *waw* or *yod*. You already know a few III-*Waw/Yod* verbs but may not recognize them as such because of the loss of the historic *waw* or *yod*. In the lexical forms you memorize, the final *waw* or *yod* has dropped and *heh* was added to mark the presence of the final vowel (for example, רָאָה, "to see," הָיָה, "to be," עָשָׂה, "to make, do"). The III-*Waw/Yod* verbs all appear in the lexicon with a final *heh* in place of the historic letter, even though the *heh* is just a vowel marker.[3] These roots should not be confused with Hebrew verbs that end with a true consonantal *heh* marked by *mappiq* (e.g., גָּבַהּ "to be high").[4] Both sets of roots appear in the lexicon with a final *heh*, but roots ending with a consonantal *heh* behave like a III-Guttural. This chapter deals only with III-*Waw/Yod* verbs.

"to answer"	עָנָה	←	*עָנַ	←	*עני	III-*Waw/Yod*
"to be high"	גָּבַהּ	←	*גָּבַה	←	*גבה	III-Guttural

You do not need to distinguish between verbs that were historically written with *waw* and those that were written with *yod*. With rare exception, roots with a historic III-*Waw* and those with a III-*Yod* both result in identical forms. For example, the verb עָנָה has multiple

3. Even when the verb appears like a strong form with the historic *waw* or *yod*, the root may be listed in the lexicon with a final *heh*. For example, שָׁלַוְתִּי ("I would be at ease") is listed in the lexicon under both שלו and שלה.

4. Remember that *mappiq* ("h-dot") indicates that *heh* is a true consonant.

meanings that derive from different historic roots that have now merged: עני* ("to answer") and ענו* ("to be humbled"). When the *waw* and *yod* dropped, these verbs followed an identical process of development that resulted in indistinguishable forms. Both are in the lexicon under עָנָה but appear as separate entries. Context will help you determine which meaning best applies.

עָנָה ← עָנַ* ← עָנַי* "to answer"

עָנָה ← עָנַ* ← עָנַו* "to be humbled"

This chapter uses the verb גָּלָה ("to uncover, remove") to illustrate how the III-*Waw/Yod* paradigms are formed. This root is chosen over more familiar verbs like עָנָה to avoid other weak features (e.g., gutturals). The root גָּלָה isolates the III-*Waw/Yod* characteristics.

III-WAW/YOD: THE BASIC PRINCIPLES

As stated in the introduction, the tendency of *waw* or *yod* to drop and coalesce affects the III-*Waw/Yod* verbs at the end of the word. More specifically, *III-*Waw/Yod *coalesces when followed by consonantal sufformatives and drops everywhere else.* This principle requires clarification before it can be applied throughout the paradigms.

III-*Waw/Yod* coalesces when followed by consonantal sufformatives and drops everywhere else.

Coalesce When Followed by Consonantal Sufformatives

Coalescing occurs in III-*Waw/Yod* roots whenever the *waw* or *yod* is followed by a consonantal sufformative. Remember that sufformatives are part of the endings you add to create the *qal* paradigm of קָטַל. Consonantal sufformatives begin with a consonant. For example, in קָטַלְתִּי ("I killed") the first person common singular sufformative תִּי starts with ת (a consonant). Conversely, in קָטְלָה ("she killed") the third person feminine singular sufformative ָה starts with a vowel (ָ) and is a vocalic sufformative.

The term "coalesce" means that the *waw/yod* merges with the preceding vowel to become a long vowel (e.g., גלי* → גָּלַיְתָ* → גָּלִיתָ "you uncovered").[5] All III-*Waw/Yod* roots coalesce using *yod* (NOT *waw*) and always coalesce with the theme vowel to become an i-class vowel, whether a *ḥireq yod* (e.g., גָּלִ֫יתָ), *tsere yod* (e.g., נִגְלֵ֫יתָ), or *segol yod* (e.g., תִּגְלֶ֫ינָה).[6] All three vowels are the natural result of contractions with *yod*.[7] Though no longer functioning as a consonant, a coalesced *yod* can help you identify the root because it reflects the historic root letter.

Drop Everywhere Else

All other forms of the III-*Waw/Yod* verb drop the *waw/yod*. "Drop" means that the *waw/yod* disappears. "Everywhere else" refers to all verb forms that do not take a consonantal sufformative, namely forms with vocalic sufformatives (e.g., יִקְטְלוּ) or with no sufformative at all (e.g., יִקְטֹל).

The dropping of the *waw/yod* can make it more difficult to recognize the verbal root because the third consonant is not represented in the form. Some forms that drop *waw/yod* leave only two visible root letters. Other forms add the letter *heh* as a vowel marker when *waw/yod* has dropped, reminding you of your vocabulary words. This letter *heh* appears throughout the paradigms because it has natural affinity with all vowel classes. Thus it can be used to mark the a-class vowel of the perfect (e.g., גָּלָה), the i-class vowel of the participle (גֹּלֶה), and the u-class vowel of the infinitive absolute (גָּלֹה).[8]

Qal as a Template for the Other Stems

In the III-*Waw/Yod* verbs, because the weakness is at the end of the verb, the characteristic features of each stem are still preserved at the front of the word. The *nun* of the *niphal* is still visible, the doubling of the *piel-hithpael* is still present, and the preformatives of the *hiphil* and *hophal* remain intact. The only thing that changes is the ending where the sufformatives attach. When you learned the strong verb, you learned to use the *qal* endings as the base for every stem. The same is true with III-*Waw/Yod* verbs.

5. See ch. 24.

6. *Qal* pf. 2ms גָּלִ֫יתָ ("you uncovered"), *niphal* pf. 2ms נִגְלֵ֫יתָ ("you uncovered yourself"), and *qal* impf. 2fp תִּגְלֶ֫ינָה ("y'all will uncover").

7. The *ḥireq yod* reflects the coalescing of *ḥireq* + *yod* (י + ◌ִ → ◌ִי) while the *tsere yod* and *segol yod* reflect historic *pataḥ* + *yod* (י + ◌ַ → ◌ֵי or ◌ֶי).

8. Notice the slight /h/ sound you hear at the end of your pronunciation of each vowel.

	Qal	*Niphal*	*Piel*	*Pual*	*Hithpael*	*Hiphil*	*Hophal*
3ms	גָּלָה	נִגְלָה	גִּלָּה	גֻּלָּה	הִתְגַּלָּה	הִגְלָה	הָגְלָה

APPLYING THE PRINCIPLES

The following discussions explain how the principle—*III-Waw/Yod coalesces when followed by consonantal sufformative and drops everywhere else*—affects each conjugation of the *qal* paradigm. The *qal* of the III-*Waw/Yod* verbs then serves as a template for the *niphal–hophal*. Features of III-*Waw/Yod* verbs that appear to be exceptions are pointed out along the way.

PERFECTS

The III-*Waw/Yod* perfects look different from both the strong verb and from one another. Yet each reflects the fundamental principle that *waw/yod* coalesces when followed by consonantal sufformatives and drops everywhere else.

Qal Perfect
גלה **"to uncover"**

(*גָּלַי →)	3ms	גָּלָה	גָּלוּ	3mp	(← *גָּלְיוּ)	DROP
(*גָּלְיָה →)	3fs	גָּלְתָה		3fp		
	2ms	גָּלִיתָ	גְּלִיתֶם	2mp		COALESCE
	2fs	גָּלִית	גְּלִיתֶן	2fp		
	1cs	גָּלִיתִי	גָּלִינוּ	1cp		

Perfects: Coalesce when Followed by Consonantal Sufformatives

In III-*Waw/Yod* perfects, forms with consonantal sufformatives coalesce the *yod* with the preceding vowel resulting in a long i-class vowel. The structure of the perfect verb explains why this happens. When a consonantal sufformative attaches to the root, the third consonant is vowelless (marked in the strong verb paradigm by a *shewa*, e.g., קָטַלְתָּ "you killed"). In III-*Waw/Yod* verbs the absence of a vowel encourages the *yod* to coalesce with the preceding vowel (e.g., גָּלִיְתָ* → גָּלִיתָ).[9]

	Coalescing		With consonantal sufformative		Root
Perfect 2ms "you uncovered"	גָּלִיתָ	←	גָּלִיְתָ*	←	גלי*

Perfects: Drop Everywhere Else

In III-*Waw/Yod* perfects, forms with no sufformative or with vocalic sufformatives drop the *waw/yod*. Hebrew adapts to the dropped consonant in different ways. You should not have to memorize these differences if you understand the explanations provided below.

Qal Perfect 3ms

The *qal* perfect 3ms has no sufformative (קָטַל). Thus, in the III-*Waw/Yod* verbs the *waw/yod* drops. However, when the *waw/yod* dropped, the short a-class theme vowel was lengthened and *heh* was added as a vowel marker (i.e., גָּלַי* → גָּלַ* → גָּלָה). This is the form that you learn for all III-*Waw/Yod* vocabulary.

	Vowel marker *heh*		*Yod* drops		
Perfect 3ms "he uncovered"	גָּלָה	←	גָּלַ*	←	גלי*

Qal Perfect 3fs

The *qal* perfect 3fs has a vocalic sufformative (ה ָ). Thus in the III-*Waw/Yod* verbs the *waw/yod* drops. If the *waw/yod* had dropped from the strong verb form (גָּלְיָה), the result would have looked exactly like the 3ms perfect (e.g., גָּלְיָה* → גָּלָה). Instead, the *waw/yod* dropped from a historic form that ended in *tav* (קטלת*).[10] This historic ending (ת ַ) later shifted throughout the language to the ה ָ ending you see in the strong form קָטְלָה. The III-*Waw/Yod* verbs retained both endings,

9. The *ḥireq yod* is thus present in more stems than just the *hiphil*. In fact, in III-*Waw/Yod hiphils* the *ḥireq yod* is not a distinctive feature of the verb stem but the result of coalescing (e.g., *qal pf.* גָּלִיתָ and *hiphil* pf. הִגְלִיתָ).

10. The historic 3fs pf. has no vocalization here (and throughout this discussion) in order to avoid the complicated development of vowels and focus only on the sufformative pertinent to this discussion. For a fuller explanation of the 3fs pf., see the following footnote.

keeping the historic תַ and adding the new sufformative הָ on top of the old ending (e.g., *גָּלַיַת → *גָּלַת → גָּלְתָה).[11] Thus the 3ms and 3fs perfects remain distinguishable (e.g., 3ms גָּלָה vs. 3fs גָּלְתָה).

	Historic הָ + תַ	*Yod* drops	Historic ending
Perfect 3fs "she uncovered"	גָּלְתָה ←	*גָּלַת ←	*גָּלִיַת

Qal Perfect 3mp

The *qal* perfect 3mp likewise has a vocalic sufformative (וּ) and drops the *waw/yod*. This adjustment is the standard pattern for III-*Waw/Yod* verbs with vocalic sufformatives. The sufformative simply slides over to fill the space left by the dropped *waw/yod* (e.g., קָטְלוּ vs. *גָּלְיוּ → גָּלוּ).

	Yod drops		
Perfect 3mp "they uncovered"	גָּלוּ ←	וּ +	*גָּלִי

Perfects: Qal as a Template for the Other Stems

In the III-*Waw/Yod* verbs, the perfect endings of the *qal* are the same as those used for the perfect in every stem. For example, the 3ms perfect has the same ending in other stems as it does in the *qal*. The only difference is that the passive stems (*niphal*, *pual*, *hophal*) consistently use *tsere yod* when the verb ends in a consonantal sufformative while the other stems have a decided preference for *ḥireq yod* (though *tsere yod* is

11. The sequence of development presented here is an abbreviation of a more complex process that includes the following stages: (1) *גַּלַיַת → (2) *גָּלַיַת → (3) *גָּלַת → (4) הָ + *גָּלַת → (5) *גָּלָתָה → (6) גָּלְתָה. The *qal* 3fs pf. began as depicted in (1), the first stage of its development. (2) At some point the near open syllable lengthened. This change could have occurred at various points but is presented here to provide the simplest starting point for the description that follows. (3) Historic *yod* then dropped before the vocalic sufformative תַ. (4) The new feminine ending הָ attached to the historic feminine ending (instead of replacing it) to avoid a form identical to the 3ms גָּלָה. (5) The accent that was historically located on the second syllable is now preserved only in pausal forms (e.g., גָּלָתָה). (6) Eventually Hebrew shifted the accent to the final syllable, resulting in the loss of the previously accented vowel. Though the reconstruction of historic forms remains somewhat hypothetical, this sequence best explains how all the features of the 3fs perfect came to be.

also seen).[12] The characteristic features of each stem are preserved at the front of the word. The following paradigms reflect the consistency of these endings across all stems (including the *hiphil* where one would expect the characteristic *ḥireq-yod* theme vowel). You do not need to memorize them once you know the *qal* form.

Table 25.1: III-*Waw/Yod* Perfects (All Stems)

	Qal	*Niphal*	*Piel*	*Pual*	*Hithpael*	*Hiphil*	*Hophal*
3ms	גָּלָה	נִגְלָה	גִּלָּה	גֻּלָּה	הִתְגַּלָּה	הִגְלָה	הָגְלָה
3fs	גָּלְתָה	נִגְלְתָה	גִּלְּתָה	גֻּלְּתָה	הִתְגַּלְּתָה	הִגְלְתָה	הָגְלְתָה
2ms	גָּלִיתָ	נִגְלֵיתָ	גִּלִּיתָ	גֻּלֵּיתָ	הִתְגַּלִּיתָ	הִגְלִיתָ	הָגְלֵיתָ
2fs	גָּלִית	נִגְלֵית	גִּלִּית	גֻּלֵּית	הִתְגַּלִּית	הִגְלִית	הָגְלֵית
1cs	גָּלִיתִי	נִגְלֵיתִי	גִּלִּיתִי	גֻּלֵּיתִי	הִתְגַּלִּיתִי	הִגְלִיתִי	הָגְלֵיתִי

IMPERFECTS The *qal* imperfects, which serve as a template for all the stems, likewise follow the principle that a III-*Waw/Yod* verb coalesces when followed by consonantal sufformatives and drops everywhere else. With consonantal sufformatives this coalescing produces a *segol yod* (יֶ). The remaining forms drop the *waw* or *yod*. When the *waw/yod* drops in forms that have no sufformative, the verbs appear with a *segol heh* (הֶ).

Imperfects: Coalesce When Followed by Consonantal Sufformatives Imperfects with consonantal sufformatives coalesce the historic *waw/yod*. The only consonantal sufformative in the imperfect paradigm is נָה, which is found in the second and third person feminine plural imperfect (e.g., תִּקְטֹלְנָה). When they coalesce, these forms appear with a *segol yod* (e.g., תִּגְלֶינָה). You learned in chapter 24 that the coalescing of *pataḥ* + *yod* produces *tsere yod* (e.g., ay → ē in *יַיְטִיב → יֵיטִיב), and in chapter 5

12. See GKC §75, Joüon §79h. The *tsere yod* probably reflects historic *pataḥ* + *yod* (י + ַ → יֵ), while the *ḥireq yod* reflects historic *ḥireq* + *yod* (י + ִ → יִ). This matches the dominant tendency for a-class theme vowels in the passive stems and i-class theme vowels in the active stems.

that *tsere yod* and *segol yod* are interchangeable. The coalescing to *segol yod* is used throughout the imperfect paradigm of III-*Waw/Yod* verbs.

	Coalescing		Strong form (2/3fp)		Root
Imperfect 2fp/3fp y'all will uncover"	תִּגְלֶינָה	←	*תִּגְלַיְנָה	←	*גלי

All the remaining III-*Waw/Yod* imperfects drop the historic *waw/yod*. Vocalic sufformatives move over to fill the space occupied by the historic *waw/yod*. Imperfects without sufformatives all appear with *segol heh*.[13]

Imperfects: Drop Everywhere Else

			No sufformative adds *heh*		Final *waw/yod* drops
Imperfect 3ms "he will uncover"	יִגְלֶה	←	ה	+	*יִגְלַי
Imperfect 2fs "you will uncover"	תִּגְלִי	←			*תִּגְלִיִי

13. Early scholars argued that III-*Waw/Yod* imperfects like יִגְלֶה developed in exactly the same manner as the perfect. The final *waw/yod* dropped and then received a vowel marker to alert readers to the presence of the theme vowel (e.g., *יִגְלִי → *יִגְלִ → יִגְלֶה). However, modern scholars now believe that יִגְלֶה actually resulted from the contraction of *yod* with a historic a-class theme vowel and that the *segol heh* (or *tsere heh*) is just an alternate representation of *tsere yod* (e.g., *יִגְלַי → *יִגְלֵי = יִגְלֶה) (GKC §75e, Joüon §79e). If the modern explanation is correct, then the principle that *III-*Waw/Yod *coalesces when followed by consonantal sufformatives and drops everywhere else* is an accurate representation of both historic development and visual appearance in all but this one aspect. Unlike other III-*Waw/Yod* verbs that lack sufformatives, verbs like יִגְלֶה actually coalesce the *yod* and "drop" it only in the sense that *heh* replaces *yod* as the vowel marker at the end of a word. Nevertheless, the lack of visible *yod* in such forms allows the guiding principle of this chapter to help beginning students despite its technical limitations.

Imperfects: Qal As a Template for the Other Stems The endings of the III-*Waw/Yod* imperfects follow the *qal* paradigm throughout all the stems.

Table 25.2: III-*Waw/Yod* Imperfects (All Stems)

	Qal	*Niphal*	*Piel*	*Pual*	*Hithpael*	*Hiphil*	*Hophal*
Drop	יִגְלֶה	יִגָּלֶה	יְגַלֶּה	יְגֻלֶּה	יִתְגַּלֶּה	יַגְלֶה	יָגְלֶה
	יִגְלוּ	יִגָּלוּ	יְגַלּוּ	יְגֻלּוּ	יִתְגַּלּוּ	יַגְלוּ	יָגְלוּ
Coalesce	תִּגְלֶינָה	תִּגָּלֶינָה	תְּגַלֶּינָה	תְּגֻלֶּינָה	תִּתְגַּלֶּינָה	תַּגְלֶינָה	תָּגְלֶינָה

JUSSIVES AND WAW CONSECUTIVES The jussives and *waw* consecutive imperfects are presented together because they are both short forms. Other than the initial □וַ of the *waw* consecutive, they look the same. These forms will not necessarily be more difficult to recognize, but they are more complex to discuss. Regardless of how the forms appear, they follow the normal functions of the jussive or *waw* consecutive imperfect.

To simplify the data, all the examples of III-*Waw/Yod* short forms use גלה so that you can focus on the characteristics of each form without being distracted by different roots. Some forms do not occur with גלה and may be difficult to pronounce with these consonants. Biblical Hebrew examples are presented in footnotes so that you can see the effect upon pronunciation.

What Are Short Forms? Jussives and *waw* consecutive imperfects tend to prefer a form that is shorter than the imperfect. In the strong verb, the distinction between long and short forms only appears in the *hiphil*, where the long forms contain pure long vowels (with vowel markers) in contrast to short forms that lack those pure long vowels (e.g., *hiphil* impf. יַקְטִיל vs. *hiphil waw* consec. וַיַּקְטֵל). In weak verbs, short forms are more prominent. The III-*Waw/Yod* short forms do not have the *segol heh* of the imperfect (e.g., *qal waw* consec. וַיִּגֶל vs. impf. יִגְלֶה).[14] While most III-*Waw/Yod* jussives and *waw* consecutive imperfects appear as short forms, they can also appear as long forms in the biblical text.

Short forms		Long forms	
N/A		יִגְלֶה	*Qal* impf. 3ms "he will uncover"
וַיִּגְלְ	or	וַיִּגְלֶה	*Qal waw* consec. impf. "and he uncovered"

Regardless of the form these verbs take, always parse them according to their function. Some Hebrew resource tools make a distinction between imperfects and "imperfects with jussive function." This can be helpful in research because it allows scholars to isolate passages that use long forms and short forms. However, for the sake of translation and parsing it gives the impression that the author chose to use a true imperfect to capture a jussive meaning when it is just as likely that the dynamics of language have created a blurring of forms.

Recognizing Short Forms

The loss of *segol heh* in the short forms can slow your initial recognition of the verb by not giving you all the information you are used to seeing. Yet these short forms still preserve key information at the front of the verb that helps identify them. For example, the *qal* short form וַיִּ֫גֶל (without *segol heh*) has an i-class preformative vowel. This i-class vowel rules out every stem except the *qal* and *niphal*. The lack of doubling in the first root letter further rules out a *niphal*. Thus, the verb must be a *qal waw* consecutive. Given the fact that the verb is strong at the beginning (compare *qal* יִקְטֹל with וַיִּ֫גֶל), the weakness must be at the end of the root, in other words, III-*Waw/Yod*. If it were a *niphal* short form, the verb would retain the initial features of the strong form (compare *niphal* יִקָּטֵל with וַיִּ֫גָּל).

Short forms of the *piel–hithpael* lose the characteristic *dagesh forte* of the second root consonant because doubling cannot be heard at the end of the word. Though students rely heavily on the *dagesh* in these

14. The Masoretes added a final *shewa* in their vocalization of forms like וַיִּגְלְ to reinforce that both consonants are vowelless.

stems, these short forms should be recognizable because of their characteristic preformatives (e.g., *piel* יְגַלֶּה → יְגַל and *hithpael* יִתְגַּלֶּה → יִתְגַּל). In short forms you will need to pay attention to all the features that might help you link a form with its strong verb equivalent.

Jussive (short form)		Imperfect	
יִגָּל	←	יִגָּלֶה	*Niphal* 3ms
יְגַל	←	יְגַלֶּה	*Piel* 3ms
יִתְגַּל	←	יִתְגַּלֶּה	*Hithpael* 3ms

Short Forms with Consonant Clusters (Qal and Hiphil)

Short forms of the *qal* and *hiphil* sometimes result in two consecutive consonants at the end of the word with no vowel for either consonant (e.g., וַיִּגְלְ). These consonant clusters are created because, without *segol heh,* the two remaining root letters have no vowel.[15] Occasionally you will see short forms that preserve a final consonant cluster, but more often Hebrew smooths out the pronunciation. The following discussion will help you recognize the relationship between the short forms and the strong verb patterns, but the information need not be memorized. To simplify the discussion the same root (גלה) is used to represent all the options you will encounter even though this root will not appear in all these forms.

In the *qal*, the III-*Waw/Yod* short forms appear in the biblical text in the following ways: with no adjustment (וַיִּגְלְ), with a lengthened preformative vowel (וַיֵּגְלְ), with the addition of a helping vowel (וַיִּגֶל), or with both a lengthened preformative vowel and an added helping vowel (וַיֵּגֶל).[16] In all of these forms the i-class preformative vowel indicates that the verb is a *qal*, and the presence of only two root consonants suggests that a final *waw/yod* has dropped.

15. Every other stem has a vowel under the first root consonant eliminating the possibility of a consonant cluster (e.g., jussives of *niphal* יִקָּטֵל, *piel* יְקַטֵּל, *pual* יְקֻטַּל, *hithpael* יִתְקַטֵּל). Conversely, the *qal* and *hiphil* have no vowel under the first root consonant (e.g., jussives of *qal* יִקְטֹל, *hiphil* יַקְטֵל), thus creating a consonant cluster whenever *segol heh* is not present. There are no relevant examples of the *hophal* in the biblical text.

Hiphil short forms use some of these same adjustments but are based on the a-class preformative vowel of the *hiphil* imperfect. *Hiphil* short forms appear without adjustment (וַיַּגְלְ) or with a helping vowel (וַיֶּגֶל).[17] *Hiphil* short forms with a helping vowel do not look like they reflect an a-class preformative vowel unless you recall the segolate patterns of Hebrew nouns. Segolate nouns add a *segol* helping vowel to eliminate the consonant cluster and then harmonize the a-class vowel with *segol* to ease pronunciation.

Vowel harmonized		Helping vowel added		Consonant cluster	
מֶלֶךְ	←	*מַלֶךְ	←	*מַלְךְ	Segolate nouns
וַיֶּגֶל	←	*וַיַּגֶל	←	*וַיַּגְלְ	*Hiphil* short form

Thus when you encounter a jussive or *waw* consecutive short form vocalized like a segolate noun, the form is reflecting an a-class preformative and is a *hiphil* (וַיֶּגֶל).

To complicate matters further, remember that the historic *qal* had an a-class preformative, just like the *hiphil*. Many of the most common III-*Waw/Yod* verbs have a guttural as the first consonant of the root (e.g., עלה "to go up," ענה "to answer," ראה "to see"). The guttural preserves the historic a-class preformative. Since both the *hiphil* and I-Guttural *qal* verbs have an a-class preformative, sometimes only context will help you distinguish between short forms of the III-*Waw/Yod qal* and *hiphil* (e.g., וַיַּרְא can be *qal* "and he saw" or *hiphil* "and he showed"). Again, the purpose of this section is only to let you know what to expect. These are not details you need to memorize.

16. Biblical examples of these forms include וַיִּשְׁבְּ (from שׁבה "and he took captive"), וַיֵּשְׁתְּ (from שׁתה "and he drank"), וַיִּגֶל (from גלה "and he uncovered"), and וַתֵּרֶב (from רבה "and she was great").

17. Biblical examples of these *hiphil* forms include וַיַּשְׁקְ (from שׁקה "and he gave water"), and וַיֶּגֶל (from גלה "and he carried into exile").

Table 25.3: III-*Waw/Yod* Short Forms with Consonant Clusters

	Qal (i-class preformative)	*Hiphil* (a-class preformative)	*Qal* or *Hiphil* (ambiguous forms a-class + guttural)
No adjustment	וַיִּגְל	וַיַּגְל	וַיַּרְא (ראה)
Lengthened preformative	וַיֵּגְל		
Helping vowel	וַיִּגֶל		וַיַּעַל (עלה)
Helping vowel + adjustment	וַיֶּגֶל	וַיֶּגֶל	

QAL IMPERATIVES As in the strong verb, imperatives are essentially the imperfect or jussive minus the preformative (e.g., תִּגְלֶה → גְּלֵה). Most masculine singular imperatives appear in the long form with the *heh* vowel marker. The notable feature of the III-*Waw/Yod* imperative is the shift from *segol heh* in the imperfect to *tsere heh* (e.g., תִּגְלֶה → גְּלֵה). Although *segol heh* and *tsere heh* are both i-class vowels, students sometimes miss the connection between the III-*Waw/Yod* imperative and its corresponding imperfect unless they have memorized the form.

	Qal impv.		*Qal* impf.
2ms	גְּלֵה	←	תִּגְלֶה
2fs	גְּלִי	←	תִּגְלִי
2mp	גְּלוּ	←	תִּגְלוּ
2fp	גְּלֶינָה	←	תִּגְלֶינָה

On rare occasions you will encounter short form imperatives. Short form imperatives exhibit the same features as the jussives and *waw* consecutives discussed above. Thus, you will see masculine singular imperatives like the *piel* גַּל (from גַּלֵּה) and *hiphil* הֶ֫גֶל (from הַגְלֵה).[18] Although there is much less in these forms upon which to base your parsing, there are helpful hints. First, evaluate whether any of the consonants at the front or back of the word could be a preformative or sufformative/suffix. Second, when confronted with only two potential root consonants, consider a III-*Waw/Yod* verb. Third, remember that segolate patterns in verbs indicate the presence of an a-class vowel and a consonant cluster. If you can envision הֶ֫גֶל as a smoothing of הַגְל*, the *heh* and a-class preformative suggest a *hiphil* imperative.

Short form imperative		*(helping vowel)*		Long form imperative	
גַּל	←		←	גַּלֵּה	*Piel* 2ms
הֶ֫גֶל	←	הַ֫גֶל	←	הַגְלֵה	*Hiphil* 2ms

INFINITIVES

Infinitive Constructs

The III-*Waw/Yod* infinitive constructs always end in וֹת. As in all the other verb forms, the front of the word matches the strong form. Although the וֹת ending creates potential confusion with feminine plural participles, nouns, and adjectives, the III-*Waw/Yod* infinitives are very common and should be a strong consideration when encountering an וֹת ending.

גְּלוֹת	←	וֹת	+	גְּלִי	*Qal* inf. cst.
				קְטֹל	(strong)

Infinitive Absolutes

The III-*Waw/Yod* infinitive absolutes follow the pattern of the strong verb (e.g., *qal:* קָטוֹל and גָּלֹה; *piel:* קַטֵּל and גַּלֵּה). The historic *waw/yod* drops (consistent with "drops everywhere else") and in most cases replaces the *waw/yod* with a *heh* vowel marker consistent with the lexical form you memorize (e.g., גָּלֹה from גלה). Some *qal* infinitive absolutes use a *waw* rather than *heh* as the vowel marker (e.g., גָּלוֹ), a

18. Biblical examples include the *piel* צַו (from צוה "command!") and the *hiphil* הֶ֫רֶב (from רבה "increase!").

form that still reminds you of both the infinitive absolute and the historic III-*Waw/Yod* root.

Table 25.4: III-*Waw/Yod* Infinitives (All Stems)

	Qal	*Niphal*	*Piel*	*Pual*	*Hithpael*	*Hiphil*	*Hophal*
Inf. Cst.	גְּלוֹת	הִגָּלוֹת	גַּלּוֹת	גֻּלּוֹת	הִתְגַּלּוֹת	הַגְלוֹת	הָגְלוֹת
Inf. Abs.	גָּלוֹ or גָּלֹה	נִגְלֹה	גַּלֵּה	גֻּלֹּה	הִתְגַּלֵּה	הַגְלֵה	הָגְלֵה
Strong	(קָטוֹל)	(נִקְטֹל)	(קַטֵּל)	(קֻטֹּל)	(הִתְקַטֵּל)	(הַקְטֵל)	(הָקְטֵל)

PARTICIPLES Since participles have no consonantal endings, they drop *waw/yod* in all forms. Because the masculine singular has no sufformative, it will have a *segol heh* because of the addition of the *heh* vowel marker. The remaining forms simply drop the *waw/yod* and the vocalic sufformative slides into place.

The one exception is the *qal* passive participle, which retains a *yod* to avoid the two consecutive vowels that would result from the loss of *yod* (e.g., גְּלוּיָה). The long theme vowel of the passive participle is unchangeable, and a vocalic sufformative cannot attach to a long vowel without an intervening consonant. As a result, the passive participle retains the *yod*.

Table 25.5: III-*Waw/Yod* Participles (All Stems)

	Qal (active)	*Qal* (passive)	*Niphal*	*Piel*	*Pual*	*Hithpael*	*Hiphil*	*Hophal*
ms	גֹּלֶה	גָּלוּי	נִגְלֶה	מְגַלֶּה	מְגֻלֶּה	מִתְגַּלֶּה	מַגְלֶה	מָגְלֶה
fs	גֹּלָה	גְּלוּיָה	נִגְלָה	מְגַלָּה	מְגֻלָּה	מִתְגַּלָּה	מַגְלָה	מָגְלָה
mp	גֹּלִים	גְּלוּיִם	נִגְלִים	מְגַלִּים	מְגֻלִּים	מִתְגַּלִּים	מַגְלִים	מָגְלִים
fp	גֹּלוֹת	גְּלוּיוֹת	נִגְלוֹת	מְגַלּוֹת	מְגֻלּוֹת	מִתְגַּלּוֹת	מַגְלוֹת	מָגְלוֹת
		YOD RETAINED						

UNIQUE FEATURES OF THE VERB היה

The familiar verb היה behaves like all the other III-*Waw/Yod* verbs, except in the short forms. If the *qal* short forms of היה were to follow the line of development described elsewhere in this chapter, they would produce a form that is virtually impossible to pronounce (e.g., יִהְיֶה → יִהְיְ*).[19]

As a result, short forms of היה follow an adjustment in vocalization seen elsewhere in Hebrew. For example, the irregular noun בְּכִי ("weeping") shares the same underlying historic form: a monosyllable with *ḥireq* + *shewa*. The historic form of בְּכִי is preserved when suffixes are added (e.g., בִּכְיוֹ "his weeping"). Yet this historic form is impossible to pronounce when it appears alone (בִּכְי*). As a result, the vowels are switched to ease pronunciation (i.e., בִּכְי* → בְּכִי).[20]

The short forms of היה follow the same transposition of vowels described above (e.g., יִהְיֶה → יִהְיְ* → יְהִי). This adjustment in pronunciation produces the jussive and *waw* consecutive forms you saw in the text of Gen 1:3, וַיֹּאמֶר אֱלֹהִים יְהִי אוֹר וַיְהִי־אוֹר ("And God said, 'Let there be light!' and there was light"). The *waw* consecutive וַיְהִי is familiar to you from your translation exercises. The short form jussive is identical to this *waw* consecutive except that it lacks the characteristic conjunction of the *waw* consecutive.[21] When you encounter less common forms like third person feminine singular וַתְּהִי ("and she was"), first person common singular וָאֱהִי ("and I was"), or first person common plural וַנְּהִי ("and we were"), do not let the substitution of preformatives obscure their connection to the more familiar וַיְהִי.

19. The root היה occurs predominantly in the *qal*, though a few *niphal* forms exist. The structure of the *niphal* forms does not allow for the anomalies discussed in this section.

20. The word בְּכִי (with the historic i-class בִּכְי*) was used to illustrate these changes because of its similarity to the i-class preformative vowel on the jussive of היה. However, these types of nouns are very common and appear in other vowel classes as well, e.g., אֲרִי "lion" (historic a-class אַרְי*) and חֳלִי "sickness" (historic u-class חָלְי*).

21. On the loss of *dagesh forte* in the *yod* due to the *Skin 'em Levi* principle, see the discussion in ch. 3.

Biblical Hebrew		Awkward monosyllable		Imperfect (long form)
יְהִי ("let him be")	←	*יְהְיְ	←	יִהְיֶה ("he will be")
בְּכִי ("weeping")	←	*בְּכְיְ		

SUMMARY This chapter covered many concepts that can be summarized by focusing on the following principles.

1. III-*Waw/yod* coalesces when followed by consonantal sufformatives.

גָּלִיתָ	←	*גָּלַיְתָ	*Qal* pf. 2ms
תִּגְלֶינָה	←	*תִּגְלַיְנָה	*Qal* impf. 2fp

2. III-*Waw/yod* drops everywhere else.

גָּלוּ	←	*גָּלְיוּ	*Qal* pf. 3mp

3. All forms in all stems are based on the strong verb + III-*Waw/Yod qal* endings.

Qal Representative Forms with גלה

גָּלָה, גָּלְתָה	Perfect
יִגְלֶה	Imperfect
גְּלֵה	Imperative
גְּלוֹת	Infinitive Construct
גָּלֹה	Infinitive Absolute
גֹּלֶה	Participle

What Questions Should I Ask When I Read?

When you encounter a verb that appears to only have two root consonants and follows the strong paradigms at the front, consider a III-*Waw/Yod* verb because these verbs are weak at the end of the word. The first question you should ask is, "Does the word have a visible *yod* where there could once have been a historic III-*Waw/Yod*?" The *yod* will be a vowel marker, but it still preserves the historic root letter and points you in the right direction. If there is no visible *yod*, could a *waw* or *yod* have dropped, leaving only two visible root letters? (Remember, because *waw/yod* c̲oalesces with c̲onsonantal sufformatives, a *waw/yod* could drop before a vocalic sufformative or in forms where there is no sufformative.) In either case, do the two consonants plus a final *heh* correspond to a word you know or can identify in a Hebrew lexicon? Since these verbs are weak at the end of the word, the beginning of the word should follow the standard features of the strong verb unless some other weakness is present to affect vocalization. At all times, let context guide your expectation for meaning and verb form, and then let it confirm your final analysis.

REPRESENTATIVE FORMS: III-WAW/YOD VERBS

In order to best master the III-*Waw/Yod* verbs, learn the *qal* forms of this paradigm and use them as a template for identifying the other verb stems. The verb stems retain their characteristic features at the front of the verb.

III-WAW/YOD VERB CHART

QAL	NIPHAL	PIEL	PUAL	HITHPAEL	HIPHIL	HOPHAL
Perfect						
גָּלָה	נִגְלָה	גִּלָּה	גֻּלָּה	הִתְגַּלָּה	הִגְלָה	הָגְלָה
גָּלְתָה	נִגְלְתָה	גִּלְּתָה	גֻּלְּתָה	הִתְגַּלְּתָה	הִגְלְתָה	הָגְלְתָה
גָּלִ֫יתָ	נִגְלֵ֫יתָ	גִּלִּ֫יתָ	גֻּלֵּ֫יתָ	הִתְגַּלִּ֫יתָ	הִגְלִ֫יתָ	הָגְלֵ֫יתָ
גָּלִ֫ית	נִגְלֵ֫ית	גִּלִּ֫ית	גֻּלֵּ֫ית	הִתְגַּלִּ֫ית	הִגְלִ֫ית	הָגְלֵ֫ית
גָּלִ֫יתִי	נִגְלֵ֫יתִי	גִּלִּ֫יתִי	גֻּלֵּ֫יתִי	הִתְגַּלִּ֫יתִי	הִגְלִ֫יתִי	הָגְלֵ֫יתִי
גָּלוּ	נִגְלוּ	גִּלּוּ	גֻּלּוּ	הִתְגַּלּוּ	הִגְלוּ	הָגְלוּ
גְּלִיתֶם	נִגְלֵיתֶם	גִּלִּיתֶם	גֻּלֵּיתֶם	הִתְגַּלִּיתֶם	הִגְלִיתֶם	הָגְלֵיתֶם
גְּלִיתֶן	נִגְלֵיתֶן	גִּלִּיתֶן	גֻּלֵּיתֶן	הִתְגַּלִּיתֶן	הִגְלִיתֶן	הָגְלֵיתֶן
גָּלִ֫ינוּ	נִגְלֵ֫ינוּ	גִּלִּ֫ינוּ	גֻּלֵּ֫ינוּ	הִתְגַּלִּ֫ינוּ	הִגְלִ֫ינוּ	הָגְלֵ֫ינוּ
Imperfect						
יִגְלֶה	יִגָּלֶה	יְגַלֶּה	יְגֻלֶּה	יִתְגַּלֶּה	יַגְלֶה	יָגְלֶה
תִּגְלֶה	תִּגָּלֶה	תְּגַלֶּה	תְּגֻלֶּה	תִּתְגַּלֶּה	תַּגְלֶה	תָּגְלֶה
תִּגְלֶה	תִּגָּלֶה	תְּגַלֶּה	תְּגֻלֶּה	תִּתְגַּלֶּה	תַּגְלֶה	תָּגְלֶה
תִּגְלִי	תִּגָּלִי	תְּגַלִּי	תְּגֻלִּי	תִּתְגַּלִּי	תַּגְלִי	תָּגְלִי
אֶגְלֶה	אֶגָּלֶה	אֲגַלֶּה	אֲגֻלֶּה	אֶתְגַּלֶּה	אַגְלֶה	אָגְלֶה
יִגְלוּ	יִגָּלוּ	יְגַלּוּ	יְגֻלּוּ	יִתְגַּלּוּ	יַגְלוּ	יָגְלוּ
תִּגְלֶ֫ינָה	תִּגָּלֶ֫ינָה	תְּגַלֶּ֫ינָה	תְּגֻלֶּ֫ינָה	תִּתְגַּלֶּ֫ינָה	תַּגְלֶ֫ינָה	תָּגְלֶ֫ינָה
תִּגְלוּ	תִּגָּלוּ	תְּגַלּוּ	תְּגֻלּוּ	תִּתְגַּלּוּ	תַּגְלוּ	תָּגְלוּ
תִּגְלֶ֫ינָה	תִּגָּלֶ֫ינָה	תְּגַלֶּ֫ינָה	תְּגֻלֶּ֫ינָה	תִּתְגַּלֶּ֫ינָה	תַּגְלֶ֫ינָה	תָּגְלֶ֫ינָה
נִגְלֶה	נִגָּלֶה	נְגַלֶּה	נְגֻלֶּה	נִתְגַּלֶּה	נַגְלֶה	נָגְלֶה
Waw Consec.						
וַ֫יִּגֶל	וַיִּגָּל	וַיְגַל		וַיִּתְגַּל	וַ֫יֶּגֶל	
וַתִּ֫גֶל	וַתִּגָּל	וַתְּגַל		וַתִּתְגַּל	וַ֫תֶּגֶל	
וַתִּ֫גֶל	וַתִּגָּל	וַתְּגַל		וַתִּתְגַּל	וַ֫תֶּגֶל	
וַתִּגְלִי	וַתִּגָּלִי	וַתְּגַלִּי		וַתִּתְגַּלִּי	וַתַּגְלִי	
וָאֵ֫גֶל	וָאֶגָּלֶה	וָאֲגַלֶּה		וָאֶתְגַּל	וָ֫אֶגֶל	
וַיִּגְלוּ	וַיִּגָּלוּ	וַיְגַלּוּ		וַיִּתְגַּלּוּ	וַיַּגְלוּ	
וַתִּגְלֶ֫ינָה	וַתִּגָּלֶ֫ינָה	וַתְּגַלֶּ֫ינָה		וַתִּתְגַּלֶּ֫ינָה	וַתַּגְלֶ֫ינָה	
וַתִּגְלוּ	וַתִּגָּלוּ	וַתְּגַלּוּ		וַתִּתְגַּלּוּ	וַתַּגְלוּ	
וַתִּגְלֶ֫ינָה	וַתִּגָּלֶ֫ינָה	וַתְּגַלֶּ֫ינָה		וַתִּתְגַּלֶּ֫ינָה	וַתַּגְלֶ֫ינָה	
וַנִּגְלֶה	וַנִּגָּלֶה	וַנְּגַלֶּה		וַנִּתְגַּל	וַ֫נֶּגֶל	

QAL	NIPHAL	PIEL	PUAL	HITHPAEL	HIPHIL	HOPHAL
Imperative						
גְּלֵה	הִגָּלֵה	גַּלֵּה		הִתְגַּלֵּה	הַגְלֵה	
גְּלִי	הִגָּלִי	גַּלִּי		הִתְגַּלִּי	הַגְלִי	
גְּלוּ	הִגָּלוּ	גַּלּוּ		הִתְגַּלּוּ	הַגְלוּ	
גְּלֶינָה	הִגָּלֶינָה	גַּלֶּינָה		הִתְגַּלֶּינָה	הַגְלֶינָה	
Infinitive Construct						
גְּלוֹת	הִגָּלוֹת	גַּלּוֹת	גֻּלּוֹת	הִתְגַּלּוֹת	הַגְלוֹת	הָגְלוֹת
Infinitive Absolute						
גָּלֹה	נִגְלֹה	גַּלֵּה	גֻּלֹּה	הִתְגַּלֵּה	הַגְלֵה	הָגְלֵה
Participle						
גֹּלֶה	נִגְלֶה	מְגַלֶּה	מְגֻלֶּה	מִתְגַּלֶּה	מַגְלֶה	מָגְלֶה
גֹּלָה	נִגְלָה	מְגַלָּה	מְגֻלָּה	מִתְגַּלָּה	מַגְלָה	מָגְלָה
גֹּלִים	נִגְלִים	מְגַלִּים	מְגֻלִּים	מִתְגַּלִּים	מַגְלִים	מָגְלִים
גֹּלוֹת	נִגְלוֹת	מְגַלּוֹת	מְגֻלּוֹת	מִתְגַּלּוֹת	מַגְלוֹת	מָגְלוֹת
גָּלוּי						
גְּלוּיָה						
גְּלוּיִם						
גְּלוּיוֹת						

THE היה VERB CHART

Inf. Cst. הֱיוֹת ***Inf. Abs.*** הָיֹה / הָיוֹ

	Perfect	*Impf.*		*Waw Consec.*	*Jussive*	*Impv.*	*Participle*
he (3ms)	הָיָה (*היי)	יִהְיֶה	(*יִהְיִ) →	וַיְהִי	יְהִי		הֹוֶה
she (3fs)	הָיְתָה	תִּהְיֶה	(*תִּהְיִ) →	וַתְּהִי	תְּהִי		הוֹיָה
you (2ms)	הָיִ֫יתָ	תִּהְיֶה	(*תִּהְיִ) →	וַתְּהִי	תְּהִי	→ הֱיֵה	
you (2fs)	הָיִ֫ית	תִּהְיִי		וַתִּהְיִי	תִּהְיִי	→ הֲיִי	
I (1cs)	הָיִ֫יתִי	אֶהְיֶה	(*אֶהְיִ) →	וָאֶהְיֶה/וָאֱהִי	אֱהִי		
they (3mp)	הָיוּ	יִהְיוּ		וַיִּהְיוּ	יִהְיוּ		
they (3fp)		תִּהְיֶ֫ינָה		וַתִּהְיֶ֫ינָה	תִּהְיֶ֫ינָה		
you (2mp)	הֱיִיתֶם	תִּהְיוּ		וַתִּהְיוּ	תִּהְיוּ	→ הֱיוּ	
you (2fp)	הֱיִיתֶן	תִּהְיֶ֫ינָה		וַתִּהְיֶ֫ינָה	תִּהְיֶ֫ינָה	→ N/A	
we (1cp)	הָיִ֫ינוּ	נִהְיֶה	(*נִהְיִ) →	וַנִּהְיֶה/וַנְּהִי	נְהִי		

CHAPTER 26

I-*Waw/Yod* Verbs

This chapter deals with roots containing *waw* or *yod* as the first consonant (e.g., ושב* "to sit, dwell" and יטב "to be good"). Most I-*Waw/Yod* verbs historically started with *waw*.[1] Over time Hebrew rejected the use of *waw* at the beginning of a word and replaced it with *yod*, perhaps in an attempt to avoid confusion with the conjunction. Though the *waw* still appears in some forms when another letter begins the word (i.e., a preformative), all I-*Waw/Yod* verbs appear with *yod* in the lexicon regardless of their historic spelling.

יָשַׁב ← ושב*
"to sit, dwell"

יָטַב ← יטב
"to be good"

In some stems, original I-*Waw* roots behave differently than original I-*Yod* roots. However, if you understand the principles outlined in this chapter, you do not need to know whether a root began with historic *waw* or *yod*. To simplify the presentation in this chapter, the roots ישב (original *waw*) and יטב (original *yod*) are used as representative roots even though some of the forms do not occur in these roots.

1. There are only a handful of original I-*Yod* verbs. While you need not remember them, they can be fit into the following mnemonic: It *is good* (יטב) and *right* (ישר) *to suckle* (ינק) a baby when he *wakes* (יקץ) and *wails* (ילל). Then *use your right hand* (ימן) to burp him.

I-Waw/Yod: The Basic Principles

You have learned that *vowelless* waw *and* yod *like to drop or coalesce.* On the other hand, any *waw* or *yod* with its own vowel continues to function as a true consonant. Thus, forms with a vowel under the first consonant of the root look just like the strong forms (e.g., *qal* pf. יָטַב "he is good"). Strong forms occur throughout the stems but are concentrated in the *piel, pual,* and *hithpael* where the first root consonant has a vowel in every paradigm (e.g., *piel* impf. יְיַשֵּׁב "he will cause to dwell"). Since strong forms are easily recognizable, this chapter focuses on forms that are weak.

Everywhere that the strong forms have a silent *shewa* under the first root consonant (e.g., *qal* impf. יִקְטֹל), the I-*Waw/Yod* is vowelless and is free to drop or coalesce (e.g., qal impf. יִיְטַב* → יִיטַב). In I-*Waw/Yod* verbs, vowelless *waw/yod* coalesces with the preformative, except in the *qal* where I-*Waw* drops. To summarize what happens in I-*Waw/Yod* verbs:

Vowelless I-*Waw/Yod* coalesces with preformative vowels.
Exception: Vowelless I-*Waw* *qal* drops.

Chapter 25 presented the five possible combinations in which *waw* and *yod* can merge with the preceding vowel to create a new long vowel. All coalescing in I-*Waw/Yod* verbs is based on these combinations. Any other combinations are incompatible and do not appear.

וֹ	←	◌ַוְ	aw → ō
◌ֵי	←	◌ַיְ	ay → ē (*tsere*)
◌ֶי	←	◌ַיְ	ay → ē (*segol*)
◌ִי	←	◌ִיְ	iy → ī
וּ	←	◌ֻוְ	uw → ū

Roots that historically began with *waw* behave differently in the *qal* where the i-class preformative vowel is incompatible with *waw*. In general, when the first root consonant would be vowelless in the *qal* strong verb, the I-*Waw* drops and any preformative lengthens.

Qal impf. ישׁב "you will dwell"   *תִּוְשֵׁב → *תִּשֵׁב → תֵּשֵׁב

APPLYING THE PRINCIPLES

Since the weakness of a I-*Waw/Yod* verb appears at the beginning of the word where the verb stems differ most, the stems are affected differently. The following presentation approaches each verb stem independently in the order you learned them. *Waw* and *yod* are presented separately in stems where they produce different results. Concentrate on understanding the explanations rather than memorizing the particulars.

The nice thing about I-*Waw/Yod* verbs is that some indication of the original *waw/yod* almost always remains visible in the text. Any *waw/yod* with a vowel remains in the same form as the strong verb (e.g., *qal* pf. יָטַב). A vowelless *waw/yod* generally coalesces and remains visible in the text, though it is now a vowel marker rather than a true consonant (e.g., *qal* impf. *יִיְטַב → יִיטַב "he will be good"). When coalescing occurs, you will be able to identify the original underlying vowel from the four combinations that produce coalescing illustrated on the previous page. This vowel can help you identify the verb stem. Even when the original *waw* drops in the *qal*, a lengthened preformative vowel provides a clue that a root letter is missing (e.g., *qal* impf. 3ms *יִוְשֵׁב → יֵשֵׁב "he will dwell").[2]

QAL I-WAW DROPS

I-Waw/Yod *coalesces with preformative vowels,* ***except in the*** **qal** ***where I-Waw drops.*** Since the *qal* stem is the most common, and most of the I-*Waw/Yod qal* verbs originally started with *waw*, *qal* I-*Waw* verbs are discussed first. Forms like the *qal* perfect (יָשַׁב), participle (ישֵׁב, i.e., יֹשֵׁב),[3] and infinitive absolute (יָשׁוֹב) carry a vowel and behave just like the strong form. In these forms you do not need to determine whether they originally began with *waw* or *yod* because they all appear with *yod*. However, *qal* forms where the original *waw* would be vowelless in the strong form drop the *waw*. Thus the imperfect and jussive (e.g. יִקְטֹל) and the imperative and infinitive construct (e.g., קְטֹל) all drop the *waw*.

2. A lengthened preformative indicates a weakness in one of the first two consonants. So far in the grammar this only includes I-*Waw/Yod* verbs. You will not have such lengthening when a verb is only weak at the end (e.g., III-*Waw/Yod*).

3. In the biblical text the dot of the *shin* often represents both vowel and consonant (e.g., ישֵׁב). They are written separately here for the sake of clarity.

Qal Imperfect (I-Waw) The best way to remember that I-*Waw* drops in the *qal* imperfect is to note that *waw* has no affinity with the i-class preformative vowel of the strong verb (יִקְטֹל). *Ḥireq* and *waw* are not compatible in sound and will not merge (think "*Ew! That won't work!*").[4] Thus the I-*Waw* *qal* drops rather than coalesces. For example, in יִוְשֵׁב* *ḥireq* + *waw* are incompatible (*Ew!*), the ו drops, and the preformative vowel lengthens to יֵשֵׁב.[5] To avoid confusion between the *yod* preformative and *yod* of the root, the following illustration highlights these changes using the second masculine singular form.

	Preformative lengthens		*Waw* drops		Original I-*Waw*
Qal impf. ישׁב "you will dwell"	תֵּשֵׁב	←	תִּשֵׁב*	←	תִּוְשֵׁב*

The *qal* imperfect יֵשֵׁב explains the appearance of the related forms: jussive, *waw* consecutive imperfect, imperative, and infinitive construct.

Qal Jussive/Waw (I-Waw) The I-*Waw* *qal* jussives are identical to the imperfect (יֵשֵׁב). The *waw* consecutive imperfect is similar, though the accent shifts towards the beginning of the verb (typical of many weak verbs). This accent shift leaves a short vowel in the final closed unaccented syllable (וַיֵּשֶׁב).

Qal Imperative (I-Waw) Since imperatives look like the imperfect minus the preformative, the I-*Waw* *qal* imperative is exactly what you would expect (e.g., impf. תֵּשֵׁב → impv. שֵׁב "dwell!").[6]

4. Contrast the compatibility of *ḥireq* + *yod* (ִי) and *ḥireq* + *waw* (ִוְ). The first is one smooth flowing sound while the second contains two distinct sounds that are not easily pronounced.

5. This explanation of יֵשֵׁב assumes that *waw* dropped to avoid the awkward *ḥireq* + *waw* ("*Ew!*") after the shift from *y<u>a</u>qtol* to *y<u>i</u>qtol* had already occurred (יַוְשֵׁב* → יִוְשֵׁב* → יֵשֵׁב). Other scholars argue that since this preformative vowel never reduces in distant open syllables (e.g., אֵדָעֲךָ), the vowel must be a pure long vowel resulting from coalescing an historic ay → ē that is written defectively in the *qal* (יַיְשֵׁב* → יֵישֵׁב* → יֵשֵׁב) (GKC §69b n. 1; Joüon §75c). However, since ישׁב is a historic I-*Waw* verb this grammar adopts the former explanation of the verb's development.

6. One might expect the I-*Waw* *qal* imperative to follow the strong pattern (קְטֹל) because the initial *waw*/*yod* has a vocal *shewa*. However, the I-*Waw* *qal* forms the imperative off the imperfect by removing the preformative (שֵׁב NOT יְשֵׁב*).

	Qal impv.		*Qal* impf.
2ms	שֵׁב	←	תֵּשֵׁב
2fs	שְׁבִי	←	תֵּשְׁבִי
2mp	שְׁבוּ	←	תֵּשְׁבוּ
2fp	שֵׁ֫בְנָה	←	תֵּשֵׁ֫בְנָה

Qal Infinitive Construct (I-Waw)

The I-*Waw* *qal* infinitive construct שֶׁ֫בֶת ("dwelling") is less intuitive, not only losing the I-*Waw* but also gaining a letter that is not part of the root. Further, the infinitive construct looks different when suffixes are attached (שִׁבְתִּי "my dwelling"). Fortunately, these forms follow basic patterns of Hebrew word formation. The following discussion explains how these forms fit within the patterns you have already learned.

The strong verbs evidence a close relationship between the imperfect, imperative, and infinitive construct (e.g., impf. יִקְטֹל, impv. קְטֹל, inf. cst. קְטֹל). Likewise, the I-*Waw* infinitive construct is closely related in form to the imperfect יֵשֵׁב and imperative שֵׁב (shown above). All three forms of ישב drop the historic *waw* (ושב*) and preserve the i-class theme vowel. Since *tsere* results from a historic short vowel, שִׁב* serves as the base for each form.[7]

The infinitive construct uses שִׁב* together with a final *tav* (i.e., שִׁבת*). This extra *tav* is similar to the addition of וֹת to the infinitive constructs of the III-*Waw/Yod* verbs (e.g., *qal* inf. cst. גְּלוֹת). While the וֹת ending is unique to the III-*Waw/Yod* infinitive constructs, a simple ת is frequently added to infinitive constructs that have lost a root letter. The resulting שִׁבת*, with its awkward final consonant cluster, is then modified just like segolate nouns. A helping vowel is provided to smooth out pronunciation and the vowels are then harmonized (שִׁבת* → שִׁ֫בֶת* → שֶׁ֫בֶת). Like segolate nouns, a *pataḥ* helping vowel is used with gutturals (דַּ֫עַת from ידע "to know"). The unmodified base שִׁבְתּ* is preserved

7. The imperfect יֵשֵׁב and imperative שֵׁב both have a long theme vowel but without the vowel marker that would indicate a historic pure long vowel. These forms thus reflect lengthening of original short vowels (שִׁב*).

whenever the infinitive appears with suffixes (e.g., שִׁבְתִּי "my sitting") because the suffix breaks up the consonant cluster.

Qal inf. cst. ושׁב* "dwelling"	שֶׁבֶת	←	שְׁבֶת	←	שׁבְת*
	harmonize vowels		*helping vowel*		tav *added to create infinitive construct*

Qal inf. cst. ושׁב* + 1cs suffix "my dwelling"	שִׁבְתִּי	←	שׁבְת*
	plus suffix		tav *added to create infinitive construct*

In summary, the I-*Waw qal* will not contract *ḥireq* and *waw* (remember, *"Ew! That won't work!"*). A I-*Waw* verb will drop in the *qal* instead of coalescing. Also, remember that the forms of the imperfect, imperative, and infinitive construct are all related though distinct: יֵשֵׁב (impf.), שֵׁב (impv.), and שֶׁבֶת (inf. cst. from שׁבת*).

I-WAW/YOD COALESCES WITH PREFORMATIVE

Qal verbs that originally began with *waw* are the only I-*Waw/Yod* verbs that drop the historic consonant. All remaining forms discussed in this chapter follow the predominant I-*Waw/Yod* pattern, namely ***vowelless waw/yod coalesces with preformative vowels.***

Qal with I-Yod

Historic I-*Yod* verbs are formed differently than historic I-*Waw* verbs. I-*Yod* verbs in which the *yod* carries its own vowel remain just like the strong verb (e.g., *qal* perfect יָטַב "it was good"). Wherever the initial *yod* would be vowelless in the *qal* strong verb, the *yod* coalesces with the preformative vowel (יִיְטַב* → יִיטַב).[8] If there is no preformative with which to coalesce, the *yod* remains and is voiced with a vocal *shewa* like the strong verb (e.g., *qal* impv. יְטַב "be good"). In other words,

8. Though only a handful of roots originally started with *yod*, forms blur in popular speech. Some historic I-*Waw* roots adopt the pattern of I-*Yod* forms יֵשֵׁב. This simplifies your analysis, since these forms have a visible *yod* and reflect the lexical form.

coalescing only occurs when the *yod* would have a silent *shewa* in the strong form.

Strong	יָטַב	Perfect (has vowel)
Strong	יְטַב	Imperative (no preformative/vocal *shewa*)
Coalesce	יִיטַב ← *יִיְטַב	Imperfect 3ms (preformative + silent *shewa*)

Niphal Paradigm

I-*Waw/Yod niphal* verbs use *waw* throughout the entire paradigm regardless of whether the root historically began with *waw* or *yod*. This use of *waw* is typical of I-*Waw/Yod* passive stems (*niphal* and *hophal*).[9] In cases where an initial *waw/yod* has its own vowel, the verb will look like a strong verb, though it will use *waw* instead of yod and may take some getting used to (e.g., *niphal* impf. יִוָּשֵׁב). When you see a *waw* standing where the first root letter should appear, think of *waw* and *yod* as virtually interchangeable in order to make an association with your vocabulary, which always uses *yod* (ישׁב).

In forms where an initial *waw/yod* would be vowelless, *waw* will coalesce with the preformative vowel. This coalescing occurs with the historic a-class preformative vowel of the *niphal* (*נַקְטַל; see ch. 24) rather than the i-class vowel of the strong verb. Thus the *pataḥ waw* coalesces to *ḥolem waw* (*נַוְשַׁב → נוֹשַׁב *niphal* pf. 3ms). As with all pure long vowels, remember to watch for defective spelling (נוֹשַׁב = נֹשַׁב).

(aw → ō)

Niphal perfect 3ms "it was inhabited" — נוֹשַׁב ← *נַוְשַׁב

or נֹשַׁב
(written defectively)

9. There are rare exceptions (e.g., Gen 8:12 *niphal* וַיִּיָּחֶל "and he stayed"). The *pual* behaves like the strong forms with *yod* throughout.

Even though the *nun* is consistent with the *niphal*, the *ḥolem waw* (וֹ) does not immediately seem to correlate to the i-class preformative of the *niphal* strong verb or even its historic a-class vowel. While potentially confusing, the *ḥolem waw* (וֹ) actually provides two clues about parsing. First, because *ḥolem waw* (וֹ) can be the result of coalescing *pataḥ* with *waw* (וְ ַ), it serves as evidence of a historic a-class vowel (נַוְשַׁב* → נוֹשַׁב). Second, even though the *waw* is a vowel marker, allow it to remind you of I-*Waw/Yod* roots (נוֹשַׁב from ישׁב). The *nun* preformative and context will further help you identify these verbs as *niphal*.

Identification	Clues		Text
יִוָּשֵׁב "it will be inhabited"	ישׁב ⟵	י/ו = ו	יִוָּשֵׁב
	Niphal impf. 3ms ⟵	(יִקָּטֵל) *niph.* feature	

Identification	Clues		Text
נוֹשַׁב "it was inhabited"	ישׁב ⟵	וֹ think י/ו	נוֹשַׁב
	Niphal pf. 3ms ⟵	(נַוְשַׁב*) contraction	

Piel, Pual, and Hithpael Paradigms In the *piel, pual,* and *hithpael,* a I-*Waw/Yod* verb always has a vowel under the first consonant of the root. As a result, you will not see weak forms in these stems. In each case, a *yod* appears as the first consonant of the root (like the vocabulary form), and the word looks just like the strong verb (e.g., *piel* impf. יְקַטֵּל and יְיַשֵּׁב).

Hiphil Paradigms The I-*Waw/Yod hiphil* does not preserve the standard distinction between the perfect i-class (e.g., הִקְטִיל) and all the remaining a-class forms (e.g., יַקְטִיל). Instead, all *hiphil* I-*Waw/Yod* verbs are based off an a-class preformative vowel. This a-class vowel coalesces with either *waw* or *yod* depending on the historic form of the root. Roots that once began with *waw* coalesce from aw → ō (הַוְשִׁיב* to הוֹשִׁיב). Roots that originally began with *yod* coalesce from ay → ē (הַיְטִיב* to הֵיטִיב). In either case, these vowels can appear with defective spelling (e.g., הֹשִׁיב and הֵטִיב).

In the *hiphil*, as with the *niphal*, learn to recognize *ḥolem waw* (וֹ) as an indication both of a I-*Waw* verb (ו = ו/י) and of potential coalescing of *pataḥ* + *waw* (וֹ = וְ ַ). Likewise, the vowel marker in the *tsere yod* (י ֵ) reminds you of the historic root letter and indicates the potential coalescing of *pataḥ* + *yod* (י ֵ = יְ ַ). In either case, you do not need to determine the historic root letters because both appear in the lexicon under *yod*.[10]

(aw → ō and ay → ē)

Hiphil imperfect 3ms "he will cause to dwell"	יוֹשִׁיב	←	*יַוְשִׁיב
Hiphil imperfect 3ms "he will cause good"	יֵיטִיב	←	*יַיְטִיב

Hophal Paradigms

The *hophal*, like the passive *niphal*, uses *waw* in all I-*Waw/Yod* verbs. This *waw* coalesces with the historic u-class preformative of the *hophal* to produce a long ū (*הֻוְשַׁב → הוּשַׁב).[11] When written defectively with *qibbuts* (e.g., הוּשַׁב = הֻשַׁב), the fact that the *qibbuts* is in an open unaccented syllable indicates a defective spelling of a long vowel. (A true short vowel would be in a closed unaccented syllable.) If you are thinking about vowel classes rather than specific vowels, you will recognize that the long ū is the same vowel class as the strong verb (הָקְטַל) and fits the *hophal* u-a vowel pattern.

(uw → ū)

Hophal imperfect 3ms "he will made to dwell"	יוּשַׁב	←	*יֻוְשַׁב

10. Again it should not be surprising to find a blurring of forms in popular speech. Some I-*Waw* roots follow the I-*Yod* forms and vice versa. Either way the *waw/yod* will lead you back to roots listed under *yod* in the lexicon.

11. In ch. 5 all vowels are divided into three vowel classes: a-class, i-class, and u-class. The three vowel classes represent the three original vowels. The other vowels are a later development. Thus the *hophal* would not have had a short /o/ (originally there was not one) but a short /u/ (*הֻקְטַל).

EXCEPTIONS In addition to the basic principle for I-*Waw/Yod* verbs presented above, you will encounter irregularities.

Assimilation in I-Waw/Yod Verbs A few I-*Waw/Yod* assimilate the *waw/yod* to the following consonant, just like vowelless *nun* discussed in the overview of weak verbs in chapter 24. Assimilation of *waw/yod* usually occurs when the second root consonant is a *tsade*. For example, along with the expected I-*Waw/Yod* form יִיצַק (from יצק) one more often finds יִצֹּק (*qal* "he will pour out"). While the verb looks like it comes from נצק, it actually comes from יצק. Though the assimilation of *nun* will naturally be your first option in forms like this, you should consider the less common assimilation of *yod* when roots with *nun* do not provide any relevant meaning.

Coalesce	יִיצַק	←	יִיְצַק	*Qal* impf. 3ms יצק "he will pour out"
Assimilate	יִצֹּק	←	יִיְצֹק	

Irregular Forms (הלך and יכל) The familiar verb הלך ("to walk") is actually derived from two roots with the same meaning—הלך and ילך (originally ולך*)—though both appear in the lexicon as הלך. The verb "to walk" is formed from הלך in some paradigms (e.g., pf. הָלַךְ) and from the root ילך in other paradigms (e.g., impf. יִוְלֵךְ → יֵלֵךְ). The former behaves like a I-Guttural, and the latter behaves like a I-*Waw*. This is why you have seen הָלַךְ in the perfect and יֵלֵךְ in the imperfect (a I-*Waw* pattern) in your translations. Both of these forms are parsed as if they come from הלך.

Another common verb יכל ("to be able, prevail") has an irregular form. In the *qal* perfect this verb looks just like a regular stative *qal* (e.g., יָכֹל "he is able"). However, in the imperfect it takes a unique u-class preformative vowel (e.g., יוּכַל). Most Hebrew resources identify יוּכַל as a *qal*. However, other scholars suggest that יוּכַל is the expected I-*Waw/Yod hophal* that has lost its causative meaning and has become the functional equivalent of a *qal*.[12] For your purposes you can treat it as a simple *qal*.

12. In favor of יוּכַל being a *hophal* is the fact that the u-class preformative vowel is extremely difficult to explain given the historic i-class preformative vowel of the *qal* stative imperfects (cf. יִכְבַּד). Explanations based on the coalescing of a historic a-class vowel (*יַוְכַל → *יוֹכַל substituted with יוּכַל) are thus problematic from the start. On the loss of causative meaning in the *hophal* see the verb יקד ("to be in flames"), which appears only in the *qal* and

SUMMARY

In I-*Waw*/Yod roots the vowelless I-*Waw/Yod* coalesces with preformative vowels, except in the *qal* where I-*Waw* drops.

1. I-*Waw/Yod* verbs are all listed in lexicons under *yod.*

2. Vowelless I-*Waw/Yod* coalesces with preformative vowels.

   All coalescing occurs according to the following patterns:

◌וֹ	←	◌ַוְ	aw → ō
◌ֵי	←	◌ַיְ	ay → ē *(tsere)*
◌ֶי	←	◌ַיְ	ay → ē *(segol)*
◌ִי	←	◌ִיְ	iy → ī
◌וּ	←	◌ֻוְ	uw → ū

3. Exception: I-*Waw qal* drops.[13]

   Imperfects lengthen the preformative (יֵשֵׁב)

   Imperatives are built off the imperfect (שֵׁב)

   Infinitives add *tav* and act like segolates (שֶׁבֶת)

4. Remember underlying preformative vowels.

   Niphal a-class (historic נַקְטַל* thus נַוְ* → נוֹ)

   Hiphil a-class (all forms, thus הַוְ → הוֹ and הַיְ → הֵי)

   Hophal u-class (historic הֻקְטַל* thus הֻוְ* → הוּ)

What Questions Should I Ask When I Read?

I-*Waw/Yod* verbs are a bit easier to identify than most III-*Waw/Yod* verbs because they retain some indication of the first root letter. More often than not, you will rightly suspect that you are looking at a root beginning with *yod*. This chapter equips you to verify your hunch. Remember, you do not have to create these forms or determine which

hophal and has the same meaning for both stems (*qal* impf. יִיקַד and *hophal* impf. יוּקַד = "he will be in flames"). See GKC §69r; Joüon §75i.

13. Remember that *ḥireq* of the *qal* preformative will not coalesce with *waw*—think "Ew!"

verbs were originally *waw* or originally *yod* in order to identify the verbs you see in the text. Simply work with the forms you encounter and parse all I-*Waw/Yod* verbs as roots starting with *yod*.

If the *waw/yod* is visible as a pure long vowel following a preformative, allow it to remind you of the first root letter (e.g., יוֹשִׁיב from ישׁב) and then ask yourself what vowel underlies the coalesced pure long vowel (e.g., וֹ = a-class + *waw*). The underlying vowel will lead you to your stem (e.g., a-class = *hiphil*).

The more difficult forms are those in which a *waw* has dropped (only in the *qal*). If you cannot match a verb (תֵּשֵׁב) to a vocabulary form (NOT תשׁב) or strong verb vowel pattern (NOT קָטַל), ask if there is a preformative or sufformative on the verb (תֵּשֵׁב). Remember, you now have a new sufformative to consider, namely the use of the *tav* as a sufformative on infinitive constructs (שֶׁ֫בֶת). When you isolate the two remaining root letters, then a final *tav*, a lengthened preformative vowel, or vowels adjusted to the segolate vowel pattern confirm that something has dropped. Consider I-*Waw/Yod* verbs. At all times, let context guide your findings and confirm your final analysis.

REPRESENTATIVE FORMS: I-WAW/YOD VERBS

	Qal (I-*Waw*)	*Qal* (I-*Yod*)	*Niphal*	*Piel–Hithpael*	*Hiphil* (I-*Waw*)	*Hiphil* (I-*Yod*)	*Hophal*
Perfect	יָשַׁב	יָטַב	נוֹשַׁב	STRONG	הוֹשִׁיב	הֵיטִיב	הוּשַׁב
Imperfect	יֵשֵׁב	יִיטַב	יִוָּשֵׁב		יוֹשִׁיב	יֵיטִיב	יוּשַׁב
Waw Consec.	וַיֵּ֫שֶׁב	וַיִּיטַב	וַיִּוָּשֵׁב		וַיּ֫וֹשֶׁב	וַיֵּ֫יטֶב	וַיּוּשַׁב
Imperative	שֵׁב		הִוָּשֵׁב		הוֹשֵׁב	הֵיטֵב	
Inf. Cst.	שֶׁ֫בֶת	יְטַב	הִוָּשֵׁב		הוֹשִׁיב	הֵיטִיב	הוּשַׁב
Inf. Abs.	יָשׁוֹב	יָטוֹב			הוֹשֵׁב	הֵיטֵב	
Participle	יֹשֵׁב	יֹטֵב	נוֹשָׁב		מוֹשִׁיב	מֵיטִיב	מוּשָׁב
	waw drops (no affinity, think "Ew!")	iy → ī	aw → ō		aw → ō	ay → ē	uw → ū

I-WAW/YOD VERB CHART

DROP	COALESCE				
QAL (I-Waw)	***QAL (I-Yod)***	***NIPHAL***	***HIPHIL (I-Waw)***	***HIPHIL (I-Yod)***	***HOPHAL***
Perfect					
יָשַׁב	יָטַב	נוֹשַׁב	הוֹשִׁיב	הֵיטִיב	הוּשַׁב
יָֽשְׁבָה	יָֽטְבָה	נוֹשְׁבָה	הוֹשִׁיבָה	הֵיטִ֫יבָה	הוּשְׁבָה
יָשַׁ֫בְתָּ	יָטַ֫בְתָּ	נוֹשַׁ֫בְתָּ	הוֹשַׁ֫בְתָּ	הֵיטַ֫בְתָּ	הוּשַׁ֫בְתָּ
יָשַׁ֫בְתְּ	יָטַ֫בְתְּ	נוֹשַׁ֫בְתְּ	הוֹשַׁ֫בְתְּ	הֵיטַ֫בְתְּ	הוּשַׁ֫בְתְּ
יָשַׁ֫בְתִּי	יָטַ֫בְתִּי	נוֹשַׁ֫בְתִּי	הוֹשַׁ֫בְתִּי	הֵיטַ֫בְתִּי	הוּשַׁ֫בְתִּי
יָֽשְׁבוּ	יָֽטְבוּ	נוֹשְׁבוּ	הוֹשִׁ֫יבוּ	הֵיטִ֫יבוּ	הוּשְׁבוּ
יְשַׁבְתֶּם	יְטַבְתֶּם	נוֹשַׁבְתֶּם	הוֹשַׁבְתֶּם	הֵיטַבְתֶּם	הוּשַׁבְתֶּם
יְשַׁבְתֶּן	יְטַבְתֶּן	נוֹשַׁבְתֶּן	הוֹשַׁבְתֶּן	הֵיטַבְתֶּן	הוּשַׁבְתֶּן
יָשַׁ֫בְנוּ	יָטַ֫בְנוּ	נוֹשַׁ֫בְנוּ	הוֹשַׁ֫בְנוּ	הֵיטַ֫בְנוּ	הוּשַׁ֫בְנוּ
Imperfect					
יֵשֵׁב	יִיטַב	יִוָּשֵׁב	יוֹשִׁיב	יֵיטִיב	יוּשַׁב
תֵּשֵׁב	תִּיטַב	תִּוָּשֵׁב	תּוֹשִׁיב	תֵּיטִיב	תּוּשַׁב
תֵּשֵׁב	תִּיטַב	תִּוָּשֵׁב	תּוֹשִׁיב	תֵּיטִיב	תּוּשַׁב
תֵּשְׁבִי	תִּיטְבִי	תִּוָּשְׁבִי	תּוֹשִׁ֫יבִי	תֵּיטִ֫יבִי	תּוּשְׁבִי
אֵשֵׁב	אִיטַב	אִוָּשֵׁב	אוֹשִׁיב	אֵיטִיב	אוּשַׁב
יֵשְׁבוּ	יִיטְבוּ	יִוָּשְׁבוּ	יוֹשִׁ֫יבוּ	יֵיטִ֫יבוּ	יוּשְׁבוּ
תֵּשַׁ֫בְנָה	תִּיטַ֫בְנָה	תִּוָּשַׁ֫בְנָה	תּוֹשֵׁ֫בְנָה	תֵּיטֵ֫בְנָה	תּוּשַׁ֫בְנָה
תֵּשְׁבוּ	תִּיטְבוּ	תִּוָּשְׁבוּ	תּוֹשִׁ֫יבוּ	תֵּיטִ֫יבוּ	תּוּשְׁבוּ
תֵּשַׁ֫בְנָה	תִּיטַ֫בְנָה	תִּוָּשַׁ֫בְנָה	תּוֹשֵׁ֫בְנָה	תֵּיטֵ֫בְנָה	תּוּשַׁ֫בְנָה
נֵשֵׁב	נִיטַב	נִוָּשֵׁב	נוֹשִׁיב	נֵיטִיב	נוּשַׁב
Imperative					
שֵׁב	יְטַב	הִוָּשֵׁב	הוֹשֵׁב	הֵיטֵב	
שְׁבִי	יִטְבִי	הִוָּשְׁבִי	הוֹשִׁ֫יבִי	הֵיטִ֫יבִי	
שְׁבוּ	יִטְבוּ	הִוָּשְׁבוּ	הוֹשִׁ֫יבוּ	הֵיטִ֫יבוּ	
שֵׁ֫בְנָה	יְטַ֫בְנָה	הִוָּשַׁ֫בְנָה	הוֹשֵׁ֫בְנָה	הֵיטֵ֫בְנָה	

Inf. Cst.					
שֶׁ֫בֶת	יְטַב	הִוָּשֵׁב	הוֹשִׁיב	הֵיטִיב	הוּשַׁב
Inf. Abs.					
יָשׁוֹב	יָטוֹב	הִוָּשֵׁב	הוֹשֵׁב	הֵיטֵב	הוּשֵׁב
Participle					
יֹשֵׁב	יֹטֵב	נוֹשָׁב	מוֹשִׁיב	מֵיטִיב	מוּשָׁב
יֹשְׁבָה	יֹטְבָה	נוֹשָׁבָה	מוֹשִׁיבָה	מֵיטִיבָה	מוּשָׁבָה
יֹשְׁבִים	יֹטְבִים	נוֹשָׁבִים	מוֹשִׁיבִים	מֵיטִיבִים	מוּשָׁבִים
יֹשְׁבוֹת	יֹטְבוֹת	נוֹשָׁבוֹת	מוֹשִׁיבוֹת	מֵיטִיבוֹת	מוּשָׁבוֹת
יָשׁוּב					
יְשׁוּבָה					
יְשׁוּבִים					
יְשׁוּבוֹת					

CHAPTER 27

II-*Waw/Yod* Verbs: Introduction and *Qal* Stem

This chapter addresses verbs where *waw/yod* stands in the middle position of the root (II-*Waw/Yod*). You have already encountered a number of these roots in your translation exercises, for example, בּוֹא ("to go in, come"), שִׂים ("to put, place"), and קוּם ("to arise, stand"). Your frequent exposure to these words and your understanding of the strong verb provide a solid foundation for learning to read II-*Waw/Yod* verbs.

The *qal* infinitive construct serves as the lexical form of II-*Waw/Yod* verbs (e.g., בּוֹא, שִׂים, קוּם). The *qal* infinitive construct is used instead of the *qal* perfect 3ms (e.g., קָטַל), the usual lexical form, because it includes all three root letters. Technically, the *waw/yod* in the infinitive construct קוּם serves as a vowel marker (not a true consonant), but it helps a student see the historic *waw/yod* of the verbal root.

WEAKNESSES OF II-WAW/YOD

The II-*Waw/Yod* roots are affected by the principle that "*waw* and *yod* like to drop or coalesce." The presentation below explains the formation of II-*Waw/Yod* verbs against the backdrop of dropping and coalescing as they affect these verbs at the front, middle, and end of the verb. The II-*Waw/Yod* verbs vary from the strong verbs: (1) In the middle of the form when the *waw/yod* drops or coalesces, (2) at the beginning of the word when the dropping or coalescing leaves the preformative vowel in a vulnerable open syllable, and (3) at the end of the word when sufformatives are attached. These variations from the strong form are natural by-products of pronunciation and syllabification and do not need to be memorized. The adjustments that occur are all based on concepts you already know.

Weak at the Middle: Waw/Yod Drops or Coalesces

II-*Waw/Yod* verbs are, by nature, weak in the middle of the verb. When the middle *waw/yod* is lost, whether through dropping or coalescing, the theme vowel shifts to the first consonant of the root.

			III	II	I	Preformative
Strong	יִקְטֹל	=	ל	טֹ	קְ	יִ
Coalesced (קום)	יָקוּם	=	ם		קוּ	יָ
Dropped (קום)	וַיָּ֫קָם	=	ם		קָ	וַיָּ֫

Weak at the Front: Open Preformative Syllables (Vowel Rules)

II-*Waw/Yod* verbs are also weak at the front of the verb. Whenever the preformative vowel stands in a closed unaccented syllable, it is short (e.g., הִקְ|טִיל *hiphil* pf.).[1] Since the first root consonant in II-*Waw/Yod* verbs carries the theme vowel, it cannot close the preformative syllable (see above). Thus, the preformative vowel of II-*Waw/Yod* verbs is left in an open unaccented syllable. This open unaccented syllable follows the standard rules of vowel change, lengthening in a near open syllable (e.g., הֵ|קִים *hiphil* pf.) and reducing in a distant open syllable (הֲ|קִי|מָ֫|נוּ *hiphil* pf. + 1cp suffix).

Strong *Hiphil* pf. 3ms	הִקְטִיל	Closed unaccented → short
Hiphil pf. (קום)	הֵקִים	Near open → lengthens
Hiphil pf. (קום) + 1cp suff.	הֲקִימָ֫נוּ	Distant open → reduces

The open preformative syllable also results in the preservation of historic vowels in the *qal* and *niphal* (historic *qal* impf. יַקְטֵל* vs. strong יִקְטֹל and *niphal* historic נַקְטַל* vs. strong נִקְטַל). The shift from historic a-class to i-class preformatives only occurred in closed unaccented syllables. The open preformative syllable of II-*Waw/Yod* verbs could not

1. The *hiphil* provides the simplest example but the principle applies to any of the stems.

shift and retained the historic preformative vowels. Therefore, when you see a-class preformative vowels, consider *qal* or *niphal* in addition to the *hiphil* as possible parsing options.

Impf.		
Historic *qal*	*יַקְ | טֻל	
Strong verb *qal*	יִקְ | טֹל	Closed → shifts to i-class
II-*Waw/Yod qal*	יָ | קוּם	Open → retains a-class

Weak at the Back: Helping Vowels with Consonantal Sufformatives

II-*Waw/Yod* verbs can also be impacted at the back of the verb. The dropping or coalescing of *waw/yod* often results in a single-syllable root that can be awkward to pronounce when consonantal sufformatives are added. The II-*Waw/Yod* verbs sometimes add a helping vowel to smooth out pronunciation. These helping vowels are not consistently applied but are common. Perfects use a *ḥolem waw* as the helping vowel (e.g., *hiphil* pf. 2ms הֲקִימ֫וֹתָ). The remaining paradigms use *segol yod* (e.g., *hiphil* impf. 2fp תְּקִימֶ֫ינָה).[2] Helping vowels take the accent, unless trumped by the so-called heavy sufformatives. Either way, the preformative is left in a distant open syllable that reduces (e.g., *hiphil* pf. 2ms הֲקִימ֫וֹתָ and 2mp הֲקִימוֹתֶ֫ם).

Perfect	הֲקִימ֫וֹתָ	*Hiphil* pf. 2ms קום
Other forms	תְּקִימֶ֫ינָה	*Hiphil* impf. 2ms קום

II-WAW/YOD: THE BASIC PRINCIPLES

The adjustments at the beginning, middle, and end of II-*Waw/Yod* verbs are natural by-products of a root moving from three consonants (two syllables) to two consonants (one syllable). The following discussion describes how each verb stem responds to both accommodate for pronunciation and maintain the distinctive features of each stem. The

2. III-*Waw/Yod* verbs also have a *segol yod* before the consonantal sufformative. In those cases, *segol yod* is actually part of the root and results from coalescing the theme vowel with the final *waw/yod* (*qal* impf. *תִּגְלַ֫יְנָה → תִּגְלֶ֫ינָה from גלה). The helping vowels of II-*Waw/Yod* verbs are not part of the root but are added to smooth out pronunciation.

II-*Waw/Yod* verbs preserve the original consonantal *waw/yod* only in the *piel, pual,* and *hithpael,* allowing them to behave like strong forms (e.g., *piel* pf. צִוָּה "he commanded" from צוה). All other II-*Waw/Yod* verbs, including alternate patterns that often replace the *piel, pual,* and *hithpael,* drop or coalesce the *waw/yod* and reflect the theme vowel of the strong form.[3] The *waw/yod* coalesces in certain forms of the *qal* and throughout the *niphal.* All other forms drop the *waw/yod.*

Qal	Drop	Coalesce
Niphal	Coalesce	
Piel–Hithpael	Drop (except strong)	
Hiphil	Drop	
Hophal	Drop	

The recurring feature of the II-*Waw/Yod* verbs is that *the perfect and the participle are related in form, and the infinitive construct provides a starting point for everything else.* These associations are not new but are stronger in the II-*Waw/Yod* verbs than in their strong verb counterparts.

II-*Waw/Yod* → **1) Perfects / Participles (related)**
II-*Waw/Yod* → **2) Everything else (related to inf. cst.)**

QAL PARADIGM

The majority of II-*Waw/Yod* verbs that you encounter will be in the *qal,* the stem that contains the most vowel variation of all verb stems. These variations are even more apparent in the II-*Waw/Yod* verbs because some vowels result from dropping *waw/yod* (e.g., *qal* pf. קָם) and others from coalescing (e.g., *qal* inf. cst. קוּם). In addition, the same form can appear with full or defective spelling, thus blurring the distinction between dropping and coalescing (e.g., *qal* pf. בּוֹא or בָּא respectively, "he came"). Students often find the array of vowels daunting and

3. Biblical Hebrew often uses reduplicated forms (discussed below) to adjust for the II-*Waw/Yod* weakness.

unpredictable.[4] The following discussion of the II-*Waw/Yod qal* highlights the continuity between the *qal* strong verb and II-*Waw/Yod* verbs.

Vowel Variation

The vowel variation within II-*Waw/Yod* verbs is directly related to the strong verb paradigms. You learned the *qal* by memorizing קָטַל (pf.) and יִקְטֹל (impf.). However, you also learned that the *qal* perfect can take a-, i-, or u-class theme vowels in the stative. Likewise the *qal* imperfect can have a-, i-, and u-class theme vowels in the active verbs. Finally, you learned that the historic forms used different preformative vowels to distinguish between active and stative verbs (e.g., *יַקְטֻל vs. יִכְבַּד). Just as you were not required to memorize the vowel variation in the *qal* strong verbs, do not try to memorize each form that a II-*Waw/Yod qal* takes. We review them here to reassure you that the vowel variation in the II-*Waw/Yod* verbs is the same vowel variation you were introduced to in the *qal* strong verb.

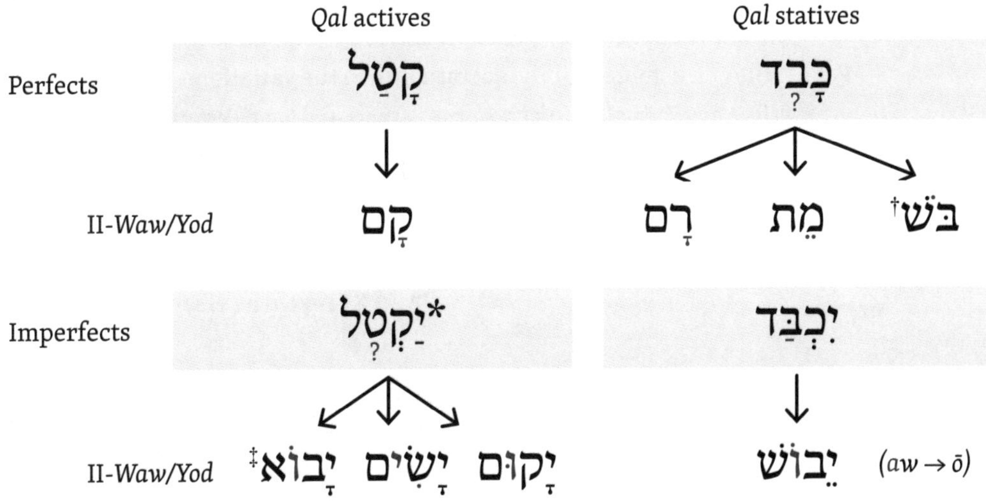

† Reflects u-class. *Qal* statives with u-class theme vowel will also appear with the full spelling (בּוֹשׁ).

‡ Reflects a-class. This *ḥolem waw* וֹ is the coalescing of an a-class vowel with *waw* (aw → ō).

Do not let the details overwhelm you. You will often be able to recognize the root based on your familiarity with vocabulary. The more constant elements like preformatives and sufformatives will help refine your

4. E.g., שִׂים ("to put, place") can appear with virtually any of the vowels: שָׂם (pf. or act. ptc.), שִׂים (inf. cst.), יָשֵׂם (juss.), וַיָּשֶׂם (*waw* consec.), שׂוֹם (inf. abs.), and שׂוּם (pass. ptc.).

identification of the form. For example, the word יָקוּמוּ can be identified by its preformative and sufformative as a 3mp imperfect from the root קוּם ("they will arise").

Basic Approach to Qal: "Short" and "Long" Forms

The patterns of dropping and coalescing in II-*Waw/Yod* verbs are less helpful than the patterns for I- and III-*Waw/Yod* verbs (see preceding chapters) because sometimes forms that drop the *waw/yod* can look just like forms that coalesce. For example, the *qal* infinitive construct בּוֹא is the result of coalescing (בַּוא*), while the *qal* infinitive absolute, also בּוֹא, is the result of dropping and adopting the vowel of the strong form (קָטוֹל). This chapter uses the patterns of dropping and coalescing as a backdrop but frames the discussion toward what you see on the page. Forms without the *waw/yod* visually present in the verb are called "short" (e.g., *qal* pf. קָם), while forms with *waw/yod* are referred to as "long" (e.g., *qal* inf. cst. קוּם).[5]

The terms "short" and "long" are a loose generalization based on what is expected in the form and are designed to help you focus on the consistencies of the *qal* rather than the variations. When you see a II-*Waw/Yod qal*, think *two forms—short and long. Perfects and participles are short; the remaining forms are long.*

II-*Waw/Yod qal*
- **1) Perfects/Participles—Short**
- **2) Everything else—Long**

Full versus Defective Spelling

The guiding principle that perfects and participles are short and infinitive constructs and all other forms are long has proven a helpful framework for students. While it works much of the time, it is not comprehensive. The presentation of these verbs as "short" and "long" is complicated by the inconsistency with which Hebrew applies vowel markers. "Short" forms can be written with full spelling (e.g., *qal* pf. בֹּשׁ instead of בּוֹשׁ, "he was ashamed") and "long" forms can be written

5. The use of the terms "short" and "long" overlaps with the tendency of II-*Waw/Yod* verbs to drop or coalesce, but that overlap is only partial. More accurately, the terms short and long are linked to the presence or absence of pure long vowels. The pure long vowels result from either coalescing (e.g., *u* + *w* contracts to יָקוּם) or adopting the pure long theme vowel of the strong verb (e.g., *qal* inf. abs. קוֹם from קָטוֹל). Unless full or defective spelling blurs these distinctions (e.g., *qal* impf. יָקֻמוּ instead of impf. יָקוּמוּ), the II-*Waw/Yod* perfect and participle usually appear as short forms and the rest as long forms (except the expected short forms of the jussive/*waw* consecutive).

with defective spelling (e.g., *qal* impf. יָקוּ֫מוּ instead of יָקֻ֫מוּ, “they will arise”). When you encounter *qal* II-*Waw/Yod* verbs, let the general principle provide a starting point, but allow both context and the formation of the word (e.g., preformatives or sufformatives) to confirm or override your initial assessment.

Short Forms: Qal Perfect/Participles

The “short” forms of the II-*Waw/Yod qal* are found in the perfect and participle. The *qal* perfect is formed by dropping the *waw* or *yod* (e.g., קוּם → קָם) and preserving the theme vowel of the strong verb: a-class for actives and a-, i-, or u-class for statives. The *qal* active perfects preserve the a-class theme vowel of the strong verb (e.g., קָטַל) regardless of the vowel present in the vocabulary form of the II-*Waw/Yod* root. Thus the active verbs בּוֹא, שִׂים, and קוּם become בָּא, שָׂם, and קָם in the *qal* perfect (קָטַל). Likewise, the stative roots רוּם, מוּת, and בּוֹשׁ reflect the spectrum of stative theme vowels: a-class רָם (“he was high”), i-class מֵת (“he was dead”), and u-class בֹּשׁ (“he was ashamed”). You need not remember which verbs take which vowel. Just know that a *qal* perfect can appear with any vowel class and usually appears as a short form.

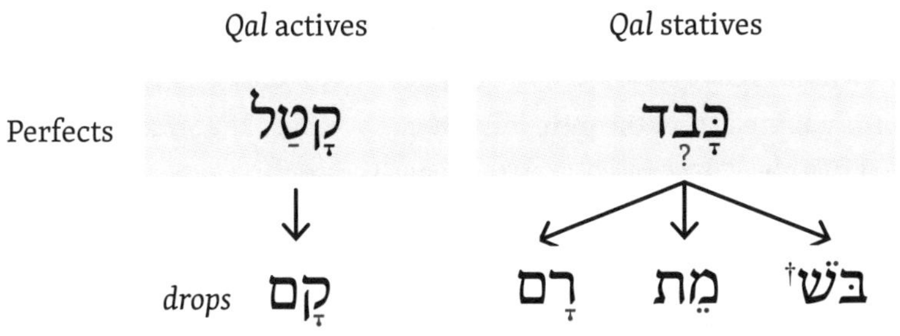

† *Qal* statives with u-class theme vowel commonly appear with the full spelling (בּוֹשׁ).

Once you know the *qal* perfect of a II-*Waw/Yod* verb, you know the participle. The II-*Waw/Yod qal* participle is the same as the *qal* perfect. The initial form in each paradigm is identical (gray shading below) and can only be distinguished by context. The remaining forms are distinguished by accent and the unique endings of the perfect and participle. The perfects take the endings you learned for the *qal* strong verb (e.g., קָם, קָ֫מָה, קַ֫מְתָּ, קַ֫מְתְּ, קַ֫מְתִּי). The participles take the gender and number endings you learned for nouns (e.g., קָם, קָמָה, קָמִים, קָמוֹת).

	Qal perfect (cf. קָטַל)	*Qal* participle (cf. קֹטֵל)		
3ms	קָם	קָם	ms	
3fs	קָ֫מָה	קָמָ֫ה	fs	Different accent
2ms	קַ֫מְתָּ	קָמִים	mp	
2fs	קַ֫מְתְּ	קָמוֹת	fp	Different endings
1cs	קַ֫מְתִּי			

Forms with the feminine ending ָה are distinguished by the placement of the accent (e.g., *qal* pf. 3fs קָ֫מָה vs. ptc. fs קָמָ֫ה). The participles, as verbal adjectives, are accented on the final syllable consistent with nouns and adjectives. Perfects, like other verbs, were historically accented further toward the front of the word.[6]

Long Forms: Everything Else The remaining forms of the II-*Waw/Yod qal* paradigm are characterized by "long" forms exhibiting a *waw/yod* vowel marker. Regardless of whether that *waw/yod* is the result of coalescing (e.g., uw → ū יָקוּם) or is adopted from the pure long theme vowel of the strong form (e.g., *qal* inf. abs. קוֹם from קָטוֹל), the *waw/yod* reminds you to consider a II-*Waw/Yod* root (קום).

Qal Infinitive Construct and Derived Forms The *qal* infinitive construct is the form you learn for your vocabulary. As in the strong paradigms, the infinitive construct serves as the base for the imperfects, jussives, *waw* consecutives, and imperatives. The *qal* imperfect reflects the addition of preformatives and sufformatives to the infinitive construct. The jussives and *waw* consecutives are often identical to the imperfect, although some appear as short forms. Since the imperatives are simply the imperfect minus the preformative, the imperative is just like the infinitive construct. Since all of these forms are related, the infinitive construct and derived forms exhibit the same vowel class.

6. Remember that you often see this historic placement of the accent (toward the front of the word) at major points of pause in the verse (e.g., standard form שָֽׁמְרָה "she kept" vs. pausal form שָׁמָ֫רָה).

	Qal inf. cst. (vocab)	*Qal* imperfect	*Qal* jussive	*Qal waw* consec.	*Qal* imperative
u-class†	קוּם	יָקוּם	יָ֫קוּמוּ	וַיָּ֫קוּמוּ	קוּם

† Thus also a-class בּוֹא, יָבוֹא, יָבֹ֫אוּ, וַיָּבֹ֫אוּ, בּוֹא and i-class שִׂים, יָשִׂים, יָשִׂ֫ימוּ, וַיָּשִׂ֫ימוּ, שִׂים.

This relationship between the infinitive construct and derived forms is consistent whether the theme vowel is a-class, i-class, or u-class (בּוֹא, שִׂים, קוּם). Thus the vocabulary words display the theme vowel of all derived forms. The variation in vowel class is simply a reflection of the strong verb patterns.

	Qal actives			*Qal* statives	
Imperfects	*יַקְטֻל (?)			יִכְבַּד	
	↙	↓	↘	↓	
coalesce	יָבוֹא†	יָשִׂים	יָקוּם	יֵבוֹשׁ†	*(aw → ō)*
Inf. Cst./Impv.	בּוֹא	שִׂים	קוּם	בּוֹשׁ	*(aw → ō)*

† The *ḥolem waw* in יָבוֹא and יֵבוֹשׁ represents the coalescing of an a-class vowel with *waw*.

Note also that the II-*Waw/Yod* imperfects retain the historic preformative vowels of the *qal* verb: a-class for the actives (e.g., יָקוּם) and i-class for the statives (יֵבוֹשׁ).

Short Form Jussives and Waw Consecutives

Sometimes the imperfect, jussive, and *waw* consecutive are identical in form, just like in the *qal* strong verb. However, sometimes the jussive and *waw* consecutive appear as short forms. These short forms are exceptions to the guiding principle that *II-*Waw/Yod qal *perfects and participles are short and the remaining forms are long.* Do not let the following details overwhelm you. Whether long or short, the theme vowels of all of these forms follow the vowel class of the infinitive construct.

For those who want to know more precisely when to expect a II-*Waw/Yod* short form, note the following guidelines:

1. *Forms with a sufformative coalesce in all three paradigms, resulting in long forms,* for example, imperfect יָקוּמוּ, jussive יָקוּמוּ, and *waw* consecutive וַיָּקוּמוּ (though all can be written defectively as יָקֻמוּ).
2. *Forms without a sufformative affect each paradigm uniquely.* Thus the imperfects, jussives, and *waw* consecutives are visibly distinct when these forms lack sufformatives (i.e., 3ms, 3fs, 2ms).
   - *Imperfect forms without sufformatives coalesce the* waw/yod, *resulting in long forms* (e.g., יָקוּם or יָקֻם with defective spelling).
   - *Jussive forms without sufformatives drop the* waw/yod, *resulting in short forms.* The theme vowel typically occurs in an accented syllable as a lengthened short vowel (e.g., יָקֹם or יָקוֹם with full spelling).
   - Waw *consecutives without sufformatives drop the* waw/yod, *resulting in short forms.* Futher, in *waw* consecutives the theme vowels appears in a closed unaccented syllable and is short (e.g., *waw* consecutive וַיָּקָם).

	Biblical Hebrew		Historic Form	
Qal Imperfect	יָקוּם	←	*יַקְוֻם	*Coalesce*
Qal Jussive	יָקֹם	←	*יַקֻם	*Drop (accented long)*
Qal Waw Consec.	וַיָּקָם†	←	*וַיַּקֻם	*Drop (unaccented short)*

† The *qibbuts* of the historic form changes to *qamets qaton* (ָ) because, with rare exceptions, Hebrew reserves *qibbuts* for use before doubled consonants.

Even these rules are not without exception. II-*Waw/Yod* roots with *ḥolem waw* (e.g., בּוֹא) retain the long ō, even in the instances where one would expect a short form, for example, *qal* imperfect יָבוֹא, jussive יָבוֹא, *waw* consecutive וַיָּבוֹא (or written defectively as יָבֹא).

Qal Infinitive Absolute

The infinitive absolute also appears as a long form, though it is not derived from the infinitive construct. Technically the infinitive absolute drops *waw/yod* and adopts the *ḥolem waw* of the strong infinitive absolute (קָטוֹל). This holds true for any II-*Waw/Yod* root regardless of the vowel in the infinitive construct (בּוֹא, שִׂים, קוּם become בּוֹא, שׂוֹם, קוֹם).

	II-*Waw/Yod*		Strong
Qal Infinitive Absolute	קוֹם	←	קָטוֹל

Qal Passive Participle

The *qal* paradigm is unique in that it has both an active and passive participle within the same verb stem.[7] In the strong verb this passive participle is קָטוּל. In II-*Waw/Yod* verbs the first root letter must carry the theme vowel of this passive participle (קוּם). Although the pure long u-class vowel is technically the result of dropping *waw/yod* and adopting the vowel of the strong verb, it is grouped with the "long" forms because of the presence of the vowel marker that helps students make an association with the II-*Waw/Yod* root.

	II-*Waw/Yod*		Strong
Qal Passive Participle	קוּם	←	קָטוּל

SUMMARY

The II-*Waw/Yod qal* verbs include more visual diversity than most paradigms. When dealing with these forms it can help to think of *waw* and *yod* as somewhat interchangeable (e.g., inf. cst. שִׂים and inf. abs. שׂוֹם both reflect the root שׂים). Though full and defective spelling may affect the appearance of the forms, the general principle is that the II-*Waw/Yod qal* has *two basic forms—short and long. Perfects and participles are short; (most) everything else is long.*

7. The passive of the *qal* can be expressed as a *niphal*, but the *qal* also has its own passive participle.

Qal II-Waw/Yod

"Short"	קָם	Perfect
	קָם	Participle
"Long"	קוּם	Infinitive Construct
	יָקוּם	Imperfect
	יָקֽוּמוּ	Jussive (*short* יָקֹם)
	וַיָּקֽוּמוּ	*Waw* Consecutive (*short* וַיָּ֫קָם)
	קוּם	Imperative
	קוּם	Passive Participle (from strong קָטוּל)
	קוֹם	Inf. Abs. (from strong קָטוֹל)

What Questions Should I Ask When I Read?

For all the complexity of explanation, the II-*Waw/Yod* verbs are not too difficult to spot in the text. You will often see some reminder of the original *waw/yod*, even if the *waw/yod* is not technically part of the root. Another advantage to II-*Waw/Yod* verbs is that most of them are roots that are familiar (e.g., קוּם, בּוֹא, שׁוּב). Because of how common some of these roots are, you are already familiar with forms that do not have a *waw/yod* present (e.g., pf./ptc. בָּא). When you suspect you are seeing a II-*Waw/Yod* verb, think: *"II-Waw/Yod: Two forms—perfect and participle are short; others are long."* Then see if the text matches your expectation. This general rule will serve you well as long as you remember there are exceptions.

Final comment: You have now had enough grammar to tell the difference between יֵשֵׁב and שׁוּב. These roots are similar enough, common enough, and basic enough in meaning that sometimes not even context helps you distinguish them. (Did he *sit*, or did he *return*?) Now that you have learned characteristics of both weak verb types, you can tell them apart. When you come across a form in the text your basic principles help orient you.

יֵשֵׁב *Qal* impf.	I-*Waw/Yod* (ישׁב)	☐ coalesces ☑ **but drops in I-*Waw qal***
	I-*Waw/Yod* (שׁוּב)	☐ perfect & participle are "short" ☐ inf. cst. ... are "long"

CHAPTER 28

II-*Waw/Yod* Verbs: *Niphal—Hophal* Stems

The previous chapter introduced the II-*Waw/Yod* verbs and covered the *qal* paradigm. This chapter addresses the II-*Waw/Yod* verbs in the remaining stems: *niphal, piel, pual, hithpael, hiphil, hophal,* and the reduplicated stems (i.e., *polel, polal, hithpolel, pilpel,* and *polpal*).

NIPHAL PARADIGM

The II-*Waw/Yod niphal,* like other II-*Waw/Yod* verbs is grouped into two sets of related forms: (1) the perfect and participle, and (2) everything else. Like the strong verbs, all *niphal* forms preserve the characteristic *nun* of the *niphal.* The perfect and participle have a visible *nun* (e.g., pf. נִקְטַל and ptc. נִקְטָל) while the infinitive construct and remaining forms have an assimilated *nun* (e.g., inf. cst. הִקָּטֵל). Besides the preservation of the *nun,* the prominent feature of the II-*Waw/Yod niphal* is the coalescing of aw → ō (וֹ) that occurs as the theme vowel in all forms.

For those who remember concepts better when they understand why they happen, the consistent presence of the *ḥolem waw* theme vowel in the II-*Waw/Yod niphal* is always the result of coalescing. In the perfect *niphal* and participle, the historic a-class theme vowel (נַקְטַל*) coalesces with the *waw/yod,* resulting in a *ḥolem waw* theme vowel (e.g., נַקְוַם* → נַקַום* → נָקוֹם).[1] In the infinitive construct and remaining forms, the a-class vowel under the first root consonant of the strong form (*niphal* inf. cst. הִקָּטֵל) coalesces with *waw* (inf. cst. הִקַּום* → הִקּוֹם). The II-*Waw/Yod* verbs use coalescing of the a-class vowel and *waw*

1. For the sake of pronunciation, the theme vowel shifts from its expected position under the *waw* to stand under the *qoph.* The shift in vowel position is reconstructed as the best explanation for the long ō in the Biblical Hebrew form (aw → ō).

throughout the *niphal* paradigm even when the lexical root is originally *yod* (e.g., בִּין "to understand" becomes נָבוֹן).

	Biblical Hebrew		*Waw* coalesces		Historic form
Niphal perfect	נָקוֹם	←	*נַקַוֹם	=	*נַקְטַל
Niphal inf. cst.	הִקּוֹם	←	*הִקַּוֹם	=	הִקָּטֵל

Niphal Perfects and Participles

The *niphal* perfect and participle reflect the historic a-class preformative vowel of this verb stem (e.g., *נַקַוֹם). Remember that in II-*Waw/Yod* verbs the theme vowel is carried by the first consonant of the root, leaving the preformative in an open unaccented syllable that requires a long vowel (e.g., נָקוֹם). Because the perfect and participle are related in the *niphal*, just as they are in the II-*Waw/Yod qal*, the initial forms in each paradigm are identical (gray shading below). The feminine forms with the ָה ending are accented differently in the perfect and participle.[2] The other forms exhibit the endings of the perfect and participle.

In the *niphal*, the preformative is affected by the vowel rules. Whenever the preformative vowel stands in a near open syllable, it lengthens. In a distant open syllable, it reduces. This creates another distinction between feminine forms with the ָה ending (pf. נָ|קֽוֹ|מָה vs. ptc. נְ|קוֹ|מָ֫ה).

As seen in the II-*Waw/Yod qal*, II-*Waw/Yod* verbs often take helping vowels before consonantal sufformatives, with perfects taking a *ḥolem waw* (וֹ). Participles do not take helping vowels because they do not have consonantal sufformatives (i.e., all begin with vowels ָה , ִים , and וֹת). Helping vowels affect the shape of the perfect by drawing the accent toward the end of the word, thus causing the preformative to reduce. They also affect the theme vowel. When a helping vowel is added, the theme vowel shifts from the expected וֹ to וּ (compare pf. 3ms נָקוֹם and

2. The participles, as verbal adjectives, are accented on the final syllable consistent with nouns and adjectives. Perfects, like other verbs, were historically accented further toward the front of the word. Remember that you often see this historic placement of the accent (toward the front of the word) at major points of pause in the verse (e.g., *qal* pf. 3fs שָֽׁמְרָה "she kept" vs. pausal form שָׁמָ֫רָה).

2ms נְקוּמֹ֫תָ). Note that both וֹ and וּ are u-class vowels. This shift creates a distinction between the *niphal* perfect and participle, a distinction that is especially helpful in distinguishing between the second person feminine singular perfect נְקוּמוֹת and the feminine plural participle נְקוֹמוֹת (though context also helps).

	Niphal Perfect	*Niphal* Participle		
3ms	נָקוֹם	נָקוֹם	ms	
3fs	נָקֹ֫ומָה	נְקוֹמָ֫ה	fs	different accent
2ms	נְקוּמֹ֫תָ	נְקוֹמִים	mp	helping vowel shifts theme vowel to וּ
2fs	נְקוּמוֹת	נְקוֹמוֹת	fp	

Niphal Infinitive Construct and Related Forms

The *niphal* infinitive construct and related forms all appear with the *dagesh* from the assimilated *nun* of the *niphal* and the coalesced theme vowel characteristic of all II-*Waw/Yod niphal* verbs (e.g., *niphal* inf. cst. הִקּוֹם). The imperfect adds the preformatives familiar to you from the strong verb, "covering" the *heh* preformative of the infinitive (*niphal* inf. cst. הִקּוֹם → impf. יִקּוֹם).[3] The jussive and *waw* consecutive are identical in form to the imperfect. The imperative lacks the preformative of the imperfect and reverts back to the *heh* preformative of the infinitive construct (*niphal* impf. תִּקּוֹם → impv. הִקּוֹם). The infinitive absolute takes the long ō vowel from the strong verb (*niphal* strong הִקָּטֹל and II-*Waw/Yod* הִקּוֹם), in this case appearing identical to the infinitive construct.

Though the formation of the *niphal* forms is complex, the final forms exhibit common features. Every form reflects the characteristic *nun* of the *niphal*, and the theme vowel is consistently וֹ (unless a וֹ helping vowel shifts the theme vowel to וּ).

3. The *segol-yod* helping vowel is used with the 2/3fp imperfect (ending in נָה) predominantly in the *qal* and *hiphil* (GKC §72i).

Niphal II-_Waw/Yod_

Nun visible	נָקוֹם	Perfect (*with helping vowel* נְקוּמ֫וֹתָ)
	נָקוֹם	Participle
Assimilation	הִקּוֹם	Infinitive Construct
	יִקּוֹם	Imperfect
	יִקּוֹם	Jussive
	וַיִּקּוֹם	*Waw* Consecutive
	הִקּוֹם	Imperative
	הִקּוֹם	Infinitive Absolute

PIEL, PUAL, HITHPAEL, AND REDUPLICATED STEMS

The *waw/yod* are not as conducive to doubling in the *piel, pual,* and *hithpael* as are strong consonants. Thus while the II-*Waw/Yod* verbs can appear as strong form *piel, pual,* and *hithpael,* Biblical Hebrew tends to use reduplicated stems that convey the same core meaning.

Strong Verb Pattern (Piel, Pual, Hithpael)

Some II-*Waw/Yod* verbs follow the strong *piel, pual,* and *hithpael* patterns. Most of these verbs are both II- and III-*Waw/Yod* verbs (e.g., צוה "to command"). These doubly weak verbs adopt the endings of the III-*Waw/Yod* verbs and treat the *waw/yod* in second position as strong. For example, the *piel* pf. 1cs of צוה is צִוִּיתִי (when ו has its own vowel, it cannot be a *shureq* and must be a doubled *waw*). It is rare to find *piel, pual,* and *hithpael* strong forms in roots that are strictly II-*Waw/Yod.* Since these verbs treat the middle *waw/yod* as strong, there is no need to discuss them further.

Reduplicated Stems

II-*Waw/Yod* verbs often replace the *piel, pual,* and *hithpael* with reduplicated stems that have the same meaning. These stems are created by dropping the *waw/yod* and reduplicating (writing twice) one or both of the remaining consonants (e.g., קֹמֵם or כִּלְכֵּל from קוּם "to arise, stand" and כּוּל "to support, nourish," respectively).

On rare occasion, roots occur in both the strong *piel-hithpael* and the reduplicated *polel-hithpolel* with subtle differences in meaning. For example, the root קוּם ("to arise, stand") appears in the *piel* meaning "confirm, ratify" and in the corresponding *polel* to mean "raise up (ruins)." Both meanings reflect the idea of causing something to stand, but the different stems convey different nuances (see ch. 21).

Reduplication #1 (Polel, Polal, and Hithpolel)

The *polel*, *polal*, and *hithpolel* are often used in place of the *piel*, *pual*, and *hithpael*. The vowel patterns of these stems are applied to any II-*Waw/Yod* root regardless of the theme vowel represented in its lexical form (e.g., בּוֹא, שִׂים, קוּם). The reduplication of the final root consonant (e.g., קֹמֵם or with full spelling קוֹמֵם) is reminiscent of the characteristic doubling of the strong verb (e.g., קִטֵּל). The names of each stem reflect the vowel patterns.

	Alternate stem (קוּם)		Strong verb
Polel	קוֹמֵם	=	*Piel*
Polal	קוֹמַם	=	*Pual*
Hithpolel	הִתְקוֹמֵם	=	*Hithpael*

These vowels patterns are applied consistently to every paradigm within the stem (pf., ptc., impf., etc.). This consistency makes the *polel-hithpolel* easier to recognize, but inevitably many forms become indistinguishable apart from context. For example, a form like קוֹמֵם could be a *polel* perfect, infinitive construct, imperative, infinitive absolute, or even a *qal* participle of קמם* (if such a root were to exist). Further, many forms of the active *polel* conjugation appear identical to the passive *polal* (highlighted in gray in the following table).[4]

4. Forms without endings preserve a vowel distinction between the active and passive. Forms with endings lose that distinction because, like the strong verb, vocalic sufformatives cause reduction of the theme vowel (cf. *piel* קִטְּלָה) and consonantal sufformatives use a standardized *pataḥ* throughout the stems (cf. *piel* קִטַּלְתָּ).

	Polel Perfect	*Polal* Perfect	*Polel* Imperfect	*Polal* Imperfect
3ms	קוֹמֵם	קוֹמַם	יְקוֹמֵם	יְקוֹמַם
3fs	קוֹמְמָה	קוֹמְמָה	תְּקוֹמֵם	תְּקוֹמַם
2ms	קוֹמַמְתָּ	קוֹמַמְתָּ	תְּקוֹמֵם	תְּקוֹמַם
2fs	קוֹמַמְתְּ	קוֹמַמְתְּ	תְּקוֹמְמִי	תְּקוֹמְמִי
1cs	קוֹמַמְתִּי	קוֹמַמְתִּי	אֲקוֹמֵם	אֲקוֹמַם
	etc.	etc.	etc.	etc.

The use of the vowel marker in the full spelling (קוֹמֵם) is unrelated to the *waw/yod* of the root, but it may help you think in terms of a II-*Waw/Yod* root.[5]

Polel* II-*Waw/Yod

קוֹמֵם	Perfect
מְקוֹמֵם	Participle
קוֹמֵם	Infinitive Construct
יְקוֹמֵם	Imperfect
יְקוֹמֵם	Jussive
וַיְקוֹמֵם	*Waw* Consecutive
קוֹמֵם	Imperative
קוֹמֵם	Infinitive Absolute (*piel* strong קַטֵּל)

5. Geminates (ch. 29) use these stems as well.

Reduplication #2 (Pilpel and Polpal)

In rare instances the II-*Waw/Yod* roots reduplicate both the first and last letters of the root to produce an active *pilpel* stem (e.g., pf. כִּלְכֵּל) and a passive *polpal* stem (e.g., pf. כָּלְכַּל). These stems are identical to the *piel* and *pual* in meaning. The active *pilpel* mirrors the *piel* in taking i-class in the perfect (קִטֵּל and כִּלְכֵּל) and a-class everywhere else (יְקַטֵּל and יְכַלְכֵּל). Likewise, the passive *polpal* and *pual* take u-class vowels throughout (קֻטַּל and כָּלְכַּל). The *pilpel* and *polpal* occur most often with כול ("to support, nourish").[6] Because these forms are unique in appearance and sound, you should have little trouble recognizing them.

	Pilpel (*Piel*)	*Polpal* (*Pual*)
Perfect	כִּלְכֵּל	כָּלְכַּל
Imperfect	יְכַלְכֵּל	יְכָלְכַּל

HIPHIL PARADIGM

The *hiphil* II-*Waw/Yod* verbs follow expected patterns. Like the *hiphil* strong forms, these verbs take the i-class theme vowel (often *ḥireq yod*). Consistent with the principle of II-*Waw/Yod* verbs, the first root consonant carries the theme vowel, leaving preformative vowels to adjust according to the vowel rules—lengthening in a near open syllable (e.g., 3ms pf. הֵ|קִים) and reducing in a distant open syllable (e.g., mp ptc. מְ|קִי|מִים).[7]

Hiphil Perfects and Participles

The basic principle that perfects and participles are related in II-*Waw/Yod* verbs is reflected in the *hiphil*. Instead of the strong pattern (where *hiphil* preformatives take i-class in the perfect and a-class everywhere else),[8] the II-*Waw/Yod* perfect and participle both take i-class preformative vowels (e.g., הֵקִים and מֵקִים). The participle is always distinguishable because of its preformative מ.

6. In II-*Waw/Yod* roots there are only twenty-seven instances of the *pilpel* and one occurrence of the *polpal*. All but three instances occur with the root כול ("to support, nourish"). You have already encountered this root in the Joseph narrative (Gen 47:12; 50:21) and will encounter it again in Ruth 4:15.

7. Some preformative vowels do not reduce, even in distant open syllables (i.e., *hiphil* pf. *waw* consec. וְהֵבֵאתָ).

8. E.g., pf. הִקְטִיל vs. ptc. מַקְטִיל.

Hiphil Infinitive Construct and Related Forms

The remaining forms have the expected a + i vowel pattern of the *hiphil* strong forms (cf. *hiphil* inf. cst. הַקְטִיל and הָקִים). The i-class theme vowel varies, using *ḥireq-yod* in the long forms (יָקִים), and *tsere* in the short form jussives, imperatives, and *waw* consecutive (יָקֵם). The long and short forms are discussed in more detail below. In *waw* consecutive forms without sufformatives, the accent retracts and shifts to the preformative, leaving the theme vowel in a closed unaccented syllable. Since closed unaccented syllables take short vowels, the *hiphil* i-class theme vowel is reflected by *segol* (e.g., *hiphil waw* consec. וַיָּקֶם).

Hiphil Helping Vowels

Hiphil II-*Waw/Yod* verbs frequently use helping vowels to smooth out pronunciation when consonantal sufformatives are added. The perfects take a long ō helping vowel (e.g., הֲקִימוֹתָ or defective הֲקִימֹתָ). All other conjugations use *segol yod*, though this helping vowel is not consistently applied (e.g., *hiphil* impf. 3fp תְּקִימֶינָה and תָּקֵמְנָה). The use of a connecting vowel causes the reduction of distant open preformative vowels (e.g., תְּ|קִי|מֶי|נָה).

Hiphil Short Forms

In the *qal* II-*Waw/Yod* verbs, forms written with the *waw/yod* were labeled "long" and forms without the *waw/yod* were labeled "short." In the *hiphil*, the *waw/yod* of the root has dropped in every paradigm. However, because many forms preserve the characteristic *ḥireq yod* of the *hiphil*, the terms short and long are still helpful for describing what visually appears in the form.

The presence of *ḥireq yod* in the II-*Waw/Yod hiphil* often reminds students of the II-*Waw/Yod* root—an added bonus. However, since the i-class theme vowel in these forms is actually the theme vowel of the *hiphil* (not the *waw/yod* of the root), the presence or absence of *ḥireq yod* follows the pattern established in the strong verb. Throughout the *hiphil* stem, forms that include *ḥireq yod* in the strong verb also take *ḥireq yod* in the II-*Waw/Yod hiphil*. Conversely, forms that are short in the *hiphil* strong verb are also short (without *ḥireq yod*) in *hiphil* II-*Waw/Yod* verbs.[9] Other than cases of defective or full spelling, exceptions occur when a helping vowel is added before consonantal sufformatives. The connecting vowel acts as a vocalic ending. Vocalic endings take *ḥireq-yod* in the *hiphil* even if the paradigm usually takes short forms.

9. See illustration on p. 258.

Forms with helping vowels appear as long forms and take the characteristic *ḥireq yod* (or *tsere yod*) of the *hiphil* (e.g., *hiphil* impf. תְּקִימֶ֫ינָה vs. strong תַּקְטֵ֫לְנָה).

Hiphil versus Qal (a-i Vowel Pattern)

The vowel pattern of the *hiphil* occasionally overlaps with the *qal*. Since all *hiphil* paradigms require a preformative and an i-class theme vowel, this overlap occurs only in *qal* verbs that take a preformative and in roots with i-class vowels (e.g., שִׂים, NOT בּוֹא or קוּם). Imperfects, jussives, and *waw* consecutives of an i-class root (e.g., שִׂים) are identical in the *qal* and the *hiphil*. Context alone will distinguish whether a verb like יָשִׂים means "he will place" (*qal*) or "he will cause to place" (*hiphil*).

Hiphil* II-*Waw/Yod

i-class	הֵקִים	Perfect	
	מֵקִים	Participle	
a-class	הָקִים	Infinitive Construct	
	יָקִים	Imperfect	
	יָקֵם	Jussive (*strong* יַקְטֵל)	*ḥireq yod* returns with vocalic sufformatives (e.g., וַיָּקִ֫ימוּ)
	וַיָּ֫קֶם	*Waw* Consecutive	
	הָקֵם	Imperative (*strong* הַקְטֵל)	
	הָקֵם	Infinitive Absolute (*strong* הַקְטֵל)	

HOPHAL PARADIGM

The II-*Waw/Yod hophal* is formed by dropping the *waw/yod* and adjusting the preformative to long ū (הוּקַם)—preserving the historic u-class preformative הָקְטַל*. This form is already familiar from the coalescing that occurs in I-*Waw/Yod* verbs (הֻוְשַׁב* → הוּשַׁב). The I-*Waw/Yod* and II-*Waw/Yod* verbs thus produce identical forms in the *hophal*. For example, הוּשַׁב is a *hophal* of either ישׁב (an unlikely sense) or שׁוּב ("he was caused to return" or "he was brought back"). Context determines which vocabulary word is most appropriate.

The *hophal* takes a consistent pattern throughout the paradigms. This consistency makes the *hophal* easy to recognize.

	Preformative lengthens		*Waw* drops			
Hophal pf./inf. cst.	הוּקַם	←	*הֻקַם	←	*הֻקְוַם	= *הֻקְטַל

Note that the *hophal* infinitive absolute adopts the *tsere* theme vowel just as it does in the strong verb (strong הָקְטֵל and II-*Waw/Yod* הוּקֵם).

Hophal* II-*Waw/Yod

הוּקַם	Perfect
מוּקָם	Participle
הוּקַם	Infinitive Construct
יוּקַם	Imperfect
וַיּוּקַם	*Waw* Consecutive
	Imperative (N/A)
הוּקֵם	Infinitive Absolute (*strong* הָקְטֵל)

SUMMARY The II-*Waw/Yod* verbs build upon information already familiar to you: the strong verbs, the historic forms of the *qal* and *niphal*, the vowel changes dictated by the vowel rules, and the tendency of *waw/yod* to drop or coalesce. The guiding principles specific to II-*Waw/Yod* verbs include:

1. Two *waw/yod* verbs lead to two options: (1) perfect and participle and (2) everything else. In the *qal*, perfects and participles are short and everything else is long.

II-*Waw/Yod* →	1) <u>P</u>erfects/<u>P</u>articiples	*Qal* "short" (קָם)
II-*Waw/Yod* →	2) Everything else	*Qal* "long" (קוּם)

2. The lexical form is the *qal* infinitive construct (e.g., בּוֹא, קוּם, שִׂים)
3. Preformative vowels appear in open unaccented syllables and thus:
   - preserve historical preformative vowels of *qal* and *niphal* (e.g., *qal* impf. יָקוּם).
   - adjust according to the vowel rules (e.g., lengthen הֵקִים *hiphil* pf., and reduce הֲקִימֹ֫נוּ *hiphil* pf. + 1cp suff.).
4. Helping vowels are sometimes added: וֹ for perfect and ֵי for the rest (e.g., *hiphil* pf. הֲקִימ֫וֹתָ and *hiphil* impf. תְּקִימֶ֫ינָה).
5. In place of *piel*, *pual*, and *hithpael*, II-*Waw/Yod* verbs often use reduplicated stems: *polel*, *polal*, *hithpolel* (קוֹמֵם, קוֹמַם, הִתְקוֹמֵם)

What Questions Should I Ask When I Read?

Any analysis of Hebrew verbs begins with an attempt to identify the root. The II-*Waw/Yod* verbs usually provide you with only two root consonants. Fortunately, theme vowels often include *waw/yod* as a vowel marker to help you intuitively consider a II-*Waw/Yod* verb. Once you suspect you are looking at a II-*Waw/Yod* verb, use the following principle to work your way through the word. *The II-*Waw/Yod *verbs lead to two options: (1) perfect and participle and (2) everything else. In general,* qal *perfects and participles are short (קָם) and everything else is long (קוּם).*

Every conjugation and every stem retains its key features even though the weakness in the middle of the II-*Waw/Yod* verbs impacts the whole word. Be especially alert to open preformative syllables that shift according to the vowel rules and to preformatives that reflect the historic a-class vowels of the *qal* and *niphal*. Because distant open preformative syllables can reduce to *shewa*, you will sometimes be forced to rely upon other indicators of verb stem. Finally, do not be confused if you see a helping vowel before a consonantal sufformative. These vowels are added only to ease pronunciation.

Most important of all, *do not give up if you do not parse a word correctly on your first try!* As you have seen in this chapter, some forms have more than one possible parsing. You do not have to get it right the first time. In fact, it can help to know what your options are. Your familiarity with vocabulary and sensitivity to context will help guide your translation.

The detailed explanations of the II-*Waw/Yod* verbs risk making Hebrew sound overly complicated and mathematical. But language is a living entity—with adaptation and irregularity resulting from centuries of use. If you think of its patterns as natural adjustments in pronunciation rather than rules to memorize, they will help you recognize forms that match what the context drives you to expect.

REPRESENTATIVE FORMS: II-WAW/YOD VERBS

	Qal	*Niphal*	*Polel*	*Polal*	*Hithpolel*	*Hiphil*	*Hophal*
Perfect	קָם	נָקוֹם	קוֹמֵם	קוֹמַם	הִתְקוֹמֵם	הֵקִים	הוּקַם
Participle	קָם (lexical form)	נָקוֹם	מְקוֹמֵם	מְקוֹמָם	מִתְקוֹמֵם	מֵקִים	מוּקָם
Inf. Cst.	קוּם	הִקּוֹם	קוֹמֵם	קוֹמַם	הִתְקוֹמֵם	הָקִים	הוּקַם
Imperfect	יָקוּם	יִקּוֹם	יְקוֹמֵם	יְקוֹמַם	יִתְקוֹמֵם	יָקִים	יוּקַם
Jussive	יָקֹם	יִקּוֹם	יְקוֹמֵם		יִתְקוֹמֵם	יָקֵם	
Waw Consec.	וַיָּ֫קָם	וַיִּקּוֹם	וַיְקוֹמֵם	וַיְקוֹמַם	וַיִּתְקוֹמֵם	וַיָּ֫קֶם	וַיּוּקַם
Impv.	קוּם	הִקּוֹם	קוֹמֵם		הִתְקוֹמֵם	הָקֵם	
Inf. Abs.	קוֹם	הִקּוֹם	קוֹמֵם	קוֹמַם	הִתְקוֹמֵם	הָקֵם	הוּקֵם

II-WAW/YOD VERB CHART

QAL

	Act. /a/	Act. /i/	Act. /u/	Stat. /i/	Stat. /u/
Perfect	בָּא	שָׂם	קָם	מֵת	בּוֹשׁ
	בָּ֫אָה	שָׂ֫מָה	קָ֫מָה	מֵ֫תָה	בּ֫וֹשָׁה
	בָּ֫אתָ	שַׂ֫מְתָּ	קַ֫מְתָּ	מַ֫תָּה(†)	בּ֫וֹשְׁתָּ
	בָּ֫את	שַׂ֫מְתְּ	קַ֫מְתְּ	מַ֫תְּ	בּ֫וֹשְׁתְּ
	בָּ֫אתִי	שַׂ֫מְתִּי	קַ֫מְתִּי	מַ֫תִּי	בּ֫וֹשְׁתִּי
	בָּ֫אוּ	שָׂ֫מוּ	קָ֫מוּ	מֵ֫תוּ	בּ֫וֹשׁוּ
	בָּאתֶם	שַׂמְתֶּם	קַמְתֶּם	מַתֶּם	בּוֹשְׁתֶּם
	בָּאתֶן	שַׂמְתֶּן	קַמְתֶּן	מַתֶּן	בּוֹשְׁתֶּן
	בָּ֫אנוּ	שַׂ֫מְנוּ	קַ֫מְנוּ	מַ֫תְנוּ	בּ֫וֹשְׁנוּ
Participle (act.)	בָּא	שָׂם	קָם	מֵת	בּוֹשׁ
	בָּאָ֫ה	שָׂמָ֫ה	קָמָ֫ה	מֵתָ֫ה	בּוֹשָׁ֫ה
	בָּאִים	שָׂמִים	קָמִים	מֵתִים	בּוֹשִׁים
	בָּאוֹת	שָׂמוֹת	קָמוֹת	מֵתוֹת	בּוֹשׁוֹת
(pass.)		שׂוּם	קוּם		
Imperfect	יָבוֹא	יָשִׂים	יָקוּם		יֵבוֹשׁ
	תָּבוֹא	תָּשִׂים	תָּקוּם	(‡)	תֵּבוֹשׁ
	תָּבוֹא	תָּשִׂים	תָּקוּם		תֵּבוֹשׁ
	תָּב֫וֹאִי	תָּשִׂ֫ימִי	תָּק֫וּמִי		תֵּב֫וֹשִׁי
	אָבוֹא	אָשִׂים	אָקוּם		אֵבוֹשׁ
	יָב֫וֹאוּ	יָשִׂ֫ימוּ	יָק֫וּמוּ		יֵב֫וֹשׁוּ
	תָּב֫וֹאנָה(❖)	תָּשֵׂ֫מְנָה	תְּקוּמֶ֫ינָה		תֵּב֫וֹשְׁנָה
	תָּב֫וֹאוּ	תָּשִׂ֫ימוּ	תָּק֫וּמוּ		תֵּב֫וֹשׁוּ
	תָּב֫וֹאנָה	תָּשֵׂ֫מְנָה	תְּקוּמֶ֫ינָה		תֵּב֫וֹשְׁנָה
	נָבוֹא	נָשִׂים	נָקוּם		נֵבוֹשׁ
Imperative	בּוֹא	שִׂים	קוּם		בּ֫וֹשׁ
	בּ֫וֹאִי	שִׂ֫ימִי	ק֫וּמִי		בּ֫וֹשִׁי
	בּ֫וֹאוּ	שִׂ֫ימוּ	ק֫וּמוּ		בּ֫וֹשׁוּ
	בֹּ֫אנָה	שֵׂ֫מְנָה	קוּמֶ֫ינָה		בּ֫וֹשְׁנָה
Inf. Cst.	בּוֹא	שִׂים	קוּם		בּוֹשׁ
Inf. Abs.	בּוֹא	שׂוֹם	קוֹם		בּוֹשׁ

(†) Many of the *qal* pf. forms of מות reflect assimilation of the last root letter *tav* into the *tav* of the sufformative (e.g., מַ֫תְתָּ → מַ֫תָּה).

(‡) The perfect and participle of מות follow a stative pattern (e.g., "be dead"), but all other forms follow the active u-class pattern like קום (e.g., "to die").

(❖) Helping vowels are not consistently applied (compare תְּקוּמֶ֫ינָה).

= lexical forms

	NIPHAL	POLEL (Piel)	POLAL (Pual)	HITHPOLEL (Hithpael)	HIPHIL	HOPHAL
Perfect	נָקוֹם	קוֹמֵם	קוֹמַם	הִתְקוֹמֵם	הֵקִים	הוּקַם
	נָק֫וֹמָה	קוֹמְמָה	קוֹמְמָה	הִתְקוֹמְמָה	הֵק֫ימָה	הוּקְמָה
	נְקוּמ֫וֹתָ	קוֹמַ֫מְתָּ	קוֹמַ֫מְתָּ	הִתְקוֹמַ֫מְתָּ	הֲקִימ֫וֹתָ	הוּקַ֫מְתָּ
	נְקוּמ֫וֹת	קוֹמַ֫מְתְּ	קוֹמַ֫מְתְּ	הִתְקוֹמַ֫מְתְּ	הֲקִימ֫וֹת	הוּקַ֫מְתְּ
	נְקוּמ֫וֹתִי	קוֹמַ֫מְתִּי	קוֹמַ֫מְתִּי	הִתְקוֹמַ֫מְתִּי	הֲקִימ֫וֹתִי	הוּקַ֫מְתִּי
	נָק֫וֹמוּ	קוֹמְמוּ	קוֹמְמוּ	הִתְקוֹמְמוּ	הֵק֫ימוּ	הוּקְמוּ
	נְקוּמוֹתֶם	קוֹמַמְתֶּם	קוֹמַמְתֶּם	הִתְקוֹמַמְתֶּם	הֲקִימוֹתֶם	הוּקַמְתֶּם
	נְקוּמוֹתֶן	קוֹמַמְתֶּן	קוֹמַמְתֶּן	הִתְקוֹמַמְתֶּן	הֲקִימוֹתֶן	הוּקַמְתֶּן
	נְקוּמ֫וֹנוּ	קוֹמַ֫מְנוּ	קוֹמַ֫מְנוּ	הִתְקוֹמַ֫מְנוּ	הֲקִימ֫וֹנוּ	הוּקַ֫מְנוּ
Participle	נָקוֹם	מְקוֹמֵם	מְקוֹמָם	מִתְקוֹמֵם	מֵקִים	מוּקָם
	נְקוֹמָ֫ה	מְקוֹמְמָה	מְקוֹמָמָה	מִתְקוֹמְמָה	מְקִימָה	מוּקָמָה
	נְקוֹמִים	מְקוֹמְמִים	מְקוֹמָמִים	מִתְקוֹמְמִים	מְקִימִים	מוּקָמִים
	נְקוֹמוֹת	מְקוֹמְמוֹת	מְקוֹמָמוֹת	מִתְקוֹמְמוֹת	מְקִימוֹת	מוּקָמוֹת
Imperfect	יִקּוֹם	יְקוֹמֵם	יְקוֹמַם	יִתְקוֹמֵם	יָקִים	יוּקַם
	תִּקּוֹם	תְּקוֹמֵם	תְּקוֹמַם	תִּתְקוֹמֵם	תָּקִים	תּוּקַם
	תִּקּוֹם	תְּקוֹמֵם	תְּקוֹמַם	תִּתְקוֹמֵם	תָּקִים	תּוּקַם
	תִּקּ֫וֹמִי	תְּקוֹמְמִי	תְּקוֹמְמִי	תִּתְקוֹמְמִי	תָּק֫ימִי	תּוּקְמִי
	אֶקּוֹם	אֲקוֹמֵם	אֲקוֹמַם	אֶתְקוֹמֵם	אָקִים	אוּקַם
	יִקּ֫וֹמוּ	יְקוֹמְמוּ	יְקוֹמְמוּ	יִתְקוֹמְמוּ	יָק֫ימוּ	יוּקְמוּ
	תִּקּ֫וֹמְנָה	תְּקוֹמֵ֫מְנָה	תְּקוֹמַ֫מְנָה	תִּתְקוֹמַ֫מְנָה	תָּקֵ֫מְנָה	תּוּקַ֫מְנָה
	תִּקּ֫וֹמוּ	תְּקוֹמְמוּ	תְּקוֹמְמוּ	תִּתְקוֹמְמוּ	תָּק֫ימוּ	תּוּקְמוּ
	תִּקּ֫וֹמְנָה	תְּקוֹמֵ֫מְנָה	תְּקוֹמַ֫מְנָה	תִּתְקוֹמַ֫מְנָה	תָּקֵ֫מְנָה	תּוּקַ֫מְנָה
	נִקּוֹם	נְקוֹמֵם	נְקוֹמַם	נִתְקוֹמֵם	נָקִים	נוּקַם
Imperative	הִקּוֹם	קוֹמֵם		הִתְקוֹמֵם	הָקֵם	
	הִקּ֫וֹמִי	קוֹמְמִי		הִתְקוֹמְמִי	הָק֫ימִי	
	הִקּ֫וֹמוּ	קוֹמְמוּ		הִתְקוֹמְמוּ	הָק֫ימוּ	
	הִקּ֫וֹמְנָה	קוֹמֵ֫מְנָה		הִתְקוֹמַ֫מְנָה	הָקֵ֫מְנָה	
Inf. Cst.	הִקּוֹם	קוֹמֵם	קוֹמַם	הִתְקוֹמֵם	הָקִים	הוּקַם
Inf. Abs.	הִקּוֹם	קוֹמֵם	קוֹמַם	הִתְקוֹמֵם	הָקֵם	הוּקֵם

CHAPTER 29

Geminate Verbs

Geminate verbs are comprised of roots whose second and third consonants are identical (e.g., סבב). Sometimes these roots behave just like the strong verb (e.g., סָבַב). But most of the time you will find that Hebrew reflects the two identical consonants using *dagesh* rather than writing the consonants twice (e.g., סַבּוּ instead of סָבְבוּ). Regardless of whether geminate verbs display two or three root letters, they are parsed using the triconsonantal pattern. Thus סַב is a *qal* pf. from a root that appears in the lexicon as סבב.

GEMINATES: THE BASIC PRINCIPLES

The geminate verbs follow one of three patterns:[1]

1. ***Can* appear as a strong verb (סָבַב = *qal* pf., compare קָטַל).**
2. ***Occasionally* have doubled first consonant (יִסֹּב = *qal* impf., compare יִקְטֹל).**
3. ***Usually* have doubled second consonant (סַבּוּ = *qal* pf., compare קָטְלוּ).**

1. On rare occasions you will also run across forms that double both the first and second consonant (e.g., *hophal* pf. 3fs הָשַּׁמָּה from שׁמם "to be desolate").

Geminates *Can* Follow Strong Verb Forms

The geminate roots can behave like strong forms (e.g., *qal* סָבַב and *piel* הִלֵּל). Because they follow expected patterns, these forms require no additional explanation.

סָבְבוּ = קָטְלוּ *Qal* pf. 3mp

Geminates *Occasionally* Double the First Consonant

Occasionally, geminate verbs are formed by doubling the first consonant of the root (e.g., יִסֹּבוּ = יִסְסְבוּ* from סבב). Grammarians believe that geminate verbs originally had two root consonants (e.g., סב). Doubling the first consonant of the root is one approach to adjusting these roots toward the standard triconsonantal pattern.

יִסֹּבוּ = *יִסְסְבוּ ← יִקְטְלוּ *Qal* impf.

Doubling the first root letter produces a stable verb form. The short preformative vowels are preserved in closed unaccented syllables; sufformatives do not need helping vowels; and theme vowels lengthen and reduce according to the patterns of the strong verb. However, doubling the first root letter creates forms that are easily confused with other verb patterns. This geminate pattern looks like both I-*Nun* verbs and certain I-*Waw/Yod* verbs (cf., יִפֹּל from נפל "to fall").

Despite its stability, this pattern is incompatible with stems that have inherent doubling (*piel*, *pual*, *hithpael*, and some forms of the *niphal*). Doubling the first consonant conflicts with the assimilation of *nun* in the *niphal*, so this pattern does not occur in the *niphal*. Similarly, the preformative of the *piel*, *pual*, and *hithpael* cannot be followed by a doubled consonant. These stems are instead written with three root letters, either using the strong *piel*, *pual*, and *hithpael* (e.g., *piel* הִלֵּל "he praised") or the reduplicated *polel*, *polal*, and *hithpolel* (e.g., *polel* סוֹבֵב "he encircled").[2]

Besides the doubled first consonant, the most notable feature of this pattern is the use of *qibbuts* in the *hophal* (הֻסַב instead of הָקְטַל).

2. These stems are sometimes labeled as *poʿel*, *poʿal*, and *hithpoʿel*. But since geminates probably originated with only two root consonants (e.g., סב), the terms *polel*, *polal*, and *hithpolel* better reflect their origin and highlight the continuity between the geminates and II-*Waw/Yod* verbs in these stems.

Hebrew prefers to use the short u-class *qibbuts* before doubled consonants. These *hophal* forms look like *pual* strong verbs, but vocabulary and context will rule out strong roots.

In summary, geminates occasionally double the first consonant, but the resulting forms look like I-*Nun* verbs. The keys to remembering each stem are as follows:

Qal: Doubled first consonant. No other changes. (יִסֹּב)

Hiphil: Doubled first consonant. No other changes. (יַסִּיב)

Hophal: Doubled first consonant. *Qibbuts* preformative. (יֻסַּב)

(*Niphal, Piel, Pual, Hithpael* do not occur with this pattern.)

Geminates *Usually* Double the Second Consonant

Geminates are usually formed by doubling the second root consonant. Hebrew does not represent doubling at the end of a word, so when a geminate form does not have a sufformative, the doubling is not marked.

סַב	=	סָבַב	←	קָטַל	*Qal* pf. 3ms
סַבּוּ	=	סָבְבוּ	←	קָטְלוּ	*Qal* pf. 3mp

Implications of Doubling the Second Consonant

Geminate roots formed by doubling the second root consonant appear as a single syllable. Thus they share features with II-*Waw*/*Yod* verbs. The theme vowel shifts to the first consonant of the root, leaving the preformative in an open unaccented syllable. This open syllable preserves the historic preformative vowels of the *qal* and *niphal*, and all preformatives adjust according to the vowel rules: lengthening in near open syllables (e.g., יָ|סֹב *qal* impf.) and reducing in distant open syllables (e.g., תְּ|סֻ|בֶּ֫י|נָה *qal* impf.). The doubled consonant at the end of the root requires a connecting vowel with consonantal sufformatives (to avoid three consonants in a row). Each of these features is discussed below.

Doubling Does Not Show at the End of the Word

Dagesh forte does not appear at the end of a geminate verb until a sufformative or suffix is added (e.g., סַב vs. סַבּוּ). Remember that the *dagesh forte* does not appear at the end of a word.

With sufformative	Without sufformative	
סַ֫בּוּ	סַב	*Qal* perfect

Gutturals Do Not Double

Since gutturals do not double, geminates with א, ע, and ר typically reflect compensatory lengthening. Geminates with ה and ח generally undergo "honorary" doubling. For example, רַעּוּ* becomes רָעוּ ("they were evil") and שַׁחּוּ* becomes שַׁחוּ ("they were humbled").

Consonantal Sufformatives Require Helping Vowels before Doubling

Doubling produces a special problem when consonantal sufformatives are added because it results in three consecutive consonants—a scenario that is impossible to pronounce (e.g., סַבְבְתָּ*). Geminates resolve this problem by adding a helping vowel. Like II-*Waw/Yod* verbs, perfects use *ḥolem waw* (וֹ), while the remaining forms use *segol yod* (יֶ).

Qal pf. 2ms	סַבּ֫וֹתָ
Qal impf. 2fp	תְּסֻבֶּ֫ינָה

Connecting vowels take the accent (e.g., סַבּ֫וֹתָ) except when followed by a heavy sufformative (e.g., סַבּוֹתֶם). With vocalic sufformatives, the root is accented (e.g., יָ֫סֹבּוּ).

QAL PARADIGM: DOUBLED SECOND CONSONANT

The doubling of the second consonant is the most common pattern for geminates. The remainder of this chapter presents the specific characteristics of this standard pattern in each stem, beginning in the *qal*.

Qal Perfects

The *qal* perfect takes the theme vowel of the strong verb: actives take a-class and statives take a-, i-, and u-class. The *dagesh* appears in the second root consonant when sufformatives are added, and consonantal sufformatives take helping vowels.

	Singular	Plural	
3m	סַב	סַבּוּ	
3f	סַבָּה		
2m	סַבּוֹתָ	סַבּוֹתֶם	with helping vowels
2f	סַבּוֹת	סַבּוֹתֶן	with helping vowels
1c	סַבּוֹתִי	סַבּוֹנוּ	with helping vowels

Geminate *qal* perfects use short a-class vowels to distinguish geminate forms from II-*Waw/Yod* roots, which take a long vowel (e.g., geminate סַב vs. II-*Waw* קָם).[3]

	Geminate (סבב)	II-*Waw/Yod* (קום)
Qal pf. 3ms	סַב	קָם

Qal Infinitive Construct and Related Forms

The vowel variation of geminate verbs in the infinitive construct and related forms is the same as that found in the *qal* strong verb. Actives can appear with any theme vowel, and statives use a-class. In forms with a preformative, the open preformative syllable preserves the historic patterns of the active and stative *qal* imperfects (יַקְטֻל* and יִכְבַּד).

Geminate *Qal*		Historic *Qal*	
יָסֹב (סבב)	←	יַקְטֻל*	*Active*
יֵקַל (קלל)	←	יִכְבַּד	*Stative*

3. One way to conceptualize the difference between the *qal* geminate and II-*Waw/Yod* verbs is to view a geminate verb as so solidly closed by the doubled consonant that the vowel will not lengthen.

Preformative vowels lengthen or reduce according to the vowel rules. The *dagesh* appears in the second root consonant when sufformatives are added, and sufformatives take helping vowels.

Inf. Cst.		Impf.	Juss./Cohort.	Impv.	*Waw* Consec.
סֹב	3ms	יָסֹב	יָסֹב		וַיָּסָב
	3fs	תָּסֹב	תָּסֹב		וַתָּסָב
	2ms	תָּסֹב	תָּסֹב	סֹב	וַתָּסָב
	2fs	תָּסֹבִי	תָּסֹבִי	סֹבִי	וַתָּסֹבִי
	1cs	אָסֹב	אָסֹבָה		וָאָסֹבָה
	2fp	תְּסֻבֶּ֫ינָה	תְּסֻבֶּ֫ינָה	סֻבֶּ֫ינָה	וַתְּסֻבֶּ֫ינָה

In *waw* consecutives and feminine plural imperfects, the theme vowel appears in a closed unaccented syllable and must be short (e.g., וַיָּסָב pron. *vay-ya´-sov*). Remember that before a doubled consonant, Hebrew prefers to represent short u-class vowels as *qibbuts* (תְּסֻבֶּ֫ינָה).[4]

One difficulty is that the feminine plural imperfect looks like *piel* or *pual* forms of the III-*Waw/Yod* verbs. For example, תְּסֻבֶּ֫ינָה (*qal* impf. 2fp סבב) looks like a *pual* 2fp imperfect from סבה*.

תְּסֻבֶּ֫ינָה

Option 1

(1) תּ□□□נָה = impf. 2fp/3fp

(2) תְּסֻבֶּ֫ינָה = *pual* יְקֻטַּל

(3) תְּסֻבֶּ֫ינָה (III-*Waw/yod* coalesce with cons. sufform.)

(4) תְּסֻבֶּ֫ינָה = סבה *(doesn't exist)*

Option 2

(1) תּ□□□נָה = impf. 2fp/3fp

(2) תְּסֻבֶּ֫ינָה = *qal* יִקְטֻל*
- distant open reduces
- two-letter root (*shewa* lost)
- u-class theme vowel

(3) תְּסֻבֶּ֫ינָה = helping vowel added

(4) תְּסֻבֶּ֫ינָה = סבב

4. Think of *qibbuts* preceding a *dagesh* as the "connect four" rule (e.g., תְּסֻבֶּ֫ינָה).

Qal Participle and Infinitive Absolute

The *qal* participles and infinitive absolute do not represent doubling with a *dagesh*. They look like strong verbs: סֹבֵב (act. ptc.), סָבוּב (pass. ptc.), and סָבוֹב (inf. abs.).

NIPHAL PARADIGM: DOUBLED SECOND CONSONANT

As expected, all forms of the *niphal* geminates preserve evidence of the *nun* of the *niphal* (e.g., *niphal* pf. נָסַב and impf. יִסַּב). Each feature of the forms is consistent with the geminate patterns and historic vowels.

Niphal Perfects and Participles

Niphal geminate verbs preserve the historic a-class vowel of the *niphal* perfect and participle (e.g., נַקְטַל*).[5] The single-syllable root leaves the preformative vowel in an open syllable that adjusts according to the vowel rules (e.g., *niphal* pf. נַסַב → נָסַב). The *niphal* participle is distinguished from the perfect by the long theme vowel in the masculine singular (e.g., ptc. נָסָב vs. pf. נָסַב) just as in the strong verb (e.g., ptc. נִקְטָל vs. pf. נִקְטַל). The feminine singular is distinguished by accent, and the masculine plural by its noun ending, but the feminine plural is identical to the 2fs perfect because of the helping vowel.

	Niphal Perfect	*Niphal* Participle		
3ms	נָסַב	נָסָב	ms	
3fs	נָסַבָּה	נְסַבָּה	fs	
2ms	נְסַבּוֹתָ	נְסַבִּים	mp	
2fs	נְסַבּוֹת	נְסַבּוֹת	fp	Identical forms
1cs	נְסַבּוֹתִי			

The main challenge is that the *niphal* perfect of a geminate (e.g., נָסַב from סבב) looks like a strong *qal* perfect (from נסב*). Concentrate on recognizing possible alternatives when an initial assessment does not work.

Niphal Infinitive Construct and Related Forms

In the *niphal* infinitive constructs and related forms, geminate roots retain the characteristic *niphal* doubling (from the assimilated *nun*) and

5. See the discussion of the original preformative vowels in ch. 24.

a-class vowel associated with the first consonant of the root (compare *niphal* strong יִקָּטֵל and יִסַּב).

Inf. Cst.		Impf.	Juss./Cohort.	Impv.	*Waw* Consec.
הִסַּב	3ms	יִסַּב	יִסַּב		וַיִּסַּב
	3fs	תִּסַּב	תִּסַּב		וַתִּסַּב
	2ms	תִּסַּב	תִּסַּב	הִסַּב	וַתִּסַּב
	2fs	תִּסַּ֫בִּי	תִּסַּ֫בִּי	הִסַּ֫בִּי	וַתִּסַּ֫בִּי
	1cs	אֶסַּב	אֶסַּ֫בָּה		וָאֶסַּב
	2fp	תִּסַּבֶּ֫ינָה	תִּסַּבֶּ֫ינָה	הִסַּבֶּ֫ינָה	וַתִּסַּבֶּ֫ינָה

POLEL, POLAL, HITHPOLEL PARADIGMS: REDUPLICATED SECOND CONSONANT

In the *polel* (active), *polal* (passive), and *hithpolel* (reflexive) stems, the geminates replace doubling with reduplication.[6] The *polel* and *polal* are only distinguishable in forms that have no sufformatives (סוֹבֵב vs. סוֹבַב). All other forms are identical (represented by gray shading below), and context must distinguish between active and passive.

	Polel Perfect	*Polal* Perfect	*Polel* Imperfect	*Polal* Imperfect
3ms	סוֹבֵב	סוֹבַב	יְסוֹבֵב	יְסוֹבַב
3fs	סוֹבְבָה	סוֹבְבָה	תְּסוֹבֵב	תְּסוֹבַב
2ms	סוֹבַ֫בְתָּ	סוֹבַ֫בְתָּ	תְּסוֹבֵב	תְּסוֹבַב
2fs	סוֹבַ֫בְתְּ	סוֹבַ֫בְתְּ	תְּסוֹבְבִי	תְּסוֹבְבִי
1cs	סוֹבַ֫בְתִּי	סוֹבַ֫בְתִּי	אֲסוֹבֵב	אֲסוֹבַב

6. Remember that Hebrew does not like to place *dentals* like ת before an "s" sound (*sibilants*). As a result, the two sounds switch places (תס → סת), a phenomenon called *metathesis*. Thus the *hithpolel* of סבב appears as הִסְתּוֹבֵב rather than הִתְסוֹבֵב*. Consider this the "p-sghetti" (spaghetti) rule. For details, see ch. 19.

The *polel*, *polal*, and *hithpolel* stems are used with both geminates and II-*Waw/Yod* verbs. The simplicity and uniformity of the patterns makes the stems easy to recognize, but the only way to distinguish between a geminate and II-*Waw/Yod* root is vocabulary and context.

As with II-*Waw/Yod* roots, the geminate verbs can use the *polel–hithpolel* as a substitute for the *piel–hithpael* or use both forms to convey different nuances of meaning. For example, the root סבב appears in the *piel* meaning "to transform" (cause to be turned) while the *polel* means "to encompass or go around." Both ideas are variations of the idea of turning.

HIPHIL PARADIGM: DOUBLED SECOND CONSONANT

Hiphil Never Uses Ḥireq yod Theme Vowel

In addition to the standard geminate tendencies, the *hiphil* geminates never occur with *ḥireq yod*. The i-class theme vowel is used throughout the entire paradigm but appears as a simple long vowel (e.g., הֵסֵ֫בּוּ) or a short vowel (e.g., הֲסִבֹּ֫תָ). The short vowel occurs when the accent shifts to create a closed unaccented syllable.

	Geminate (סבב)	Strong	
Preformative lengthens i-class theme (NOT ִי)	הֵסֵב	הִקְטִיל	*Hiphil* Perfect (i + i)
Preformative lengthens i-class theme (NOT ִי)	הָסֵב	הַקְטִיל	*Hiphil* Inf. Cst. (a + i)

The loss of the distinctive *ḥireq yod* together with the other geminate features result in some *hiphil* verbs that do not look like the strong form.

Adjusted features	Geminate (סבב)	Strong	
Preformative reduces *Short i-class vowel* *Visible doubling* *Helping vowel takes accent*	הֲסִבּ֫וֹתָ	הִקְטַ֫לְתָּ Remember, strong *hiphil* follows *qal* theme vowel with consonantal sufformatives	*Hiphil* Perfect (2ms)

It may take some time to get used to these verbs. Rely heavily on the strong features like preformatives, sufformatives, and expected vowel patterns of the *hiphil* stem. Then allow the structure of the word to explain the variations in the weak verb form.

Hiphil Participle Uses i-class Preformative

Geminate *hiphil* participles take an i-class preformative like the perfect (e.g., pf. הֵסֵב → ptc. מֵסֵב) rather than the a-class preformative vowel of the strong verb (e.g., מַקְטִיל). This affinity between the *hiphil* perfect and participle also occurs in the II-*Waw/Yod* verbs, but the II-*Waw/Yod* verbs appear with *ḥireq yod* (e.g., מֵקִים *hiphil* ptc. from קוּם) while the geminates do not (e.g., מֵסֵב from סבב).

	Geminate	Strong	
i-class	הֵסֵב	הִקְטִיל	Perfect
	מֵסֵב	מַקְטִיל	Participle
a-class	הָסֵב	הַקְטִיל	Infinitive Construct
	יָסֵב	יַקְטִיל	Imperfect

HOPHAL PARADIGM: DOUBLED SECOND CONSONANT

The *hophal* geminates use the same vowel classes as the strong verb: u-class preformative with an a-class theme vowel in all paradigms except the infinitive absolute which takes the same *tsere* theme vowel as the strong verb. The open preformative syllable consistently takes a pure long *shureq* that never reduces (e.g., הוּסַב from סבב). This pattern is the same as the *hophal* of the I-*Waw/Yod* verbs (יוּשַׁב from ישב) and the II-*Waw/Yod* verbs (e.g., יוּקַם from קום). Thus context and meaning will again determine which type of root is being used.

	Geminates	Strong
Hophal Pf./Inf. Cst. (and related forms)	הוּסַב	הָקְטַל
Hophal Inf. Abs.	הוּסֵב	הָקְטֵל

SUMMARY

The geminate patterns are driven by the needs of pronunciation and follow familiar features of Hebrew word structure.

1. *Can* appear as a strong verb (סָבַב = *qal* pf., compare קָטַל).
2. *Occasionally* have doubled first consonant (יִסֹּב = *qal* impf., compare יִקְטֹל).
3. *Usually* have doubled second consonant (סַבּוּ = *qal* pf., compare קָטְלוּ).

The typical geminate pattern doubles the second consonant of the root. The preformative vowel appears in an open syllable, preserving historic vowels and adjusting according to the vowel rules (e.g., יָסֹב from *qal* יַקְטֻל*). Consonantal sufformatives need helping vowels (וֹ in the perfects and יֶ everywhere else). These helping vowels pull the accent toward the end of the word, leaving the preformative in a distant open syllable (e.g., *hiphil* pf. 2ms הֲסִבֹּתָ).

Keep in mind that

- Doubling does not show at the end of a word (סַב vs. סַ֫בּוּ)
- *Qal* geminates take *pataḥ* (סַב vs. II-*Waw/Yod qamets* קָם)
- *Polel, polal, hithpolel* commonly used in place of *piel-hithpael*
- *Hiphil* does not use *ḥireq yod*

What Questions Should I Ask When I Read?

This chapter presents clues that help you determine if a verb with only two visible consonants is a geminate root like סבב (vs. I, II, III-*Waw/Yod)*. If one of the two consonants is doubled, especially when it is not marking a *niphal* or *piel-hithpael,* consider a geminate root. If you suspect a geminate form because of your vocabulary, but do not see doubling, ask if another feature of pronunciation prohibits doubling—e.g., doubling is not heard at the end of a word or a guttural may reject doubling. Note also that the *pataḥ* theme vowel of the *qal* perfect סַב helps you consider a geminate root (vs. II-*Waw/Yod* קָם).

REPRESENTATIVE FORMS: GEMINATE VERBS

	Qal		*Niphal*	*Polel*	*Polal*	*Hithpolel*	*Hiphil*	*Hophal*
	Act.	Stat.		*(Piel)*	*(Pual)*	*(Hithpael)*		
Perfect	סַב סַ֫בָּה	קַל קַ֫לָּה	נָסַב נָסַ֫בָּה	סוֹבֵב	סוֹבַב	הִסְתּוֹבֵב	הֵסֵב הֵסֵ֫בָּה	הוּסַב הוּסַ֫בָּה
Participle	סֹבֵב (act.) סָבוּב (pass.)		נָסָב נְסַבָּה	מְסוֹבֵב	מְסוֹבָב	מִסְתּוֹבֵב	מֵסֵב מְסִבָּה	מוּסָב מוּסַבָּה
Imperfect	יָסֹב יָסֹ֫בּוּ	יֵקַל יֵקַ֫לּוּ	יִסַּב יִסַּ֫בּוּ	יְסוֹבֵב	יְסוֹבַב	יִסְתּוֹבֵב	יָסֵב יָסֵ֫בּוּ	יוּסַב יוּסַ֫בּוּ
Waw Consec.	וַיָּ֫סָב						וַיָּ֫סֶב	
Imperative	סֹב סֹ֫בִּי	קַל קַ֫לִּי	הִסַּב הִסַּ֫בִּי	סוֹבֵב		הִסְתּוֹבֵב	הָסֵב	
Inf. Cst.	סֹב	קַל	הִסַּב	סוֹבֵב	סוֹבַב	הִסְתּוֹבֵב	הָסֵב	הוּסַב
Inf. Abs.	סָבוֹב	קָלוֹל	הִסֹּב	סוֹבֵב	סוֹבַב	הִסְתּוֹבֵב	הָסֵב	הוּסֵב

GEMINATE VERB CHART (PRIMARY PATTERN)

	QAL		*NIPHAL*	*POLEL*	*POLAL*	*HITHPOLEL*	*HIPHIL*	*HOPHAL*
	Active	***Stative***		*(Piel)*	*(Pual)*	*(Hithpael)*		
Perfect	סַב	קַל	נָסַב	סוֹבֵב	סוֹבַב	הִסְתּוֹבֵב	הֵסֵב	הוּסַב
	סַ֫בָּה	קַ֫לָּה	נָסַ֫בָּה	סוֹבְבָה	סוֹבְבָה	הִסְתּוֹבְבָה	הֵסֵ֫בָּה	הוּסַ֫בָּה
	סַבּ֫וֹתָ	קַלּ֫וֹתָ	נְסַבּ֫וֹתָ	סוֹבַ֫בְתָּ	סוֹבַ֫בְתָּ	הִסְתּוֹבַ֫בְתָּ	הֲסִבּ֫וֹתָ	הוּסַבּ֫וֹתָ
	סַבּ֫וֹת	קַלּ֫וֹת	נְסַבּ֫וֹת	סוֹבַ֫בְתְּ	סוֹבַ֫בְתְּ	הִסְתּוֹבַ֫בְתְּ	הֲסִבּ֫וֹת	הוּסַבּ֫וֹת
	סַבּ֫וֹתִי	קַלּ֫וֹתִי	נְסַבּ֫וֹתִי	סוֹבַ֫בְתִּי	סוֹבַ֫בְתִּי	הִסְתּוֹבַ֫בְתִּי	הֲסִבּ֫וֹתִי	הוּסַבּ֫וֹתִי
	סַ֫בּוּ	קַ֫לּוּ	נָסַ֫בּוּ	סוֹבְבוּ	סוֹבְבוּ	הִסְתּוֹבְבוּ	הֵסֵ֫בּוּ	הוּסַ֫בּוּ
	סַבּוֹתֶם	קַלּוֹתֶם	נְסַבּוֹתֶם	סוֹבַבְתֶּם	סוֹבַבְתֶּם	הִסְתּוֹבַבְתֶּם	הֲסִבּוֹתֶם	הוּסַבּוֹתֶם
	סַבּוֹתֶן	קַלּוֹתֶן	נְסַבּוֹתֶן	סוֹבַבְתֶּן	סוֹבַבְתֶּן	הִסְתּוֹבַבְתֶּן	הֲסִבּוֹתֶן	הוּסַבּוֹתֶן
	סַבּ֫וֹנוּ	קַלּ֫וֹנוּ	נְסַבּ֫וֹנוּ	סוֹבַ֫בְנוּ	סוֹבַ֫בְנוּ	הִסְתּוֹבַ֫בְנוּ	הֲסִבּ֫וֹנוּ	הוּסַבּ֫וֹנוּ
Participle	סֹבֵב		נָסָב	מְסוֹבֵב	מְסוֹבָב	מִסְתּוֹבֵב	מֵסֵב	מוּסָב
			נְסַבָּ֫ה	מְסוֹבְבָה	מְסוֹבָבָה	מִסְתּוֹבְבָה	מְסִבָּה	מוּסַבָּה
	(pass. סָבוּב)		נְסַבִּים	מְסוֹבְבִים	מְסוֹבָבִים	מִסְתּוֹבְבִים	מְסִבִּים	מוּסַבִּים
			נְסַבּוֹת	מְסוֹבְבוֹת	מְסוֹבָבוֹת	מִסְתּוֹבְבוֹת	מְסִבּוֹת	מוּסַבּוֹת
Imperfect	יָסֹב	יֵקַל	יִסַּב	יְסוֹבֵב	יְסוֹבַב	יִסְתּוֹבֵב	יָסֵב	יוּסַב
	תָּסֹב	תֵּקַל	תִּסַּב	תְּסוֹבֵב	תְּסוֹבַב	תִּסְתּוֹבֵב	תָּסֵב	תּוּסַב
	תָּסֹב	תֵּקַל	תִּסַּב	תְּסוֹבֵב	תְּסוֹבַב	תִּסְתּוֹבֵב	תָּסֵב	תּוּסַב
	תָּסֹ֫בִּי	תֵּקַ֫לִּי	תִּסַּ֫בִּי	תְּסוֹבְבִי	תְּסוֹבְבִי	תִּסְתּוֹבְבִי	תָּסֵ֫בִּי	תּוּסַ֫בִּי
	אָסֹב	אֵקַל	אֶסַּב	אֲסוֹבֵב	אֲסוֹבַב	אֶסְתּוֹבֵב	אָסֵב	אוּסַב
	יָסֹ֫בּוּ	יֵקַ֫לּוּ	יִסַּ֫בּוּ	יְסוֹבְבוּ	יְסוֹבְבוּ	יִסְתּוֹבְבוּ	יָסֵ֫בּוּ	יוּסַ֫בּוּ
	תְּסֻבֶּ֫ינָה	תְּקַלֶּ֫ינָה	תִּסַּבֶּ֫ינָה	תְּסוֹבֵ֫בְנָה	תְּסוֹבַ֫בְנָה	תִּסְתּוֹבַ֫בְנָה	תְּסִבֶּ֫ינָה	תּוּסַבֶּ֫ינָה
	תָּסֹ֫בּוּ	תֵּקַ֫לּוּ	תִּסַּ֫בּוּ	תְּסוֹבְבוּ	תְּסוֹבְבוּ	תִּסְתּוֹבְבוּ	תָּסֵ֫בּוּ	תּוּסַ֫בּוּ
	תְּסֻבֶּ֫ינָה	תְּקַלֶּ֫ינָה	תִּסַּבֶּ֫ינָה	תְּסוֹבֵ֫בְנָה	תְּסוֹבַ֫בְנָה	תִּסְתּוֹבַ֫בְנָה	תְּסִבֶּ֫ינָה	תּוּסַבֶּ֫ינָה
	נָסֹב	נֵקַל	נִסַּב	נְסוֹבֵב	נְסוֹבַב	נִסְתּוֹבֵב	נָסֵב	נוּסַב
Imperative	סֹב	קַל	הִסַּב	סוֹבֵב		הִסְתּוֹבֵב	הָסֵב	
	סֹ֫בִּי	קַ֫לִּי	הִסַּ֫בִּי	סוֹבְבִי		הִסְתּוֹבְבִי	הָסֵ֫בִּי	
	סֹ֫בּוּ	קַ֫לּוּ	הִסַּ֫בּוּ	סוֹבְבוּ		הִסְתּוֹבְבוּ	הָסֵ֫בּוּ	
	סֻבֶּ֫ינָה	קַלֶּ֫ינָה	הִסַּבֶּ֫ינָה	סוֹבֵ֫בְנָה		הִסְתּוֹבַ֫בְנָה	הֲסִבֶּ֫ינָה	
Inf. Cst.	סֹב	קַל	הִסַּב	סוֹבֵב	סוֹבַב	הִסְתּוֹבֵב	הָסֵב	הוּסַב
Inf. Abs.	סֹב	קָלוֹל	הִסֹּב	סוֹבֵב	סוֹבַב	הִסְתּוֹבֵב	הָסֵב	הוּסֵב

CHAPTER 30

I-*Nun* Verbs

This chapter covers verbs whose roots begin with *nun* (e.g., נטשׁ "to forsake"). The recurring pattern is that *a* nun *with silent* shewa *assimilates.*[1] The term *assimilation* means that a letter too weak to maintain its own sound takes on the sound of an adjacent consonant. The assimilation of *nun* is a feature that you have already encountered. For example, vowelless *nun* assimilates when the preposition מִן ("from") is attached to a word—e.g., *מִנְמֶּלֶךְ → מִמֶּלֶךְ. Without a vowel sound to anchor its position in the word, the /n/ sound is lost and replaced by the /m/ that follows—מִמֶּלֶךְ.

The same principle applies to I-*Nun* verbs. Wherever *nun* would have a silent *shewa* in the strong form, the *nun* takes on the characteristics of the following consonant. This doubling of the next consonant is then represented by a *dagesh forte* (e.g., יִטֹּשׁ "he will forsake").[2]

יִטֹּשׁ ← *יִטְטֹשׁ ← *יִנְטֹשׁ *Qal* impf. נטשׁ

While the *dagesh* represents the doubled second consonant, in this case another *tet,* it is also accurate to think of this *dagesh* as evidence of a *nun.*

In I-*Nun* verbs *a* nun *with silent* shewa *assimilates* (יִפֹּל)
***unless followed by a guttural* (יִנְאַף).**

1. Assimilation happens in English as well. The "n" of the Latin prefix *in-* ("not") assimilates when it is attached to certain letters (e.g., "inseparable" vs. "irresponsible").

2. The assimilation of *nun* described here is also seen in nouns that are derived from these roots. For example, from the roots נתן ("give") and נסע ("travel") you find the derivatives "gift" (מַתָּנָה = *מַנְתָּנָה) and "journey" (מַסַּע = *מַנְסַע).

I-NUN: THE BASIC PRINCIPLES

In I-Nun verbs a nun with silent shewa assimilates unless followed by a guttural. In accordance with this principle, assimilation occurs regardless of verb stem or paradigm. To anticipate where I-*Nun* verbs assimilate, scan the strong verb paradigms to see where *shewa* appears under the first consonant of the root. For example, the *qal* and *niphal* both exhibit assimilation but in different paradigms.

Qal Perfect	*Qal* Imperfect	*Niphal* Perfect	*Niphal* Imperfect
קָטַל	יִקְטֹל	נִקְטַל	יִקָּטֵל

Conversely, any form with a vowel sound (vowel or a vocal *shewa*) under the *nun* behaves as a strong verb (e.g., *qal* pf. 3ms נָפַל and 2mp נְפַלְתֶּם). The *nun* is retained in order to carry the vowel sound. As a result, the *piel, pual,* and *hithpael* and many forms of the *qal* and *niphal* do not assimilate (e.g., *hithpael* הִתְנַפֵּל).

I-Nun With Silent Shewa Assimilates

The practical result of assimilation is that the *nun* no longer appears and the next consonant is written with a *dagesh forte.* Since the *dagesh* provides a visible indication where a *nun* once stood, it helps students to think of the *dagesh forte* as a hidden *nun.*

*יִנְטַשׁ	*Qal* strong pattern
↓	
יִטַּשׁ	*Qal* Impf. נטשׁ

In addition to preserving evidence of the *nun,* the *dagesh* preserves the original closed syllable and preformative vowel of the strong form. Preformative vowels thus remain in stable syllables and do not need to adjust. The I-*Nun* verbs behave like strong verbs in all other aspects. Thus, the *qal* and *niphal* forms of נטשׁ become:

	Qal Perfect	*Qal* Imperfect	*Niphal* Perfect	*Niphal* Imperfect
Strong	קָטַל	יִקְטֹל	נִקְטַל	יִקָּטֵל
	↓	↓	↓	↓
I-*Nun*	נָטַשׁ	יִטַּשׁ	נִטַּשׁ	יִנָּטֵשׁ

No Assimilation When Followed by a Guttural

Nun does not assimilate when the second consonant of the root is a guttural (e.g., *qal* impf. 2ms לֹא תִנְאָף; Exod 20:14). Instead the verb follows the strong verb pattern. In rare cases, a I-*Nun* verb whose second root letter is a guttural employs compensatory lengthening or implicit doubling (e.g., *niphal* pf. 3ms נִחַם "he was sorry," NOT נִנְחַם*).

Qal Perfect	*Qal* Imperfect
תִּנְאַף	תִּקְטֹל
"you commit adultery"	

I-Nun Qal Infinitive Construct and Related Forms

The *qal* imperative and infinitive construct of the I-*Nun* verbs can take one of two forms, with *nun* (e.g., נְפֹל) and without *nun* (e.g., שַׁק). Some I-*Nun* imperatives and infinitive constructs are formed off the *qal* strong verb. Since the imperative and infinitive construct both have vocal *shewa* in the strong form (e.g., קְטֹל), the *nun* is retained (נְפֹל impv. "fall!" or inf. cst. "falling").

Other I-*Nun* imperatives and infinitive constructs are formed off the I-*Nun* imperfect (e.g., *qal* impf. תִּשַּׁק from נשק "to kiss"). Remember, you learned to form the imperative by dropping the preformative of the imperfect (שַׁק → תִּשַּׁק "kiss!"). Since the *nun* was assimilated in the imperfect, it does not appear in the imperative, yet the *dagesh forte*, indicative of assimilated *nun*, does not appear in the first consonant of a word (e.g., *qal* impv. שַׁק). The infinitive construct uses the same base as the imperative (e.g., impv. גַּשׁ from נגשׁ "to approach") but adds a final *tav* and adjusts the vowels according to the same pattern as segolate nouns (e.g., גַּשׁ → גַּשְׁתּ* → גַּשֶׁת* → גֶּשֶׁת).[3] The *tav* sufformative and segolate pattern is also used in I-*Waw/Yod* infinitive constructs (e.g., *qal* impf. יֵשֵׁב → inf. cst. שֶׁבֶת from ישׁב "to dwell"). Sometimes the same I-*Nun* root can appear according to either pattern of formation.

3. Note that the *dagesh* in גַּשׁ is a *dagesh lene* (NOT *dagesh forte*).

Infinitive		Imperative		
נְפֹל		נְפֹל		Strong pattern *(vocal shewa = no assimilation)*
גֶּשֶׁת	←	גַּשׁ	←	Impf. base *(impf.)* תִּגַּשׁ
נְשֹׁק *(strong pattern)*		שַׁק *(off impf.)*		Mixed *(same root uses different patterns)*

The underlying vowel pattern of the I-*Nun qal* infinitive construct (e.g., גַּשְׁת*) reappears when suffixes are added (e.g., גַּשְׁתִּי "***my*** approaching"). Remembering how these infinitive constructs are formed will help you recognize that גֶּשֶׁת ("approaching") and גַּשְׁתִּי ("my approaching") are both *qal* infinitive constructs from נגשׁ.

Infinitive Construct (נגשׁ)

"drawing near"	גֶּשֶׁת	←	גַּשֶׁת	←	גַּשְׁת*
	harmonize vowels		helping vowel		*tav* added to create inf. cst.
"my drawing near"			גַּשְׁתִּי	←	גַּשְׁת*
			plus suffix (same form)		*tav* added to create inf. cst.

The Hophal Uses Short /u/ Rather Than Short /o/

The only other significant change in appearance caused by the assimilation of *nun* occurs in the *hophal*. The assimilation of vowelless *nun* creates a stable syllable structure that generally preserves the same preformative vowel as the strong verb. However, because Hebrew prefers to use *qibbuts* before doubled consonants (הָקְטַל vs. הֻגַּשׁ from נגשׁ "to draw near"), the *hophal* of I-*Nun* verbs uses short /u/ rather than short /o/. Thus, many I-*Nun hophal* forms look like *pual* verbs.

Hophal of נגשׁ			*Hophal* Strong
הֻגַּשׁ	←	*הָנְגַּשׁ	הָקְטַל
qibbuts before doubled consonants			

Rather than memorizing this feature, simply remember that short /o/ and short /u/ are both u-class vowels that are interchangeably used depending upon the environment in which they appear.[4] Also note that the same form may have more than one parsing option.

Skin 'em Levi (קנמ לוי-"s") Consonants May Drop Dagesh Forte

Some forms drop the characteristic doubling that alerts you to the presence of a I-*Nun* verb. Several consonants tend to lose the *dagesh forte* when followed by a *shewa*. The mnemonic *Skin 'em Levi* (קנם לוי-"s") designates the /s/ sounds (ס-צ-שׂ-שׁ) and other letters that, when followed by *shewa*, do not always appear with *dagesh forte* when one is expected.

Actual form	Expected form	
יִסְעוּ	יִסְּעוּ	"they will set out" (נסע)

Because the expected form of the verb would include a *dagesh forte*, these forms without *dagesh* should be pronounced in accordance with the expected vocal *shewa*. For example, the verb יִסְעוּ ("they will set out"from נסע) should be pronounced *yis*^{e}*-ū* (NOT *yis-ū*). The Masoretic vocalization indicates that they did not hear the doubling, despite the presence of a vocal *shewa*. It does not mean that they were restructuring the word.

4. Think of *qibbuts* preceding a *dagesh* as the "connect four" rule (e.g., *hophal* pf. הֻגַּשׁ "he was brought near").

IRREGULAR I-NUN VERBS

The Verb לקח Acts Like a I-Nun Verb

The verb לקח is irregular because it does not begin with *nun* but behaves exactly like a I-*Nun* verb. The assimilation of *lamed* does not happen in any other Hebrew verb. It may be helpful to remember the unique assimilation of לקח if you associate this verb with its antonym נתן (i.e., *give* and *take*).

Infinitive		Imperative		Imperfect	Perfect
קַ֫חַת†	←	קַח	←	תִּקַּח	לָקַח
קַחְתִּי				(תִּלְקַח*)	

with suffix "my taking"

† The use of *pataḥ* (קַ֫חַת vs. גֶּ֫שֶׁת) is due to the guttural ח.

The Verb נתן Assimilates Final Vowelless Nun

A vowelless *nun* also assimilates in other positions. For example, the verb נתן assimilates its final *nun.* When it assimilates, this *nun* appears as *dagesh forte* in the sufformative that follows. Because the *dagesh forte* often replaces *dagesh lene,* the assimilated *nun* is less noticeable (e.g., נָתַ֫תָּ → נָתַ֫נְתָּ*). The assimilation of final vowelless *nun* can occur in any form of נתן regardless of stem.[5]

The *qal* infinitive construct of נתן can assimilate both the initial and final *nun,* leaving only one visible root consonant. The infinitive construct is formed by removing the preformative from the I-*Nun* imperfect (תִּתֵּן → תֵּן) and adding the *tav* sufformative of I-*Nun* infinitive constructs (ת + תֵּן = תֵּת). The vowelless *nun* assimilates into the *tav,* although *dagesh forte* only appears if suffixes are added (e.g., תִּתִּי "***my*** giving"). As a result, the infinitive construct often leaves only one root letter visible (e.g., תֵּת or תִּתִּי from נתן).[6]

5. Though rare outside of נתן, this phenomenon takes place with other verbs as well. Cf. Gen. 4:23 הַאְזֵ֫נָּה (הַאְזֵנְנָה* = *hiphil* impv. 2fp אזן "hear").

6. Note that the *dagesh* in תֵּן is a *dagesh lene* (NOT *dagesh forte*). In the second form, *ḥireq* replaces *tsere* in the closed unaccented syllable.

Inf. Cst.		Imperative		Imperfect	Perfect
תֵּת†	←	תֵּן	←	תִּתֵּן	נָתַתָּ
(תֵּנֶת*)				(2ms תִּנְתֵּן*)	(2ms נָתַנְתָּ*)
תִּתִּי *with suffix* "my giving"					

† The initial *tav* has a *dagesh lene,* and doubling is not represented at the end of words.

The following chart provides samples of the *qal* forms of נתן for you to examine. Note especially that the *dagesh* in the perfects with consonantal sufformatives is a *dagesh forte* because it follows a vowel and that it represents an assimilated *nun* (e.g., נָתַ֫תָּ = נָתַ֫נְתָּ*).

		Qal Pf.	*Qal* Impf.	*Qal* Impv.	*Qal* Inf. Cst.
נגשׁ		נָגַשׁ	יִגַּשׁ	גַּשׁ	גֶּ֫שֶׁת
		↓	↓	↓	↓
נתן	3ms	נָתַן	יִתֵּן		תֵּת
	3fs	נָתְנָה	תִּתֵּן		(תֵּנֶת)
	2ms	נָתַ֫תָּ	תִּתֵּן	תֵּן or תְּנָה†	
	2fs	נָתַתְּ	תִּתְּנִי	תְּנִי	
	1cs	נָתַ֫תִּי	אֶתֵּן		

† Roughly half of the imperatives of נתן use the long form תְּנָה (cf. *qal* impv. קָטְלָה).

The Qal Passive—נתן and לקח

Chapter 21 presented rare verb stems that appear in the Hebrew Bible, including the historic *qal* passive. Two of the most common *qal* passive verbs are נתן and לקח, verbs affected by the I-*Nun* patterns. The *qal* passive is characterized by the u + a vowel pattern common to all passive verbs and is sometimes mistaken for the *pual* or *hophal.* For example, לֻקַּח looks like a *pual* of לקח. However, the contexts in which these forms appear require a meaning that reflects the simple passive of a *qal* (i.e., "he was/will be taken").[7] When the context indicates a simple passive action instead of the passive meaning of a *piel* or *hiphil,* translate these forms as *qal* passives.

Historic *qal* passive		
לֻקַּח	Perfect	Looks like strong *pual* (קֻטַּל)
יֻקַּח	Imperfect	Looks like I-*Nun hophal* (יֻגַּשׁ)

SUMMARY The primary feature of I-*Nun* verbs is that *nun* with silent *shewa* assimilates (יִפֹּל) unless followed by a guttural (יִנְאַף). This principle is consistently applied and represents the primary adjustment for I-*Nun* verbs. A few other I-*Nun* features to keep in mind are:

1. *Qal* imperatives and infinitive constructs take one of two forms—with *nun* (e.g., נְפֹל) and without *nun* (e.g., impv. גַּשׁ and inf. cst. גֶּשֶׁת).
2. *Hophal* uses the *qibbuts* preformative before the doubled consonant (e.g., הֻגַּשׁ).
3. *Skin 'em Levi* consonants (קנמ לוי-"S") may drop *dagesh forte* (יִסְעוּ instead of יִסְּעוּ).
4. Remember לקח behaves like I-*Nun* verbs, and נתן assimilates final *nun.*

What Questions Should I Ask When I Read? I-*Nun* verbs are some of the easiest to identify. Many occur just like the strong form, and the others usually retain evidence of the *nun* through the presence of *dagesh forte.* The presence of *dagesh forte* reminds you to consider an assimilated *nun.*

One potential difficulty is that assimilation in I-*Nun* verbs results in the same form as geminate verbs that double the first root consonant (and rarely also in I-*Waw/Yod* verbs). When you encounter doubling with only two visible root consonants, consider first the more

7. For example, Gen 2:23, "And the man said, 'This now is bone of my bones and flesh of my flesh. She will be called woman because *she was taken* (לֻקֳחָה) out of man.'"

frequent I-*Nun* verbs, then geminates, and last the rare assimilation in I-*Waw/Yod* verbs.

יִטֹּשׁ	"he will forsake"	I-*Nun* (נטשׁ)
יִסֹּב	"he will turn"	Geminate (סבב)
יִצֹּק	"he will pour"	I-*Waw/Yod* (יצק)

The greatest difficulty with I-*Nun* verbs comes from losing two of the three root consonants (e.g., תֵּת "giving" inf. cst. of נתן). When you see a verb with only one visible root consonant, it is a I-*Nun* verb that has also lost its third root letter. The three most common roots that leave only one visible root letter are נתן ("give"), נכה ("strike"), and נטה ("stretch out"). For example, the word וַיַּךְ is a *qal* or *hiphil waw* consecutive imperfect from נכה.

וַיַּךְ	"and he struck" (נכה)

The advantage of these roots is that they are frequent and are so difficult the first time you read them that you never forget them.

REPRESENTATIVE FORMS: I-NUN VERBS

	Qal		*Qal* Pass.	*Niphal*	*Hiphil*	*Hophal*
Perfect	נָטַשׁ		לֻקַּח	נִגַּשׁ	הִגִּישׁ	הֻגַּשׁ
Imperfect	יִטֹּשׁ		יֻקַּח	יִנָּגֵשׁ	יַגִּישׁ	יֻגַּשׁ
Waw Consecutive	וַיִּטֹּשׁ	*Formed off the imperfect* (תִּגַּשׁ)		וַיִּנָּגֵשׁ	וַיַּגֵּשׁ	וַיֻּגַּשׁ
Imperative	נְטֹשׁ	גַּשׁ		הִנָּגֵשׁ	הַגֵּשׁ	
Infinitive Construct	נְטֹשׁ	גֶּשֶׁת		הִנָּגֵשׁ	הַגִּישׁ	הֻגַּשׁ
Infinitive Absolute	נָטוֹשׁ			נִגֹּשׁ	הַגֵּשׁ	הֻגֵּשׁ
Participle	נֹטֵשׁ			נִגָּשׁ	מַגִּישׁ	מֻגָּשׁ

I-NUN VERB CHART

	QAL		NIPHAL	HIPHIL	HOPHAL
Perfect	נָפַל		נִגַּשׁ	הִגִּישׁ	הֻגַּשׁ
	נָפְלָה		נִגְּשָׁה	הִגִּישָׁה	הֻגְּשָׁה
	נָפַלְתָּ		נִגַּשְׁתָּ	הִגַּשְׁתָּ	הֻגַּשְׁתָּ
	נָפַלְתְּ		נִגַּשְׁתְּ	הִגַּשְׁתְּ	הֻגַּשְׁתְּ
	נָפַלְתִּי		נִגַּשְׁתִּי	הִגַּשְׁתִּי	הֻגַּשְׁתִּי
	נָפְלוּ		נִגְּשׁוּ	הִגִּישׁוּ	הֻגְּשׁוּ
	נְפַלְתֶּם		נִגַּשְׁתֶּם	הִגַּשְׁתֶּם	הֻגַּשְׁתֶּם
	נְפַלְתֶּן		נִגַּשְׁתֶּן	הִגַּשְׁתֶּן	הֻגַּשְׁתֶּן
	נָפַלְנוּ		נִגַּשְׁנוּ	הִגַּשְׁנוּ	הֻגַּשְׁנוּ
Imperfect	יִפֹּל		יִנָּגֵשׁ	יַגִּישׁ	יֻגַּשׁ
	תִּפֹּל		תִּנָּגֵשׁ	תַּגִּישׁ	תֻּגַּשׁ
	תִּפֹּל		תִּנָּגֵשׁ	תַּגִּישׁ	תֻּגַּשׁ
	תִּפְּלִי		תִּנָּגְשִׁי	תַּגִּישִׁי	תֻּגְּשִׁי
	אֶפֹּל		אֶנָּגֵשׁ	אַגִּישׁ	אֻגַּשׁ
	יִפְּלוּ		יִנָּגְשׁוּ	יַגִּישׁוּ	יֻגְּשׁוּ
	תִּפֹּלְנָה		תִּנָּגַשְׁנָה	תַּגֵּשְׁנָה	תֻּגַּשְׁנָה
	תִּפְּלוּ		תִּנָּגְשׁוּ	תַּגִּישׁוּ	תֻּגְּשׁוּ
	תִּפֹּלְנָה		תִּנָּגַשְׁנָה	תַּגֵּשְׁנָה	תֻּגַּשְׁנָה
	נִפֹּל		נִנָּגֵשׁ	נַגִּישׁ	נֻגַּשׁ
		formed off the impf. תִּגַּשׁ			
Imperative	נְפֹל	גַּשׁ	הִנָּגֵשׁ	הַגֵּשׁ	
	נִפְלִי	גְּשִׁי	הִנָּגְשִׁי	הַגִּישִׁי	
	נִפְלוּ	גְּשׁוּ	הִנָּגְשׁוּ	הַגִּישׁוּ	
	נְפֹלְנָה	גַּשְׁנָה	הִנָּגַשְׁנָה	הַגֵּשְׁנָה	
Inf. Cst.	נְפֹל	גֶּשֶׁת	הִנָּגֵשׁ	הַגִּישׁ	הֻגַּשׁ
Inf. Abs.	נָפוֹל		נִגֹּשׁ/הִנָּגֵשׁ	הַגֵּשׁ	הֻגֵּשׁ
Participle	נֹפֵל		נִגָּשׁ	מַגִּישׁ	מֻגָּשׁ
	נֹפְלָה		נִגָּשָׁה	מַגִּישָׁה	מֻגָּשָׁה
	נֹפְלִים		נִגָּשִׁים	מַגִּישִׁים	מֻגָּשִׁים
	נֹפְלוֹת		נִגָּשׁוֹת	מַגִּישׁוֹת	מֻגָּשׁוֹת

CHAPTER 31

I-Guttural Verbs

The final three chapters of the grammar focus on verbs that have a guttural as one of the root letters. The introduction to weak verbs (ch. 23) provided the principles necessary to recognize most roots with gutturals. The final chapters refine these concepts as they specifically apply to verbs with gutturals in the first, second, and third root consonants (I, II, and III-Guttural verbs).

I-GUTTURAL: BASIC PRINCIPLES

The I-Guttural verbs include those that begin with the true gutturals (א, ה, ח, ע) and the consonant ר because it often behaves like gutturals. These letters exhibit four characteristics that are already familiar to you—three characteristics common to all gutturals and one characteristic specific to the letter *aleph*.

1. **Gutturals do not double.**
2. **Gutturals prefer a-class vowels.**
3. **Gutturals often take composite *shewa*.**
4. ***Aleph* likes to quiesce (lose its consonantal value).**

These features are not all present in every verb but can be expected in certain contexts. The inability to double the first consonant of the root is directly applicable to certain forms of the *niphal* (e.g., *niphal* impf. יִקָּטֵל). Further, because the guttural is in the first position of the root, it is perfectly poised to influence retention of historic a-class preformative vowels and to require composite *shewa* in place of regular *shewa* (e.g., *qal* impf. יַעֲמֹד vs. יִקְטֹל). Finally, in many I-*Aleph* verbs the *aleph* appears at the end of a syllable where it can quiesce (e.g., *qal* inf. cst. לֵאמֹר vs. לִקְטֹל).

GUTTURALS DO NOT DOUBLE (NIPHAL)

The only place where doubling is affected in a I-Guttural verb is in the *niphal*, where doubling of the first consonant of the root is a characteristic feature. In these forms the guttural rejects the doubling and the preformative vowel lengthens to compensate (e.g., יֵחָשֵׁב "it will be considered").[1] The key is to remain alert when you notice a guttural letter in your root and consider the changes that could have occurred because of its presence.

GUTTURALS TAKE COMPOSITE SHEWA

A dominant feature of I-Guttural verbs is the use of composite *shewa*. The composite *shewa* is common in I-Guttural verbs because the first root consonant is frequently vowelless in the strong verb paradigms (e.g., יִקְטֹל). This means that a I-Guttural verb often contains a vowelless guttural , and these vowelless gutturals prefer a composite *shewa* (e.g., יֶאֱסֹר).

Composite Shewa Influenced by the Preceding Vowel

The vowel class of a composite *shewa* in a I-Guttural verb is determined by the preceding preformative vowel. In other words, gutturals do not just assert their preference for the a-class composite *shewa*, or in the case of *aleph* an i-class composite *shewa*. Instead, the composite *shewa* matches the vowel class of the preformative of the verb stem. In the case of the *qal* and *niphal*, the influence of the guttural may result in the retention of the historic a-class preformative vowel (compare יַקְטֻל* with יַעֲמֹד). As illustrated in the diagram below, each preformative vowel appears with a corresponding composite *shewa*.

1. The I-Gutturals exhibit compensatory lengthening in the *niphal* with all guttural consonants, including ה and ח.

Composite *Shewa* Influenced by Preceding Vowels

	Strong verb	I-Guttural
Qal impf. (historic)	*יַקְטֵל	יַעֲמֹד
Qal impf. (strong)	יִקְטֹל	יֶאֱסֹר
Hophal impf.	יָקְטַל	יָעֳמַד

Note that Hebrew has only three composite *shewas*, one for each vowel class. An a-class preformative is matched by ֲ , an i-class preformative by ֱ , and a u-class preformative by ֳ .

When nothing dictates which composite *shewa* to choose, the gutturals revert to their usual preference. Most gutturals prefer an a-class composite *shewa* (e.g., *qal* impv. עֲמֹד). However, *aleph* often exhibits a preference for the i-class vowel. Note, for example, the *qal* imperfect (אֶחֱבֹשׁ vs. יַעֲמֹד) and the *qal* imperative (אֱמֹר vs. עֲמֹד).

The principle outlined above does not state that gutturals require composite *shewa*. Gutturals merely *prefer* composite *shewa*. Sometimes I-Gutturals take a regular *shewa* just like the strong verb (e.g., יַעְטֶה, יֶאְסֹר, נֶהְפַּךְ). These should pose no problem.

Hebrew Cannot Have Two Vocal Shewas in a Row

Hebrew does not allow two vocal *shewas* in a row. When you learned to add prepositions onto words (ch. 7), you discovered that a word beginning with *shewa* cannot take the standard vowelless preposition (e.g., לְ + שְׁמוּאֵל). Instead, the first *shewa* upgrades to a full vowel to smooth out pronunciation (*לְשְׁמוּאֵל → לִשְׁמוּאֵל).

The use of a composite *shewa* (which is always vocal) in I-Guttural verbs sometimes creates situations where the suitable combination of silent *shewa* + vocal *shewa* in the strong verb (e.g., יִקְטְלוּ) creates an awkward combination of two vocal *shewas* in I-Guttural verbs (e.g., יִקְטְלוּ vs. *יֶחֱזְקוּ). When this happens, the composite *shewa* upgrades to a full vowel to help ease pronunciation (e.g., יֶחֱזְקוּ → יֶחֶזְקוּ), similar to what you saw with prepositions.

	Shewa upgrades		With composite *shewa*	Strong verb
Qal impf. (3mp)	יֶחֶזְקוּ	←	*יֶחֱזְקוּ	(יִקְטְלוּ)

vocal *shewa*
silent *shewa*

When a composite *shewa* upgrades to a full vowel, it does so only as an aid to pronunciation. The syllabification of the word remains consistent with its historic form. For example, יֶחֶזְקוּ is syllabified in the same manner as its strong verb counterpart יִקְ|טְ|לוּ (*yiq-tᵉ-lū*). Because the upgraded composite *shewa* is merely a helping vowel, the preformative syllable of this word is still theoretically closed יֶחֶ|זְ|קוּ. The upgraded Hebrew vowel was only made to ease pronunciation. Thus the *shewa* in יֶחֶזְקוּ is pronounced according to the strong form it represents and is vocal (i.e., *ye-ḥe-zᵉ-qū* NOT *ye-ḥez-qū*). The short vowels under the first two consonants of this word appear to break the vowel rules that you learned, that is, that closed unaccented syllables take short vowels. The upgraded vowel is only a helping vowel, and the preformative syllable is still theoretically closed.

ALEPH LIKES TO QUIESCE (CANAANITE SHIFT)

Several unique features of I-*Aleph* verbs are due to changes brought about by the tendency for *aleph* to quiesce. You should have little problem recognizing these anomalies because of your frequent exposure to the verb אמר in forms like לֵאמֹר ("to say" or "saying") and וַיֹּאמֶר ("and he said").

Aleph Quiesces (לֵאמֹר)

One place where quiescent *aleph* typically affects the final form of the word is the *qal* infinitive construct לֵאמֹר ("saying"). This form is nothing more than an adjustment of the anticipated I-Guttural form לֶאֱמֹר*. When the *aleph* quiesces, the preceding vowel lengthens to accommodate the open unaccented syllable (e.g., לֵאמֹר ← לֶאֱמֹר*). This form of the infinitive is generally seen only with the root אמר.

לֵאמֹר ← לֶאֱמֹר*

Canaanite Shift (וַיֹּאמֶר)

Another familiar form that looks different than what you learned is the *waw* consecutive imperfect וַיֹּאמֶר ("and he said"). The *qal* imperfect of אמר was historically יַאְמַר*, in keeping with the historic active *qal* patterns. When *aleph* quiesced, the preceding vowel lengthened (יָאמַר*). At some point in the development of the Hebrew language, almost all long ā vowels shifted to long ō. This change from ā → ō is referred to as the *Canaanite Shift* because it is a phenomenon common to the languages of Canaan but is not found in related languages outside Canaan (e.g., Hebrew לֹא vs. Aramaic לָא "not"). This shift from ā → ō produced the form you see today (יֹאמַר ← יָאמַר*).

	Waw Consec. impf.	Canaanite Shift	*Aleph* quiesces	Historic pattern
(pausal form)	וַיֹּאמַר	יֹאמַר ←	יָאמַר* ←	יַאְמַר*
(usual form)	וַיֹּאמֶר			

This shift from ā → ō consistently occurs in a few common I-*Aleph* verbs.[3] The remaining I-*Aleph* verbs may take this form but usually look just like any other I-Guttural verb where *aleph* does not quiesce (e.g. יֶאֱסֹף).

Aleph Drops (אֹאמְרָה → אֹמְרָה)

Two other forms that can prove a bit tricky are the first person singular *qal* imperfect and cohortative. Based on the familiar וַיֹּאמֶר (or וַיֹּאמַר in pause), one expects the imperfect and cohortative to be אֹאמַר and אֹאמְרָה respectively. While this is technically correct, the quiescent *aleph* of the root likes to drop out of these forms completely. The dropping of the *aleph* thus produces אֹמַר ("I will say") and אֹמְרָה ("let me say"). Though technically part of the 1cs preformative, the *aleph* provides a visual reminder of the I-*Aleph* root.

אֹמַר = Imperfect — not ptc. (אֹמֵר)

אֹמְרָה = Cohortative (אֹאמְרָה*) — or ptc. fs (אֹמְרָה)

2. The vowel chart in ch. 5 notes that true historic long ā vowels are extremely rare in Biblical Hebrew. Their rarity is due to the fact that original long ā shifted to ō during the Canaanite Shift. Long ā vowels that appear in Biblical Hebrew are generally lengthened short vowels.

3. It is consistently seen in five verbs: אבד, אבה, אכל, אמר, and אפה.

SUMMARY Main principles:

1. Gutturals do not double.
2. Gutturals prefer a-class vowels.
3. Gutturals often take composite *shewa.*
4. *Aleph* likes to quiesce (lose its consonantal value).

Keep in mind:

- Hebrew cannot have two vocal *shewas* in a row (יֶחֶזְקוּ NOT יֶחֶזְקוּ*)
- Remember the special forms of I-*Aleph* verbs (אָמַר, לֵאמֹר, וַיֹּאמֶר)

What Questions Should I Ask When I Read?

Unlike consonants that drop, coalesce, or double, the gutturals remain visibly present, allowing you to identify the verbal root. The feature of gutturals most likely to affect your recognition of the verb form is their lack of doubling. When you see a guttural, ask yourself if the vowel preceding it could result from compensatory lengthening and thus correspond with the strong verb *niphal* (יִקָּטֵל). The second feature to consider is whether the gutturals' preference for a-class vowels might preserve historic vowel patterns. Remember, an a-class preformative vowel can appear in the *hiphil* or the historic *qal* and *niphal.*

Now that you have been introduced to most of the weak verb tendencies, watch out for verbs that combine the weakness of a I-Guttural with weakness in other positions. For example, the initial guttural of the root could be combined with a III-*Waw/Yod* עָשָׂה ("to make do"), II-*Waw/Yod* חוּס ("to pity), or a Geminate חָלַל ("to pollute, defile"). In such cases, the verb in the biblical text exhibits features of both weaknesses (e.g., עֲשִׂיתֶם is a *qal* pf. 2mp from עשׂה, "you made").

REPRESENTATIVE FORMS: I-GUTTURAL AND I-ALEPH VERBS

	I-Guttural					I-Aleph	
	Qal		*Niphal*	*Hiphil*	*Hophal*	*Qal*	
	active	stative					
Perfect	עָמַד	חָזַק	נֶעֱמַד†	הֶעֱמִיד	הָעֳמַד	אָכַל	אָמַר
Impf.	יַעֲמֹד *yaqtul*	יֶחֱזַק *yiqtal*	יֵעָמֵד	יַעֲמִיד	יָעֳמַד	יֹאכַל	יֹאמַר
Waw Consec.	וַיַּעֲמֹד	וַיֶּחֱזַק	וַיֵּעָמֵד	וַיַּעֲמֵד	וַיָּעֳמַד	וַיֹּאכַל	וַיֹּ֫אמֶר וַיֹּאמַ֫ר
Impv.	עֲמֹד	חֲזַק‡	הֵעָמֵד	הַעֲמֵד		אֱכֹל	אֱמֹר‡
Coh.	אֶעֶמְדָה	אֶחֶזְקָה	אֵעָֽמְדָה	אַעֲמִ֫ידָה		אֹכְלָה	אֹמְרָה
Inf. Cst.	עֲמֹד	חֲזַק	הֵעָמֵד	הַעֲמִיד	הָעֳמַד	אֱכֹל	אֱמֹר (לֵאמֹר)
Inf. Abs.	עָמוֹד	חָזוֹק	הֵעָמֹד	הַעֲמֵד	הָעֳמֵד	אָכוֹל	אָמוֹר
Ptc.	עֹמֵד	חָזֵק	נֶעֱמָד	מַעֲמִיד	מָעֳמָד	אֹכֵל	אֹמֵר

† For some reason the original a-class preformative vowel is retained in some forms but not in others.

‡ Notice that I-Gutturals generally prefer the a-class composite *shewa*, but the I-*Aleph* verbs prefer the i-class composite *shewa*.

I-GUTTURAL VERB CHART

	QAL		NIPHAL	HIPHIL	HOPHAL	QAL (I-Aleph)
Perfect						
	עָמַד	חָזַק	נֶעֱמַד	הֶעֱמִיד	הָעֳמַד	אָכַל
	עָֽמְדָה	חָֽזְקָה	נֶעֶמְדָה	הֶעֱמִידָה	הָעָמְדָה	אָֽכְלָה
	עָמַדְתָּ	חָזַקְתָּ	נֶעֱמַדְתָּ	הֶעֱמַדְתָּ	הָעֳמַדְתָּ	אָכַלְתָּ
	עָמַדְתְּ	חָזַקְתְּ	נֶעֱמַדְתְּ	הֶעֱמַדְתְּ	הָעֳמַדְתְּ	אָכַלְתְּ
	עָמַדְתִּי	חָזַקְתִּי	נֶעֱמַדְתִּי	הֶעֱמַדְתִּי	הָעֳמַדְתִּי	אָכַלְתִּי
	עָֽמְדוּ	חָֽזְקוּ	נֶעֶמְדוּ	הֶעֱמִידוּ	הָעָמְדוּ	אָֽכְלוּ
	עֲמַדְתֶּם	חֲזַקְתֶּם	נֶעֱמַדְתֶּם	הֶעֱמַדְתֶּם	הָעֳמַדְתֶּם	אֲכַלְתֶּם
	עֲמַדְתֶּן	חֲזַקְתֶּן	נֶעֱמַדְתֶּן	הֶעֱמַדְתֶּן	הָעֳמַדְתֶּן	אֲכַלְתֶּן
	עָמַדְנוּ	חָזַקְנוּ	נֶעֱמַדְנוּ	הֶעֱמַדְנוּ	הָעֳמַדְנוּ	אָכַלְנוּ
Imperfect						
	יַעֲמֹד	יֶחֱזַק	יֵעָמֵד	יַעֲמִיד	יָעֳמַד	יֹאכַל
	תַּעֲמֹד	תֶּחֱזַק	תֵּעָמֵד	תַּעֲמִיד	תָּעֳמַד	תֹּאכַל
	תַּעֲמֹד	תֶּחֱזַק	תֵּעָמֵד	תַּעֲמִיד	תָּעֳמַד	תֹּאכַל
	תַּעַמְדִי	תֶּחֶזְקִי	תֵּעָֽמְדִי	תַּעֲמִידִי	תָּעָמְדִי	תֹּאכְלִי
	אֶעֱמֹד	אֶחֱזַק	אֵעָמֵד	אַעֲמִיד	אָעֳמַד	אֹכַל (= אֹאכַל)
	יַעַמְדוּ	יֶחֶזְקוּ	יֵעָֽמְדוּ	יַעֲמִידוּ	יָעָמְדוּ	יֹאכְלוּ
	תַּעֲמֹדְנָה	תֶּחֱזַקְנָה	תֵּעָמַדְנָה	תַּעֲמֵדְנָה	תָּעֳמַדְנָה	תֹּאכַלְנָה
	תַּעַמְדוּ	תֶּחֶזְקוּ	תֵּעָֽמְדוּ	תַּעֲמִידוּ	תָּעָמְדוּ	תֹּאכְלוּ
	תַּעֲמֹדְנָה	תֶּחֱזַקְנָה	תֵּעָמַדְנָה	תַּעֲמֵדְנָה	תָּעֳמַדְנָה	תֹּאכַלְנָה
	נַעֲמֹד	נֶחֱזַק	נֵעָמֵד	נַעֲמִיד	נָעֳמַד	נֹאכַל
Imperative						
	עֲמֹד	חֲזַק	הֵעָמֵד	הַעֲמֵד		אֱכֹל
	עִמְדִי	חִזְקִי	הֵעָֽמְדִי	הַעֲמִידִי		אִכְלִי
	עִמְדוּ	חִזְקוּ	הֵעָֽמְדוּ	הַעֲמִידוּ		אִכְלוּ
	עֲמֹדְנָה	חֲזַקְנָה	הֵעָמַדְנָה	הַעֲמֵדְנָה		אֱכֹלְנָה
Inf. Cst.						
	עֲמֹד	חֲזַק	הֵעָמֵד	הַעֲמִיד	הָעֳמַד	אֱכֹל
Inf. Abs.						
	עָמוֹד	חָזוֹק	הֵעָמֹד נַעֲמֹד	הַעֲמֵד	הָעֳמֵד	אָכוֹל

QAL	NIPHAL	HIPHIL	HOPHAL	QAL (I-Aleph)
Participle				
עֹמֵד	נֶעֱמָד	מַעֲמִיד	מָעֳמָד	אֹכֵל
עֹמְדָה	נֶעֱמָדָה	מַעֲמִידָה	מָעֳמָדָה	אֹכְלָה
עֹמְדִים	נֶעֱמָדִים	מַעֲמִידִים	מָעֳמָדִים	אֹכְלִים
עֹמְדוֹת	נֶעֱמָדוֹת	מַעֲמִידוֹת	מָעֳמָדוֹת	אֹכְלוֹת

CHAPTER 32

II-Guttural Verbs

Verbal roots with the gutturals or the consonant ר appearing as the second root consonant (II-Guttural verbs) exhibit the same characteristics as those encountered in I-Guttural verbs. II-Guttural verbs differ from the strong verb based on the conditions surrounding the second root letter.

II-GUTTURAL: BASIC PRINCIPLES

Gutturals exhibit four tendencies; however only three apply to II-Guttural verbs.

1. **Gutturals do not double.**
2. **Gutturals prefer a-class vowels.**
3. **Gutturals often take composite shewa.**
4. Aleph *likes to quiesce (lose its consonantal value).*

The tendency of *aleph* to quiesce (lose its consonantal value) does not occur in II-Guttural verbs. In the historic forms of all verbs, the second consonant carried a vowel—preserved in Biblical Hebrew forms by a vowel or a vocal *shewa.* Because *aleph* cannot quiesce when it has a vowel of its own, *aleph* in the middle of a root functions as a regular guttural.

GUTTURALS DO NOT DOUBLE (PIEL–HITHPAEL)

The inability of gutturals to double impacts all *piel, pual,* and *hithpael* verbs. In most cases the preceding vowel lengthens to "compensate" for what should have been a closed unaccented syllable (e.g., *piel* impf. יְקַטֵּל vs. יְבָרֵךְ "he will bless"). In other cases, the vowel remains unchanged as if doubling is still in effect (e.g., *piel* impf. יְקַטֵּל vs. יְכַהֵן "he serves as a priest"). This "implicit doubling" typically occurs with the "h" consonants ה and ח (i.e., honorary doubling), though it can occur with other gutturals as well.[1] When you encounter a guttural in the second position of the root, look for a long vowel that could signal compensation for doubling or be alert for short vowels that do not stand in the expected closed unaccented syllable . Those features indicate that you are dealing with a *piel*, *pual*, or *hithpael*. The following chart illustrates both compensatory lengthening and honorary doubling using the verbs ברך ("to bless") and כהן ("to act as a priest") even though these roots may not appear in all these forms.

	Strong verb	Compensatory lengthening	Honorary doubling
Piel pf.	קִטֵּל	בֵּרֵךְ	כִּהֵן
Piel impf.	יְקַטֵּל	יְבָרֵךְ	יְכַהֵן
Pual impf.	יְקֻטַּל	יְבֹרַךְ	יְכֻהַן

Since compensatory lengthening and implicit doubling represent the closed unaccented syllable of the *piel*, *pual*, and *hithpael*, these syllables are stable and unchangeable. No matter what form the verb takes, the vowel adjustments remain to help signal a *piel*, *pual*, or *hithpael*. In other words, even when sufformatives or suffixes are added, the resulting distant open syllable is still considered historically closed and does not reduce (e.g., כִּהַנְתֶּם).

GUTTURALS PREFER A-CLASS VOWELS

A guttural's general preference for a-class vowels occasionally results in a verb appearing with an a-class theme vowel in place of the expected vowel of the strong verb. For example, the *piel* perfect of ברך ("to bless") appears with the expected theme vowel of the *piel* strong verb (בֵּרֵךְ) for קִטֵּל but also appears as בֵּרַךְ. The a-class theme vowel in בֵּרַךְ is a by-product of a guttural's preference for a-class vowels.

1. For example, verbs with ע as the second consonant of the root tend to prefer implicit doubling in the *piel* but compensatory lengthening in the *pual* and *hithpael*.

The remaining elements of the form confirm that בֵּרַךְ is still a *piel.* When you encounter verb forms that do not match what you learned in the strong verb, look for gutturals that might be subtly impacting the form of the verb.

GUTTURALS PREFER COMPOSITE SHEWA

II-Guttural verbs also tend to exhibit composite *shewa* in forms where the strong verb has a vocal *shewa* (e.g., יִקְטְלוּ vs. יִבְחֲרוּ). As long as you remember that *a* shewa *is a* shewa *is a* shewa and that the composite *shewa* is there to aid in the pronunciation of the guttural, you should have little trouble identifying and translating these verb forms.

SUMMARY

Learn to look for potential weak consonants when you examine verbs. Then consider the basic principles for gutturals and *resh* that you have learned.

1. Gutturals do not double (e.g., בֵּרֵךְ and כִּהֵן).
2. Gutturals prefer a-class vowels (e.g., בֵּרֵךְ vs. בֵּרַךְ).
3. Gutturals often take composite *shewa* (e.g., יִבְחֲרוּ).
4. *Aleph* likes to quiesce (lose its consonantal value).

What Questions Should I Ask When I Read?

The main consideration for II-Guttural verbs is their effect on the *piel, pual,* and *hithpael* stems. The characteristic doubling that you have come to rely on does not appear with a guttural. Look for compensatory lengthening or honorary doubling of the preceding vowel (e.g., *piel* impf. יְבָרֵךְ and יְכַהֵן respectively). Even though honorary doubling means there are no changes to the vowels, you can still recognize its presence by the short vowel in an open unaccented syllable. The other preferences for a-class vowels and composite *shewa* are not going to affect your recognition of the root or verb form.

Watch out for the combination of other weaknesses coupled with gutturals in the second position—e.g., III-*Waw/Yod* רָאָה ("to see"), I-*Waw/Yod* יָהַב ("to give"), Geminate רָעַע ("to be bad"), I-*Nun* נָחַם ("to be sorry, console oneself"), and I-Guttural אָחַז ("to seize, hold"). In such cases, the verb in the biblical text exhibits features of both weaknesses (e.g., וַיֹּאחֲזוּ is a *qal waw* consec. impf. 3mp from אחז, "and they seized").

REPRESENTATIVE FORMS: II-GUTTURAL VERBS

	Qal	*Niphal*	*Piel*	*Pual*	*Hithpael*
Perfect	בָּחַר	נִבְחַר	בֵּרֵךְ	בֹּרַךְ	הִתְבָּרֵךְ
			בֵּרַךְ		
Impf.	יִבְחַר	יִבָּחֵר	יְבָרֵךְ	יְבֹרַךְ	יִתְבָּרֵךְ
Waw Consec.	וַיִּבְחַר	וַיִּבָּחֵר	וַיְבָ֫רֶךְ	וַיְבֹרַךְ	וַיִּתְבָּרֵךְ
Impv.	בְּחַר	הִבָּחֵר	בָּרֵךְ		הִתְבָּרֵךְ
Inf. Cst.	בְּחַר	הִבָּחֵר	בָּרֵךְ	בֹּרַךְ	הִתְבָּרֵךְ
Inf. Abs.	בָּחוֹר	נִבְחֹר	בָּרֵךְ		הִתְבָּרֵךְ
Ptc.	בֹּחֵר	נִבְחָר	מְבָרֵךְ	מְבֹרָךְ	מִתְבָּרֵךְ

II-GUTTURAL VERB CHART

	QAL	NIPHAL	PIEL	PUAL	HITHPAEL
Perfect					
	בָּחַר	נִבְחַר	בֵּרֵךְ (בֵּרַךְ)	בֹּרַךְ	הִתְבָּרֵךְ
	בָּֽחֲרָה	נִבְחֲרָה	בֵּרְכָה	בֹּרְכָה	הִתְבָּֽרְכָה
	בָּחַ֫רְתָּ	נִבְחַ֫רְתָּ	בֵּרַ֫כְתָּ	בֹּרַ֫כְתָּ	הִתְבָּרַ֫כְתָּ
	בָּחַ֫רְתְּ	נִבְחַ֫רְתְּ	בֵּרַ֫כְתְּ	בֹּרַ֫כְתְּ	הִתְבָּרַ֫כְתְּ
	בָּחַ֫רְתִּי	נִבְחַ֫רְתִּי	בֵּרַ֫כְתִּי	בֹּרַ֫כְתִּי	הִתְבָּרַ֫כְתִּי
	בָּֽחֲרוּ	נִבְחֲרוּ	בֵּרְכוּ	בֹּרְכוּ	הִתְבָּֽרְכוּ
	בְּחַרְתֶּם	נִבְחַרְתֶּם	בֵּרַכְתֶּם	בֹּרַכְתֶּם	הִתְבָּרַכְתֶּם
	בְּחַרְתֶּן	נִבְחַרְתֶּן	בֵּרַכְתֶּן	בֹּרַכְתֶּן	הִתְבָּרַכְתֶּן
	בָּחַ֫רְנוּ	נִבְחַ֫רְנוּ	בֵּרַ֫כְנוּ	בֹּרַ֫כְנוּ	הִתְבָּרַ֫כְנוּ
Imperfect					
	יִבְחַר	יִבָּחֵר	יְבָרֵךְ	יְבֹרַךְ	יִתְבָּרֵךְ
	תִּבְחַר	תִּבָּחֵר	תְּבָרֵךְ	תְּבֹרַךְ	תִּתְבָּרֵךְ
	תִּבְחַר	תִּבָּחֵר	תְּבָרֵךְ	תְּבֹרַךְ	תִּתְבָּרֵךְ
	תִּבְחֲרִי	תִּבָּֽחֲרִי	תְּבָֽרְכִי	תְּבֹֽרְכִי	תִּתְבָּֽרְכִי
	אֶבְחַר	אֶבָּחֵר	אֲבָרֵךְ	אֲבֹרַךְ	אֶתְבָּרֵךְ
	יִבְחֲרוּ	יִבָּֽחֲרוּ	יְבָֽרְכוּ	יְבֹֽרְכוּ	יִתְבָּֽרְכוּ
	תִּבְחַ֫רְנָה	תִּבָּחַ֫רְנָה	תְּבָרַ֫כְנָה	תְּבֹרַ֫כְנָה	תִּתְבָּרַ֫כְנָה
	תִּבְחֲרוּ	תִּבָּֽחֲרוּ	תְּבָֽרְכוּ	תְּבֹֽרְכוּ	תִּתְבָּֽרְכוּ
	תִּבְחַ֫רְנָה	תִּבָּחַ֫רְנָה	תְּבָרַ֫כְנָה	תְּבֹרַ֫כְנָה	תִּתְבָּרַ֫כְנָה
	נִבְחַר	נִבָּחֵר	נְבָרֵךְ	נְבֹרַךְ	נִתְבָּרֵךְ
Imperative					
	בְּחַר	הִבָּחֵר	בָּרֵךְ		הִתְבָּרֵךְ
	בַּחֲרִי	הִבָּֽחֲרִי	בָּֽרְכִי		הִתְבָּֽרְכִי
	בַּחֲרוּ	הִבָּֽחֲרוּ	בָּֽרְכוּ		הִתְבָּֽרְכוּ
	בְּחַ֫רְנָה	הִבָּחַ֫רְנָה	בָּרַ֫כְנָה		הִתְבָּרַ֫כְנָה
Inf. Cst.					
	בְּחַר	הִבָּחֵר	בָּרֵךְ	בֹּרַךְ	הִתְבָּרֵךְ
Inf. Abs.					
	בָּחוֹר	נִבְחֹר/הִבָּחֹר	בָּרֵךְ	בֹּרַךְ	הִתְבָּרֵךְ

	QAL	NIPHAL	PIEL	PUAL	HITHPAEL
Participle					
	בֹּחֵר	נִבְחָר	מְבָרֵךְ	מְבֹרָךְ	מִתְבָּרֵךְ
	בֹּחֲרָה	נִבְחָרָה	מְבָֽרְכָה	מְבֹרָכָה	מִתְבָּֽרְכָה
	בֹּחֲרִים	נִבְחָרִים	מְבָֽרְכִים	מְבֹרָכִים	מִתְבָּֽרְכִים
	בֹּחֲרוֹת	נִבְחָרוֹת	מְבָֽרְכוֹת	מְבֹרָכוֹת	מִתְבָּֽרְכוֹת

CHAPTER 33

III-Guttural and III-*Aleph* Verbs

As you have seen in the last two lessons, roots with guttural letters exhibit a number of predictable characteristics.

1. *Gutturals* do not double.
2. **Gutturals prefer a-class vowels.**
3. *Gutturals* often take composite *shewa.*
4. ***Aleph* likes to quiesce (lose its consonantal value).**

III-GUTTURAL: BASIC PRINCIPLES

These features are not all prominent in III-Guttural verbs. The strong verb paradigms do not call for doubling of the third consonant of the root, though the final consonant may be doubled in weak verb stems. Moreover, the transition from root to sufformative does not typically require a composite *shewa* (e.g., שָׁמַעְתִּי) like one sees in the transition from the preformative to root (e.g., יַעֲמֹד). As a result, III-Guttural verbs primarily exhibit a preference for a-class theme vowels and the quiescing of *aleph* inevitable in III-*Aleph* verbs.

GUTTURALS PREFER A-CLASS VOWELS

The III-Guttural verbs display a consistent preference for a-class theme vowels, whether that be the original theme vowel, a replacement for other vowels, or the addition of an a-class helping vowel to ease pronunciation. The reason for this preference is that the a-class vowel is pronounced in the back of the throat close to where the guttural is produced and creates a helpful transition in sound. If the strong verb already has an a-class theme vowel, there is no need for change (e.g., *pual* שֻׁלַּח). But forms that usually take other theme vowels typically substitute an a-class theme vowel in place of the standard pattern (e.g., שִׁלַּח vs. קִטֵּל). As a result, the a-class theme vowel is the common theme vowel of III-Guttural verbs.

Helping Vowels

While III-Guttural verbs typically trade out the i-class and u-class theme vowels of the strong verb in favor of an a-class vowel, some forms use a helping vowel to smooth out the transition into the guttural (e.g., יַשְׁלִ֫יחַ vs. יַקְטִיל). You learned this helping vowel by the name furtive *pataḥ*. This furtive *pataḥ* is unnecessary when sufformatives are added because pronunciation is already smoothed out when the guttural picks up a new syllable (e.g., מַשְׁלִ֫יחִים). As a result, the helping vowel generally appears only when the guttural is the last sound heard in the verb (e.g., *hiphil* pf. הִשְׁלִ֫יחַ).

The only other place where III-Guttural verbs need a helping vowel is in the 2fs perfect (e.g., קָטַ֫לְתְּ). The awkward consonant cluster at the end of this word is exacerbated by the presence of gutturals. As a result, the 2fs perfect in any verb stem adds a helping vowel in III-Guttural verbs (e.g., *qal* שָׁלַ֫חְתְּ → שָׁלַ֫חַתְּ "you sent"). The fact that this helping vowel is not part of the historic structure of the verb is evident from the *dagesh* at the end of the word. Since *dagesh forte* is not used at the end of words, the *dagesh* in שָׁלַ֫חַתְּ must be a *dagesh lene* (*BeGaD-KePhaT* dot). Yet *dagesh lene* is unexpected after a vowel. This anomaly alerts you to the presence of a helping vowel added solely for pronunciation purposes. Reliance on the sufformative and recognition that gutturals prefer a-class vowels should allow you to recognize the 2fs perfect of III-Gutturals.

	Helping vowel		Expected strong form
"you sent"	שָׁלַ֫חַתְּ	←	*שָׁלַ֫חְתְּ

The III-Guttural verbs that consistently use a helping vowel instead of substituting an a-class theme vowel are: (1) The participles and infinitive absolutes of all verb stems (e.g., *qal* ptc. שֹׁלֵחַ), (2) *hiphil* forms with *ḥireq yod* (e.g., *hiphil* pf. הִשְׁלִ֫יחַ), and (3) the *qal* infinitive construct (שְׁלֹחַ). Because of these helping vowels, forms that would be identical in the strong verb take a distinct vocalization in the III-Guttural verbs. For example, the strong form קְטֹל could be a *qal* imperative or infinitive construct. In III-Guttural roots, these forms can be differentiated by the helping vowel. The *qal* imperative שְׁלַח takes an a-class theme vowel and does not need a helping vowel. The *qal* infinitive construct שְׁלֹחַ is one of the forms that does take a helping vowel. You do not need to know which forms take a helping vowel. Though knowing which forms take a helping vowel can reduce your parsing options, it is sufficient to know what the helping vowels are and why they are there.

QUIESCING OF ALEPH (III-ALEPH)

III-*Aleph* verbs act differently than the other III-Guttural verbs. III-*Aleph* quiesces (loses its consonantal value) whenever it appears at the end of a syllable, i.e., at the end of a verb or before a consonantal sufformative (e.g., מָצָ֫אתִי). When *aleph* quiesces at the end of a word, it takes a long theme vowel. Many theme vowels are already long (e.g., קְטֹל and מְצֵא), but short a-class theme vowels lengthen (e.g., קָטַל → מָצָא).

קָטַל → מָצָא (quiescent *aleph* takes long vowel)

The *aleph* also quiesces when the verb has consonantal sufformatives. Other than the *qal*, all perfects with consonantal sufformatives take a long /ē/ theme vowel throughout the stems (e.g., *piel* 1cs pf. מִצֵּ֫אתִי), and the imperfect and related forms consistently take a short /e/ theme vowel with consonantal sufformatives (e.g., *piel* 2fp pf. תְּמַצֶּאנָה). The *qal* perfect utilizes long /ā/ and long /ē/ in order to maintain a distinction between active and stative forms. The active verbs have an a-class vowel and the stative verbs have the same i-class vowel (e.g., מָצָ֫אתִי "I found" vs. מָלֵ֫אתִי "I am full") as all the other stems.

מִצֵּ֫אתִי Perfects usually /ē/

מָצָ֫אתִי (*Qal* Active /ā/)

מָלֵ֫אתִי (*Qal* Stative /ē/)

יְמַצֶּ֫אנָה Others /e/

Though memorizing the parsing implications for each vowel pattern above helps in the recognition of forms, reliance on preformatives and sufformatives is usually sufficient. Your goal with this level of detail should be to understand the overall concepts so that seeing a vowel other than that of the expected strong form does not inhibit your recognition of the verb.

SUMMARY III-Guttural:

1. Generally take an a-class theme vowel in all paradigms.
2. Exceptions take a helping vowel to transition from the long vowel of the verb into the guttural (e.g., *hiphil* pf. הִשְׁלִיחַ).

III-*Aleph:*

1. Quiesce whenever the *aleph* would close a syllable in the strong form (end of a word and before consonantal sufformatives).
2. Vowels adjust to accommodate quiescing (e.g., *qal* pf. 3ms מָצָא and piel pf. מִצֵּאתִי).

What Next? If you have put in the time to read through this grammar and work through the exercises, you have acquired a life-long skill. Because this approach to Hebrew focuses on how the language works rather than mass memory of paradigms, you may grow rusty but you will not lose this skill.

In trying to maintain their Hebrew, students frequently set unreasonable objectives for reading and become discouraged by failing to meet those goals. Life is going to get in the way, so you need an approach that is sustainable. We suggest that you select one day of the week that is most convenient for reading Hebrew and that you select a reasonable time limit (not a passage length). Start in whatever book or passage you wish to translate and work through the passage until your time limit expires. During the rest of the week, daily read the same text you translated. Having already translated the passage it should take only a few minutes each subsequent day. In this way you will consistently read Hebrew and will reinforce your Hebrew skills in manageable bits. Also, if your "daily reading" happens only two or three times a week, you just reviewed a single passage three times. That is success!

Do not consider Hebrew a skill to master, but a language to engage. Remember that your purpose for learning Hebrew in the first place was to experience the joy of reading the biblical text. In that light, allow yourself to concentrate on the text for meaning and reflection, especially in your subsequent readings.

REPRESENTATIVE FORMS: III-GUTTURAL VERBS

	Qal	*Niphal*	*Piel*	*Pual*	*Hithpael*	*Hiphil*	*Hophal*
Pf.	שָׁלַח	נִשְׁלַח	שִׁלַּח	שֻׁלַּח	הִשְׁתַּלַּח	הִשְׁלִיחַ	הָשְׁלַח
(2fs)	שָׁלַחַתְּ	→ etc.					
Impf.	יִשְׁלַח	יִשָּׁלַח	יְשַׁלַּח	יְשֻׁלַּח	יִשְׁתַּלַּח	יַשְׁלִיחַ	יָשְׁלַח
Waw Consec.	וַיִּשְׁלַח	וַיִּשָּׁלַח	וַיְשַׁלַּח	וַיְשֻׁלַּח	וַיִּשְׁתַּלַּח	וַיַּשְׁלַח	וַיָּשְׁלַח
Impv.	שְׁלַח	הִשָּׁלַח	שַׁלַּח		הִשְׁתַּלַּח	הַשְׁלַח	
Inf. Cst.	שְׁלֹחַ	הִשָּׁלַח	שַׁלַּח		הִשְׁתַּלַּח	הַשְׁלִיחַ	
Inf. Abs.	שָׁלוֹחַ	נִשְׁלֹחַ	שַׁלֵּחַ			הַשְׁלֵחַ	הָשְׁלֵחַ
Ptc.	שֹׁלֵחַ	נִשְׁלָח	מְשַׁלֵּחַ	מְשֻׁלָּח	מִשְׁתַּלֵּחַ	מַשְׁלִיחַ	מָשְׁלָח

Gray Shading = Forms that typically exhibit the a-class helping vowel.

1. Participle and infinitive absolute (all stems)
2. *Hiphil* forms that take *ḥireq yod* theme vowel
3. *Qal* infinitive construct
4. Perfect 2fs (all stems)

REPRESENTATIVE FORMS: III-ALEPH VERBS

	Qal stative	*Qal* active	*Niphal*	*Piel*	*Pual*	*Hithpael*	*Hiphil*	*Hophal*
Perfect	מָלֵא	מָצָא	נִמְצָא	מִצֵּא	מֻצָּא	הִתְמַצֵּא	הִמְצִיא	הָמְצָא
(1cs)	מָלֵאתִי	מָצָאתִי	נִמְצֵאתִי	→ etc.				
Impf.		יִמְצָא	יִמָּצֵא	יְמַצֵּא	יְמֻצָּא	יִתְמַצֵּא	יַמְצִיא	יָמְצָא
(2fp)		תִּמְצֶאנָה	→ etc.					
Impv.		מְצָא	הִמָּצֵא	מַצֵּא		הִתְמַצֵּא	הַמְצֵא	
(2fp)		מְצֶאנָה	→ etc.					
Inf. Cst.		מְצֹא	הִמָּצֵא	מַצֵּא		הִתְמַצֵּא	הַמְצִיא	הָמְצָא
Inf. Abs.		מָצוֹא	נִמְצֹא	מַצֹּא		הִתְמַצֵּא	הַמְצֵא	הָמְצֵא
Ptc.		מֹצֵא	נִמְצָא	מְמַצֵּא	מְמֻצָּא	מִתְמַצֵּא	מַמְצִיא	מָמְצָא

Aleph would close a syllable

No Endings

מָצָא long vowels in all forms

Consonantal Endings

מִצֵּאתִי Perfects usually /ē/ (except *qal* active מָצָאתִי)

יְמַצֶּאנָה Remaining forms use /e/

Aleph opens a syllable

Vocalic Endings

מָצְאוּ Like strong verb

III-GUTTURAL VERB CHART

	QAL	NIPHAL	PIEL	PUAL	HITHPAEL	HIPHIL	HOPHAL
Perfect							
	שָׁלַח	נִשְׁלַח	שִׁלַּח	שֻׁלַּח	הִשְׁתַּלַּח	הִשְׁלִיחַ	הָשְׁלַח
	שָֽׁלְחָה	נִשְׁלְחָה	שִׁלְּחָה	שֻֽׁלְּחָה	הִשְׁתַּלְּחָה	הִשְׁלִ֫יחָה	הָשְׁלְחָה
	שָׁלַ֫חְתָּ	נִשְׁלַ֫חְתָּ	שִׁלַּ֫חְתָּ	שֻׁלַּ֫חְתָּ	הִשְׁתַּלַּ֫חְתָּ	הִשְׁלַ֫חְתָּ	הָשְׁלַ֫חְתָּ
	שָׁלַ֫חְתְּ	נִשְׁלַ֫חְתְּ	שִׁלַּ֫חְתְּ	שֻׁלַּ֫חְתְּ	הִשְׁתַּלַּ֫חְתְּ	הִשְׁלַ֫חְתְּ	הָשְׁלַ֫חְתְּ
	שָׁלַ֫חְתִּי	נִשְׁלַ֫חְתִּי	שִׁלַּ֫חְתִּי	שֻׁלַּ֫חְתִּי	הִשְׁתַּלַּ֫חְתִּי	הִשְׁלַ֫חְתִּי	הָשְׁלַ֫חְתִּי
	שָֽׁלְחוּ	נִשְׁלְחוּ	שִׁלְּחוּ	שֻֽׁלְּחוּ	הִשְׁתַּלְּחוּ	הִשְׁלִ֫יחוּ	הָשְׁלְחוּ
	שְׁלַחְתֶּם	נִשְׁלַחְתֶּם	שִׁלַּחְתֶּם	שֻׁלַּחְתֶּם	הִשְׁתַּלַּחְתֶּם	הִשְׁלַחְתֶּם	הָשְׁלַחְתֶּם
	שְׁלַחְתֶּן	נִשְׁלַחְתֶּן	שִׁלַּחְתֶּן	שֻׁלַּחְתֶּן	הִשְׁתַּלַּחְתֶּן	הִשְׁלַחְתֶּן	הָשְׁלַחְתֶּן
	שָׁלַ֫חְנוּ	נִשְׁלַ֫חְנוּ	שִׁלַּ֫חְנוּ	שֻׁלַּ֫חְנוּ	הִשְׁתַּלַּ֫חְנוּ	הִשְׁלַ֫חְנוּ	הָשְׁלַ֫חְנוּ
Imperfect							
	יִשְׁלַח	יִשָּׁלַח	יְשַׁלַּח	יְשֻׁלַּח	יִשְׁתַּלַּח	יַשְׁלִיחַ	יָשְׁלַח
	תִּשְׁלַח	תִּשָּׁלַח	תְּשַׁלַּח	תְּשֻׁלַּח	תִּשְׁתַּלַּח	תַּשְׁלִיחַ	תָּשְׁלַח
	תִּשְׁלַח	תִּשָּׁלַח	תְּשַׁלַּח	תְּשֻׁלַּח	תִּשְׁתַּלַּח	תַּשְׁלִיחַ	תָּשְׁלַח
	תִּשְׁלְחִי	תִּשָּׁלְחִי	תְּשַׁלְּחִי	תְּשֻׁלְּחִי	תִּשְׁתַּלְּחִי	תַּשְׁלִ֫יחִי	תָּשְׁלְחִי
	אֶשְׁלַח	אֶשָּׁלַח	אֲשַׁלַּח	אֲשֻׁלַּח	אֶשְׁתַּלַּח	אַשְׁלִיחַ	אָשְׁלַח
	יִשְׁלְחוּ	יִשָּׁלְחוּ	יְשַׁלְּחוּ	יְשֻׁלְּחוּ	יִשְׁתַּלְּחוּ	יַשְׁלִ֫יחוּ	יָשְׁלְחוּ
	תִּשְׁלַ֫חְנָה	תִּשָּׁלַ֫חְנָה	תְּשַׁלַּ֫חְנָה	תְּשֻׁלַּ֫חְנָה	תִּשְׁתַּלַּ֫חְנָה	תַּשְׁלַ֫חְנָה	תָּשְׁלַ֫חְנָה
	תִּשְׁלְחוּ	תִּשָּׁלְחוּ	תְּשַׁלְּחוּ	תְּשֻׁלְּחוּ	תִּשְׁתַּלְּחוּ	תַּשְׁלִ֫יחוּ	תָּשְׁלְחוּ
	תִּשְׁלַ֫חְנָה	תִּשָּׁלַ֫חְנָה	תְּשַׁלַּ֫חְנָה	תְּשֻׁלַּ֫חְנָה	תִּשְׁתַּלַּ֫חְנָה	תַּשְׁלַ֫חְנָה	תָּשְׁלַ֫חְנָה
	נִשְׁלַח	נִשָּׁלַח	נְשַׁלַּח	נְשֻׁלַּח	נִשְׁתַּלַּח	נַשְׁלִיחַ	נָשְׁלַח
Imperative							
	שְׁלַח	הִשָּׁלַח	שַׁלַּח		הִשְׁתַּלַּח	הַשְׁלַח	
	שִׁלְחִי	הִשָּׁלְחִי	שַׁלְּחִי		הִשְׁתַּלְּחִי	הַשְׁלִ֫יחִי	
	שִׁלְחוּ	הִשָּׁלְחוּ	שַׁלְּחוּ		הִשְׁתַּלְּחוּ	הַשְׁלִ֫יחוּ	
	שְׁלַ֫חְנָה	הִשָּׁלַ֫חְנָה	שַׁלַּ֫חְנָה		הִשְׁתַּלַּ֫חְנָה	הַשְׁלַ֫חְנָה	
Inf. Cst.							
	שְׁלֹחַ	הִשָּׁלַח	שַׁלַּח	שֻׁלַּח	הִשְׁתַּלַּח	הַשְׁלִיחַ	הָשְׁלַח
Inf. Abs.							
	שָׁלוֹחַ	נִשְׁלֹחַ	שַׁלֵּחַ	שֻׁלֹּח	הִשְׁתַּלֵּחַ	הַשְׁלֵחַ	הָשְׁלֵחַ

	QAL	NIPHAL	PIEL	PUAL	HITHPAEL	HIPHIL	HOPHAL
Participle							
	שֹׁלֵחַ	נִשְׁלָח	מְשַׁלֵּחַ	מְשֻׁלָּח	מִשְׁתַּלֵּחַ	מַשְׁלִיחַ	מָשְׁלָח
	שֹׁלְחָה	נִשְׁלָחָה	מְשַׁלְּחָה	מְשֻׁלָּחָה	מִשְׁתַּלְּחָה	מַשְׁלִיחָה	מָשְׁלָחָה
	שֹׁלְחִים	נִשְׁלָחִים	מְשַׁלְּחִים	מְשֻׁלָּחִים	מִשְׁתַּלְּחִים	מַשְׁלִיחִים	מָשְׁלָחִים
	שֹׁלְחוֹת	נִשְׁלָחוֹת	מְשַׁלְּחוֹת	מְשֻׁלָּחוֹת	מִשְׁתַּלְּחוֹת	מַשְׁלִיחוֹת	מָשְׁלָחוֹת

III-ALEPH VERB CHART

	QAL	NIPHAL	PIEL	PUAL	HITHPAEL	HIPHIL	HOPHAL
Perfect							
	מָצָא	נִמְצָא	מִצֵּא	מֻצָּא	הִתְמַצֵּא	הִמְצִיא	הָמְצָא
	מָֽצְאָה	נִמְצְאָה	מִצְּאָה	מֻצְּאָה	הִתְמַצְּאָה	הִמְצִיאָה	הָמְצְאָה
	מָצָאתָ	נִמְצֵאתָ	מִצֵּאתָ	מֻצֵּאתָ	הִתְמַצֵּאתָ	הִמְצֵאתָ	הָמְצֵאתָ
	מָצָאת	נִמְצֵאת	מִצֵּאת	מֻצֵּאת	הִתְמַצֵּאת	הִמְצֵאת	הָמְצֵאת
	מָצָאתִי	נִמְצֵאתִי	מִצֵּאתִי	מֻצֵּאתִי	הִתְמַצֵּאתִי	הִמְצֵאתִי	הָמְצֵאתִי
	מָֽצְאוּ	נִמְצְאוּ	מִצְּאוּ	מֻצְּאוּ	הִתְמַצְּאוּ	הִמְצִיאוּ	הָמְצְאוּ
	מְצָאתֶם	נִמְצֵאתֶם	מִצֵּאתֶם	מֻצֵּאתֶם	הִתְמַצֵּאתֶם	הִמְצֵאתֶם	הָמְצֵאתֶם
	מְצָאתֶן	נִמְצֵאתֶן	מִצֵּאתֶן	מֻצֵּאתֶן	הִתְמַצֵּאתֶן	הִמְצֵאתֶן	הָמְצֵאתֶן
	מָצָאנוּ	נִמְצֵאנוּ	מִצֵּאנוּ	מֻצֵּאנוּ	הִתְמַצֵּאנוּ	הִמְצֵאנוּ	הָמְצֵאנוּ
Imperfect							
	יִמְצָא	יִמָּצֵא	יְמַצֵּא	יְמֻצָּא	יִתְמַצֵּא	יַמְצִיא	יָמְצָא
	תִּמְצָא	תִּמָּצֵא	תְּמַצֵּא	תְּמֻצָּא	תִּתְמַצֵּא	תַּמְצִיא	תָּמְצָא
	תִּמְצָא	תִּמָּצֵא	תְּמַצֵּא	תְּמֻצָּא	תִּתְמַצֵּא	תַּמְצִיא	תָּמְצָא
	תִּמְצְאִי	תִּמָּֽצְאִי	תְּמַצְּאִי	תְּמֻצְּאִי	תִּתְמַצְּאִי	תַּמְצִיאִי	תָּמְצְאִי
	אֶמְצָא	אֶמָּצֵא	אֲמַצֵּא	אֲמֻצָּא	אֶתְמַצֵּא	אַמְצִיא	אָמְצָא
	יִמְצְאוּ	יִמָּֽצְאוּ	יְמַצְּאוּ	יְמֻצְּאוּ	יִתְמַצְּאוּ	יַמְצִיאוּ	יָמְצְאוּ
	תִּמְצֶאנָה	תִּמָּצֶאנָה	תְּמַצֶּאנָה	תְּמֻצֶּאנָה	תִּתְמַצֶּאנָה	תַּמְצֶאנָה	תָּמְצֶאנָה
	תִּמְצְאוּ	תִּמָּֽצְאוּ	תְּמַצְּאוּ	תְּמֻצְּאוּ	תִּתְמַצְּאוּ	תַּמְצִיאוּ	תָּמְצְאוּ
	תִּמְצֶאנָה	תִּמָּצֶאנָה	תְּמַצֶּאנָה	תְּמֻצֶּאנָה	תִּתְמַצֶּאנָה	תַּמְצֶאנָה	תָּמְצֶאנָה
	נִמְצָא	נִמָּצֵא	נְמַצֵּא	נְמֻצָּא	נִתְמַצֵּא	נַמְצִיא	נָמְצָא
Impv.							
	מְצָא	הִמָּצֵא	מַצֵּא		הִתְמַצֵּא	הַמְצֵא	
	מִצְאִי	הִמָּֽצְאִי	מַצְּאִי		הִתְמַצְּאִי	הַמְצִיאִי	
	מִצְאוּ	הִמָּֽצְאוּ	מַצְּאוּ		הִתְמַצְּאוּ	הַמְצִיאוּ	
	מְצֶאנָה	הִמָּצֶאנָה	מַצֶּאנָה		הִתְמַצֶּאנָה	הַמְצֶאנָה	
Inf. Cst.							
	מְצֹא	הִמָּצֵא	מַצֵּא	מֻצָּא	הִתְמַצֵּא	הַמְצִיא	הָמְצָא
Inf. Abs.							
	מָצוֹא	נִמְצֹא	מַצֹּא	מֻצָּא	הִתְמַצֵּא	הַמְצֵא	הָמְצֵא

	QAL	NIPHAL	PIEL	PUAL	HITHPAEL	HIPHIL	HOPHAL
Participle							
	מֹצֵא	נִמְצָא	מְמַצֵּא	מְמֻצָּא	מִתְמַצֵּא	מַמְצִיא	מָמְצָא
	מֹצְאָה	נִמְצָאָה	מְמַצְּאָה	מְמֻצָּאָה	מִתְמַצְּאָה	מַמְצִיאָה	מָמְצָאָה
	מֹצְאִים	נִמְצָאִים	מְמַצְּאִים	מְמֻצָּאִים	מִתְמַצְּאִים	מַמְצִיאִים	מָמְצָאִים
	מֹצְאוֹת	נִמְצָאוֹת	מְמַצְּאוֹת	מְמֻצָּאוֹת	מִתְמַצְּאוֹת	מַמְצִיאוֹת	מָמְצָאוֹת

APPENDIX 1

Introduction to the Hebrew Bible

THE HEBREW BIBLE AND ENGLISH TRANSLATIONS

The order of the books in English translations is different from that found in Hebrew Bibles. Though both contain the same content, Hebrew groups the material into twenty-four books, as opposed to English translations that are divided into thirty-nine books (e.g, 1-2 Samuel is viewed as one book).

Arrangement of the Hebrew Canon

HEBREW BIBLE (BHS)
(24 Books)

Law
Genesis
Exodus
Leviticus
Numbers
Deuteronomy

Prophets

Former	Latter
Joshua	Isaiah
Judges	Jeremiah
Samuel	Ezekiel
Kings	Twelve Minor Prophets

Writings

Poetry	Scrolls	History
Psalms	Ruth	Daniel
Job	Song	Ezra/Neh
Prov	Eccl	Chr
	Lam	Esther
	Esther	

ENGLISH TRANSLATIONS
(39 Books)

Law
Genesis
Exodus
Leviticus
Numbers
Deuteronomy

History

Joshua	II Kings
Judges	I Chronicles
Ruth	II Chronicles
I Samuel	Ezra
II Samuel	Nehemiah
I Kings	Esther

Poetry
Job
Psalms
Proverbs
Ecclesiastes
Song of Songs

Prophets

	Minor Prophets	
Isaiah		
Jeremiah	Hos	Nah
Lam	Joel	Hab
Ezekiel	Amos	Zeph
Daniel	Obad	Hag
	Jonah	Zech
	Micah	Mal

The three sections of the Hebrew Bible are referred to as the Law (*Torah*), the Prophets (*N^{e}vi'im*), and the Writings (*K^{e}tuvim*). You may sometimes see a reference to the Hebrew Bible calling it the Tanak, which is an acronym based on the first letter in the name of each section of the Hebrew canon. The *Torah* or Pentateuch ("Five Scrolls") has the same arrangement in all Bibles. The Prophets and the Writings are consistent in their contents but vary widely from manuscript to manuscript in the arrangement of books within each section.[1]

Names of Hebrew Books

Sometimes Hebrew language resources refer to the biblical books by their Hebrew names. Some books are named after their major character while others are based off a key word or phrase from the first verse of the book. You should be able to recognize the titles of books derived from personal names, but others will be more difficult. The list below provides the Hebrew titles along with the English equivalent when the Hebrew does not match the English name. Though books that are divided into "First" and "Second" in English translations are treated as one book in Hebrew, they are often referred to as א and ב (1 and 2) in the page headings of the Hebrew Bible.

1. For a discussion of the various manuscripts and their arrangements of the Prophets and Writings, see Roger T. Beckwith, *The Old Testament Canon of the New Testament Church and Its Background in Early Judaism* (Grand Rapids: Eerdmans, 1985).

Genesis	בְּרֵאשִׁית	***In the beginning*** God created . . . (1:1)
Exodus	שְׁמוֹת	And these are ***the names of*** the sons of Israel . . . (1:1)
Leviticus	וַיִּקְרָא	And the Lord ***called*** to Moses . . . (1:1)
Numbers	בְּמִדְבַּר	And the Lord spoke to Moses ***in the wilderness of*** Sinai . . . (1:1)
Deuteronomy	דְּבָרִים	These are the ***words*** which Moses spoke . . . (1:1)
Joshua	יְהוֹשֻׁעַ	
Judges	שֹׁפְטִים	
Samuel	שְׁמוּאֵל	
Kings	מְלָכִים	
Isaiah	יְשַׁעְיָהוּ	
Jeremiah	יִרְמְיָהוּ	
Ezekiel	יְחֶזְקֵאל	
Hosea	הוֹשֵׁעַ	
Joel	יוֹאֵל	
Amos	עָמוֹס	
Obadiah	עֹבַדְיָה	
Jonah	יוֹנָה	
Micah	מִיכָה	
Nahum	נַחוּם	
Habakkuk	חֲבַקּוּק	
Zephaniah	צְפַנְיָה	
Haggai	חַגַּי	
Zechariah	זְכַרְיָה	
Malachi	מַלְאָכִי	
Psalms	תְּהִלִּים	
Proverbs	מִשְׁלֵי	***The proverbs of*** Solomon . . . (1:1)
Job	אִיּוֹב	
Ruth	רוּת	
Song of Songs	שִׁיר הַשִּׁירִים	
Lamentations	אֵיכָה	***How*** alone sits the city . . . (1:1)
Ecclesiastes	קֹהֶלֶת	The words of ***the Preacher*** . . . (1:1)
Esther	אֶסְתֵּר	
Daniel	דָּנִיֵּאל	
Ezra	עֶזְרָא	
Nehemiah	נְחֶמְיָה	
Chronicles	דִּבְרֵי הַיָּמִים	(lit. *the matters of the days*)

Chapter and Verse Divisions

Chapter and verse divisions in the Hebrew Bible are much the same as those in English translations. However, they sometimes differ, and citation in Hebrew reference tools may not always correspond with the verse references as you know them. For example, Joel appears with four chapters in Hebrew and three chapters in English though they contain the same content. Moreover, Psalm 3:1 (Eng) corresponds to 3:2 (Heb) because psalm headings are assigned a verse number in Hebrew. Many resources alert you to these differences, but if you get stuck, look a little before or after the text you are studying.

FEATURES OF THE HEBREW BIBLE

The Text

Most printed editions of the Hebrew Bible, including *Biblia Hebraica Stuttgartensia (BHS)*, are based on the Leningrad Codex (1008 CE).[2] Though the Dead Sea Scroll discoveries predate this text by a thousand years, this reliable manuscript is the earliest complete copy of the Hebrew Bible.[3] Printed editions replicate both the text of the Leningrad Codex and a number of extra features provided by the Masoretes that copied it (discussed below). Moreover, critical editions that are used for research add a section at the bottom of each page, called a critical apparatus, listing readings from other manuscripts that support or depart from the Leningrad Codex.[4] An overview of the critical apparatus is best found in an introduction to textual criticism (see bibliography).

Liturgical Notations

Some Hebrew Bibles (like *BHS*) include abbreviations in the margins that serve as division markers for the annual reading cycles. These marginal notations ס and פרש represent the groupings of two distinct

2. K. Elliger and W. Rudolph, *Biblia Hebraica Stuttgartensia*, 5th ed. revised by A. Schenker (Stuttgart: Deutsche Bibelgesellschaft, 1997).

3. The *Hebrew University Bible* [HUB] prefers to use the partially damaged Aleppo Codex (980 CE) where possible. An introduction to the methodology and format of this edition can be found in M. H. Goshen-Gottstein, *The Book of Isaiah: Sample Edition with Introduction* (Jerusalem: Magnus Press, 1965) 7–45.

4. The most commonly used critical edition is *BHS*. A new edition called *Biblia Hebraica Quinta (BHQ)* is in progress, with a number of volumes already published. For a general introduction to the project with critical texts of Ruth and Esther, texts read in the *Learning Biblical Hebrew Workbook*, see A. Schenker, ed., *Biblia Hebraica Quinta: General Introduction and Megilloth*, Fascicle 18 (Stuttgart: Deutsche Bibelgesellschaft, 2004). Another type of critical edition, an *eclectic text* ("selected text"), does not represent a text appearing in any single manuscript but rather scholars' best reconstruction from all the available manuscripts. The variant readings used to produce such an edition are again organized and listed in a critical apparatus so that the reader can assess the data. See Michael V. Fox, *Proverbs: An Eclectic Edition with Introduction and Textual Commentary* (Atlanta, GA: SBL Press, 2015).

5. The division of the Pentateuch into 154–167 sections in the Palestinian tradition or 53–54 divisions in the Babylonian tradition is due to variations in how the passages are grouped when read in the synagogue.

reading traditions, a Palestinian reading tradition and a Babylonian reading tradition.

The large ס that appears in the inner margin represents one "section" or *seder* (סֵ֫דֶר) of a three-year reading cycle. The rabbis in Palestine divided the Torah into 154–167 sections (סְדָרִים) so that the Torah would be read in the synagogue once every three to three and one-half years. The *seder* notation is sometimes followed by a Hebrew number identifying its place in the book (e.g., [כ֫] ס = section 20). The same *seder* markings occur in the Prophets and Writings although the precise significance of these divisions is uncertain.

The abbreviation פרשׁ is also placed in the inner margin and represents one "division" or *parashah* (פָּרָשָׁה) of the Babylonian reading cycle. The rabbis in Babylon divided up the Torah into 53 divisions (פָּרָשׁוֹת; today there are 54) so that it was read in the synagogue once every year.[5] The *parashah* division is not used outside of the Pentateuch.

Section Breaks

In addition to the notations in the margin, Hebrew Bibles place a פ or ס within the text to indicate section breaks. These section breaks (*parashiyot*) are comparable to English paragraphs. To mark a major section break, the scribes left the rest of the line open. Eventually scribes inserted the letter פ (for Aramaic פְּתוּחָא "open") to signify the open line of a major section break. To mark a minor section break, the scribes left a gap but continued writing on the same line following that gap. These minor section breaks are marked with ס (standing for the Aramaic word סְתוּמָא "closed") to indicate a closed gap in the line. While section breaks are consistently seen in manuscripts, their placement is not standardized. You will also notice that the verse divisions (which were added later) do not always correspond with these section breaks.

The Ketiv/Qere

Hebrew Bibles also have a method for marking alternate readings within the text. These markings identify instances of what is called *ketiv/qere* (from כתב "to write" and קרא "to read"). As scribes were copying the text, they occasionally came to consonants in their base text that did not match their reading tradition. To preserve the integrity of the text, scribes wrote the consonantal text just as it was written in their base text (the *ketiv*) but supplied the vowels of the word required by their long-standing reading tradition (the *qere*). When you encounter a *ketiv/qere* it is possible that one is an error, but it is also possible that both preserve valid reading traditions.

Words affected by *ketiv/qere* are presented in different ways. In editions like *BHS*, the consonants in the text are pointed with the vowels of the word in the scribe's reading tradition. The word in the Hebrew text is then marked with a circle on top, and the notation קׄ in the margin provides the reader with the consonants that go with those vowels. In student-friendly editions like the *Reader's Hebrew Bible*, the words appear back-to-back.[6] The word the scribe saw written (*ketiv*) appears first with the vowels that belong to that word. The word the scribe wanted read (*qere*) appears immediately following in brackets with its appropriate vowels. In the following illustrations, gray is used to represent what the scribe saw in the text and red to represent his reading tradition.

Ruth 1:8

קׄ יעשׂ	יַעְ֫שֹׂ֫ה יְהוָ֨ה עִמָּכֶם֙ חֶ֔סֶד	*BHS*
	יַעֲשֶׂ֣ה [יַ֣עַשׂ] יְהוָ֨ה עִמָּכֶם֙ חֶ֔סֶד	*Readers*

Both examples above indicate that the scribe saw יעשׂה in his base text ("he will do"), but his reading tradition led him to expect the word יַ֣עַשׂ ("may he do").

Perpetual Qere

Most of the *qere* readings are indicated by a notation in the text. However, some *qere* readings are so common that the readers' familiarity with them was assumed. For example, the pronoun הוא is used for both masculine and feminine forms in the Pentateuch and thus is pointed either as הוּא ("him") or הִוא (for הִיא "her"). Other examples of the perpetual *qere* include the word Jerusalem (יְרוּשָׁלַ֫ם read as יְרוּשָׁלַ֫יִם) and God's personal name (יְהוָה read as אֲדֹנָי).[7] No marginal spellings are provided for these words.

6. A. Philip Brown II and Bryan W. Smith, eds. *A Reader's Hebrew Bible* (Grand Rapids: Zondervan, 2008).

7. For further discussion, see Exercise 3B in the *Learning Biblical Hebrew Workbook*.

APPENDIX 2

Hebrew Accents

In addition to adding the vowel pointing to Hebrew texts, the Masoretes included a system of accents. Two different sets of accents are used, one for Job, Psalms, and Proverbs and the other for all the other books of the Hebrew Bible. On a basic level the principles and major accents of these sets are similar, making it possible to discuss both sets together. The accentuation system in the Hebrew Bible serves three different purposes: (1) to indicate the stressed syllables for pronunciation, (2) to mark word groupings (syntax), and (3) to provide musical notations for chanting the text in the synagogue.

INDICATE STRESSED SYLLABLES FOR PRONUNCIATION

One of the functions of the Hebrew accents is to mark the syllable that receives the stress in any given word (see arrows below). Regardless of the appearance, most accents identify the stressed syllable. Note, for example, the Hebrew text of Gen 1:1.

בְּרֵאשִׁ֖ית בָּרָ֣א אֱלֹהִ֑ים אֵ֥ת הַשָּׁמַ֖יִם וְאֵ֥ת הָאָֽרֶץ׃

↑ ↑ ↑ ↑ ↑ ↑ ↑

A handful of accents are not linked to any syllable but stand immediately before or after the word. One accent is repeated when the stress is not on the end of the word (e.g., Gen 1:2 תֹ֙הוּ֙ וָבֹ֔הוּ pronounced ***tō***′-*hū*), but other times you have to rely on your knowledge of word formation and pronunciation. For example, the accent in עֲבָדֶיךָ֙ ("your servants") always appears at the end of the word. Only a knowledge of suffix endings alerts you to the correct pronunciation of עֲבָדֶיךָ֙ as *a-vā-**dē*′**-kā*.

MARK WORD GROUPINGS

Another function of the Masoretic accents is to indicate the natural word groupings within the sentence. The representation of thought units is accomplished by using two different kinds of accents: (1) *disjunctive accents* that mark subtle breaks or pauses in the sentence structure, and (2) *conjunctive accents* that connect a word to what follows. The basic accents of each type are listed below in order of relative weight. This list is not exhaustive but includes those accents most helpful for determining how the Masoretes understood the relationship between words.[1]

Disjunctive Accents

:□□̩□ — *Soph pasuq* (:□□□) and *silluq* (□□̩□) The *silluq* with *soph pasuq* falls on the final word of each verse. The *silluq* marks the accented syllable, and the *soph pasuq* marks the "end of the verse."[2]

□□֑□ — *Atnaḥ:* The *atnaḥ* marks the main pause within the verse.

□□֥□֫ — *Oleh veyored: This accent is used only in Job, Psalms, and Proverbs.* When used, it replaces *atnaḥ* to mark the main pause in longer verses, with *atnaḥ* then providing a secondary break between *oleh v*[e]*yored* and the end of the verse.

□□֔□ & □□֕□ — *Zaqeph qaton* (□□֔□) and *zaqeph gadol* (□□֕□): These accent marks subdivide each half of the verse created by the *atnaḥ*. Because the *zaqeph gadol* (□□֕□) is restricted as to when it can occur, the *zaqeph qaton* (□□֔□) is more

1. Some printed copies of *BHS* include a bookmark called "Tabula Accentum" that offers a quick reference to the Masoretic accents (e.g., K. Elliger and W. Rudolph, *Biblia Hebraica Stuttgartensia*, 5th ed. revised by A. Schenker [Stuttgart: Deutsche Bibelgesellschaft, 1997]).

2. The *silluq* is similar in appearance to the *metheg* ("bridle"), but *silluq* is easily identified as it always appears in the last word of the verse.

common. These two accents do not appear in Job, Psalms, and Proverbs.

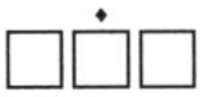

Revia: The *revia* is used to further subdivide the units of thought within the verse.

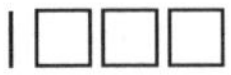

Paseq: The *paseq* marks a *slight* pause within the *lowest* subdivisions of a verse. It is included here because students wonder what it means. While the *paseq* is disjunctive, it is so weak that its significance is nearly inperceptiable (at least relative to its appearance).

The disjunctive accents aid in the translation process by alerting the reader to a traditional understanding of the thought breaks in a verse. If you hit a disjunctive accent, be sure that you have a unit of thought. It will not necessarily be a complete clause (subject + verb), but it should be a complete phrase. The disjunctive accents allow you to focus on a limited number of words at a time and provide boundaries for connecting ideas within the verse.

Conjunctive Accents

The conjunctive accents serve to *join* words into thought groups. Unlike disjunctives that signal a break in thought, conjunctive accents indicate that you need to keep reading; the author has not yet completed a thought. The most common conjunctives are recognizable because they look like they are pointing you forward to the next word.

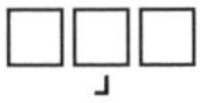

Munaḥ

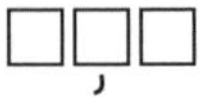

Merka = read on to the next word

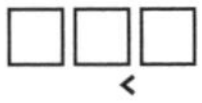

Mahpak

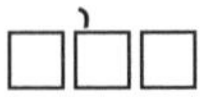

Azla

CANTILLATION MARKS

Another function of the accents in the Hebrew Bible is to provide melodies for chanting (or singing) the Hebrew text in the synagogue. In general, each accent mark represents a musical melody (called a *trope*) that is sung every time you encounter that accent. However, the melodies vary for each section of the Hebrew Bible (the Pentateuch, the Prophets, and the Scrolls, namely Song of Songs, Ruth, Lamentations, Ecclesiastes, Esther). They also differ somewhat between the various Jewish traditions (e.g., Ashkenazi, Sephardi, Yemenite). Further, a few accents have multiple melodies, and the correct one is chosen in conjunction with the type of accent that follows. Thus Hebrew cantillation is a highly specialized art and requires considerable training.

Below you will find the tropes for Deut 6:4–5. The initial note (or *upbeat*) is used on every unaccented syllable prior to the accented syllable. The melody itself is sung on the accent. For a fuller discussion of Hebrew chanting see *Haftarah Chanting*.[3]

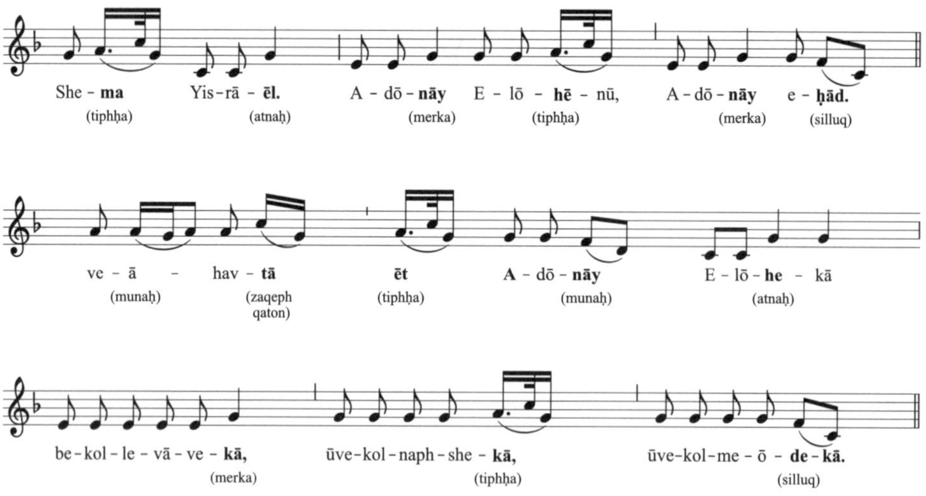

PASSSAGES WITH DOUBLE ACCENTS

Some texts are marked with two different reading traditions simultaneously—Genesis 35:22 and the two passages containing the Decalogue or Ten Commandments (Exod 20:2–17 and Deut 5:6–22).[4] In each case, the same set of accents (the set for the majority of books in the Hebrew Bible) is applied twice, once for each reading tradition.

3. Pinchas Spiro, *Haftarah Chanting*, rev. ed. (New York: Board of Jewish Education of Greater New York, 1994).

4. Generally speaking, the two cantillation patterns in the Decalogue affect whether you hear individual verses or hear ten statements (Ten Commandments).

To illustrate what this looks like in the text, consider the simplest example. In Gen 35:22 the words אָבִ֑י "his father") and יִשְׂרָאֵ֑ל "Israel") each have two major accents. The *atnaḥ* under אָבִ֑י ("his father") is paired with the *silluq* under יִשְׂרָאֵ֑ל ("Israel") and indicates a tradition that ends the verse after the phrase "and Israel heard" in the middle of line two below (signalled also by the פ paragraph break). The *atnaḥ* under יִשְׂרָאֵ֑ל ("Israel") reflects a second reading tradition that is paired with the second *silluq* to end the verse after the phrase, "and Jacob had twelve sons" (signalled also by the *soph pasuq* :).

22 וַיְהִ֗י בִּשְׁכֹּ֤ן יִשְׂרָאֵל֙ בָּאָ֣רֶץ הַהִ֔וא וַיֵּ֣לֶךְ רְאוּבֵ֗ן וַיִּשְׁכַּ֕ב אֶת־ב
פִּילֶ֣גֶשׁ אָבִ֑יו וַיִּשְׁמַ֖ע יִשְׂרָאֵ֑ל פ וַיִּהְי֥וּ בְנֵֽי־יַעֲקֹ֖ב שְׁנֵ֥ים עָשָֽׂר׃
23 בְּנֵ֣י לֵאָ֔ה בְּכ֥וֹר יַעֲקֹ֖ב רְאוּבֵ֑ן וְשִׁמְעוֹן֙ וְלֵוִ֣י וִיהוּדָ֔ה וְיִשָּׂשכָ֖ר ...

Tradition A, marked by the red accents, creates a natural break between the recounting of Reuben's disgraceful act and the following list of Jacob's sons. Tradition B continues to the end of verse 22 so that the reader's last thought is on the introduction of Jacob's other children.

Tradition A

Reuben went and slept with Bilhah,
his father's concubine,
and Israel heard.

Now Jacob had twelve sons:
The sons of Leah: Reuben . . .

Tradition B

Reuben went and slept with Bilhah,
his father's concubine.
and Israel heard.
But Jacob had twelve sons.

The sons of Leah: Reuben . . .

The differences emphasized in the translations above reflect the role of the accents in preserving early interpretations of the text. Keep in mind that the accents are a later addition. Though not definitive,[5] these accents reflect an ancient reading tradition that predates their insertion into the text and need be given careful consideration.

5. Alternate traditions related to the interpretation of phrases, verses, and entire passages are embedded in ancient translations like the Greek Septuagint and Aramaic Targums and preserved in discussions in rabbinic works.

APPENDIX 3

How to Create a Grammatical Diagram

One technique that is quite helpful for analyzing Hebrew texts is the use of grammatical diagrams. Diagramming is more effective in certain genres, but it has positive benefits for any passage. It forces you to consciously consider the relationship between the various phrases of the passage and to trace the author's flow of thought. Note the following example:

Genesis 1

↓ In the beginning
God created the heavens and the earth.

> *The decision to indent these phrases reflects a realization that they indicate the context or circumstance in which the main action takes place, i.e., they are subordinate to the main clause.*

Now the earth was formless and void
and darkness was over the surface of the deep
and the spirit of God was hovering over the face of the waters.

And God said, "Let there be light."
And there was light.
And God saw that the light was good.
And God separated between the light and the darkness.
And God called the light day
And the darkness he called night.

Ideally a grammatical diagram should be created from the original text as an expression of how the text should be interpreted. If someone does not know Hebrew, a grammatical diagram can be done from an English translation as well. However, you must realize that an English grammatical diagram is one step further removed in the exegetical process. English grammatical diagrams show you how *other people* have interpreted the text so that you can begin the process of analysis and interpretation on your own. English grammatical diagrams are best done with several different translations of a passage as a means of identifying the issues of interpretation that need to be resolved. Differences between the English versions highlight where scholars have differences of opinion.

While there can be many technical and complex elements to a grammatical diagram, the core idea is quite basic. Diagramming is simply a visual alignment of the phrases and clauses so that you can see parallel ideas, related points, supporting ideas, and so on. Stated another way, it is a visual representation of the author's flow of thought.

STEP 1: SELECT A PASSAGE

As you begin, make sure that the passage you are studying contains a cohesive unit of thought. Also keep in mind that each segment is part of a larger context. That context will have a significant bearing upon how you interpret the passage, just as your diagram will impact your assessment of that broader context. For example, let's take a portion of text from the book of Deuteronomy.

Deuteronomy 4:5–8

5 See, I have taught you statutes and judgments, as the LORD my God commanded
me, so that you should do them in the midst of the land that you are entering to
possess. 6 Keep them and do them, for that will be your wisdom and your under-
standing in the sight of the peoples who will hear all these statutes and will say,
"Surely this great nation is a wise and understanding people." 7 For what great
nation is there that has a god so near to it as the LORD our God, whenever we
call upon him? 8 And what great nation is there that has righteous statutes and
judgments like all this teaching that I am setting before you today?

5 רְאֵה ׀ לִמַּדְתִּי אֶתְכֶם חֻקִּים וּמִשְׁפָּטִים כַּאֲשֶׁר צִוַּנִי יְהוָה אֱלֹהָי לַעֲשׂוֹת
כֵּן בְּקֶרֶב הָאָרֶץ אֲשֶׁר אַתֶּם בָּאִים שָׁמָּה לְרִשְׁתָּהּ׃ 6 וּשְׁמַרְתֶּם וַעֲשִׂיתֶם
כִּי הִוא חָכְמַתְכֶם וּבִינַתְכֶם לְעֵינֵי הָעַמִּים אֲשֶׁר יִשְׁמְעוּן אֵת כָּל־הַחֻקִּים
הָאֵלֶּה וְאָמְרוּ רַק עַם־חָכָם וְנָבוֹן הַגּוֹי הַגָּדוֹל הַזֶּה׃ 7 כִּי מִי־גוֹי גָּדוֹל אֲשֶׁר־
לוֹ אֱלֹהִים קְרֹבִים אֵלָיו כַּיהוָה אֱלֹהֵינוּ בְּכָל־קָרְאֵנוּ אֵלָיו׃ 8 וּמִי גּוֹי גָּדוֹל אֲשֶׁר־
לוֹ חֻקִּים וּמִשְׁפָּטִים צַדִּיקִם כְּכֹל הַתּוֹרָה הַזֹּאת אֲשֶׁר אָנֹכִי נֹתֵן לִפְנֵיכֶם הַיּוֹם׃

STEP 2: ISOLATE THE CLAUSES

The next step in the process is to isolate each individual clause (subject + verb + modifiers) and place it on its own line. The easiest way to identify clauses is by spotting each verb. Each verb is placed on its own line along with the words that are associated with it.

NOTE: For those diagramming in Hebrew, remember to isolate all verbs whether stated or implied. A verbless clause is still a clause.

5 ***See,***
I have ***taught*** you statutes and judgments,
as the Lord my God ***commanded*** me,
so that you ***should do*** them in the midst of the land
that you ***are entering*** to possess.
6 ***Keep*** them
and ***do*** them,
for that ***will be*** your wisdom and your understanding in the sight of the peoples
who ***will hear*** all these statutes
and ***will say,***
"Surely this great nation ***is*** a wise and understanding people"
7 For what great nation ***is*** there
that ***has*** a god so near to it as the Lord our God,
whenever we ***call*** upon him?
8 And what great nation ***is*** there
that ***has*** righteous statutes and judgments like all this teaching
that I ***am setting*** before you today?

5 רְאֵה ׀
לִמַּדְתִּי אֶתְכֶם חֻקִּים וּמִשְׁפָּטִים
כַּאֲשֶׁר צִוַּנִי יְהוָה אֱלֹהָי
לַעֲשׂוֹת כֵּן בְּקֶרֶב הָאָרֶץ
אֲשֶׁר אַתֶּם בָּאִים שָׁמָּה לְרִשְׁתָּהּ׃
6 וּשְׁמַרְתֶּם
וַעֲשִׂיתֶם
כִּי הִוא חָכְמַתְכֶם וּבִינַתְכֶם לְעֵינֵי הָעַמִּים
אֲשֶׁר יִשְׁמְעוּן אֵת כָּל־הַחֻקִּים הָאֵלֶּה
וְאָמְרוּ
רַק עַם־חָכָם וְנָבוֹן הַגּוֹי הַגָּדוֹל הַזֶּה׃
7 כִּי מִי־גוֹי גָּדוֹל
אֲשֶׁר־לוֹ אֱלֹהִים קְרֹבִים אֵלָיו כַּיהוָה אֱלֹהֵינוּ
בְּכָל־קָרְאֵנוּ אֵלָיו׃
8 וּמִי גּוֹי גָּדוֹל
אֲשֶׁר־לוֹ חֻקִּים וּמִשְׁפָּטִים צַדִּיקִם כְּכֹל הַתּוֹרָה הַזֹּאת
אֲשֶׁר אָנֹכִי נֹתֵן לִפְנֵיכֶם הַיּוֹם׃

STEP 3: DIAGRAM THE CLAUSES

Now that you have the clauses separated, begin from the first clause and arrange the clauses in a manner that reflects the development and relationship of ideas. This identification is accomplished through the use of indenting subordinate phrases and visually displaying the relationship between clauses by means of arrows and lines. Moreover, the final product should allow you to read the passage from top to bottom in the same order as it appears in the biblical text (even if you have to get creative with the use of dashes, arrows, and ellipses).

Main Clauses Belong at the Outer Margin

Main clauses provide the primary sequence of events or the core ideas in a discussion. The main clauses should appear at the outer margin of the page. For English grammatical diagrams this means leaving these clauses at the far left of the page. Hebrew grammatical diagrams will place them at the far right of the page.

Supporting Items are Indented

Information that refines the main clause is indented whether it appears before or after the main clause. These indented clauses are referred to as subordinate (think "supporting"). Key words like כִּי ("because, that") and אֲשֶׁר ("that, which") are frequently used to signal a supporting clause. Words and phrases that describe elements of the main clause (like adjectives or adverbs) may also be set apart on a separate line and indented. These elements should be indented so that they appear directly beneath the main word they modify. The "rules" here are not precise, and sometimes it is easier to leave smaller units on the same line with the larger clause. Remember, the approach to diagramming presented here focuses on how the main ideas in the text relate to one another.

Align Parallel Ideas

Places where the text says the same thing in various ways (called *apposition* or restatement) can be stacked to help you better see the relationship of the parts. For example, in Gen 22:2 God told Abraham "Take your son, your only one whom you love, Isaac, and go to the land of Moriah." We might want to stack several of these restated items for greater clarity.

```
Take|your son,
    |         ↑ your only one
    |         | whom you love,
    |Isaac,
and go to the land of Moriah
```

The apposition of "your son" and "Isaac" is marked by a solid line to visually highlight their parallel relationship. Likewise, the identifiers "your only one" and "whom you love" are both indented to the same degree and are linked by an arrow pointing to the word they describe. When we capture this apposition on a grammatical level, we consciously recognize that God is calling attention to the cost of this request.

Isolate Adverbial Phrases and Clauses: How? When? Where? Why?

You should also isolate phrases that explain the verb. A phrase that is adverbial (i.e., it modifies the verb) answers the questions: How? When? Where? Why? If a phrase answers these questions, it should be placed on its own line.

Identify Adjective Clauses: Who? Which? What Kind? How Many?

Adjectival clauses ask questions that are distinct from those asked by adverbs. Adjectives answer the questions: Who? Which? What kind? How many? Generally speaking, you will not isolate words or phrases that function adjectivally (e.g., "righteous"). We often leave these with the main clause to avoid fragmenting the basic idea. However, we do isolate adjectival clauses (i.e., those with a verb). This is especially common with adjectival clauses introduced by the relative pronoun "which, that, who" (אֲשֶׁר).

Set Off Dialogue in Boxes

When a text includes direct speech (i.e., a quotation), use a dialogue box to set the entire quotation apart. The dialogue box indicates that this material functions as a unit in the diagram. For example, instead of "they will say ***it***," Deut 4:6 asserts, "And they will say, ***Surely this great nation is …***" The entire quotation functions as the object of the verb. The dialogue box allows you to see the role of the unit and to analyze the development of ideas within the quotation itself.

Carefully Analyze the Options

As you think through each clause, carefully evaluate the ways that a particular clause might relate to the surrounding context. (Is it offering a parallel idea? Is it offering support to a clause that precedes or follows?, etc.) For indented material, use an up arrow to indicate a connection with the preceding clauses (↑), a down arrow to indicate a connection with the following clauses (↓), and vertical lines and extended arrows to join multiple components together (|). Remember that adverbial phrases and clauses should be aligned with the verb, adjective, or other adverb that they modify. Adjectival clauses should be aligned with the noun or pronoun they modify.

The following pages present completed grammatical diagrams of Deut 4:5–8 in both English and Hebrew. Examine them carefully to help learn the process of creating a grammatical diagram.

USING THE DIAGRAM AS A TOOL FOR MEANING

The primary purpose of a grammatical diagram is not to produce a visual representation of the passage but to force you to consciously consider the relationship between clauses.

Weighing the Interpretive Options

In some cases grammar and context may allow for more than one way to represent the ideas; and these alternatives can significantly affect the way that you understand the passage. Do not be discouraged when there is more than one viable option. In fact, recognizing the strengths of different options promotes humility and an understanding of why some interpret the text differently than you do. For example, in Deut 4:5–8 there are two ways that you can associate v. 7 with the preceding verse.

Option One

DO THESE LAWS BECAUSE YOU HAVE A PRIVILEGED RELATIONSHIP WITH GOD

6 **Keep them**
and do them,
↑ for that will be | your wisdom (= Why?)
↑ | and your understanding
| in the sight of the peoples (= Where?)
↑ who will hear all these statutes (= Who?)
| and will say, ‘Surely this great nations is a wise and understanding people.’
7 | **For what great nation is there** (= Why?)
↑ **that has a god so near to it . . .**

If you approach the passage in the manner depicted above, then God's people are asked to perform God's laws because of the privileged relationship that they have with God. No other nation has such an intimate relationship with the God of the universe or any of their own gods, and so they should not trivialize that unique status by failing to live in a manner pleasing to God.

Option Two

THE NATIONS WILL BE AMAZED BECAUSE YOUR RELATIONSHIP WITH GOD IS SO UNLIKE THEIR OWN

6 Keep them
and do them,
↑ for that will be | your wisdom (= Why?)
↑ | and your understanding
| in the sight of **the peoples** (= Where?)
↑ **who will hear** all these statutes (= Who?)
| and **will say**, | 'Surely this great nation is a a wise and understanding people.'
↑
7 | **For what great nation is there** (= Why?)
↑ **that has a god so near to it** . . .

This second approach implies that the nations will be amazed at the wisdom and understanding displayed by the people of God because it is so unique in relation to their own experience with their deities. The wisdom and understanding that they perceive will not be based on Israel's own merit but on the character of God and the fact that he granted Israel special access to him and a personal revelation of his character reflected in his instructions for their conduct.

Finding the Main Point

As you work through any passage, remember that the layout itself does not determine or indicate significance. The main verbs on the outside margin do not necessarily indicate the focus of the passage. Sometimes the main clauses are merely the framework for the idea the author is developing. The grammatical diagram simply illustrates the flow of thought. The heart and theme of the passage must be determined by the context and details of the text.

DEUTERONOMY 4:5–8 (GRAMMATICAL DIAGRAM)

5 See,
I have taught you statutes and judgments,
↑ as the LORD my God commanded me, (= How?)
so that you should do them (= Why?)
↑ in the midst of the land (= Where?)
↑ that you are entering to possess. (= Which?)

6 Keep them
and do them,
↑ for that will be | your wisdom (= Why?)
and your understanding
↑ in the sight of the peoples (= Where?)
↑ who | will hear all these statutes (= Who?)
and will say, ‘Surely this great nation is a wise and understanding people.’
↑
7 For what great nation is there (= Why?)
↑ that has a god so near to it (= Which?)
↑ as the LORD our God, (= How?)
whenever we call upon him? (= When?)

8 And what great nation is there (= Why?)
↑ that has righteous statutes and judgments (= Which?)
↑ like all this teaching (= What kind?)
↑ that I am setting before you today? (= Which?)

DEUTERONOMY 4:5–8 (GRAMMATICAL DIAGRAM)

5 רְאֵה ׀
לִמַּדְתִּי אֶתְכֶם חֻקִּים וּמִשְׁפָּטִים
↑ כַּאֲשֶׁר צִוַּנִי יְהוָה אֱלֹהָי (= How?)
לַעֲשׂוֹת כֵּן (= Why?)
↑ בְּקֶרֶב הָאָרֶץ (= Where?)
↑ אֲשֶׁר אַתֶּם בָּאִים שָׁמָּה לְרִשְׁתָּהּ׃ (= Which?)

6 וּשְׁמַרְתֶּם
וַעֲשִׂיתֶם
↑ כִּי הִוא חָכְמַתְכֶם וּבִינַתְכֶם (= Why?)
↑ לְעֵינֵי הָעַמִּים (= Where?)
↑ אֲשֶׁר | יִשְׁמְעוּן אֵת כָּל־הַחֻקִּים הָאֵלֶּה (= Who?)
| וְאָמְרוּ [רַק עַם־חָכָם וְנָבוֹן הַגּוֹי הַגָּדוֹל הַזֶּה׃]

↑
7 כִּי מִי־גוֹי גָּדוֹל (= Why?)
↑ אֲשֶׁר־לוֹ אֱלֹהִים קְרֹבִים אֵלָיו (= Which?)
↑ כַּיהוָה אֱלֹהֵינוּ (= How?)
בְּכָל־קָרְאֵנוּ אֵלָיו׃ (= When?)

8 וּמִי גּוֹי גָּדוֹל (= Why?)
↑ אֲשֶׁר־לוֹ חֻקִּים וּמִשְׁפָּטִים צַדִּיקִם (= Which?)
↑ כְּכֹל הַתּוֹרָה הַזֹּאת (= What kind?)
↑ אֲשֶׁר אָנֹכִי נֹתֵן לִפְנֵיכֶם הַיּוֹם׃ (= Which?)

APPENDIX 4

How to Create a Thematic Outline

A thematic outline allows you to reflect on the focus of the author's message. A thematic outline is not a summary of content. Your translation already represents *what the passage says.* Your diagram reflects *how the author says it.* The goal of a thematic outline is to describe *why the author says it this way.* Thematic outlines can vary widely in terms of how a reader expresses her or his observations and reflections on the text. The variations may focus on highlighting different nuances, but readers who diagram the passage in the same manner will reflect the same basic interpretation of the author's message.

A thematic outline forces you to move beyond content and requires that you consider both the author's intentions and the persuasive force of the text. If you have done your grammatical diagram well, the thematic outline should materialize quite naturally from the questions you asked of the text while diagramming. The thematic outline should be simple and concise and may be artistic and creative. Regardless, it should be worded in such a way that it guides the reader through the author's flow of thought. You will find that the grammatical diagram and thematic outline both help in determining how you might teach or discuss a passage.

The treatment of Deut 4 on the following page illustrates the transition from grammatical diagram to thematic outline. Ideally, a thematic outline will evidence the passage's relationship to the broader context. For simplicity, the following outline addresses the passage as self-contained.

DEUTERONOMY 4:5–8 (THEMATIC OUTLINE)

Grammatical Diagram

5 See,
I have taught you statutes and judgments,
↑ as the LORD my God commanded me, (= How?)
so that you should do them (= Why?)
↑ in the midst of the land (= Where?)
↑ that you are entering to possess. (= Which?)

6 Keep them
and do them,
↑ for that will be | your wisdom (= Why?)
and your understanding
↑ in the sight of the peoples (= Where?)
↑ who | will hear all these statutes (= Who?)
and will say, 'Surely this great nation is a wise and understanding people.'
↑
7 For what great nation is there (= Why?)
↑ that has a god so near to it (= Which?)
↑ as the LORD our God, (= How?)
whenever we call upon him? (= When?)
8 And what great nation is there (= Why?)
↑ that has righteous statutes and judgments (= Which?)
↑ like all this teaching (= What kind?)
↑ that I am setting before you today? (= Which?)

Thematic Outline

I. Torah given to the people
- from God
- for the future
(implicit assurance of a future)

II. Invitation to obey
- because Torah reflects wisdom to the nations
- because Torah evidences divine presence unparalleled among the nations
- because Torah promotes justice & equity surpassing that of the nations

DEUTERONOMY 4:5–8 (THEMATIC OUTLINE)

Thematic Outline	Grammatical Diagram
I. Torah given to the people • from God • for the future (implicit assurance of a future)	5 רְאֵה ׀ לִמַּדְתִּי אֶתְכֶם חֻקִּים וּמִשְׁפָּטִים (= How?) ↑כַּאֲשֶׁר צִוַּנִי יְהוָה אֱלֹהָי (= Why?) לַעֲשׂוֹת כֵּן (= Where?) ↑בְּקֶרֶב הָאָרֶץ (= Which?) ↑אֲשֶׁר אַתֶּם בָּאִים שָׁמָּה לְרִשְׁתָּהּ׃
II. Invitation to obey • because Torah reflects wisdom tp the nations.	6 וּשְׁמַרְתֶּם וַעֲשִׂיתֶם (= Why?) ↑כִּי הִוא חָכְמַתְכֶם וּבִינַתְכֶם (= Where?) ↑לְעֵינֵי הָעַמִּים ↑אֲשֶׁר | (= Who?) יִשְׁמְעוּן אֵת כָּל־הַחֻקִּים הָאֵלֶּה וְאָמְרוּ | רַק עַם־חָכָם וְנָבוֹן הַגּוֹי הַגָּדוֹל הַזֶּה׃
• because Torah evidences divine presence unparalleled among the nations	7 ↑ (= Why?) כִּי מִי־גוֹי גָּדוֹל (= Which?) ↑אֲשֶׁר־לוֹ אֱלֹהִים קְרֹבִים אֵלָיו (= How?) ↑כַּיהוָה אֱלֹהֵינוּ (= When?) בְּכָל־קָרְאֵנוּ אֵלָיו׃
• because Torah promotes justice & equity surpassing that of the nations	8 (= Why?) וּמִי גּוֹי גָּדוֹל (= Which?) ↑אֲשֶׁר־לוֹ חֻקִּים וּמִשְׁפָּטִים צַדִּיקִם (= What kind?) ↑כְּכֹל הַתּוֹרָה הַזֹּאת (= Which?) ↑אֲשֶׁר אָנֹכִי נֹתֵן לִפְנֵיכֶם הַיּוֹם׃

Following a survey of the history of Israel's disobedience in contrast to God's faithfulness (Deut 1-4) and preceeding the formal instruction (Deut 4), Moses addresses the people in light of their relationship to Torah (Deut 4:5-8). The positive content of these verses both underscores their significance and suggests that the commands to "do" and "obey" are an invitation to participate in something astounding.[1] The commandments come directly from God, are given to the people for their new land (with implied assurance of that land), will be internationally recognized for their wisdom, evidence God's presence with his people, and promote justice and equity surpassing any yet known among the nations.

1. See also Daniel Block, "The Grace of Torah: The Mosaic Prescription for Life (Deut 4:1-8; 6:20-25)," in *How I Love Your Torah, O Lord!: Studies in the Book of Deuteronomy* (Eugene, OR: Wipf & Stock, 2011), 1–20.

APPENDIX 5

Transliteration

The following discussion explains the transliteration system used in many articles and books to represent Hebrew words using English letters. In order to make the information more accessible to English readers, many commentaries and reference works do not use the Hebrew alphabet when printing words or phrases from the biblical text. Instead they use transliteration. Transliteration attempts to represent each Hebrew character with a single English equivalent so that you can tell exactly how a word is spelled in the Hebrew text.[1]

TRANSLITERATION OF HEBREW CONSONANTS

Most of the Hebrew transliterations are fairly easy to remember (e.g., ב = b). However, some features of transliteration are not as straightforward. Letters that have no sound in English are represented by symbols (e.g., א = ʾ and ע = ʿ). Hebrew letters with similar sounds are distinguished by diacritical markings (e.g., ט, ת = ṭ, t respectively). For other letters, the simplest way to represent the sound with English characters would mistakenly lead one to think that there are two letters present (e.g., שׁ = š, NOT sh, which would imply סה). Finally, some transliteration symbols reflect the way the letter was originally pronounced rather than its modern pronunciation (e.g., ו = w, NOT v). Note that transliteration does not distinguish between medial and final forms (e.g., both מ and ם = m).

Here are a few hints to help you remember the English equivalents. For א = ʾ and ע = ʿ remember that the symbol for א curves left (think

1. When dealing with older scholarly works you may encounter subtle variations in the transliteration systems, but they have been standardized in recent years. With technological upgrades it has also become more common to include the Hebrew font in published materials.

aleph = "*a-left*"). The forms with the dot beneath them indicate hard sounds. The consonant ḥ = hard 'h' or ח.[2] Remember that ס = s, but the /s/ sounds that are distinguished by dots on top of the Hebrew character (שׂ/שׁ) are similarly distinguished by diacritical markings on top in English transliteration (ś/š). It may help to note that the diacritical mark on ś for שׂ points down to where the dot would appear on the Hebrew letter.

Transliteration of Hebrew Consonants

א	ʾ	מ	m
בּ/ב	b/ḇ (pronounced *b/v*)	נ	n
גּ/ג	g/ḡ	ס	s
דּ/ד	d/ḏ	ע	ʿ
ה	h	פּ/פ	p/p̄
ו	w (or *v*)	צ	ṣ (hard *s*)
ז	z	ק	q
ח	ḥ (hard *h*)	ר	r
ט	ṭ (hard *t*)	שׂ	ś
י	y	שׁ	š
כּ/כ	k/ḵ	תּ/ת	t/ṯ
ל	l		

Watch out for the *BeGaD-KePhaT* letters. The correspondence between the dot in *BeGaD-KePhaT* letters (indicating hard pronunciation) and the English transliteration is sometimes confusing because they seem reversed. If the Hebrew letter has a dot, the transliteration has no marking (e.g., כּ = k). But if there is nothing in Hebrew (no dot), then it gets a marking (a line) in English (e.g., ḵ = כ). In an oversimplification,

2. You will not really hear a difference between ט and ת, but the former is technically a hard /t/.

with *BeGaD-KePhaT* letters, the Hebrew and the transliteration never have both a dot and a line.

TRANSLITERATION OF HEBREW VOWELS

In transliteration, Hebrew vowels are distinguished between long and short vowels, between vowels with and without a vowel marker (ו, י, or ה), and between silent and vocal *shewa*. Even though technically all *shewas* represent the absence of a vowel ("a *shewa* is a *shewa* is a *shewa*"), silent *shewa* remains unmarked but vocal *shewa* is typically represented by superscript e (X^e). Since the composite *shewa* is shorter than a short vowel, transliteration uses the crescent for composite *shewas* (ă), no diacritical markings for short vowels (a), the macron for long vowels (ā), and the circumflex to reflect the presence of vowel markers (â).

Note that â represents *qamets* plus a vowel marker (ָה , while āh represents *qamets* plus consonantal *heh* (ָהּ). However, when *heh* serves as a vowel marker for other vowels, it is represented with 'h' to indicate that the natural vowel marker is not used. For example, because *yod* has affinity with *tsere* and is the most natural choice for a vowel marker, transliteration distinguishes between רֹעֵה = rōʿēh and רֹעֵי = rōʿê.

Transliteration of Hebrew Vowels

Shewa		Short vowels		Long vowels		Long vowels with vowel marker		
ă	◌ֲ	a	◌ַ	ā	◌ָ	â	ָה	*at end of word*
ĕ	◌ֱ	e	◌ֶ	ē	◌ֵ	ê	ֵי / ֶי	
		i	◌ִ			î	ִי	
ŏ	◌ֳ	o	◌ָ	ō	◌ֹ	ô	וֹ	
		u	◌ֻ			û	וּ	

X^e ◌ְ (vocal)

X ◌ְ (silent)

EXERCISE FOR APPENDIX 5

The exercises include an optional transliteration assignment that provides practice converting the Hebrew characters into English transliteration and converting English transliteration back into Hebrew (see Exercise AP-5 in the workbook).

APPENDIX 6

Verb Paradigms

QAL VERB CHART

Inf. Cst. קְטֹל ↓ **Inf. Abs.** קָטוֹל

	Pf.	*Impf.*	*Juss.*		*Impv.*	*Active Ptc.*
he (3ms)	קָטַל	יִקְטֹל	יִקְטֹל			קֹטֵל
she (3fs)	קָטְלָה	תִּקְטֹל	תִּקְטֹל			קֹטְלָה (קֹטֶלֶת)
you (2ms)	קָטַלְתָּ	תִּקְטֹל	תִּקְטֹל	→	קְטֹל (קָטְלָה)	קֹטְלִים
you (2fs)	קָטַלְתְּ	תִּקְטְלִי	תִּקְטְלִי	→	קִטְלִי	קֹטְלוֹת
I (1cs)	קָטַלְתִּי	אֶקְטֹל	אֶקְטְלָה			
						Passive Ptc.
they (3mp)	קָטְלוּ	יִקְטְלוּ	יִקְטְלוּ			קָטוּל
they (3fp)		תִּקְטֹלְנָה	תִּקְטֹלְנָה			קְטוּלָה
you (2mp)	קְטַלְתֶּם	תִּקְטְלוּ	תִּקְטְלוּ	→	קִטְלוּ	קְטוּלִים
you (2fp)	קְטַלְתֶּן	תִּקְטֹלְנָה	תִּקְטֹלְנָה	→	קְטֹלְנָה	קְטוּלוֹת
we (1cp)	קָטַלְנוּ	נִקְטֹל	נִקְטְלָה			

NIPHAL VERB CHART

② הִקָּטֵל *Inf. Cst.* ③ נִקְטֹל / הִקָּטֹל *Inf. Abs.*

↓

	Pf.	*Impf.*	*Juss.*		*Impv.*	*Ptc.*
he (3ms)	① נִקְטַל	יִקָּטֵל	יִקָּטֵל			④ נִקְטָל
she (3fs)	נִקְטְלָה	תִּקָּטֵל	תִּקָּטֵל			נִקְטָלָה
you (2ms)	נִקְטַ֫לְתָּ	תִּקָּטֵל	תִּקָּטֵל	→	הִקָּטֵל	נִקְטָלִים
you (2fs)	נִקְטַ֫לְתְּ	תִּקָּטְלִי	תִּקָּטְלִי	→	הִקָּטְלִי	נִקְטָלוֹת
I (1cs)	נִקְטַ֫לְתִּי	אֶקָּטֵל	אֶקָּטְלָה			
they (3mp)	נִקְטְלוּ	יִקָּטְלוּ	יִקָּטְלוּ			
they (3fp)		תִּקָּטַ֫לְנָה	תִּקָּטַ֫לְנָה			
you (2mp)	נִקְטַלְתֶּם	תִּקָּטְלוּ	תִּקָּטְלוּ	→	הִקָּטְלוּ	
you (2fp)	נִקְטַלְתֶּן	תִּקָּטַ֫לְנָה	תִּקָּטַ֫לְנָה	→	הִקָּטַ֫לְנָה	
we (1cp)	נִקְטַ֫לְנוּ	נִקָּטֵל	נִקָּטְלָה			

PIEL VERB CHART

② קַטֵּל *Inf. Cst.* ↓

③ קַטֵּל (קַטֹּל) *Inf. Abs.*

	Pf.	*Impf.*	*Juss.*		*Impv.*	*Ptc.*
he (3ms)	① קִטֵּל	יְקַטֵּל	יְקַטֵּל			④ מְקַטֵּל
she (3fs)	קִטְּלָה	תְּקַטֵּל	תְּקַטֵּל			מְקַטֶּלֶת
you (2ms)	קִטַּלְתָּ	תְּקַטֵּל	תְּקַטֵּל	→	קַטֵּל	מְקַטְּלִים
you (2fs)	קִטַּלְתְּ	תְּקַטְּלִי	תְּקַטְּלִי	→	קַטְּלִי	מְקַטְּלוֹת
I (1cs)	קִטַּלְתִּי	אֲקַטֵּל	אֲקַטְּלָה			
they (3mp)	קִטְּלוּ	יְקַטְּלוּ	יְקַטְּלוּ			
they (3fp)		תְּקַטֵּלְנָה	תְּקַטֵּלְנָה			
you (2mp)	קִטַּלְתֶּם	תְּקַטְּלוּ	תְּקַטְּלוּ	→	קַטְּלוּ	
you (2fp)	קִטַּלְתֶּן	תְּקַטֵּלְנָה	תְּקַטֵּלְנָה	→	קַטֵּלְנָה	
we (1cp)	קִטַּלְנוּ	נְקַטֵּל	נְקַטְּלָה			

PUAL VERB CHART

② קֻטַּל *Inf. Cst.*

③ קֻטֹּל *Inf. Abs.*

	Pf.	*Impf.*	*Ptc.*
he (3ms)	① קֻטַּל	יְקֻטַּל	④ מְקֻטָּל
she (3fs)	קֻטְּלָה	תְּקֻטַּל	מְקֻטָּלָה
you (2ms)	קֻטַּלְתָּ	תְּקֻטַּל	מְקֻטָּלִים
you (2fs)	קֻטַּלְתְּ	תְּקֻטְּלִי	מְקֻטָּלוֹת
I (1cs)	קֻטַּלְתִּי	אֲקֻטַּל	
they (3mp)	קֻטְּלוּ	יְקֻטְּלוּ	
they (3fp)		תְּקֻטַּלְנָה	
you (2mp)	קֻטַּלְתֶּם	תְּקֻטְּלוּ	
you (2fp)	קֻטַּלְתֶּן	תְּקֻטַּלְנָה	
we (1cp)	קֻטַּלְנוּ	נְקֻטַּל	

HITHPAEL VERB CHART

② הִתְקַטֵּל *Inf. Cst.* ↓ ③ הִתְקַטֵּל *Inf. Abs.*

	Pf.	*Impf.*	*Juss.*		*Impv.*	*Ptc.*
he (3ms)	① הִתְקַטֵּל	יִתְקַטֵּל	יִתְקַטֵּל			④ מִתְקַטֵּל
she (3fs)	הִתְקַטְּלָה	תִּתְקַטֵּל	תִּתְקַטֵּל			מִתְקַטְּלָה
you (2ms)	הִתְקַטַּ֫לְתָּ	תִּתְקַטֵּל	תִּתְקַטֵּל	→	הִתְקַטֵּל	מִתְקַטְּלִים
you (2fs)	הִתְקַטַּ֫לְתְּ	תִּתְקַטְּלִי	תִּתְקַטְּלִי	→	הִתְקַטְּלִי	מִתְקַטְּלוֹת
I (1cs)	הִתְקַטַּ֫לְתִּי	אֶתְקַטֵּל	אֶתְקַטְּלָה			
they (3mp)	הִתְקַטְּלוּ	יִתְקַטְּלוּ	יִתְקַטְּלוּ			
they (3fp)		תִּתְקַטֵּ֫לְנָה	תִּתְקַטֵּ֫לְנָה			
you (2mp)	הִתְקַטַּלְתֶּם	תִּתְקַטְּלוּ	תִּתְקַטְּלוּ	→	הִתְקַטְּלוּ	
you (2fp)	הִתְקַטַּלְתֶּן	תִּתְקַטֵּ֫לְנָה	תִּתְקַטֵּ֫לְנָה	→	הִתְקַטֵּ֫לְנָה	
we (1cp)	הִתְקַטַּ֫לְנוּ	נִתְקַטֵּל	נִתְקַטְּלָה			

HIPHIL VERB CHART

② הַקְטִיל *Inf. Cst.* ↓ ③ הַקְטֵל *Inf. Abs.*

	Pf.	*Impf.*	*Juss.*		*Impv.*	*Ptc.*
he (3ms)	① הִקְטִיל	יַקְטִיל	יַקְטֵל			④ מַקְטִיל
she (3fs)	הִקְטִ֫ילָה	תַּקְטִיל	תַּקְטֵל			מַקְטִילָה
you (2ms)	הִקְטַ֫לְתָּ	תַּקְטִיל	תַּקְטֵל	→	הַקְטֵל	מַקְטִילִים
you (2fs)	הִקְטַ֫לְתְּ	תַּקְטִ֫ילִי	תַּקְטִ֫ילִי	→	הַקְטִ֫ילִי	מַקְטִילוֹת
I (1cs)	הִקְטַ֫לְתִּי	אַקְטִיל	אַקְטִ֫ילָה			
they (3mp)	הִקְטִ֫ילוּ	יַקְטִ֫ילוּ	יַקְטִ֫ילוּ			
they (3fp)		תַּקְטֵ֫לְנָה	תַּקְטֵ֫לְנָה			
you (2mp)	הִקְטַלְתֶּם	תַּקְטִ֫ילוּ	תַּקְטִ֫ילוּ	→	הַקְטִ֫ילוּ	
you (2fp)	הִקְטַלְתֶּן	תַּקְטֵ֫לְנָה	תַּקְטֵ֫לְנָה	→	הַקְטֵ֫לְנָה	
we (1cp)	הִקְטַ֫לְנוּ	נַקְטִיל	נַקְטִ֫ילָה			

Remember: The *hiphil* has a characteristic *ḥireq-yod* except when: (1) forms with consonantal sufformatives take short /a/ in the perfect (like the *qal*) and *tsere* everywhere else, and (2) short forms with no ending take *tsere*.

HOPHAL VERB CHART

② הָקְטַל *Inf. Cst.*

↓

③ הָקְטֵל *Inf. Abs.*

matches Hiphil

	Pf.	*Impf.*	*Ptc.*
he (3ms)	① הָקְטַל	יָקְטַל	④ מָקְטָל
she (3fs)	הָקְטְלָה	תָּקְטַל	מָקְטָלָה
you (2ms)	הָקְטַ֫לְתָּ	תָּקְטַל	מָקְטָלִים
you (2fs)	הָקְטַ֫לְתְּ	תָּקְטְלִי	מָקְטָלוֹת
I (1cs)	הָקְטַ֫לְתִּי	אָקְטַל	
they (3mp)	הָקְטְלוּ	יָקְטְלוּ	
they (3fp)		תָּקְטַ֫לְנָה	
you (2mp)	הָקְטַלְתֶּם	תָּקְטְלוּ	
you (2fp)	הָקְטַלְתֶּן	תָּקְטַ֫לְנָה	
we (1cp)	הָקְטַ֫לְנוּ	נָקְטַל	

Bibliography

NOTE: Many language resources are known by author's last names or by abbreviations. Helpful abbreviations are listed in brackets after the bibliographic information.

WORKS CITED

Beckwith, Roger T. *The Old Testament Canon of the New Testament Church and Its Background in Early Judaism.* Grand Rapids: Eerdmans, 1985.

Block, Daniel. *How I Love Your Torah, O Lord!: Studies in the Book of Deuteronomy.* Eugene, OR: Wipf & Stock, 2011.

Brown, A. Philip, II, and Bryan W. Smith, eds. *A Reader's Hebrew Bible.* Grand Rapids: Zondervan, 2008. [*Reader's Bible*]

Elliger, K. and W. Rudolph. *Biblia Hebraica Stuttgartensia.* 5th ed. Revised by A. Schenker. Stuttgart: Deutsche Bibelgesellschaft, 1997. [*BHS*]

Fox, Michael V. *Proverbs: An Eclectic Edition with Introduction and Textual Commentary*. The Hebrew Bible: A Critical Edition. Atlanta, GA: SBL Press, 2015.

Gesenius, Wilhelm. *Gesenius' Hebrew Grammar*. Edited by E. Kautzsch. Translated and edited by A. E. Cowley. 2nd Eng. ed. Oxford: Clarendon Press, 1910. [GKC]

Goshen-Gottstein, M. H. *The Book of Isaiah: Sample Edition with Introduction.* Jerusalem: Magnus Press, 1965.

Joüon, Paul, and T. Muraoka. *A Grammar of Biblical Hebrew*. Revised English ed. Roma: Pontificio istituto biblico, 2006. [Joüon]

Manuel, Paul. "Notes on Hebrew Grammar." Class notes for Hebrew 103. University of Wisconsin-Madison, fall, 1988.

Rainey, Anson F. "The Ancient Hebrew Prefix Conjugation in the Light of Amarnah Canaanite." *Hebrew Studies* 27 (1986): 4–19.

Robar, Elizabeth. *The Verb and the Paragraph in Biblical Hebrew*. Leiden: Brill, 2015.

Schenker, A. ed. *Biblia Hebraica Quinta: General Introduction and Megilloth*, Fascicle 18. Stuttgart: Deutsche Bibelgesellschaft, 2004. [*BHQ*]

Spiro, Pinchas. *Haftarah Chanting*. Rev. ed. New York: Board of Jewish Education of Greater New York, 1994.

Waltke, Bruce K., and Michael Patrick O'Connor. *An Introduction to Biblical Hebrew Syntax*. Winona Lake, IN: Eisenbrauns, 1990. [Waltke-O'Connor]

Williams, Ronald J. "The Passive Qal Theme in Hebrew." Pages 43–50 in *Essays on the Ancient Semitic World*. Edited by John W. Wevers and D. B. Redford. Toronto: University of Toronto Press, 1970.

Yeivin, Israel. *Introduction to the Tiberian Masorah*. Translated and edited by E. J. Revell. Missoula, MT: Scholars Press, 1980.

SELECT RESOURCES FOR STUDENTS

Hebrew Bibles

Brown, A. Philip, II, and Bryan W. Smith, eds. *A Reader's Hebrew Bible*. Grand Rapids: Zondervan, 2008. [*Reader's Bible*]

Elliger, K. and W. Rudolph. *Biblia Hebraica Stuttgartensia*. Study edition. 5th ed. Revised by A. Schenker. Stuttgart: Deutsche Bibelgesellschaft, 1997. [*BHS*]

Schenker, A. ed. *Biblia Hebraica Quinta: General Introduction and Megilloth*, Fascicle 18. Stuttgart: Deutsche Bibelgesellschaft, 2004. [*BHQ*]

Lexicons

Brown, Francis, Samuel Rolles Driver, and Charles Augustus Briggs. *A Hebrew and English Lexicon of the Old Testament, with an Appendix Containing the Biblical Aramaic*. Oxford: Oxford University Press, 1906. [BDB]

Holladay, William L, ed. *A Concise Hebrew and Aramaic Lexicon of the Old Testament*. Leiden: E. J. Brill, 1988. [Holladay]

Koehler, L. and W. Baumgartner. *The Hebrew and Aramaic Lexicon of the Old Testament*. 2 vols. Leiden: Brill, 2001. [*HALOT* or KB]

Reference Grammars

Gesenius, Wilhelm. *Gesenius' Hebrew Grammar*. Edited by Emil Kautzsch. Translated and edited by A. E. Cowley. 2nd Eng. ed. Oxford: Clarendon Press, 1910. [GKC]

Joüon, Paul, and T. Muraoka. *A Grammar of Biblical Hebrew*. Revised English ed. Roma: Pontificio istituto biblico, 2006. [Joüon]

Waltke, Bruce K., and Michael O'Connor. *An Introduction to Biblical Hebrew Syntax.* Winona Lake, IN: Eisenbrauns, 1990. [Waltke-O'Connor]

Concordances

Even-Shoshan, Abraham. *A New Concordance of the Old Testament.* Grand Rapids: Baker, 1989. [Even-Shoshan]

Kohlenberger, John, and James A. Swanson. *The Hebrew-English Concordance to the Old Testament, with the NIV.* Grand Rapids: Zondervan, 1998.

Hebrew Accents

Spiro, Pinchas, *Haftarah Chanting.* Rev. ed. New York: Board of Jewish Education of Greater New York, 1994.

Yeivin, Israel. *Introduction to the Tiberian Masorah.* Translated and edited by E. J. Revell. Scholars Press, 1980.

Textual Criticism

Fox, Michael V. *Proverbs: An Eclectic Edition with Introduction and Textual Commentary*. The Hebrew Bible: A Critical Edition. Atlanta, GA: SBL Press, 2015.

Goshen-Gottstein, M. H. *The Book of Isaiah: Sample Edition with Introduction.* Jerusalem: Magnus Press, 1965.

McCarter, P. Kyle. *Textual Criticism: Recovering the Text of the Hebrew Bible*. Philadelphia: Fortress, 1985.

Tov, Emanuel. *Scribal Practices and Approaches Reflected in the Texts Found in the Judean Desert*. Atlanta, GA: Society of Biblical Literature, 2004.

Tov, Emanuel. *Textual Criticism of the Hebrew Bible*. 3rd rev. exp. ed. Minneapolis: Fortress, 2011.

Subject Index